POLACOS IN ARGENTINA

JEWS AND JUDAISM: HISTORY AND CULTURE

POLACOS IN ARGENTINA

POLISH JEWS, INTERWAR MIGRATION, AND THE EMERGENCE OF TRANSATLANTIC JEWISH CULTURE

Mariusz Kałczewiak

THE UNIVERSITY OF ALABAMA PRESS
Tuscaloosa

The University of Alabama Press
Tuscaloosa, Alabama 35487-0380
uapress.ua.edu

Typeface: Garamond and Futura

Cover image: Polish passenger ship, the MS *Sobieski*
Cover design: David Nees

Cataloging-in-Publication data is available from the Library of Congress.
ISBN: 978-0-8173-2039-3
E-ISBN: 978-0-8173-9269-7

לאהובי עירד
To my always loving Irad

Contents

Illustrations

FIGURES

TABLES

Acknowledgments

This book is a product of five years of intellectual journeys between Warsaw and Buenos Aires. Countless friends and colleagues have accompanied me across borders and continents, in Poland, Israel, Germany, Argentina, and the United States. It was unbelievably exciting to follow the footsteps of Jewish migrants and to analyze their journey from Europe to Latin America. I dedicate this book to the memory of Polish Jews who bravely crossed the Atlantic and constructed "Jewish Argentina" in all its diverse facets.

My special thanks go to Raanan Rein of Tel Aviv University who has been for me a best possible guide through Argentine history. He has always been attentive, helping, and inspiring. Raanan helped me to grow as a scholar, to avoid black and white divisions, and not to take things for granted but to constantly dig for deeper meanings. He encouraged me to be critical and was confident in my attempt to merge Eastern European and Latin American history. I thank three respective directors of the Zvi Yavetz School of Historical Studies at Tel Aviv University: Billy Melman, Leo Corry, and Aviad Kleinberg. Thank you for welcoming me in Tel Aviv and making my studies smooth and pleasant. In Germany, Peter Haslinger of Justus Liebig University in Giessen has helped me to sharpen the eastern European aspects of my research and taught me how to maneuver through the labyrinths of the German academic system.

This research could not be realized without financial help of diverse institutions. Between 2012 and 2015, the Graduate Center for the Study of Culture of Justus Liebig University in Giessen, Germany, provided me with generous scholarship support, including a travel stipend, which allowed me to research in Buenos Aires for several months. The Shlomo Glas and Fanny Balaban-Glas Foundation, as well Tel Aviv University's Goldstein-Goren Diaspora Research Center, allowed me to pursue my studies in financial comfort in 2015 and 2016. Tel Aviv University has supported me with numerous travel grants, as well as funded me with a scholarship during the write-up phase. I am happy to acknowledge the financial support of the Center of Jewish History in New York, POLIN Museum of the History of Polish Jews, Smathers Library at the University of

Florida, and the Center for Research on Polish Jews and Israel-Poland Relations of Tel Aviv University.

This book would not have become what it is without numerous conversations with colleagues around the world. I express my sincere gratitude to Kamil Kijek, Magalena Kozłowska, and Claudia Stern for reading the introduction and their insightful thoughts about Polish and Latin American Jews. I thank Hana Wirth-Nesher and Scott Ury for being curious and critical guides through the world of Yiddish letters and of Eastern European Jewish history. My Yiddish teachers, Abraham Lichtenbaum, Karolina Szymaniak, Marek Tuszewicki, and Kobi Weitzner, allowed me to understand the language spoken by Polish Jews in Argentina and in Poland. I have been privileged to be a *lajsero* and participate in biannual conferences of the Latin American Jewish Studies Association (LAJSA). I thank Naomi Lindstrom for carefully reading and reviewing my manuscript. Adriana M. Brodsky, Leonardo Senkman, Marcos Silber, and colleagues at the Sverdlin Institute for Latin American History and Culture (Tel Aviv University) provided me with insightful comments on Argentine history. In Poland, Polish Association for Yiddish Studies and Polish Association for Jewish Studies invited me for conferences where I could present and discuss my ideas. The congresses of European Association for Jewish Studies, as well as biannual Poland-Israel Workshops in the History and Culture of Polish Jews have been amazing platforms for scholarly exchange.

I thank Ezequiel Semo, the librarian of the IWO Institute in Buenos Aires, for his wonderful help during my research in 2014. I am grateful to the archivists at the YIVO Institute for Jewish Research in New York, National Library of Poland in Warsaw, and at Biblioteca Nacional in Buenos Aires. My utmost words of gratitude go to Tomasz Frydel, Maxwell E. Greenberg, and Susan Harris for masterfully editing the manuscript. Michał Śmielak has wonderfully helped to create maps used in my book. Dan Waterman, editor in chief at University of Alabama Press has been extremely helpful in making this book available in print. I would like to thank the editors at Brill for permission to publish a revised version of an article that first appeared in *The New Ethnic Studies in Latin America* (Brill 2017). I also acknowledge the permission to publish fragments of my article that appeared earlier in *Studia Judaica* (vol. 33 [2014]).

I am endlessly grateful to my mother, Grażyna Kałczewiak, for showing me how to be a good and passionate teacher, no matter if one teaches Polish literature at a neighborhood elementary school or Jewish history at the university level. *Dziękuję, mamo*. My loving husband, Irad Ben Isaak, has been a constant inspiration and support throughout the research and writing process. Irad has always made me sure that I am on the right path. I dedicate this book to him with love and appreciation.

A Note on Translation, Spelling, and Transliteration

As this work relies heavily on Yiddish sources, extensive transliteration was necessary. The transliteration is usually based on the standardized YIVO transliteration system. There are several exceptions to this system. If a title or a name had an original (at the time of publication) and more easily identifiable transliterated spelling, I follow this spelling. For instance, I spelled the Buenos Aires daily newspaper as *Yidische Zaitung*, instead of *Yidishe Tsaytung*. Similarly, I transliterated the name of travel writer Peretz Hirschbein, instead of Perets Hirschbeyn, as suggested by the YIVO. By analogy, I decided to use the widely acknowledged Spanish spelling of Samuel Rollansky, rather than transliterate it from Yiddish as Shmuel Rozhansky. Geographical names appear according to their respective historical names instead of their contemporary forms, unless there is a conventional English equivalent (like Warsaw for Warszawa). Though, I use Jewish studies conventional English form Vilna instead of contemporary Vilnius or Polish Wilno. Foreign words are italicized only the first time they appear, at which point they are explained. In terms of the few cases of Hebrew transliteration, the Library of Congress system was followed. All translations are by the author unless otherwise indicated.

POLACOS IN ARGENTINA

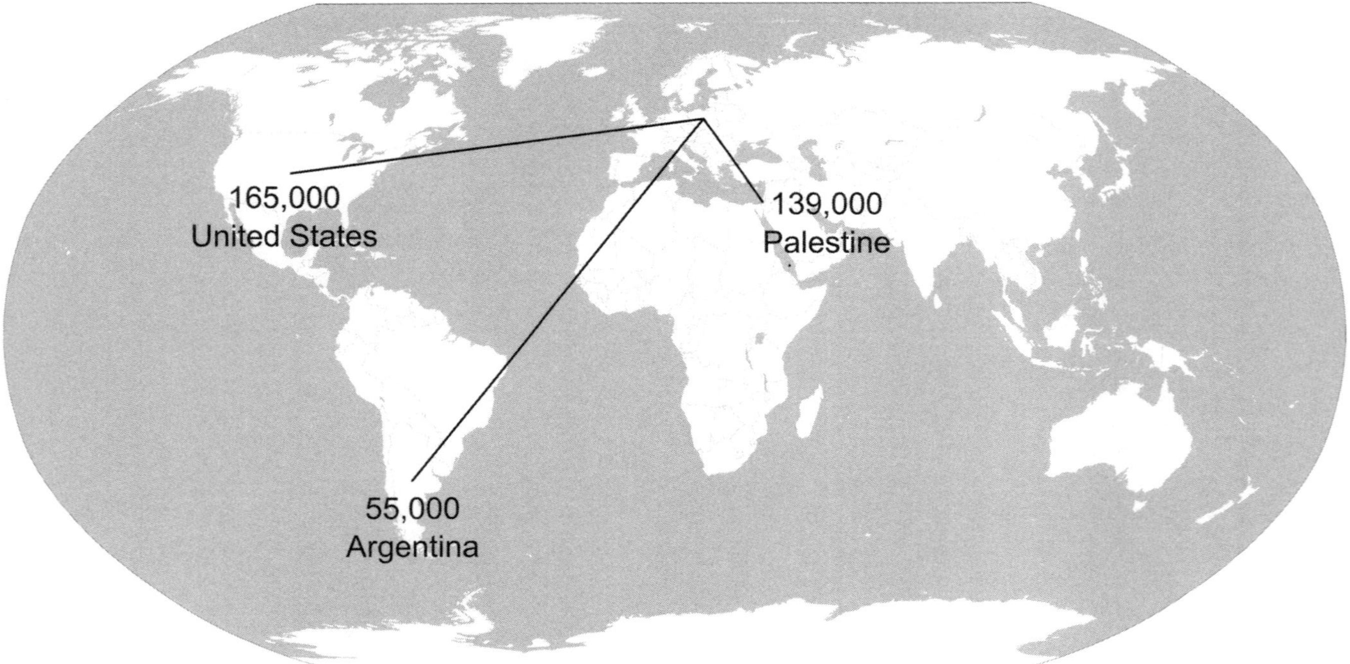

Figure 1. Jewish emigration from Poland to the United States, Palestine, and Argentina between 1919 and 1939, based on Mark Tolts, "Population and Migration. Migrations since World War I," YIVO Encyclopedia of Jews in Eastern Europe

Introduction

In 1923, a Varsovian Yiddish author Hersh Dovid Nomberg wrote: "Argentina! Once it was a word that was heard in all Jewish cities and *shtetls*, as a call of redemption, a word that made Jewish hearts tremble with happiness, expectation and hope. As a lovely spring wind, the message traveled around all Jewish places: a country for Jews, for Jewish agricultural workers, the Redeemer arose, Baron Hirsch! . . . The newspapers were agitating, this one for, the other against. . . . The intelligentsia had debated: is Argentina a competition for Zion or not? In short, for some years Argentina occupied a very prominent place for the Jewish public."[1]

Between the 1890s and 1930s, Argentina, after the United States and Palestine, became the main destination for Russian, Polish, Hungarian, Romanian, and other eastern European Ashkenazi Jews searching for safety, civil rights, and better economic prospects. One of them was Lazaro Pinchuk, from a little Polish town called Włodzimierz Wołyński. This was the mid-1920s, and Lazaro was a twenty-one-year-old man with no clear perspective of what he wanted to do in life. Suddenly, all the colleagues at his carpentry shop were speaking of Argentina. He had family members living in the United States, but the United States was just about to close its gates to new Jewish immigrants. In 1923, Lazaro decided to immigrate to Argentina by himself. The young *shtetl* boy managed to obtain a passport and Argentine visa and navigated his way from Poland to Trieste in Italy. He left all his family behind and started a new life in Buenos Aires. He moved to a new country, to a city dozens of times bigger than his hometown, with a new language and climate. Even though initially he barely earned a living as a furniture polisher, he always made sure he had enough money to buy the Yiddish left-wing daily *Di Presse*. From time to time, he saved enough to go to the Yiddish theater. The story of Lazaro is emblematic for thousands of *polacos*, Polish Jews who immigrated to Argentina in the interwar period.

This book explores their migration journey, its historical context, and social and cultural consequences. I tackle migration as a sociocultural dialogue on Jewish ethnicity, modernity, and diasporism. My study explores the evolution of transatlantic cultural migrant networks and sheds light on heterogeneous ethnonational and diasporic processes engendered through emigration. Of key importance in this research are the following issues: 1) ethnic identity in the context of migration and Jewish and Argentine national projects and 2) the emergence of a political, social, and cultural *writing space* between Jews in Poland and Jews in Argentina. This book approaches Jewish migration to Argentina and the following development of a transnational Jewish culture as a multilateral process that took place on both sides of the Atlantic. At the turn of the twentieth century, people and literature began to circulate between Poland and Argentina. Beginning in the 1890s, Poland's elitist Hebrew press began publishing Argentina-themed articles, followed by emigration pamphlets, Yiddish travel writing on Argentina, immigrants' reports, and works of fiction; a prolific "writing territory" was developed, connecting both sides of the Atlantic. In order to demonstrate these cultural entanglements, I use a framework of "Yiddishland," a geographic and cultural space inhabited by Yiddish-speaking Jews that encompassed not only Poland and Argentina but also the United States and Soviet Russia.

This book encompasses the period of intensive interwar (1914–39) immigration from Poland to Argentina, when individuals, ideas, popular beliefs, and social issues transcended geographic borders. This study starts in 1914, a year that marked the beginning of the Great War, the suspension of transatlantic passenger traffic between Europe and the Americas, and, most significantly, the end of the first era in Jewish immigration to Argentina. The fall of the Austrian, German, and Russian empires after World War I led to a reconstruction of an independent Polish state, challenging and reshaping the ethnic identifications of Jewish migrants. World War I also marked the establishment in 1916 of Agudas Ahim (later known as Poylisher Farband, or Union of Polish Jews, in Argentina), a central body uniting the Jewish residents of Argentina who shared a strong attachment to Poland, their place of origin.[2] The Polish-Jewish landsman movement was a platform for discussing the Jewish place within Argentine society and within the diasporic ethnocultural space of Yiddish speakers (Yiddishland), while also contributing to the cross-border discourse on nationalism and transnational belonging. The year 1914 also marked the arrival of Yiddish writer Peretz Hirschbein in Argentina. This Poland-born author, journalist, and global cosmopolitan was one of the few Polish Jews who visited Argentina and wrote a travelogue describing the Jewish life emerging in this country. Hirschbein's memoirs reveal a vivid portrait of how Yiddish culturists perceived Argentina, emigration, geographic expansion, and the transculturation of eastern European Jewish lives. Hirschbein himself embodied the growing entanglements between Jewish Poland and Argentina.

This book looks at migration from two ends (Argentine and Polish), challenging the linear approaches that often do not pay enough attention to premigration visions of the receiving nation or to the postmigration links maintained with the homeland. Jewish migration to the Americas was not merely an answer to pogroms and economic hardships experienced back home.[3] Migration was also catalyzed by changing economic and social structures, the erosion of the shtetl, and the political reconfigurations in Europe. Of equal significance were Argentine programs that facilitated emigration; although never geared toward Jews specifically, these programs allowed many to settle in Latin America. I build off the work of José Moya, whose study of Spanish immigration to Argentina criticized that "the notion of [a] new country's superiority and the assimilating power of its environment made pre-arrival traits more or less irrelevant."[4] Mass migration to the Americas created a form of Jewish cultural, conceptual, and textual networks, the study of which requires historians to capture both life in the host country as well as debates concerning the nature of transatlantic migration among European communities. The transnational scope of Jewish debates and practice between eastern Europe and Argentina needs to be studied as a continuous development, rather than a sudden rupture of Jewish life in Europe. This book thickens previous historiographies of Jewish migration from eastern Europe to Argentina by tracing the images of Argentina that prewar Polish Jews constructed and subsequently circulated.

As a case study, Jewish emigration from Poland to Argentina illuminates how ethnicity evolved and transformed among migrants and their children, along with the dynamics that emerged from the tension between rootedness to a new country and commitments to the Old Country. I focus on a generation of migrants—Polish Jews—who relocated to Argentina and lived there following World War I. This generation of Jews reflects a *transitory stage* in the course of individual and collective ethnic identity development. Emigration transformed Polish Jews into *Argentine Jews* and the children of these migrants became *Jewish Argentines*. Several important factors shaped the evolution of ethnic identities between first- and second-generation Jewish migrants. First, the Yiddish language, as an expression of Jewish ethnicity, was constructed around Poland-centered Jewish ethnonationalist project. It suggested a transformative path toward a progressive, secular, ethnic Jewishness that could be relevant both in eastern Europe and in the Americas. Even as Argentine Jewish culture developed in multiethnic Buenos Aires, where Jewish ethnicity was shaped vis-a-vis other migrant communities, the interwar Ashkenazi Jewish case was modified by a desire to forge a new secular Yiddish culture, often looking to Poland for influence. In this sense, the Old Country was not simply a reservoir of conservative norms but a resource of modern ideas on Jewish life in diaspora. In the realm of Yiddish culture, Poland was one of its interwar centers, while Argentina was at its periphery.

Second, the dynamics between Poland and Argentina did not always parallel the dominant narrative of Jewish immigration to the United States, wherein the new country was positively imagined as an advantageous destination with economic possibilities and high levels of democratic freedoms. In Jewish Poland, the social imaginaries of Argentina were complex, as Argentina was rarely imagined as an unambiguously desired destination and often criticized as hazardous and challenging. While Argentina offered Jews civil rights and economic opportunities, these migrants were simultaneously limited in their political mobility and social and cultural expression. At the same time in Poland, Zionist and non-Zionist visions of the Jewish future were conceptualized and hotly debated, and Jews could claim cultural rootedness, primarily through secular Yiddish literature, journalism, and scholarship. In Argentina, these aspects never reached a stage comparable with the situation in Poland. The gradual identification among Jewish migrants as Argentine Jewish was dually informed by preconceptions about Argentina formed in Poland and notions of Jewish nationhood that migrants brought from eastern Europe. Drawing from *landsman* sources, Yiddish press, and immigrant literature, I argue that that "becoming Argentine" was shaped by a process in which immigrants continuously positioned themselves between their new homeland and their home country, including their sustained involvement in eastern European matters.[5] The process of *becoming Argentine Jews* is best elucidated through the fund-raising campaigns conducted for the benefit of Jews in Poland in the 1920s and 1930s.

Jews in Argentina were shaped both by their Argentine surroundings and by "external" influences from eastern Europe. This reflected the situation for Jews who remained in Poland. Poland's Jewish society was never hermetically sealed but involved interaction, cooperation, and common practices with Christian neighbors. Jews were simultaneously the agents and the receivers of influence.[6] Similar tendencies were visible in Argentina. Life in Buenos Aires was characterized by a "cultural porosity" and a constant exchange between the Jewish and non-Jewish world, what some local Yiddishists (especially in the 1930s) interpreted as posing a certain ethnic danger. While Argentine nationalism invited Jews to imagine themselves as Argentines, social and political discourse in Poland largely placed them outside of a "Polish nation." The Argentine nation-state and its melting-pot policies that included efforts at nationalizing immigrants offered Jews the promise of secular universal citizenship and national inclusion. Simultaneously, in early twentieth-century Argentina, the local national discourse challenged Argentine Jews' ethnonational identification with compatriots in other parts of the world. Jewish migrants to Argentina were encouraged (both externally and internally) to identify with their new homeland. Despite the discrepancies between Argentine national belonging and diasporic Jewish identifications, both phenomena proved to be compatible in early twentieth-century Argentina.

In a pre-1939, globalizing Jewish world, alternative visions of Jewish ethnicity and nationalism were at play. Not all immigrant Jews quickly and without reservations embraced their new countries as loving homelands. In addition, Jewish national arguments were regularly raised not only by Zionists but also by Bundists, Diaspora Nationalists, and other political movements. As Jews migrated to the Americas, this sociopolitical aspect gained additional importance and contributed to the development of transatlantic networks and identities. This book brings together the impact of a Yiddish-centered ethnonational revival, the entanglements of diasporism, and the civic promises offered by Argentina to understand the complex experiences of Jews migrating from Poland to Argentina. More specifically, this book explores the diasporic Yiddishland nation that emerged within the cultural and textual space between Poland and Argentina. Thus, this work challenges the unilateral assumptions concerning Jewish migration to the Americas, namely that contacts between Argentine and eastern European Jews in the early twentieth century were weak or nonexistent. Traditional scholarship tends to approach the migration of eastern European Jews to the Americas exclusively from the perspective of the host country, discussing mostly the integration and acculturation of Jewish immigrants, the economic and social changes of their community, and the formation of Jewish institutions in the new country.[7] Until recently, little was known about how this east to west migration was imagined in the home country, along with the diasporic links that emerged between Polish Jews who migrated to Argentina and those who remained in Europe. I suggest an alternative approach to ethnicity in context of migration and suggest Yiddish print culture as a platform for building transatlantic networks.

The year 1939 is the closing caesura of this book. The Holocaust and the almost complete annihilation of Polish Jewry radically redefined the geographies of the Jewish world. Before 1939, Poland housed the biggest European Jewish community of around 3.3 million in 1939. After the Holocaust, Poland ceased to be a major center of Jewish life, and its links with multiple diasporic communities of Eastern European Jews became limited or, as in the case of Argentina, structurally redefined in a direction of commemoration policies. Zionism's victory and the establishment of the State of Israel challenged the diasporic ethnocultural project that Yiddish language defined. As Judith Butler put it, "Zionism exercises a hegemonic control over the concept of Jewishness" and consequently dismantles the notion of diasporic Jewishness.[8] A Yiddish cultural link that connected Jews in Poland and Argentina was largely cut off and, by the late 1940s and 1950s, was gradually replaced in Argentina by growing popular support for Zionism and Israeli statehood. Yiddish gradually lost its national and cultural meaning; its unifying power decreased while Yiddish cultural networking ceased to be relevant. My book explores the transatlantic commitments and networks that post-1939 events have largely erased from dominant narratives of Jewish-Argentine history.

Table 1. Total Jewish Immigration to Argentina, 1888–1935

Years	Jewish immigration to Argentina
1888–1900	14,700
1901–14	87,500
1915–19 (World War I)	1,600
1920–35	87,250

Sources: Based on Victor A. Mirleman, *En búsqueda de una identidad. Inmigrantes judíos en Buenos Aires, 1890–1930* (Buenos Aires: Editorial Mila, 1988), 5; and Arie Tartakower, *Dos yidishe emigratsye-problem un der yidisher velt-kongres* (Paris: Ekzekutiv-komitet forn yidishn velt-kongres, 1935), 7.

Jewish Emigration from Eastern Europe to Argentina

Between 1870 and 1930, four million immigrants arrived in Argentina, radically changing the country's demographics during the early twentieth century. In 1930, Argentina's population reached 11.9 million, up from only 1.81 million inhabitants in 1870 (see table 1).[9] Eastern European Jewish immigrants began arriving in Argentina beginning in the 1880s thanks initially to the resettlement project sponsored by German Jewish financier Baron Maurice de Hirsch. Inspired by the ideas of Jewish productivization and redemption by manual work, de Hirsch's enterprise facilitated the immigration of nearly ten thousand Jewish colonists to Argentina between the 1880s and 1920s. Argentina's stakes in Baron de Hirsch's colonization project was largely tied to the government's desire for European migrants to immigrate to and assimilate into Argentine society; the incorporation of European migrants was perceived as a process of "whitening" Argentina. The agricultural settlements in Argentina sponsored by de Hirsch became a cornerstone of Argentine Jewish mythology, even though the urban population quickly outnumbered those living in the colonies. In 1925, a mere 12.9 percent of the Jewish population inhabited the agricultural settlements.[10]

Immigration brought about a dramatic social reconstitution of Argentine society. Between 1820 and 1932, Argentina was the second receiving country after the United States and took in 6.5 million people (11.6 percent of the total number of migrants in the world) (see table 2).[11] In 1914, around half of Buenos Aires residents were foreign born; in the surrounding province, 34 percent of the population was also foreign born.[12] Argentina's population continued to grow, almost doubling in the interwar years from around 8 million in 1914 to 14 million in 1939.[13] Throughout the entire period between 1870 and 1930, immigration was responsible for around 30 percent of population growth.[14] Between 1921 and 1939, emigration from Poland increased, and soon, Polish citizens

Table 2. Immigration to Argentina, 1915–1939

Years	Italians	Spaniards	Poles (Jews and non-Jews)	Germans	Russians
1915–20	73,071	147,840	685	9,087	3,064
1921–30	534,794	399,473	128,452	60,130	11,597
1931–35	64,193	63,963	18,724	13,650	2,832
1936	6,426	9,453	7,631	2,981	1,869
1937	10,926	5,150	13,828	2,857	122
1938	17,976	13,170	14, 356	10,179	1,863
1939	14,372	14, 446	4,216	8,744	1,903
Total	**721,758**	**652,495**	**187,892**	**107,658**	**23,520**

Sources: Based on Vicente Vázquez-Presedo, *Estadísticas históricas argentinas II (Comparadas). Segunda Parte 1914–1939* (Buenos Aires: Ediciones Macchi, 1976); data from *Dirección Nacional de Migraciones.*

(Jews and non-Jews) reached the status of the third-largest immigrant community after Spaniards and Italians.[15] In 1920, Argentina was home to more than 130,000 Jews, and by 1930, Jews numbered 280,000.[16] The sociologist Jacob Shatzky estimated that around 210,000 Jews permanently settled in the country between 1901 and 1945.[17] The implementation of a near closed door immigration policy in the United States in 1924 (the Johnson-Reed Act) reoriented Jewish immigration to Latin America; in the period between 1926 and 1930, Jewish immigration to Latin America accounted for 43 percent of total Jewish migration (table 3).[18]

Precise pre-1918 statistics accounting for country-of-origin among Jewish immigrants to Argentina are mostly unavailable. Immigrants were statistically segregated according to nationality, but many of those who emigrated from the Russian and Austrian empires, and were labeled as Russians and Austrians, were in fact Jews originating from Polish lands. Yet the available archival materials suggest that emigration from Russia was a pattern most clearly visible among the empire's Polish Jews. N. Reiff believed that 44 percent of Jews emigrating from Russia to the United States came from Polish provinces; a similar percentage could be attributed to immigration to Argentina.[19] This high percentage likely correlates to the spatial concentration of Jews in the western part of the Russian Pale of Settlement, which included Polish territory. Historian Konrad Zieliński estimated that prior to 1914 approximately 11.5 percent of Jewish emigrants from the Russian-occupied Congress Poland had immigrated to Argentina.[20] Polish Jewish sociologist Arie Tartakower estimated that before 1914, two-thirds of all emigrants leaving Congress Poland were Jews.[21]

Polish emigration statistics become clearer in the post–World War I period

Table 3. Jewish Immigration to the Principal Immigration Countries, 1921–1939

Years	**United States**		**Canada**		**Argentina**		**Brazil**		**Palestine**	
	A share in world Jewish migration in given years (left) and absolute number of immigrants (right)									
1921–25	65.6%	280,283	3.4.%	14,400	9.3%	39,713	1.7%	7,139	14.0%	60,765
1926–30	31.7%	54,998	8.9%	15,300	19.5%	33,721	12.9%	22,296	5.9%	10,179
1931–35	7.6%	17,986	1.8%	4,200	5.4%	12,700	5.5%	13,075	61.7%	147,502
1936–39	29.7%	79,819	0.3%	900	5.4%	14,789	3.9%	10,600	28.1%	75,510
Total	**42.8%**	**433,086**	**3.1%**	**34,800**	**9.0%**	**100,923**	**5.2%**	**53,110**	**26.5%**	**293,956**

Source: Jacob Lestschinsky, "Jewish Migrations, 1840–1946," in *The Jews: Their History, Culture, and Religion*, ed. Louis Finkelstein, vol. 2, 1216–17 (New York: Harper Brothers, 1955).

Note: The table excludes other countries, which explains why the percentages do not equal 100 percent.

Table 4. Jewish Emigration from Poland to Argentina, 1919–1938

Year	**Number of Jewish immigrants to Argentina**	**Percent (%) of Jews in overall emigration from Poland to Argentina**
1919–22	2,553	31
1923	7,455	75
1924	4,871	73.4
1925	4,810	54.5
1926	4,750	32.9
1927	4,113	20.4
1928	4,808	21.8
1929	3,842	18.2
1930	4,882	35.4
1931	2,476	55.9
1932	1,335	64.9
1933	1,313	76.2
1934	1,472	71.6
1935	2,022	55.9
1936	2,750	46.4
1937	2,433	28.7
1938	2,175	28.3
Total	**58,060**	**35.2**

Source: Based on Marta Kowalska, "La emigración judía de Polonia a la Argentina en los años 1918–1939," *Estudios Latinoamericanos* vol. 12 (1989): 259.

(see table 4). Between 1920 and 1937, 1,820,000 people left Poland, including 395,000 Jews (22 percent).[22] Poland was one of the most important sending countries to Argentina between the 1920s and1930s. Throughout the 1920s, Poland was often the third sending country, after Spain and Italy, and represented 13 percent of total immigration to Argentina.[23] On average, Jews formed around 35 percent of Polish immigration to Argentina in interwar period, but during certain years (1923, 1924, 1933, 1934), Jews represented more than 70 percent. Beyond Jewish immigrants, numerous Christian Polish, Ukrainian, and Belorussian peasants also relocated to Argentina.[24] In the interwar years, Argentina was the third most important receiving country of Jewish emigrants following the United States and Palestine: between 1919 and 1939, the country received 110,000 eastern European Jews.[25] The Jews who immigrated to Latin America were largely of Polish origin and in the 1920s represented around 55 percent of all Jews settling in Argentina.[26] As estimated by Victor A. Mirelman the Jews of Poland formed around 70 percent of all Jewish immigration to Argentina during the years of the highest Jewish immigration (1924–30).[27]

My study focuses specifically on the experience of Polish Jews in Argentina. Whenever I use the phrase *Polish-Jewish*, I refer to the experience of Polish Jews, rather than to relations between Jews and gentile Poles. Although some would justifiably argue that it was not only Polish Jews who left Europe, it is worth thinking about Polish Jews specifically within the larger eastern European and Argentine contexts. The reemergence of an independent Poland in 1918 influenced the way Polish Jews perceived themselves and were perceived by others. For Jews in the process of migration, their subethnic identity was of key importance and was forged vis-a-vis Jews from other regions. This process of intraethnic identity formation was also at play in the context of eastern Europe, where Jewish regional identities were very powerful. In the Americas however, Jewish subethnic identities needed "to be remapped on a transnational terrain."[28] Within its 1918 to 1939 borders, Poland was home to more than three million Jews and, to a great extent, was the epicenter of Jewish life on the European continent. It held the highest share of Jewish citizens in the world (roughly 10 percent of the overall population) and despite growing anti-Semitism, it figured prominently as a political, social, and cultural center of Jewish life for smaller and younger diasporas, including Argentina. Polish Jewry was extremely heterogeneous, and various plans for improving the situation of Jews in Poland were implemented. The secularist-socialist supporters of the Bund party wanted to focus on local problems and act in the "here and now," the orthodox were interested in preserving the disintegrating traditional social structure, while the Zionists saw the Jewish future in Palestine. Emigration was also a popular option. Immigration to Argentina was the result of the social and economic transformation of Jewish Poland: industrialization, the decline of the shtetl, and ongoing secularization and Polonization of the younger generation.[29] These changes allowed other nontraditional life choices to seem possible and relevant.

As Scott Ury aptly noted, it is hard to give a clear description of who was/is a Polish Jew.[30] The Jews who lived in interwar Poland were a complex amalgam of identities and cultural choices. For the purpose of this study, I conceive of Polish Jews as those born on territories that were part of the Second Polish Republic after 1918. While many Polish Jews were religious Yiddish-speakers, *Haskalah* (the Jewish Enlightenment), acculturation, Jewish nationalisms, and proletarian struggles were redefining what it meant to be Jewish, both individually and collectively.[31] In a region of Galicia, Polonization had made profound advances before the Great War, and in 1921, around 42 percent of Jews declared their nationality as Polish. The influence of Polish nationalism within Polish Jewry challenged many identifications with orthodoxy and later Zionism. In the former Kingdom of Poland, the Polonization of the elite was outweighed by the Yiddish-speaking Hasidic orthodoxy in pre-1918 times. In the multinational Kresy in northeastern Poland, the Jewish elite had predominantly acculturated in Russian culture. During the interwar years, these diverse groups were defined as Polish Jews but maintained different individual trajectories and experiences. As Kenneth Moss noted, interwar Poland experienced a process of acculturation without assimilation.[32] While Jews spoke Polish and were rooted in Polish culture, they hardly ever were seen and perceived themselves as "regular Poles."

Those Jews who migrated to Argentina as adults shortly after World War I were born as citizens of the Russian, Austro-Hungarian, and Prussian empires but were influenced by contact with the surrounding Polish culture and Poles. It is noteworthy that some pre-1918 Jewish immigrants to Argentina identified as Polish Jews despite never having lived in independent Poland. It was their experience of immigration to Argentina that defined them as Polish Jews. The Jews from Poland (or from what came to be defined as Poland in 1918) were transformed into Polish Jews precisely when they left Poland. By settling in Argentina, the immigrants needed to conceptualize their (sub)ethnic identities. Although many Jews still saw themselves as *litvaks, galitsianers*, or Russian Jews, the independence of Poland, there-centered Zionism, and Yiddish-centered nationalism demanded that they conceptualize their self-identifications according to the new political entity. This was true both in eastern Europe, as well as for immigrants in Argentina. Further, the process of becoming Argentine and forming Jewish Argentine identities demanded a redefinition of their relationship to the place of origin and subethnic identifications. Even those Jewish immigrants who might not have defined themselves as Polish before World War I, in post-1918, Argentina began to imagine Jewish Poland (not Russia or Austro-Hungary) as an embodiment of the Jewish homeland, where Yiddish ethnonational life unfolded.

To analyze the experiences of Polish Jewish immigrants in Argentina, and the transnational Yiddish culture, I focus on the capital city of Buenos Aires, a dense site of Jewish life. This reflects the spatial distribution of the interwar arrivals who rarely ventured to the agricultural colonies. Yet, when discussing Polish-Jewish conceptualizations of Argentina, I refer to the entire Argentine territory and include the Jewish agricultural colonization. The periodization of this book encompasses two eras in Argentine history: the democratic period of mass Jewish migration that lasted from 1916 until 1930 and the 1930s with the authoritarian takeover and immigration restrictions. In 1916, Hipólito Yrigoyen of the Unión Cívica Radical rose to power, marking the beginning of a decade and a half of radical governments in Argentina. The radicals took power following the introduction of universal male suffrage in 1912. Benefiting from the evolving social structure and the rise of popular party politics, the radicals succeeded in recruiting the support of working-class masses. Two governments of Yrigoyen (1916–22, 1928–30) and of Marcelo Torcuato de Alvear (1922–28) allowed social progress for second-generation immigrants by making accessible university education (Reforma universitaria in 1918) and through the continuous development of employment in the public sector. These radical governments are considered the first democratic governments in Argentina's history.

José Félix Uriburu came to power in Argentina in 1930, which was the beginning of the so-called Infamous Decade, marked by a conservative and oligarchic backlash. The conservatives questioned the principle of universal suffrage and limited some constitutional freedoms. Argentine politics of the 1930s closely resembled the fascist governments in Europe, particularly that of Mussolini in Italy.[33] Numerous political opponents were sent to concentration camps in Ushuaia, the alliance between the government and the Catholic Church was strengthened, a paramilitary Unión Cívica Argentina was established, and the state's economic policies increasingly intervened in the industry. The early 1930s was a period of economic crisis that resulted in growing poverty, criminality, and hopelessness. In 1930, Uriburu raised the price of immigration visas from three to thirty pesos, and in 1931, immigration was limited to agricultural workers. Two years later, policy dictated that only those with job security or other financial support in Argentina would be granted entry into the country.[34] Nevertheless, the immigration from Poland continued through the 1930s, marking the decade as a period of immigrant integration into the Argentine national culture. The nationalist spirit of the era also reinforced immigrant identification with their new homeland. The economic recuperation visible from 1936 allowed immigrants to participate in Argentina's growing middle-class society, enjoying leisure activities such as trips to the cinema, dancing, and visits to the beach.[35] For Argentine Jews in the 1930s, the liberal integrationist ideals of the previous two decades were perceived as outdated. Many acculturated Jews began searching for ways of rapprochement with their Jewishness by way of Zionism, ethnic activism, and/or transnational solidarity.

Nation, Ethnicity, and Diaspora

Jewish emigration from Poland to Argentina is a lens for observing the competitive collision between diasporism and nationalism. In Poland, the early 1920s marked a period of growing Jewish Diaspora Nationalism, while the 1930s ushered in an era of Zionism; it should be noted that both movements were criticized by the antinationalist and nonnationalist orthodoxy and communists.[36] Interwar Warsaw had two key Jewish national figures: the Zionist Yitshak Grünbaum and the Yiddishist supporter of a Jewish cultural-national autonomy, Noyekh Prilutsky, with each representing different Jewish nationalisms. Polish and Argentine nation-state nationalisms conceived of the Jews within a national framework as includabe or excludable subjects, while the supporters of the Yiddish-based, diasporic Jewish nationalism offered a counternarrative of Diaspora Nationalism. The latter emphasized *doikeyt* (here-ness) and underlined that eastern Europe, or other diaspora countries, could offer a basis for an improved Jewish life. Both in Poland and Argentina, the revival of a Yiddish-centered, secular, Jewish ethnonationalism gained popularity among a considerable share of the local Jewish population. This study reconstructs how Jewish national and cultural life was influenced by migration through the analysis of transatlantic discussions that explore language, ethnicity, and nationalism.

While Zionism emphasizes the territorial foundations of Jewish identity, diasporism puts the focus on genealogy and a shared past.[37] Although the triumph of Zionism overshadowed other manifestations of Jewish nationalism, Diaspora Nationalism continues to be used as a critical framework for diaspora scholars. As Julie E. Cooper points out, Daniel and Jonathan Boyarin conceive of Jewish diasporism as a powerful countermodel to Zionist-centered Jewish identifications.[38] Building upon previous arguments made by the Boyarins, I apply the diasporic lens to unpack the diversity of Jewish-Argentine cultural identifications shaped both by Argentine experiences and the eastern European developments in the first half of the twentieth century. Following Roza Tsagarousianou, I aim to trace the connectivity and linkages that transnational migration demanded, rather than casting migrant experiences as displacement or exile.[39] I argue that Polish-Jewish migrants carved their identities both in the context of diasporism and Jewish and Argentine nationalisms. This was a simultaneous and not exclusive process. By succeeding in Argentina, they did not shed their diasporic identifications but shifted them to another level.

Despite the focus of Jewish studies on the "exile from Zion," Jews quite often felt comfortable in diaspora.[40] Despite repeated violence, Jewish communities flourished outside of their primordial homeland, whether in medieval Spain or the Hellenistic world.[41] Yerushalmi correctly noticed a duality of attachment both to the ancient land of origin and the desire to fill the place of resettlement with familiarity and to perceive it as Jewish. The notion of dual attachment relates not only to Zion and the dispersion in Europe but also to Jewish mass migration at the turn of the twentieth century. Ashkenazi Jews in diaspora often imagined Poland as an eastern European Zion, even as they were engaged in building their lives in Argentina. Focusing on the Polish city of Białystok, Kobrin traced the multilayered links between various centers of the Białystoker diaspora, including the Argentine one, bound mostly by the memories or imagined connections to their remote hometown in eastern Europe. Her study proved how a common ethnic origin remained relevant after migration and the importance of remembering a shared past. Following Rebecca Kobrin, I suggest a broader concept of Jewish diaspora, one that goes beyond Zionist longings and recenters eastern Europe at the center of an imagined Yiddish nation.[42]

These types of transnational ties remain largely unexplored in a wider context. Researchers tend to explain the historical phenomena related to Jewish lives in specific geographical areas without emphasizing the connections between different Jewish centers. Jewish experiences are often studied not only as separate from the non-Jewish setting but also without accounting for the links that connected Jews in diaspora across different continents.[43] Białystok Jews were not an exception from the broader trends present among migrating Jews. Beyond the lives of the migrants themselves, the mass migration of Jews that began in the late nineteenth century permanently reshaped the situation in their home countries. There is a need to examine the history of Argentine Ashkenazi Jews in relation to the conditions and changes in eastern Europe, which served as their ancestral homeland and an important point of reference after their emigration. This study suggests an emergence of a diasporic Jewish space that included both Poland and Argentina, within which a Polish Jewish subethnicity was debated and performed. Parallel phenomena were visible also among Sephardi immigrants to Argentina and their attachments to their Mediterranean and Middle Eastern homelands.[44]

Polish-Jewish immigrants were impacted by Argentine nationalism (which many of them quickly embraced), local perceptions of recent immigrant arrivals, as well as Jewish national movements (both Zionism and Diaspora Nationalism). At the same time, they were involved in global debates concerning Jews in eastern Europe. While transatlantic Jewish exchange happened within "one Jewish nation," the dialogue was bifurcated, both culturally and spatially, between Poland and Argentina, thus marking the process as transnational. Transnationalism allows scholars to speak of hybrid or mixed identities, as it offers a way of being constrained from the unidirectional focus of migration from one country to another.[45] Whereas *international* has come to denote the relations between states, governments, and other official bodies, *transnational* emphasizes people and groups who act across nations and share a common attribute of dispersal.[46] Although most studies of transnational phenomena refer to recent times of intensified globalization, sociologists of migration have long recognized that earlier migrants also maintained ties with their homelands. Scholars admit that "old migrations" reveal patterns of transnationalism, but these linkages rarely serve as a central point of inquiry.[47] The majority of research on historical migrations has focused on migrant adaptation in the host country, rather than how they continued to look back on their place of origin.[48]

This study applies a transnational lens to interpret an early twentieth-century historical phenomena that geographically spans the sending and receiving spheres of migration. Importantly, Jews in Argentina and in Poland were not equal partners, and the community in Poland was much more central than still peripheral Jewish Argentina. Jews emigrating from Poland to Argentina during the interwar period were transmigrants, whose multiple identities were generated from their sustained connections to both Poland and Argentina. This research builds off previous arguments made by Glick Shiller, Basch, and Blanc-Szanton that transmigrants "make decisions, feel concerns, and develop identities within networks that connect them to two societies simultaneously."[49] In the era of mass migration, multiple diasporic longings were at play and were never exclusive. Involvement with Jewish Poland did not challenge the formation of a Jewish-Argentine identity but rather contributed to the diversity of simultaneous ethnic attachments. The technological developments of the 1920s and 1930s did not allow for transnational relationships as we might imagine them today; yet, transmigrants had various ways to accommodate and resist divisive circumstances and ideologies that often shape the transnational experience.

The transnational connections between Argentina and Jewish Poland were held together through the movement of people and ideas as well as print culture. Ethnonational diasporas often develop a sense of "diaspora consciousness" marked by multiple identifications.[50] For instance, Sephardi Jews, as examined by Brodsky, exercised their loyalties to their ethnic community in Argentina and their hometowns in the Middle East or North Africa.[51] This research shows that a sense of belonging "both here and there" was a feature visible among Polish-Jewish migrants in Argentina. Despite internal and external tensions, the migrant generation voiced their dual belonging to Argentina and to the transnational and imagined polity of Yiddishland. Transnational phenomena shape, and are shaped by, the hegemonic structure of nation-states (Poland and Argentina) and by national movements (Yiddish-centered, Diaspora Nationalism, and to lesser extent Zionism) that foster ideologies of identity.[52] This research departs from the understanding that transnationalism does not hinder integration but rather results in a "complex amalgam of structures that combine elements of transnationalism and assimilation."[53]

By focusing on Polish Jews, this book underlines the power of subethnic identifications. In many cases Polish-Jewish identities were formed in dialogue with the experience of migration. Only after leaving Poland did many Jews long for a clear expression of their subethnic identities. The *Polishness* of many immigrants was overshadowed and complicated by preexisting categorizations of Jewishness among Argentines, wherein Ashkenazi Jews were defined as *rusos*, or Russians. Simultaneously, the stigma of female trafficking was attached to Jewish-Polishness, as Jewish prostitutes were popularly nicknamed *polacas*. To challenge these stereotypes, many Polish Jews sought to redefine their position in Argentina's ethnic mosaic. Polish Jews looked toward the Sephardim, an ethnic minority whose "Jewishness" often went unseen by the broader Argentine society, as they sought to define subethnic identity and demand recognition within the Jewish community. Both Sephardim and Polish Jews faced the challenge of insufficient communal recognition and were accused of separatism when they attempted to establish their subethnic institutions. Central to Sephardic consciousness was their rootedness to the Spanish Golden Age, while Polish Jews similarly dreamed of the glory of Jewish Poland. This study calls for a closer examination of Polish Jews in the Argentine context; as a case study, the Polish-Jewish experience illuminates the underlying fragments and tensions within the presumed homogeneity of Argentina's Ashkenazi majority.

Ethnicity and race obtained visible cultural and political power in Latin America.[54] Already in a colonial context, Spanish rulers were interested in keeping the racial segregation that clashed with a practical reality of running an empire. Biologically and culturally mixed categorizations emerged: mestizo, mulatto, castizo, and so on. In the nineteenth century, new immigration from Europe (including Jews) and Asia complicated the ethnic composition of Latin American republics. Race, *mestizaje*, and nation-ethnicity relations are a very fertile field of research with a clear modern trend to reclaim indigenous histories and mixed ancestry. Popular and academic literature has explored Japanese-Brazilians, Arab-Argentines, and Jewish-Argentines as *hybrid* or *hyphenated identities*.[55] Recent trends in Latin American Jewish studies have critiqued the myopic "Jews only" focus, encouraging researchers to think about Jews in relation to other communities, while examining "Argentine lives" as a whole. Earlier scholars looked at Jewish Latin American diasporas in a comparative perspective or placed them next to Canadian, South African, or European Jewish communities, but contemporary research is most interested in learning the ways in which Jews interacted within multiethnic societies.

In proposing a new research agenda for Latin American studies, Raanan Rein and Jeffrey Lesser argued that the study of Jewish experiences in Latin America should not be regarded as a study of an "exceptional case" but rather as an opportunity to explore how ethnicity influenced Latin American societies in general.[56] Although this book acknowledges similarities between the experiences of Jews and other immigrant groups as well as an obvious need to examine the Argentine lives of the immigrants, I suggest an additional lens of diasporic linkages performed across the Atlantic. I build off the argument proposed by Rein, that the increased legitimization of transnational links should lead to broadened research that would include more pluralistic and diverse forms of Latin American Jewish experiences.[57] Looking at the process of emigration, the construction of "Argentina" in Jewish Poland and the way that Argentine Jews saw themselves within the framework of the Yiddishland invites us to examine how patterns of ethnonational and diasporic identities emerged, dovetailed, and evolved. While I analyze how Polish-Jewish subethnicity in Argentina formed in dialogue with and alongside *argentinidad* (Argentineness), I also look at how diasporic linkages complicated the relationship between immigrants and the host nation.

Yiddishland and Global Jewish Ethnicities

When describing Jewish diasporism, historian and supporter of Jewish Autonomism, Simon Dubnow (1860–1941) saw Jews as a spiritual, social, and cultural nation but without political or territorial representation.[58] Consequently, his vision of Jewish Diaspora Nationalism (Autonomism) included the Yiddish language as the foundation of nation building. In the 1930s, nearly thirteen million Jews spoke Yiddish worldwide.[59] Yiddish was a crucial mark of Ashekanzi Jewish ethnicity in both Poland and Argentina during the interwar period. Drawing on Benedict Anderson's approach that sees nations as socially constructed and imagined, I see the transnational space of Yiddishland as an imagined diasporic Yiddish nation, inhabiting old and new centers of eastern European Jewishness.[60] During the interwar period, the Yiddishists around the world engaged in a debate over the future of the "homeland" of Yiddish culture. The Yiddishist discourse in Poland and beyond popularized the concept of Yiddishland, a linguistic embodiment of the eastern European diaspora. Yiddishland was imagined not only as the historic home of the Yiddish language but also included territories, or colonies, in the Americas, South Africa, Australia, and Palestine.[61] The term is very useful for examining cultural and ethnic exchanges between Poland and Argentina. The aterritoriality of Yiddishland highlights the ways that Jews in Argentina saw themselves embedded in a continuous cultural debate with eastern Europe.

This book applies the terms *Yiddishism* and *Yiddishland* as analytic tools to understand Jewish experiences in-between Poland and Argentina. Furthermore, this book engages in a discussion about language ideologies—ideas about the interplay of language, ethnicity, and nation—while exploring the meaning of language among hybridized immigrant Jewish identities. Yiddishism was a cultural-linguistic form of Jewish nationalism and a bearer of a cultural identity. It was a culturist movement that sought recognition across borders and helped Jews mark their diasporic ethnonational identity without being rooted to a singular geographic site. In essay writings, Hersh Dovid Nomberg and Der Tunkeler popularized the term that was used during the 1908 Czernowitz language conference.[62] Yiddish was one of the most successful "power for language" movements, and following the Czernowitz conference, Yiddish came to be seen as political gunpowder.[63] Yiddishism corresponded with non-Zionist political alternatives such as territorialism and Diaspora Nationalism/folkism. As Kenneth B. Moss wrote, the institution of a full-fledged, separate Jewish culture (i.e., Yiddish culture) was something peculiar to eastern European modernity. It did not have a comparative model in western Europe, where emancipation and integration were bound up with the dissolution of Jewish identities (except of religious ones), nor in the United States, where the concept of secular citizenship had purported to include

Jews into the nation. In eastern Europe, the productive potential was of a separate Jewish language and collective Jewish identities. Eastern European Jews claimed an alternative form of modernity: Yiddish-centered Jewish culture.[64] This approach also characterized Jewish immigrants in Argentina for a period of time.

Yiddish served as a basis for identity formation among Ashkenazi Jews, for those in eastern Europe and those in the new Jewish centers, and grew into an ethnonational phenomenon with its own culture, politics, and education system. Yiddish-centered cultural and national efforts were secular endeavors, spearheaded by progressive cultural nationalists with political ideologies that challenged traditional orthodoxy and conservative religious institutions. Although the imagined secular-progressive Yiddishness was not equivalent to Yiddishism (which focused on the advancement of Yiddish as a language of high and popular culture and scholarship), both terms center the intersection between language and nationality. Whereas Zionism came to be understood as "the" Jewish national movement, the efforts of proponents of secular Yiddishness were also balanced on the same Jewish national platform as the Zionists and existed alongside one another.

Various Jewish political movements, like Bundism and Labor Zionism, relied heavily on the power of Yiddish as a defining factor of linguistic, ethnic, and national identity. Yiddishism was envisioned by the Jewish intelligentsia, but their project aimed to bring the new Jewish culture to the masses. One of its first theoreticians was Chaim Zhitlowsky, who imagined the Yiddish language as a site (whether actual or imagined) of Jewish sovereignty and cultural autonomy if not nationhood.[65] For Zhitlowsky and other advocates of Yiddish, the ideal of *kultur-arbet*, or cultural work, became a slogan for popular efforts and was transformed into an agenda with a clear programmatic and pragmatic dimension. Despite, and in response to, the growing acculturation in Poland and elsewhere in the world throughout the 1920s and 1930s, Yiddishist activists increasingly engaged in debates about a transnational Yiddishland that connected eastern European Jewish communities. In many ways, Yiddishism was a response to other developing nationalist movements across countries with established Jewish minorities, namely Poland. As Dovid Katz noted, eastern European Jews used Yiddishism as a tool to acquire an advanced language of culture that empowered them and placed them on the same level as their neighbors.[66] While traditional Jewish life was eroding, Yiddish-centered movements proposed an interesting alternative, offering a new type of Jewishness that intersected with a progressive national and diasporic framework. They offered Jews an imagined cultural homeland, national language, national literature, and national goals. As Jewish realities changed, Yiddishists believed that ethnicity could be preserved by linguistic self-reflexivity.[67]

Yiddishism grew strong roots in Argentina, and the global character of the movement influenced Jewish immigrant identities in Argentina. The Yiddishland framework allowed Jews in Argentina to be in permanent cultural, political, and social exchange with Jews in Poland, the United States, and other countries. As a language spoken by a majority of Jews, Yiddish was a lingua franca that permitted communication and the transfer of cultural contents and ideas across borders. Despite being initially perceived as peripheral from the eastern European perspective, few Argentine Jews were quick to embrace the Yiddishist agenda. This ambivalence was shaped by the relatively late Jewish immigration to Argentina and the social demographics of this community. Those Polish Jews who settled in Argentina in the 1920s and 1930s grew up on the highly politicized "Jewish street" of Poland. Some arrived after journalistic and partisan experiences with Bundism, Labor Zionism, or communism. For this generation, it was obvious that Jews needed a Yiddish press to voice their interests and Jewish progressive schooling to educate the younger generations and that the task of the Yiddish press and literature was to raise ethnonational awareness. Yiddishist discourse relied on literary, pedagogical, and journalistic mediums wherein Yiddish was employed as a national language.

It should be noted that Yiddish and Yiddishism in the Argentine context should not be perceived merely as a nostalgic link to primordial language and culture. Argentina, which came to represent "the second-best immigration option," allows us to better understand the complex relations within Yiddishland and the nexus between the diasporic and the national. Argentina did not carry the same weight as the United States, and sometimes, Jewish Poland even ridiculed and marginalized it. The marginalization of Jewish Argentina incentivized Argentine Jews to participate in transnational diasporic cultural networks. The struggle for ethnic Argentine Jewish prestige and reputation was carried out on both domestic and international fronts. Like other ethnic communities in Argentina, Jews wanted to be perceived as economically powerful and ethnically proud. As such, they built ethnic institutions in Argentina and engaged in Jewish fund-raising and aid initiatives for the Old Country. The transnational engagement in Europe was marked as Argentine help and regarded as in statu nascendi Jewish-Argentineness. The same was true for representing Argentina in the global Jewish sphere; the 1937 Yidisher Kultur-Kongres in Paris is one such example.

By demanding admission to and recognition within the Yiddishland diaspora, Argentina's Jews cultivated their rootedness to Argentina. When discussing Argentina's belonging to Yiddishland, local Yiddishist Pinie Katz wrote that it was precisely the liberal laws of Argentina that allowed Yiddish culture to flourish. Katz believed in the complementarity of being Jewish and Argentine, and as a communist, he stressed the common struggle for a better and more just world among both Argentines and Jews.[68] In a 1940 essay, Katz gave voice to Jewish rootedness in Argentina, which he defined as a Jewish home. At the same time, he described Jews as a nation and Argentine Jews as part of this nation.[69] Whereas argentinidad was clearly pronounced among acculturated second-generation Jewish Argentines, the Yiddish-speaking *argentiner yidn* also developed a strong connection to their adopted country. As first-generation immigrants however, their relationship to their new Argentine homeland was marked by careful and, at times, tenuous linguistic negotiations between Spanish and Yiddish. In addition, these new Polish-Jewish Argentines were forced to contend with competing nationalisms between Argentina and Poland, along with broader processes within the Jewish diaspora.

Book Structure

The organization of the book is thematic rather than chronological. The first and second chapters engage with debates among Polish Jews concerning Argentina in order to glimpse the ways in which various actors imagined the emigration. In the first chapter, I analyze how Hebrew and Polish journals, edited and read by a local Jewish elite, conceptualized emigration to Argentina at the turn of nineteenth and twentieth centuries. Additionally, I show how state-run and Jewish emigration societies influenced the discourse on Argentina in Poland. In the first chapter, I argue that the Jewish elite intentionally portrayed Argentina in negative terms in an effort to stabilize the old hierarchies and to slow ongoing social and economic changes. At the same time, the Polish government was increasingly invested in Jewish emigration from Poland. I use the Argentine case to portray the ruptures within Polish Jewry and to present the Argentine debates as a lens for looking at the transformation it was undergoing. The conflicting images of Argentina that were created and re-created in Jewish Poland illustrate the competing interests of futureless (often working-class) youth, the interests of an integrationist elite, religious leadership, and the agenda of Polish authorities.

In the second chapter, I show how the Yiddish press played a key role in creating popular images of Argentina in Jewish Poland. Immigration to Argentina, portrayed historically (1890s) as negative, was largely normalized in the 1920s. Yiddish dailies such *Haynt* and *Der Moment* acted as emigration advisors and informed potential emigrants about the economic and social situation in Argentina. At the same time, Yiddish media outlets often exoticized Argentina, overemphasizing the country as a global mecca of Jewish prostitution. In addition, this chapter analyzes how ship companies advertised travel to Argentina, exploring the graphic strategies used to incentivize migration. I suggest that the Yiddish press acted as a textual intermediary, translating the Argentine experience to its readership in Poland. Collectively, chapters 1 and 2 offer a holistic view of how Argentina was represented and perceived in pre-1939 Poland and the ideological tensions that arose as Argentina was absorbed into the eastern European Jewish worldview.

Chapter 3 focuses on exoticization of Argentina, by way of travel writings by eastern European Yiddish authors. I analyze the travelogues of Peretz Hirschbein (*Fun vayte lender. Argentine, brazil yuni, november1914*, 1916) and Hersh Dovid Nomberg ("Di argentinishe rayze," 1924) and illuminate the portrayal of Argentina as a dangerous, wild, and abnormal space. Hirschbein's and Nomberg's travelogues and travel articles were principally geared toward eastern European Jews considering emigration, as well as those who never thought of Argentina as a relevant option. I argue that authors were bound to the expectations of their eastern Europe audience; readers sought to affirm their stereotypes of Argentina by way of the literature they consumed. Further, I situate Yiddish travelogues of Argentina into a wider panorama of European travel writing. I examine the similarities and differences between Jewish travel writers and those who represented the colonial empires. Furthermore, I underline the proximity between travelers and those whom they researched (immigrant Jews) to argue that Hirschbein and Nomberg, as Jews, often had different agendas from that of their western European counterparts.

In chapter 4, I examine how diverse actors in Poland and Argentina worked to include Argentina in the imagined entity of Yiddishland. I analyze the portrayals of Argentina in the high-brow, Warsaw-based Yiddish literary journal *Literarishe Bleter*. The journal offered a unique representation of Argentina and its Jews that was not essentialized, nor exoticized; rather this journal of interwar Poland represented Jews in Argentina as fellow citizens of a diasporic Yiddish nation. Next, the travels of Polish Jewish representatives to Argentina provide useful case studies to observe the expansion of the Yiddishland from eastern Europe to Latin America. For instance, Peretz Hirschbein and Hersh Dovid Nomberg shared a Yiddishist ideology and during their visits carefully observed the successes and shortcomings of the Yiddish cultural agenda in Argentina. At the same time, visits to Latin American by the well-known Yiddish writers reinforced Yiddish culture in Argentina. Hirschbein and Nomberg were received as stars of Yiddish culture after arriving in Buenos Aires. This part of the book thus deals with *traveling Yiddishism*: an ethnonational and cultural movement whose transnational scope helped to bridge Argentina's Polish Jewish population and Poland's literate public. At the same time, Argentine Jews marked the emergence of Jewish-Argentine identities by receiving the emissaries of the Old World. Local activists saw themselves as representatives of Argentina and wished to present Argentine Jewish culture as an echo of progressive Yiddish cultural trends from Poland. Hirschbein and Nomberg observed the formation of diasporic Jewish identities alongside the intersecting process of *becoming* Argentine. In sum, this chapter underlines the legacy of Yiddishism in migratory movements and underscores how travel writing elucidates the tension between the national and the diasporic.

Chapter 5 centers Argentine Jewish discussions on Argentineness, Jewishness, and the place of Jews in Argentina. My research on Argentine policies, debates concerning the Jews, Argentine Jewish essay writing, and immigrant literature illustrates that the postwar Polish-Jewish immigration wave challenged and complicated the ongoing processes of cultural integration in Argentina. The 1920s influx of Jews who experienced the Yiddish sociocultural renaissance in Poland helped to again anchor Yiddish culture in Argentina and temporarily re-Yiddishize it. This chapter argues that the negotiation of Jewish argentinidad was significantly influenced by the diasporic Yiddish agenda. I begin by introducing the immigration ideologies that developed in Argentina since the mid-nineteenth century, underscoring how Argentine leaders imagined the place of Jews within the national project. I move on to portray the circles of *israelitas argentinos* (or Jewish Argentines), the second generation of Argentina's first agricultural colonists. I analyze the cultural circle of Sociedad Hebraica Argentina (SHA), along with its charismatic leader Salomón Resnick, to highlight their active role in the process of hybridization between the Argentine and the Yiddish. Although they saw Argentina as their physical and spiritual homeland and Spanish as the quotidian language in the public sphere, many Jewish Argentines did not relinquish their commitment to eastern Europe and more specifically Jewish Poland. Resnick translated Poland's Yiddish authors, and anti-Semitism in Poland was regularly met with an outcry in the Spanish-language Jewish press. Simultaneously, the Yiddish cultural sphere in Argentina was not an insular space but an arena of hybridization where the diasporic and the local mixed. The lines between Yiddish and Jewish-Argentine cultural spheres were ambivalent.

Through chapters 6 and 7, I trace Argentine landsman history. Landsmanshaftn, associations that united Jews coming from the same town or region (landslayt), were often marginalized in the historiography and portrayed as nostalgic, backward-looking gatherings. In these two chapters, I challenge these simplifications and offer a panoramic and complex picture that underscores the role of landsmanshaftn in ethnic empowerment. I analyze the influence of the landsman movement on the development of a diasporic Polish-Jewish subethnicity, while highlighting its transnational reach to the Jews in Poland. I argue that Poylisher Farband (the landsman organization uniting Jewish immigrants from Poland) constructed a framework of belonging that demanded that Polish Jews in Argentina maintain a commitment to their native country. Ultimately, Argentine landsmanshaftn helped to shape transnational solidarity networks between dispersed Polish Jews, centering common goals, both real and imagined. The 1920s and 1930s saw an array of fund-raising initiatives to support various institutions, including secular Yiddishist schools, YIVO Institute, assistance for the poor, often including both members of the organization and the Jewish community more broadly.

Simultaneously, Argentine Jews of Polish origin did not see their engagement with Poland as an obstacle for becoming Argentine. On the contrary, ethnic engagement was a mechanism for claiming belonging to Argentina and marking the successes, cohesiveness, and vitality of the ethnic community. Landsmanshaftn offered an interstitial site of Argentine rootedness and diasporic nostalgia, a space to negotiate and define Jewish argentinidad. The transnational commitments and engagement among the Polish Jews of Argentina highlight both a *dependence* within diasporic networks and claims for *independence*, along with a desire to be recognized as Argentine Jews. I move outside a narrow scholarly focus on memorial books (*yizkor bikher*) published by the landsmanshaftn after 1945 by emphasizing the pre-1939 role of these associations in engendering sub(ethnic) identities, seeing them as a path for inclusion in a multiethnic society.

Chapter 8 focuses on the perception of eastern Europe in the context of Argentina. I explore the channels through which the Jews in Argentina were informed about the developments in eastern Europe. Additionally, I examine how Jewish Argentine ethnic leaders sought to cast a positive light on Argentina in Jewish Poland. In sum, I use Argentine Yiddish immigrant literature as a lens to explore the challenges and contradictions of building a new life in Latin America while maintaining ties to eastern Europe. Some authors offer ecstatic manifestos calling for an embrace of Argentina, only to later describe the pain of being uprooted and culturally displaced in Argentina. Central to my study is a challenge to the idea that Argentina offered a gold ticket to success or effortless "redemption" from troubles faced by Polish Jews in eastern Europe. As such, this work explores the emotional and cultural price of emigration.

1

Jewish Elites, Gentile Opinions, and the Argentine Dream

At the turn of the nineteenth and the twentieth centuries, Peretz Hirschbein, a Polish-born Yiddish writer, recalled that Argentina was "seducing" the poorest of the poor with its presumed richness and liberties. Jews in Poland allegedly began to dream about Argentina. Hirschbein paraphrased the contemporary atmosphere in the following way: "Come here [to Argentina], come here, it will be your country. . . . Here flows milk and honey. . . . You can eat bread and meat until being satiated. Sun and happiness rule here. Come here, with sons and daughters, settle down in a country of happiness, everything will be provided upon your arrival. . . . Come quick, come quick!"[1]

The establishment of the Jewish Colonization Association (JCA) by Baron Maurice de Hirsch in the last decade of the nineteenth century sparked a debate in eastern Europe concerning the possibility of immigration to Argentina. Hirsch devoted a significant sum of money with the intention to resettle thousands of eastern European Jews to new agricultural colonies in Argentina, among other countries in the Americas. At the end of the century, the rush to Argentina was popularized primarily among impoverished Polish Jews; however, acculturated Jewish elites, with no intention of emigrating, also held stakes in this emerging migration. From the elite perspective, emigration was a new burning social problem that was approached very ambivalently. The Argentine fever of the 1890s was an answer to the same pressing social and political problems that Zionism and Jewish socialism began to address at the end of the nineteenth century. In the exact same way that Zionism was initially limited to the narrow circles of Hovevey Tsiyon (Lovers of Zion), Argentine debates did not start among ordinary people but among the educated and cultured classes. The Argentine emigration was one of the instances when they did not focus on internal issues but looked on the fates of the poor and persecuted. The discussions concerning Argentina within the Jewish elite mirrored parallel debates within Polish Catholic elite concerning the question of peasant colonization of Argentina and Brazil.

This chapter explores how external actors, Jewish elite who did not plan to emigrate, Poland's government, as well as Jewish and non-Jewish emigration activists approached the issue of Jewish emigration to Latin America. It starts by depicting the last decade of the nineteenth century and the Argentine debates in the Hebrew and Polish Jewish press and later examines how emigration to Argentina was inscribed into wider discussions on the place of Jews in Poland. The Argentine colonization initiative of de Hirsch was rooted in the Jewish elite's desire to ease the poverty of eastern European Jewry. Studying the contexts in which Jewish immigration to Argentina was approached in those early years helps to understand the developments in conceptualizing Argentina that took place in the next decades (see fig. 2).

Helping the Folk: The Polish Jewish Elite and the Question of *Erets Ha-kesef*

At the end of the nineteenth century, around 40 percent of Russian Jews relied on communal help. The May Laws of 1882 limited the number of professions available to Jews, forbade relocation, work in agriculture, and the production and sale of alcohol, consequently bringing ruin to many Jewish families in tsarist Russia.[2] In the context of the economic crisis, some eastern European *maskilim* (the followers of the Haskalah) and integrationists saw colonization in Argentina as a chance to improve the plight of the Jewish poor.[3] In some cases, pogroms functioned as the final decisive push for the ordinary Jews. Yet, the agricultural settlement project of de Hirsch was, at times, met with suspicion by Poland's Jewish elite. The ongoing industrialization of the Kingdom of Poland cast visions of pastoral agricultural settlements in Argentina in an unrealistic light and as untimely efforts that went against the modernizing economic trends of Europe. Yet, the growing economic crisis and rising level of poverty demanded the search for a solution. The tendency to approach Argentina as a site of hope for impoverished countrymen can be traced in the Jewish elite's Hebrew and Polish-language press. Both the contributors and the readers of these newspapers did not think of themselves when they talked about Argentina. The subject of their discussions was the disenfranchised, the poor, and the hopeless. In 1913, Adolf Goldflam, the president of the Warsaw Information Bureau for Emigrant Jews, said that Jewish emigrants were "dark and passive" and consequently demanded a helping hand of the privileged coreligionists.[4]

Poland's Jewish journals began featuring Argentina as early as 1888, when the Hebrew-language *Hazefirah* wrote about a group of Jews who settled in Buenos Aires.[5] In the next few years, regular reports about groups or families departing to Argentina from various corners of the Russian Empire began to appear in the newspaper. In June 1889, *Hazefirah* reported a visit to Warsaw by the Argentine consul, who encouraged emigration with promises of equal civil rights and a warm welcome in Argentina.[6] The paper published reports about the agents of de Hirsch in Paris, at times reprinting their letters in *Hazefirah*.[7] The debate

Figure 2. A map of Jewish agricultural colonies in Argentina. Colonies are marked with black dots. From *50 años de colonización judía en la Argentina* (Buenos Aires: DAIA, 1939), 151.

about Argentina continued into the 1890s and 1900s. Readers and editors took positions on the Argentine question, with some arguing that Erets Ha-kesef was rich, abundant, and free, while others, including some Zionists, emphasized the threat that emigration posed to Jewish unity and tradition.[8] Others, like Zionist author Nahum Slouschz, wrote that Argentina was made "for people, not for the spirit," rejecting claims that viewed Argentine emigration as a danger to Zionist ideology.[9] Personal letters from Argentina also appeared in *Hazefirah*.[10] Abraham Rozenfeld wrote from Colonia Mauricio, Abraham Horovitz from Moisés Ville, and Israel Fingerman from Colonia Clara.[11] Another Hebrew newspaper, *Hamagid* from Kraków, received regular correspondence from Argentina-based writer and activist Yankev Shimon (Jacobo Simón) Liachovitzky.[12] Newspapers served as the contact point between emigrants and the community in Poland. For instance, a certain Perets Faygenboym made a request in his letter to have a few religious objects, like *sidurim* (prayer books), sent to Moisés Ville.[13]

The Polish-language integrationist publication *Izraelita* approached the prospect of building a Jewish settlement in Argentina rather ambivalently. On the one hand, *Izraelita* often cited the presumably marvelous statistics of JCA colonies, pointing to the large Jewish farms and religious freedoms offered by Argentina.[14] It reported the growing number of colonists (7,551 in 1901 and 20,115 in 1910),[15] the exceptionally magnificent harvest, and remittances sent by the colonists.[16] Its chief editor, Samuel Peltyn, wrote that the idea of Jewish immigration to Argentina was laudable and would improve the fate of the Jewish masses, even "refine them."[17] Ten years later, Adolf Jakub Cohn answered in *Izraelita* how those "allowed by luck to be above the crowd and who could allow themselves to lead a lovely, thornless life in the homeland [Poland]"—meaning the upper-class readers of the journal—should react to emigration. Cohn applauded Jewish colonization in Argentina. He believed that those who "suffocate" in poverty would do anything to leave Russian Poland. The task of the Jewish elite was to assist fellow coreligionists whom "circumstances had brought to the verge of an abyss." Cohn explicitly called on the Jewish intelligentsia and bourgeoisie to facilitate emigration to Argentina.[18] On the other hand, Nahum Sokolow was convinced that emigration could not be a solution for the entire Jewish folk, even not the poor with no prospects. Sokolow believed that Polish maskilim knew their people better than western European men of charity (as de Hirsch) and saw more room for social work in Poland rather than rushing to emigration. Some regarded emigration as a form of defeatism and an implicit acknowledgment that Jewish integrationist circles had nothing to offer the poor.

Izraelita had a rather one-sided approach to the conflicts between the immigrant colonists and the JCA administration. The weekly relied on information provided by English newspapers and, as an acculturationist paper, took the side of the German Jewish and English Jewish JCA functionaries rather than the ordinary eastern European settlers.[19] Sokolow, referring to the colonists' rebellion against the JCA administration, wrote that the "colonies are inhabited by the riffraff, by emigrant scumbags from Volhynia, Bessarabia and God knows where else. This is a dark and insolent crowd, easy to manipulate by any gossip, people without goals and endurance."[20] While acknowledging some initial difficulties, *Izraelita* concluded that complaints of the immigrants were often exaggerated and untrue. Answering a letter from a Moisés Ville colonist, who lamented the JCA restrictions, the weekly wrote: "These kinds of careerists and know-it-alls . . . for whom it is hard to carry the yoke of order, are a destructive force and should be deported as soon as possible. There [in Argentina] one needs simple and honest people; there you need honest minds and strong hands. . . . Delicate minds with experience in commerce would only produce intrigue, gossip and internal conflict."[21] *Izraelita*'s editors were perfectly aware of the difficulties and conflicts in Argentina but saw colonization as an endeavor worth the price of the initial pain. Sokolow wrote that constructing the "new Jew," a hard-working colonist devoted to the land, was a top priority, and in this light "any Argentine or Palestinian scandals" were of no importance.[22]

Izraelita did not directly encourage emigration but often saw it as a relevant option for masses of impoverished Jews. At the beginning of the 1880s, the journal debated whether to emigrate but, by the beginning of the twentieth century, was describing emigration as an active and ongoing process.[23] In the early twentieth century, emigration had become a Jewish reality rather than a matter of debate. Nearly every issue published articles on Jewish colonization in Argentina, reporting on statistical data that concerned settler benefits and information on agricultural production. *Izraelita* also reprinted letters of the colonists. In 1892, one of them wrote that the JCA had provided them with all comforts, including elegant bed sets. The colonist wrote that his letter was intended to fight off "the complaints of malcontents who spread lies about Argentina."[24] Taken as a whole, *Izraelita* approached Argentina with hope and came to view emigration as part of the broader positivist agenda by which the acculturated Jewish elite attempted to ease the situation of the poor Jewish masses in Poland. Yet, as the integrationists stressed, Jewish life needed to be improved in Poland, as emigration was a solution available only to a small fraction of the population.

The issue of Jewish immigration to Argentina remained a controversial subject during the entire pre-1914 period, functioning as an arena where diverse interests collided. Emigration represented hope for the poor, but at the same time, according to others, it endangered the traditional Jewish family, community structures, and norms. Orthodox circles, which shaped communal life in many towns and cities, approached immigration to Argentina or the United States critically and with suspicion.[25] Yet, even the progressive maskilim often viewed Argentina in the darkest hues. In 1891, *Hazefirah* lamented the plight of Jews from Yelizavetgrad (now Kropyvnytskiy in Ukraine), who, on their way to Argentina, were refused entry to Austrian Lemberg (Lwów in Poland in interwar years, now Lviv in Ukraine) and were sent back to Russia.[26] A few years later, the same newspaper reported on the situation of immigrants abandoning Argentine Jewish colonies due to financial problems and conflicts with the JCA administration. In one article, Sokolow offered a scathing commentary: "To the wild creatures, to the fanatics, who come from the Spaniards. Do we want to send our poor folk to them?"[27]

In 1890, as the first letters describing the situation in Argentina began flowing in, an editor of *Hazefirah* came out in a fury, accusing the emigrants of not following the paper's advice:

> Again Argentina! Even after witnesses, hundreds of confirmed witnesses, [reported] the hardship and pain that await [arrivals] in the remote country, and after we warned the unfortunate not to go to Argentina, but [now] we are helpless. Just yesterday our correspondent from Berlin reported another hundred families on their way to Argentina. It is with pain and sadness that we look on the division of the nation into those who read [our advice] and those who do not, and lament the small number of newspaper readers among the *folksmenshn*."[28]

This quote highlights the ambivalent attitude toward Argentina on the part of the Jewish elite in Poland. The *Hazefirah* article called the emigrants "miserable wanderers" and talked about those attracted by Argentina as "bats which instead of a sweet light of truth prefer the drug of death." Argentina was described as a seductive and false Garden of Eden. The daily reported about dozens of readers asking the editors about Argentina. *Hezefirah*'s advice was clear: keep calm and stay at home.

The elite's Hebrew or Polish sources from the pre-1914 era were far from optimistic and explicitly pointed to the difficulties faced by settlers. In 1910, in Galician Stanislau (now Ivano-Frankivsk in Ukraine), a book was published by Leon Chasanovitch, a writer and Labor Zionist, who traveled to the Argentine Jewish colonies.[29] His book, *Die Krise der jüdischen Kolonisation in Argentinien und der moralische Bankerott der J.C.A.-Administration* (The crisis of Jewish colonization in Argentina and the moral bankruptcy of the JCA administration), was published in German and Yiddish, suggesting that it was targeted at both the popular and acculturated readership. Chasanovitch fiercely criticized the colonization enterprise. He knew it from personal experience by living briefly in Argentina, before being deported after standing charged with anarchism. Chasanovitch accused the organization of fraud, misunderstanding the original concepts of de Hirsch, and "moral bankruptcy." Chasanovitch prodded the JCA by emphasizing that fewer Jews lived in all the Jewish colonies of Argentina than on a single street in Vilna.[30]

Yiddish writer Yitskhok Leybush Peretz emerged as the figure that united the Jewish elite with the Jewish masses concerning the Argentine question. He belonged to the cultural echelons of Jewish society but wrote in Yiddish for a broader Jewish public, often taking inspiration from the life of simple shtetl Jews. According to Samuel Rollansky, Peretz planned to travel to Argentina together with his friend Yankev Dinezon and considered founding a Yiddish newspaper there. In a letter to Dovid Falk, Peretz wrote about a separate book that he planned to devote to Argentina.[31] In 1902, Peretz entered into a debate about the JCA with literary critic Israel Isidor Elyashev (Bal Mahshoves), who described Argentine colonization as "creating an open wound on the body of the Jewish folk," arguing the negative consequences that the Palestine-Argentina dichotomy might have on the Zionist project.[32] Peretz dismissed this accusation and argued that the JCA was the only existing transnational Jewish body, "a sign of Jewish unity," and could only be beneficial to Jewish folk.[33] In another article, Peretz criticized a moral panic concerning Argentine Jewish female trafficking. In a protofeminist call, Peretz emphasized that Jewish prostitution was linked to the poverty of Jewish women in eastern Europe and Argentina and their lack of independence and chances to earn a living. Peretz noted the hypocrisy of Argentina's critics by pointing out that prostitution blossomed in every big Jewish city.[34] Although in Poland Peretz's opinions were of great importance, his articles supporting agricultural colonization went almost unnoticed in Argentina, which in that period still lacked professional Jewish media outlets. Peretz's interest in Argentina does not signify his special preference for Latin America but rather part of the ongoing discussions of that era, when, as Rollansky concluded, "Palestine and Argentina appeared as two twins."[35]

On the Same Ship: Jewish and Non-Jewish Emigration from Poland

The possibilities of immigration to Argentina were relevant not only to Jews but also to Polish and Ukrainian peasants. Between 1869 and 1939, around 150,000 Polish peasants permanently immigrated to Argentina and Brazil, with a large majority in the 1890s and 1900s.[36] "Argentine fever" in the Kingdom of Poland hit Jews and peasants precisely in the same years. Economic opportunities became increasingly scarce beginning in 1884, due to the agrarian crisis, a ban on crop exports to the UK, a ban on working in Prussia, an industrial crisis in the Łódź area, growing overpopulation in rural areas of central and eastern Poland, and the introduction of the May Laws in the case of Jews.[37] In the last decade of the nineteenth century, Argentina emerged as an emigration destination for both Jews and non-Jews. Both Jews and peasants were targeted by emigration agents, who circulated through towns and villages.

Catholic leaders, similarly to Jewish elite media outputs, initially were critical concerning the Polish peasant immigration to Latin America, mostly to Brazil. In 1891, Antoni Potocki compiled a book of letters sent by emigrants from Brazil and Argentina. The letters depicted Brazil as hell on Earth, emphasizing the striking poverty of the immigrants and their hopelessness and disillusionment. In addition, gentile Polish authors, similarly to some Jewish figures, explained the difficulties of colonization by placing the blame on the "inadequate human capital."[38] During the emigration fever of the 1890s and 1900s, popular Polish press titles, such as *Kurjer Warszawski, Gazeta Lwowska*, and *Kurier Poznański*, warned readers not to immigrate to Latin America. Press editors and their urban readers, largely alienated from the life of the peasantry, regarded emigration as "a threat" to Polishness losing its human reservoir.[39] From the perspective of Polish landowners, including the nobility and the Catholic Church, the peasant emigration was a purely negative development. It was perceived as devastating to the national economy and Poland's human resources, while depriving landowners of cheap and always available labor.

Among the critical voices, some understood the precarious situation of the peasants and advocated for and helped to organize emigration.[40] In those years, some studies examined the possibilities and influences of gentile emigration to Latin America, usually situated within a quasi-colonial discourse (partitioned Poland was obviously incapable of making any real colonial claims). During the Argentine hype preceding World War I, the Polish Emigration Society (Polskie Towarzystwo Emigracyjne) published several books featuring Argentina. In 1912, Roman Jordan's *Argentyna jako teren dla polskiego wychodźstwa: Sprawozdanie z podróży informacyjnej* (Argentina as a terrain for Polish emigration: A report from a study trip) came out in Kraków. Józef Okołowicz, another leader of the Polish Emigration Society, published *O widokach dla robotników sezonowych w Argentynie* (Concerning the prospects of seasonal workers in Argentina) in Kraków in 1911.

After the First World War, the discourse of colonization and emigration continued in independent Poland. Józef Włodek, a Polish honorary consul in Argentina, edited *Argentyna i emigracja ze szczególnym uwzględnieniem emigracji polskiej* (Argentina and emigration with a special focus on Polish emigration), published in Warsaw in 1923. In the late 1920s and early 1930s, several Polish-Spanish phrasebooks were also published in Warsaw (some by governmental institutions, some by steamship carriers). In 1937, the Emigration Syndicate issued a brochure on immigration to Argentina that, although directed mostly at Polish peasants, applauded Jewish achievements in Argentina.[41] In the same year, the Polish consul in Buenos Aires, Wacław Dostal, edited another updated volume on Argentina.[42] In 1936, the Instytut Gospodarstwa Społecznego (Institute of Social Economy) announced a memoir contest for Polish emigrants in South America. The following year, the institute published a volume that included selected testimonies.[43] They featured the difficulties of immigrant life, but also a conviction that their hard work would help them to improve their lives. The testimonies, written by ordinary people, bore witness to the challenges of everyday life. Although these publications primarily featured Polish gentile emigrants of peasant backgrounds, they drew on the general presence of Argentina in the discourse of emigration in interwar Poland.

Discussions about emigration were fostered by semiacademic and semi-policy-oriented institutions, including the Polskie Towarzystwo Emigracyjne (Polish Emigration Society, PTE), Naukowy Instytut Emigracyjny (Scientific Emigration Institute), and Liga Morska i Kolonialna (Naval and Colonial League). These bodies, rooted in pre–World War I colonization debates, saw emigration as a solution to Poland's economic problems, as well as a mechanism of colonial expansion. They organized research expeditions to Argentina, Peru, Brazil, and Canada, published policy papers, held conferences, and edited academic periodicals and monographs. The PTE, established in 1924, sought primarily to offer protection to Polish emigrants. The Scientific Emigration Institute, headed by nationalist Stanisław Gąbecki, operated between the mid-1920s and 1932 and focused on exploring new areas for Polish colonial settlement, chiefly in Latin America. In the same geographic context, the institute's Gustaw Załęcki talked about Polish "national imperialism."[44] When Latin American countries began to limit their proimmigration policies at the turn of the 1920s and into the 1930s, Mieczysław Fularski of the Naval and Colonial League debated the possibilities of colonization that remained open to Poland.[45]

For these societies, Jewish emigration was but a section of the broader Polish landscape of emigration. In 1937, Stanisław Pawłowski published *O emigracji żydów z Polski i ich kolonizacji* (On the emigration of Jews from Poland and their colonization). The sixty-eight-page publication, published by the Naval and Colonial League, focused on the various destinations for Jewish emigration from Poland and described it as an "obvious need." Pawłowski referred to the then-popular discourse of *Lebensraum* (living space) and pointed to Poland's high population growth, which made it "too tiny" for an ever-increasing population. Pawłowski pointed out that Jews were a diasporic nation, full of national awareness, therefore emigration would not harm them as a community. He advised that Palestine would make the best option for Jewish emigration—"Palestine can be in Jewish hands in just a few years"—but at the same time, supported Argentina, "where Jews showed a lot of organizational abilities," as a promising alternative. Pawłowski called on Polish emigration societies to intensify their propaganda among the Jewish public. According to Pawłowski, the Polish state should take an active role in promoting Jewish emigration, in place of what he saw as "a passive policy." He argued that Poland's foreign policy should include providing Jews with reasonable emigration possibilities yet remain linked to broader emigration plans that included non-Jews.[46]

The theme of immigration to Argentina also became a part of the anti-Semitic discourse in interwar Poland. Within the growing anti-Semitic debates, Jewish immigration to Argentina (or elsewhere) was considered the perfect solution to the "Jewish problem." This view corresponded with the discourse of Poland's presumed overpopulation and the government-backed emigration of minorities. For instance, the Narodowy Związek Chłopski (National Peasant Union, NZCh), an organization that defined the raising of national awareness among peasants as its goal, saw Jewish domination in commerce as a threat to the national rights of the Poles and called for a boycott of Jewish-owned businesses. In the words of one representative: "Without enough customers, the Jewish shopkeepers will close their businesses; the Jewish industrialists, without enough clients, will withdraw the funds earned in better times and will leave for Argentina. There they will conduct their business, where the people are hardly enlightened or smart."[47]

Jewish emigration from Poland also had its Jewish advocates. A key political figure was Ignacy Schiper, who served as deputy in the Polish parliament (Sejm) from 1919 to 1927. Schiper worked in the Warsaw Institute of Judaic Studies and contributed to the innovative sociohistorical studies on Polish Jewry, including aspects of migration. Despite being a Zionist, Schiper never planned to go to Palestine himself; yet, he understood the importance of migration for the pauperized Polish Jews. In 1925, he inquired in the Sejm about the Emigration Law that was to regulate emigration policies.[48] In 1939, his academic colleague from the Institute of Judaic Studies, Arie Tartakower, wrote important studies on Jewish migration: *Yidishe emigratsye un yidishe emigratsye-politik* (Jewish emigration and Jewish emigration policy), published in Vilna, and *Di yidishe vanderungen* (The Jewish migrations), published in Warsaw.

Government-funded emigration think tanks, like the Polish Emigration Society or Scientific Emigration Institute, also attracted Jewish demographers and politicians. Leon Alter and Mieczysław Goldsztejn published articles on Jewish emigration in the journal of the Scientific Emigration Institute.[49] Alter was among a group of gentiles and Jews who strongly advocated for the emigration of Jews from Poland and wished to see it included in a broader policy of the Polish state. He served as director of the Warsaw office of Hebrew Immigrant Aid Society (HIAS) and Head of the Emigration Department in the Ministry of Work and Social Care. In 1931, Alter traveled to Argentina in order to examine the local situation and promote emigration.[50] As the economic and political situation worsened in Poland, Alter saw the growing importance of Jewish emigration from Poland. In 1926, he argued that the Jewish livelihood in the artisan economy was threatened by industrialization, the development of cooperatives, and closure of the Russian market for Polish goods.[51] In 1937, the situation was so dire that he wrote that "a particularly intense demand for emigration is taking on the character of a psychosis."[52] When emigration was limited in more and more countries, Alter lamented that Polish Jews found themselves facing problems of exceptional severity; yet, he advised resisting any attempts at a chaotic massive emigration.[53] Conversely, he tried to exercise pressure via government channels. Similarly, some Jewish leaders cooperated closely with the Polish government as members of a delegation in the 1939 Evian Conference on Jewish refugees and migrants.[54]

The Polish Government and Argentina as a Solution to the Jewish Question

Following 1918, the government of independent Poland was another actor who participated in shaping the local discourse about Argentina. Its Argentine policies and agenda influenced the way Jewish and Christian immigration to Argentina was conceptualized and conducted. In the interwar period, Poland was interested in strengthening its economic ties with Argentina, but emigration stood at the focal point. Throughout most of the interwar period, the Jewish minority was considered a challenge to the project of a "national state for the Poles" that some leaders (especially those with ties to the National Democrat party or Endecja) preferred over the multiethnic republic that was in existence until 1939.[55] Although the 1921 constitution proclaimed equality between Jews and Christians, the reality was a far cry from it. Many Jews wanted to leave Poland, a decision that the Polish government supported. The Polish Ministry of Foreign Affairs considered promoting emigration from Poland as part of its long-term agenda, and the State Emigration Office (Państwowy Urząd Emigracyjny) and Emigration Council (Rada Emigracyjna) supervised the emigration of Jews and non-Jews alike.

Although the governing parties changed, Polish authorities regarded emigration as a solution to the country's economic problems and social tensions throughout the entire interwar period. Taking into account the problem of overpopulation in villages and the thousands of the so-called unneeded, Poland saw emigration as a reasonable mechanism of population control. These trends were visible already in the first years of independent Poland. As early as 1920, a program of minister Grabski stipulated that the state would support the "emigration of economically weak, and re-emigration of economically strong individuals."[56] Parliamentarian Antoni Szmigiel from the agrarian party Polskie Stronnictwo Ludowe "Piast" argued in 1927 that "emigration is becoming a burning issue.

There is nothing degrading in being a country of emigration, and I do not agree with those who see emigration as a misfortune for Poland. Emigration is indeed evidence of a nation's vitality, and when it is well organized, it can be a blessing."[57] Between 1916 and 1938, the unemployed, or "professionally passive," to use the official Polish terminology of the day, represented 73.5 percent of all emigrants (279,000).[58] Although Józef Okołowicz, the first director of the Emigration Office, proclaimed in 1920 that emigration should be utilized in the smallest degree possible, in fact the government, through direct and indirect channels, facilitated leaving the country for those who were interested.[59] During the 1920s, the emigration of ethnic Poles was considered by some as a form of compensation for the absence of Polish colonies. The overseas export of Polish peasants, especially to Latin America, was seen by the government not only as a solution to poverty and overpopulation but as a tool of quasi-colonial expansion. In the early 1920s, the Minister of Labor and Social Care, Franciszek Sokal, argued that emigration was unavoidable and Poland should search for places where Polish peasants could find better economic prospects. Sokal saw peasant emigration as a chance to build ethnic enclaves of Polishness outside of Poland.[60] The revived pre-1918 calls for founding a "New Poland" in Latin America, along with Polish colonial claims, could still be heard in the 1930s.

Following the world economic crisis, the political discourse of 1930s Poland saw a growing trend of "encouraging" minorities to leave the country.[61] Poland's policy supported homogenizing the national structure both through promoting Polonization and advocating for the emigration of minorities. In 1921, the government established the Emigration Council, which was supposed to be responsible for policy planning. However, the Jewish deputy to the Sejm, Ignacy Schiper, expressed the critical observation that the council "was more like an academic club that had insufficient insight into actual practices."[62] Calls for promoting Jewish emigration increased during the nationalist upheaval in the second part of the 1930s. In 1936, the problem of Jewish emigration was discussed several times in the Sejm, often under the pressure of international Jewish organizations.[63] In 1937, the Ministry of the Interior (MSW) complained to the Ministry of Foreign Affairs (MSZ) that emigration assistance was being wrongly focused on ethnic Poles.[64] In its view, the state should focus on facilitating the emigration of national minorities and introducing mechanisms to expedite it. The MSW demanded that MSZ negotiate higher entry quotas for Polish Jews with other countries. In 1938, the interministerial commission issued directives that supported precisely this fast-track for the emigration of minorities.[65] In 1939, Polish authorities were even positively disposed toward illegal, so-called tourist emigrants who overstayed their tourist visas.[66] Yet in the late 1930s, any form of emigration was becoming more and more difficult both in the case of Argentina and other countries.

Poland's government policies concerning Argentina and Jewish immigration to Argentina were also shaped by reports and correspondence arriving directly from Buenos Aires. The Polish Embassy in Argentina opened in 1922 with Władysław Mazurkiewicz as its head for more than fourteen years. The MSZ in Warsaw kept regular diplomatic correspondence with the embassy's officials. In the 1930s, MSZ published yearly reports about emigration from Poland to Argentina and Argentina's economic situation. The reports were well-researched, lengthy publications (more than 120 pages), based on Argentine sources and likely written by the Buenos Aires embassy staff. At times, the reports criticized the emigration of Jews from Poland and defined it as a policy mistake. For instance, the 1938 embassy report underscored the positive impact of Jews on the Polish and Argentine economy. The report emphasized the fact that many Jews in Poland "had a positive social and pro-state influence." Another point of emphasis was the loyalty of Jewish residents, especially the orthodox segment of Polish Jewry. The report pointed out how "beneficial" Jewish artisans and farmers were to the Argentine economy. The report underlined that Jewish immigration helped Argentina to develop, as Polish Jews were "good entrepreneurs and up-and-coming."[67] Similarly, in its brochure *Wiadomości o Argentynie* (Information on Argentina), the Emigration Syndicate stressed the attributes of "work, solidarity, perseverance and intelligence" of Jewish emigrants from Poland as playing a crucial role in Argentina.[68] Strikingly, these pro-Jewish observations of the diplomatic staff were able to coexist with the anti-Semitic tendencies in Polish politics of late 1930s.

In the 1930s, following the world economic crisis, Argentina largely closed its doors to Jewish emigration from Poland. In fact, only those already in Argentina could use the so-called *llamadas* system to invite family members to Argentina. The nationalist Argentine governments of the 1930s approached Jewish immigration with growing suspicion, which reflected anti-Semitic prejudices. This did not go unnoticed in Poland. The antimigration policies of Argentine authorities, often combined with anti-Semitic resentment of the government, were visible in diplomatic contacts with Poland and went hand in hand with the same tendencies in Europe. When the new Argentine ambassador, Rodolfo Freyre, arrived in Warsaw in 1937, he was quick to inform Polish president Ignacy Mościcki about Argentina's anti-Jewish fears. Freyre argued that the image of a Polish immigrant had begun to worsen in the last ten to fifteen years, when the "hard-working Polish peasant was exchanged by the Jew." The Jewish share in emigration from Poland in the few proceeding years indeed exceeded 50 percent. Returning to early twentieth-century accusations, the new ambassador added that the Argentine government feared that Jews would disseminate communist ideology in Argentina.[69] Mościcki expressed his understanding for Freyre's anxiety and informed him that, according to him, Polish emigration should only consist of "healthy village elements" and that "Argentine consuls could refuse Jews to board ships departing from Poland."[70]

Further, the internal correspondence between Argentine diplomats in Poland and the Argentine Ministry of Foreign Affairs was filled with clearly anti-Semitic contents. Freyre wrote to Carlos Saavedra Lamas, Argentina's minister of Foreign Affairs at the time, stating that Argentina should use Mościcki's advice and refuse issuing visas to Jews, as they "had an aversion to agricultural work" and "had dishonest commercial habits."[71] In the late 1930s, Argentine and Polish policies concerning the "Jewish problem" worked in tandem. Poland wanted Jews out, while Argentina refused to let them in. Marcos A. Savon, the Argentine consul in the Polish port city of Gdynia, wrote to Saavedra Lamas in 1937 that Argentina should impose stricter barriers to Jewish immigration from Poland, explaining that the Jews "had resentment against Christianity" and "were willing to commit the greatest crimes" and spread communism.[72] Savon further argued that Polish authorities had put Jews on a fast-track and facilitated their immigration to Argentina and elsewhere. A conflict emerged in 1938 when Argentina suddenly stopped issuing visas to Polish citizens. The Polish Ministry of Foreign Affairs was surprised and outraged by the move, which singled out Poland.[73] In dealing with the issue, the ministry suggested to the Polish consul in Buenos Aires to not elaborate on the ethnic background of the emigrants when discussing the matter with Argentine authorities. Lying that all incoming emigrants were farmers was also suggested.[74]

Conclusion

Despite financial misery and efforts of government and Jewish emigration advocates, most Polish Jews could not emigrate or were far from seriously considering emigration as a reasonable solution in interwar years. Poland remained loosely engaged in promoting emigration (both of Jews and Christians). For the most part, the policies discussed by the parliamentarians and emigration advocates were not carried out in practice. The numerous research expeditions, policy papers, and initial agreements with Brazil and Bolivia did not lead to any organized mass settlement. Most of the emigrants left Poland independently, without any government assistance. It was partly facilitated by the Polish legal framework of emigration of the interwar period, which was progressive for the time. Poland's constitution of 1921 proclaimed the right of every citizen to emigrate. The 1927 Emigration Law confirmed the "freedom to emigrate" and included several promigration paragraphs (such as free passports for the poor).[75] The law established the responsibility of the Polish state for its emigrant citizens in regulating colonization and emigration propaganda.

Wide portions of Poland's Jewry did not consider emigration a realistic solution. This was especially true for the orthodox supporters of Agudas Isroel, folkists, and part of the Bundists. Some opposed not emigration as such, but "emigrationism," the ideology that suggested emigration as the only solution for Polish Jews, which implied that leaving Poland was surrendering to anti-Semitism.[76] The number of interwar emigrants was rather low in proportion to the size of the Polish Jewish community of more 3.3 million in 1938.[77] Between 1919 and 1937, Palestine received around 155,000 immigrants from Poland (less than 5 percent of Poland's Jewish population).[78] In terms of immigration to Argentina, the numbers were not impressive either. In the interwar years, around 157,000 to 167,000 Polish citizens immigrated to Argentina, including 55,000 to 60,000 Jews. The peak of emigration to Argentina was reached between 1926 and 1930, when 91,000 people left Poland, including 22,500 Jews (25 percent).[79] Only when Argentina limited its immigration quotas did Palestine begin to dominate as the receiving country for Polish Jews. The year 1932 represented the first time when more Polish Jews immigrated to Palestine (39.8 percent) rather than Argentina (18.4. percent). Yet throughout the 1930s, Argentina was still second in terms of overseas emigration destinations for Polish Jews.[80]

The way Jewish elite and Poland's wider public discourse approached Argentina shows the context in which Jewish immigration to Argentina was being debated. Initially, emigration was perceived as a danger to communal cohesion. With time, however, it received much more understanding. Many of those privileged who were not forced to emigrate due to poverty or direct persecution acknowledged that their experiences were not universal. At the same time, Polish government and Jewish and non-Jewish migration activists worked to promote the emigration of the Jewish and Christian poor, with varying degrees of success. The next chapter explores the process of imagining Argentina, as articulated by ordinary Jews through the prolific Yiddish daily press published during the interwar years. The following chapter analyzes how the conceptual framework provided by initial elitist and governmental debates of Argentina was adjusted by those who were indeed emigrating, that is the Jewish poor and proletariat.

2

Between Hope and Fear

The Imageries of Argentina in Poland's Yiddish Channels

Ready for a Journey? Early Yiddish Emigration Guidebooks

Israel Makranski of the Poylisher Farband in Buenos Aires recalled that Jewish colonization in Argentina "shined in the dark night of Jewish life in Europe."[1]

Yet, as emigration from Russia was restricted or treated as a delict until the end of tsarist rule, coordinating individual immigration to Argentina was a major challenge for ordinary Jews. Obtaining a passport was difficult and expensive, and many young men were emigrating in order to avoid conscription to the army. Consequently, many Jews fled the empire (including Russian Poland) without legal documentation, bribing the border police or using a forged passport. Police documents reveal that emigration agents were often involved in the smuggling of goods and people. Russian emigrants usually crossed the Austrian border around the town of Brody and continued their journey by train to Hamburg or Bremen. The way via Russian Lipava or Odessa was more expensive and required the possession of a valid passport.[2] Those immigrating to Argentina under the auspices of the Jewish Colonization Association (JCA) received exceptional emigration permits. The JCA had its office in St. Petersburg and coordinated with the Russian government. In Austrian Galicia, the emigration laws of 1897 permitted emigration for anyone except those obligated to serve in the army. Consequently, most of the people leaving Russian Poland in 1905 were deserters (around 80 percent), whereas in Galician Husiatyń it was about 40 percent in 1913.[3] The deserters who could not obtain official passports relied on the help of smugglers and document forgers, many of whom were Jewish. In 1912, the Russian police arrested a gang of seventeen Jewish smugglers from Myszyniec, who were transporting Jews across the Prussian border. In 1913, the Austrian police found forty-five false passports in the emigration agency run in Stary Sambor by Salomon Weiniger.[4]

In these challenging circumstances, the immigrants sought competent emigration advice. Modern Yiddish dailies and weeklies would not become commonplace until the second decade of the twentieth century. In order to understand how immigrants gathered information on Argentina, it is important to study

Yiddish immigration guidebooks published in eastern Europe at the end of the nineteenth century. They provide a data set that shows how the Jewish public in Poland conceptualized a country that had newly appeared as a potential immigration destination. Around 1910, the Yiddish daily press became much more available in Poland, and newspapers such as *Haynt* or *Der Moment* began to play an increasingly important role in transmitting the information about Argentina. This chapter examines how immigrant guidebooks and Yiddish press shaped the way Jews in Poland imagined Argentina.

At the end of the nineteenth century, the recruitment for agricultural settlement in Argentina was dominant. To reach emigrants, the JCA established a network of information centers and traveling emigration agents. In time, the JCA's activities developed, and in 1909, it had representatives in 433 towns and cities throughout the Russian Empire, including 50 in the Kingdom of Poland, which at the end of the first decade of the century was the source of approximately 25 percent of all Russian Jewish emigrants.[5] The organization published regular reports and Spanish-Yiddish dictionaries and brochures explaining how to receive an emigration passport. From 1907 onwards, the JCA published a Yiddish biweekly *Yidisher Emigrant* (Jewish emigrant), distributing around seventy thousand copies in 1910. Similar (but independent from the JCA) counseling institutions could be found in Warsaw, predominantly run by wealthier and Polonized Jews, who regarded emigration advising and advocacy as charity work. They established the Warsaw Information Bureau for Emigrant Jews and, beginning in 1912, the Jewish Emigration Society as well.[6] The former organization was in permanent contact with the JCA, and immigrants planning to go to Argentina made up 26 percent of those seeking the organization's advice.[7] Alongside organizations that offered free emigration advice, or those associated with JCA, numerous private Jewish emigration agencies were also established to help coordinate the recruitment of both Christian and Jewish emigrants. These organizations were structured hierarchically, with branches in important ports, big cities in eastern Europe, and smaller towns. In Galicia, only 15 percent of agents were Poles in 1910, while the rest were Jews or Germans. Quite often, emigration agencies were a family business or were run by women. In Husiatyń, Pinkas Kapeller worked with his son David, while in Rawa Ruska Moses Gelber cooperated with his son-in-law. In Rohatyń, Josef and Ruchla Doller jointly represented the *Austro-Americana* ship line.[8]

The integrationist and *maskil* periodicals that discussed Argentina in the 1890s and 1900s were largely unavailable to poorer Jews, who were supposed to become the colonists of Argentina. That changed around 1910 with the emergence of a regular Yiddish-language press, geared specifically to ordinary Yiddish-speaking Jews. Earlier, a plethora of short Yiddish books describing the conditions of life in Argentina appeared throughout eastern Europe to shed some

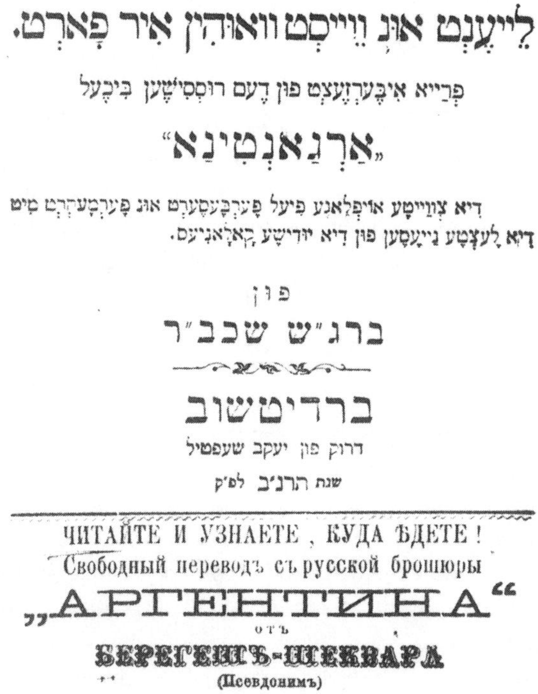
לייענט אונ ווייסט וואוהין איר פארט.

פרייא איבערזעצט פון דעם רוססישען ביכעל

„ארגאנטינא“

דיא צווייטע אויפלאגע פיעל פערבעססערט אונ פערמעהרט מיט
דיא לעצטע נייעסען פון דיא יודישע קאלאניעס.

פון

ברג״ש שכב״ר

ברדיטשוב

דרוק פון יעקב שעפטיל

שנת הרנ״ב לפ״ק

ЧИТАЙТЕ И УЗНАЙТЕ, КУДА ѢДЕТЕ!
Свободный переводъ съ русской брошюры
„АРГЕНТИНА“
отъ
БЕРЕГЕШЪ-ШЕХВАРА
(Псевдонимъ)

Figure 3. Bargash Shakhbar, *Argentina. Leyent un veyst vohin ir fort* (Berdichev, 1892)

much-needed light on Argentina. One of the first emigration guidebooks published in Yiddish was *Argentina. Leyent un veyst vohin ir fort* (Argentina: Read and know where you are going), published in Berdichev in 1892, originally in Russian and compiled by Bargash Shakhbar (a nickname). It is unclear who published the Russian original. Although the book was published in Ukrainian Berdichev, it catered principally to Polish Jews. The first pages advertised the possibility of purchasing the book in a well-known Warsaw publishing house of the Orgelbrand family, in the headquarters of Yudishe Biblyotek on Niecała Street or the Dinezon's bookstore on Nalewki Street (both in Warsaw).

Shakhbar's *Argentina* was a very realistic and accessible depiction of immigration conditions (fig. 3). It did not romanticize the process of immigration and described in detail the numerous problems, obstacles, and forms of harassment that emigrants faced during their journey. It informed its readers that in the "Argentine paradise, no one waited for the emigrants with open hands."[9] The author pointed out that promises of plots of land, farm animals, and money for starting a new life in Argentina were fulfilled only in rare cases. Due to passport or other legal difficulties, Shakhbar argued, many immigrants had been forced to return home from European port cities. The book described agents that sold false tickets to Argentina and robbers who attacked those waiting for the ship. The book continued by informing readers about the terrible travel conditions: "You will have money only for a third-class ticket. There you [will] hardly have any air to breathe, receive small portions of food and have barely anything to drink. . . . In a space for three hundred people, they [will] squeeze in five hundred or more, so that it is not uncommon for someone to suffocate."[10] The guidebook informed travelers that the salty seawater was undrinkable, that the fresh water supply was very limited, and the little that was available "was covered with a green mold and stank unbearably." Sea sickness, which "spared only maybe one in a hundred," was described in an equally terrifying way. Hundreds of sick passengers allegedly lay in the *tsvishndek* (storage area) without any help and weak from disease.

The following chapters of the book featured specific descriptions about life in Argentina: its geography, the local population, Spanish colonization, and European immigration. The author touched upon Argentine gauchos, whose "whole life was to ride a horse around the steppe."[11] Shakhbar also described Argentina's economic development. Commerce was supposed to "increase day by day," and familiar potatoes and wheat, as well as lesser-known varieties of corn and melons, were grown in Argentina. Special attention was paid to cattle, Argentina's primary export. In addition, Shakhbar portrayed Argentine imports in detail, giving the future immigrant a perspective on which trades could be practiced with success. Nevertheless, Shakhbar warned that only "those with professions, or with money" would be lucky enough to have a relatively easy start. Most immigrants worked very hard to earn the most basic quality of life. Many faced difficulties with adapting to the new climate, and lodging and food were allegedly very expensive. The author also explained that in Argentina, one needed to work very hard for bread and that nothing "here was given for free." As Shakhbar warned, many immigrants started to miss their homes after realizing that life in Argentina was no heaven. Yet, many lacked the necessary financial means to return, others "died from worrying," yet others were forbidden to go back.[12]

Shakhbar claimed that the possibilities of becoming a farmer were scarce in Argentina because the local government was made up of a group of liars, who fooled immigrants. The situation with buying land from private owners was similar: "First, you don't know the language, second, you don't know the laws, third, the officials are thieves," Shakhbar summarized.[13] However, the ending of his book was more optimistic. In referring to the experiences of eastern European Jews, he explained: "You know well what is hunger and suffering[,] . . . and you know that the way to the Garden of Eden is a way through troubles. . . . But Argentina can become that kind of *Gan Eden*." The last paragraph of the book advised high caution, as Argentina could become a paradise only for the "proper, prepared emigrants." For others, it would rather be a "graveyard." The author advised against emigrating in the given moment and instead suggested waiting for the assistance of the government and the fulfillment of a future de Hirsch project.[14] It is impossible to identify Shakhbar's cultural and economic background, thus I cannot speculate about his exact motivations. On the one hand, the book appeared in Yiddish, catering to the future emigrants, yet on the other, Shakhbar gave a rather cold assessment of the opportunities in Argentina. His negative attitude might have been based on the earliest voices that spoke about the difficulties in Argentina, formulated by a Jewish elite fearing the loss of control and authority or by the negative attitude of Russian authorities, who generally forbade emigration and had an interest in spreading cautionary narratives, such as that of Shakhbar.

At the end of the nineteenth century, similar brochures circulated throughout eastern Europe. In 1893, an analogous guidebook was published in Warsaw. The book, titled *Di beshraybung fon argentina un ire kolonyen* (Description of Argentina and its colonies) and edited by Yaakov Yedvabnik, was already in its fifth edition (the first was probably issued in 1889), which suggests a sustained interest and demand for these kinds of guidebooks (fig. 4). The book, much more detailed than Shakhbar's brochure, focused specifically on the agricultural colonies founded by Baron de Hirsch. In the space of more than a hundred pages, Yedvabnik gave a general overview of Argentina and presented the main personalities involved in Jewish colonization. The prologue describes the unusual commotion that the possibility of immigration to Argentina evoked in eastern Europe. As Yedvabnik argued, the word *Argentina* "was repeated and echoed by everyone, by the intelligentsia and by blue-collar workers. It became a kind of magic spell that was supposed to solve all Jewish problems. It was on the lips of everyone." The decade between the 1880s and 1890s was described as a unique moment when Argentina literally crashed into the lives of eastern European Jews.[15]

Yedvabnik stated that only a few people had any reliable information about Argentina and the opportunities it offered. Here and there, Jewish newspapers, such as Warsaw's *Izraelita*, published an article about the possibilities of emigration, but all in all, information was hardly available to ordinary Jews. This lack of information compelled Yedvabnik to write a guidebook for his "Jewish brothers." Yedvabnik's book was supposed to be up-to-date with the "hottest news and observations." Having never been to Argentina, he gathered his information from encyclopedias, books, and journals. Yedvabnik decided to write his book in Yiddish, in a "simple, everyday language, understandable to everyone," rather than in German, Polish, or Russian. The structure of Yedvabnik's book was similar to other books of this genre. The author began by describing the history of European colonization of the future Argentina, underlining the conflicts between the "civilized Europeans" and indigenous groups that he saw

די בעשרייבונג פאָן

אַרגענטינא

אונד איהרען קאָלאָניען

פאָן פערשיעדענע ריכטיגען קוואַללען בעאַרבייטעט

דורך

יאַקאָב יעדוואַבניק

פינפטע אויפלאַגע

גאַנצליך אומגעאַרבייטעטע

אונד

בעדייטענד פערגראָססערטע

געדרוקקט בייא אלעקסאנדער גינז.

ווארשויא

5-ОЕ ИЗД.

АРГЕНТИНА

ОЧЕРКЪ,

СОЧИНЕНІЕ

Якова Едвабника.

ВАРШАВА.

1893.

Figure 4. Yaakov Yedvabnik, *Di beshraybung fun argentina un ire kolonyen* (Warsaw, 1893)

as "wild peoples." Later, Yedvabnik described the geography of Argentina, its climate, trade, and industry. In a chapter titled "Religion and civilization," Yedvabnik informed readers that, although the dominant religion of the land was Catholicism, the government allowed everyone to practice their faith freely. He added that the Argentine government supported the development of secular science and public education was free.[16] Those who had fears about living conditions were informed that Buenos Aires was a fully "European city," with electric lamps and horse trams on most streets.

Yedvabnik's book was a mixture of practical information relevant to the workers and descriptions of the magnificence and grandeur of Buenos Aires. Yedvabnik wrote that an average worker earned between 80 to 100 rubles a month, an artisan around 30 more and an accountant around 800. In the same paragraph, he wrote that "for the most basic food" one needed to spend between 70 to 120 rubles (meaning that working-class families could barely sustain their basic needs). Writing about the travel costs, he mentioned third-class tickets and advised negotiating discounts for bigger groups of emigrants.[17] Similarly, he provided information only about food for third-class passengers. Elsewhere, paying little attention to the financial burden that purchasing a ship ticket meant for the majority of immigrants, when writing about travel conditions Yedvabnik recommended taking the most comfortable French ships. In other passages, Yedvabnik wrote about the Flores district, where the aristocracy lived, Palermo park, and the beautiful avenues lined with palm trees that "were hard to see even in Paris." His book featured a few photos, maps, and drawings that served as additional proof to his remark that "civilization was well-rooted there."[18]

A Place for Big Jewish Things? Narrating the Argentine Immigrant Experience in the Interwar Yiddish Daily Press

In independent Poland (after 1918), the usual push factors forced Jews to search for new-old safe havens. The postwar economic situation was dire, and large sectors of Polish society still rejected equal treatment of the Jewish minority. Sociologist Arie Tartakower wrote in 1935 that "emigration is the dream of hundreds of thousands, if not millions, and even Jewish cultural life is strongly connected with this main problem of contemporary Jewish social life."[19] Tartakower estimated that around 1.2 million Jews without a stable income lived in Poland. This group constituted a reservoir of potential emigrants.[20] Answering the interest in emigration, Poland's Yiddish press published countless articles that unveiled the Argentine reality not only to those who planned to emigrate but also to the general reading public. While those considering emigration purchased the emigration brochures, the news in Argentina present in the Yiddish dailies were available to anyone who bought the newspaper, which reported on a va-

Figure 5. An invitation to a lecture, "To Where Can the Jews Immigrate," given in 1926 in unknown Polish town by *Yidisher Emigrant* editor M. Krymski, DŻS IK 2f, National Library of Warsaw

riety of issues. Articles dealing with Argentina appeared in nearly all Jewish journals, independently of their ideological and linguistic profile. Sometimes journalists traveled to provincial cities and debated there the question of the era: To where can Jews immigrate (fig. 5)? This section shows that emigration from Poland to Argentina remained highly controversial among the Jewish reading public in Poland. The Yiddish press gives insightful accounts of how ambiguously this subject was approached.

Events in Argentina were followed in Poland with curiosity, and Jewish news from Argentina reached it regularly. All major Polish Jewish dailies subscribed to the Argentine Yiddish press. When the Buenos Aires *Di Yidische Zaitung* did not arrive in Poland on time, its editor Matías Stoliar turned to the Polish Embassy to clarify the issue with the authorities in Warsaw.[21] In his correspondence, we see that among the subscribers of Buenos Aires dailies were editors of numerous Yiddish periodicals published in Poland: *Unzer Tog, Di Tsayt* (both in Vilna), *Unzer Express, Literarishe Bleter, Folkstsaytung, Haynt, Der Moment* (all in Warsaw), *Nayer Folksblat, Lodzer Tagesblat* (both in Łódź), *Der Morgen* (in Lwów), YIVO Institute in Vilna, *Farayn fun yidishe literatn un zhurnalistn* (Association of Yiddish Writers and Journalists in Warsaw) in Warsaw, *Yidisher artistn farayn* (Jewish Artist Association), and several individuals.[22] This shows that the interwar Jewish media in Poland, as well as the country's Yiddish cultural elite, tracked developments in Argentina and were able to transmit Argentine subjects further to readers in Poland. Yet on several occasions, Poland's government (fearing revolutionary propaganda) banned the import of Argentine Yiddish dailies, limiting transnational dialogue between Jewish Poland and Jewish Argentina. These kinds of problems were reported in 1934 by *Di Presse*'s editor Pinie Katz.[23]

Poland's Yiddish periodicals of the interwar period reveal diverse accounts about life in Argentina. However, two aspects occupied the attention: Argentina as a potential emigration destination and Argentina as a risky country known for its Jewish criminality and prostitution. This chapter examines the leading Yiddish-language newspapers published in Warsaw in the interwar period. It focuses on the dailies *Haynt* and *Der Moment*, as well as the evening tabloid paper *Hayntige Nayes*. These publications were politically diverse and very influential within Poland's Jewish press, thus providing a window into how the majority of Jews in Warsaw and in Poland experienced Argentina. At the time, *Haynt* was closely related to the Zionist movement, whereas *Der Moment* initially stood for folkism, later becoming a national nonpartisan title.[24] Elite Jewish titles in Hebrew and Polish from the turn of the century had an extremely limited readership, while Yiddish newspapers published in the interwar years were the most popular source of information for working-class and poor Jews. At the beginning of the century, the Yiddish press in Polish lands was largely ephemeral, as the big dailies were still emerging: *Haynt* in 1908 and *Der Moment* in 1910. They reached a certain level of stability only after 1912, when their daily circulation exceeded one hundred thousand copies. In the 1920s and 1930s, they catered primarily to an urban Jewish population, those already to a certain extent distanced from the orthodoxy and in many cases belonging to a new Jewish proletariat.

The possibilities of emigration, or their lack, were abundantly mirrored in Poland's Yiddish press. By publishing various articles on immigration to Argentina, Yiddish dailies fulfilled a role of "emigration advisor," especially for those who could not or did not know how to find relevant information elsewhere. They offered almost free, relatively up-to-date, and competent advice from the sources, validated by the power of print. This function of the Jewish press was highly important due to the massive readership of Yiddish journals. In the early 1930s, *Hayntige Nayes* sold more than seventy-five thousand copies daily, and the affordable price made it accessible to practically everyone. Importantly, Warsaw's Yiddish press was read not only in the capital but also in other provinces and even worldwide.[25] As the economic and political situation in Poland worsened, the emigration question emerged as a key issue discussed by the press. When the United States closed its doors to a majority of Polish Jewish immigrants in 1924, Argentina reached its peak importance.[26] For a half decade, it was the primary country of emigration for Jews leaving Poland. Some of them, such as Argentine

Yiddish activist Samuel Rollansky, who left Poland at this time, believed that Argentina surely was a place "for big Jewish things."[27]

In answering readers' interest in Argentina-related texts, Poland's Yiddish newspapers published numerous articles about immigration to Argentina, usually in the form of short messages no more than a few sentences in length. Numerous articles described the conditions, possibilities, and requirements of immigration. Sometimes, they took the form of longer analytical texts, but usually, the Yiddish press contained various short practical pieces of information about immigration procedures and advertisements of transatlantic steamship companies offering voyages to Buenos Aires. We find them mainly in columns devoted to migration matters or in those covering international news (less often). In late 1924, *Der Moment* published a column titled "Yedies un anvayzungen far emigranten" (Information and tips for the emigrants), where immigration to Argentina was regularly mentioned. Fulfilling its informative role of emigration advisor, *Der Moment* informed potential emigrants about the documents necessary to apply for an Argentine visa.[28] It mentioned, among others, a certificate of morality, a work ability certificate, and a health certificate. Potential immigrants could also find information about officials who could provide these documents.

Der Moment quite often published information on immigration provided by various organizations coordinating immigration and colonization in Argentina. For instance, reports of the Jewish Emigration Aid Society (JEAS) appeared quite regularly, typically describing current immigration possibilities or immigration statistics (fig. 6). *Der Moment* was clearly interested in transmitting to their readers competent, valuable, and firsthand information. For many Polish Jews, immigration to Argentina was a difficult and risky endeavor, requiring financial resources and informed knowledge of current immigration procedures. Therefore, *Der Moment* tried to facilitate this process by providing reliable data and information. By publishing statistical information on Jewish immigration to Argentina, the daily provided direct and official evidence that Jews indeed settled in that remote country. Knowing that a steamship ticket was a significant financial burden for working-class Jews, Yiddish newspapers provided information on current prices of tickets and other financial issues related to immigration. For example, in May 1930, *Hayntige Nayes* notified readers about the approximate costs of settling in Argentina: "The cost of a steamship ticket to Buenos Aires is around $107. Those who do not have the required documents need to prove that they possess an additional $150 (single immigrant) or $300 (family)."[29] Apart from statistical and financial information, the Yiddish dailies reported on recent changes in immigration procedures. In a January 1924 report printed in *Der Moment*, HIAS noted that immigrants could stay up to five days in free *aynvanderungs-heym*, or immigrant houses.[30] A similar message ap-

Figure 6. JEAS (Jewish Emigration Aid Society) poster of Spanish and English courses, Warsaw, 1920s, DŻS IK 2f, National Library in Warsaw

peared in a January 1924 issue of *Haynt*, where we read about reduced residence time offered in these facilities, due to the large number of needy immigrants.[31]

For readers personally interested in emigration, articles describing the details of life and work in Argentina were especially valuable. News about wages, costs, and the standard of living or attitudes of non-Jews had a powerful influence on allowing them to envision their life in a new country. For example, in September 1924, *Der Moment* reported about excellent opportunities for bakers in the province of Buenos Aires.[32] Seeking to encourage potential migrants, the journal wrote that trained bakers could expect a simpler immigration process due to their importance for the Argentine economy. Six years later, in May 1930 (during the world economic crisis), less favorable information was provided by *Hayntige Nayes*.[33] Thanks to "well-informed" sources, the newspaper reported that the possibility of immigration to Argentina was scarce and noted that the Argentine government had recently limited the number of immigrants allowed into the country. The daily, attempting to facilitate the complicated emigration process, described an obligatory and newly introduced llamada procedure that allowed immigration only of those whose relatives in Argentina undertook to support him/her upon arrival.

Poland's Yiddish press needed to carefully balance between a cautionary tone and an encouraging one for those navigating the immigration process. An editorial criticizing emigration published in *Haynt* or *Der Moment* was a powerful tool influencing personal migration decisions, especially of those who did not have family or friends in Argentina or could not find information elsewhere. When making readers aware of the problematic situation in Argentina, and simultaneously conveying a message of *don't go to Argentina now*, Yiddish newspapers usually depicted stories of Polish Jews who decided to return from Argentina.[34] For instance, in 1924 *Der Moment* warned against emigration, describing the story of seventeen working-class families, who came back to Poland after only one year in Argentina.[35] The daily underlined the significant level of unemployment among workers in Argentine cities, which in the late 1920s was well above 10 percent.[36] The text mentioned jobless Jews from the capital, who moved to the larger agricultural colonies, but once there, they also had difficulties finding any work. Warning against leaving Poland, *Der Moment* emphasized the low wages in Argentina and the insufficient number of available flats. In October 1924, the daily covered a return of Jews unsatisfied with their lives in Argentina, describing a group of native Varsovians who, unhappy with their situation in Latin America, decided to return to Poland.[37] A *Haynt* issue from January 1924 also stressed the problematic economic situation in Argentina, especially the high rate of unemployment that was on the rise due to the big number of new immigrants.[38] Similarly, the daily pointed out that relatively few immigrants—mostly skilled workers—were able to find jobs in Argentine cities. *Haynt* reported accurately that there were no jobs for carpenters or metal workers in Argentina, and those with experience in the free professions were forced to earn their living as doormen or servants. The 1924 warnings were probably convincing. Polish-Jewish immigration dropped by approximately 50 percent in 1924 compared with the 1923 level.

Warning messages were also embedded in the political conflicts between various groups within Polish Jewry. The ambiguous discourse toward migration, characteristic of the turn of the century, was revived again in the mid-1920s. Writer and traveler Hersh Dovid Nomberg criticized the press for their excessive cautionary language. He wrote in 1926 that, like never before, emigration was a factual need of numerous pauperized Polish Jews, who could barely make ends meet. According to him, it was the most "burning problem" in Poland, as anti-Semitism was on the rise and traditional Jewish professions were disappearing. "Entire shtetls would emigrate if they could, but now only one in a hundred is lucky enough. Hundreds of others look at the emigrant with jealous eyes, like someone who managed to survive," the author wrote. Nomberg criticized Jewish leaders for not engaging enough in preparing Jews for emigration, by not teaching them agricultural professions, which was preferred by many potential emigration countries.[39] He condemned the Yiddish press for transmitting overly critical voices and challenging emigration as such.

How to Reach Argentina? Iconographies of Emigration

The advertisements produced by passenger steamship companies operating between Europe and Buenos Aires offered another way for Polish Jews to conceptualize Argentina. *Der Moment* and other Yiddish- and Polish-language Jewish newspapers regularly published advertisements of various ship companies. Argentina appeared as one of the main destinations of transatlantic cruises. In the mid-1920s, some of the most frequently advertised liners included the Italian Cosulich Line and the British Royal Mail Steam Packet Line (RMSP) and White Star Line. In the late 1930s, the Polish Linja Południowo-Amerykańska (South American Line) entered into competition with foreign carriers. This liner invited the passengers with shorter travel time, the possibility of paying in Polish currency, and no need of making a stopover in Germany, Italy, or France. The number of cruises was also increasing. Whereas in 1938, *Pułaski* left Polish Gdynia for Buenos Aires every two months, in 1939, two ships, *Chrobry* and *Sobieski*, were connecting the two cities every month.

The ads were generally similar in their structure. They contained the name of the carrier, offered destinations, the Warsaw address of the company, and the addresses of its branches in other provinces (including cities as Lwów, Grodno, Stanisławów, and Kowel). Quite often, they included information about upcoming departures, ticket prices, and all kinds of additional information for immigrants. Some ads contained black-and-white drawings—usually depicting a steamer or immigrants themselves, as in the case of RMSP ads published in *Haynt* in 1923.[40] In figure 7, we see a poor immigrant couple, burdened with bundles, probably just before heading out across the ocean, which contrasts with a depiction of a well-dressed man and woman, who probably have already succeeded in the New World. These pictures reflected common images of easy success allegedly awaiting every Jew in the Americas. We can interpret the motif as that of a hope giver—an image that visualizes stories about the wealth of America that many Polish Jews were accustomed to hearing about. The sharp contrast between departing immigrants and a couple on the American shore created an illusion that the steamship ticket for the RMSP was a simple key to wealth and success in America. This ad advertised cruises both to New York and to various Latin American destinations. The image, however, did not differentiate between these places. Success seemed possible not only in New York but also in lesser-known Argentina, Brazil, or Cuba.

In their advertisements, steamship companies usually emphasized regular and quick cruises, at other times the convenience and luxury of their steamers. For

Figure 7. Advertisement of RMSP, *Haynt*, June 21, 1923, 1

Figure 8. Advertisement of RMSP, *Haynt*, January 4, 1923, 1

instance, in February 1923, *Haynt* published a Cosulich Line ad with text in bold: "Di rayze doyert nur 19 teg!" (The trip takes just 19 days!).[41] The 1928 flyer of the Dutch Royal Lines printed the menu offered in a transit hotel in Amsterdam and informed readers in thick print which tram line to take to the headquarters of the Poylisher Farband in Buenos Aires.[42] Sometimes the ads included additional information to assure voyagers about the security and comfort of their cruise. For example, in February 1924, *Der Moment* ran an advertisement commissioned by a French company, Chargeurs Reunis.[43] The ad explained that a special envoy of the company was responsible for controlling the travel conditions of the emigrants in order to analyze the desired improvements. Moreover, probably as a special offer, Chargeurs Reunis invited the relatives of Polish

Jews already living in Argentina to send their letters and greetings to their families through them. The announcement offered the low cost of ship travel from Bordeaux to Buenos Aires, though the price was not specified. To purchase a ticket, customers were invited to personally visit the office of Chargeurs Reunis at Królewska Street in Warsaw. The invitation for personal ticket purchase, rather than through a third-party buyer, was likely an additional measure to ensure the honesty and credibility of the ship liner.

Steamship companies' announcements differed significantly from other ads published in Yiddish newspapers. There was a clear trend of placing ads of the transatlantic steamship carriers on the front pages. Only rarely are these types of ads found on the second or third page. Visible placement of the advertisement was of course supposed to attract the attention of readers who were seen as potential emigrants or as relatives of someone who had already left Poland. The placement of steamer ads also reflected the prosperity of transoceanic lines by showing that they could afford the most expensive advertising space. The advertisement on the first page of *Haynt* in January 1923 (fig. 8) was much larger than the other ads and obituaries printed in the daily.[44] It was the only one to include graphic elements—depicting a steamer proudly floating on the waves. Interestingly, this advertising by RMSP, which presented ships departing for New York, Brazil, and Argentina, divided its space evenly between North and South American destinations. Emigration to Argentina was often depicted as less important or marginal, which was communicated via a reduced font size. While the ad underlined New York as a key Jewish destination, this ad was unique in that it presented immigration to Argentina as an equally viable option. It reflected the ongoing Polish Jewish debate about emigration and, to lesser extent, a debate on emigration to the United States or Argentina specifically. The particularities of the countries seem not to matter that much.

Steamship carriers' advertisements offer a perspective on Jewish Polish conceptualization of Argentina that differ from the texts about immigration published by Yiddish dailies. In this case, Argentina became a form of "merchandise" sold to Jewish customers. Its qualities were not defined by factual information but referred rather to an imagined country on the other side of the Atlantic, a place that was better and freer and offered lucrative possibilities. Advertisements portrayed Argentina from the perspective of the steamship carriers interested in increasing their sales. Advertising was the main tool of attracting potential passengers. It seems that market-conscious vessel companies adjusted the quantity of their commercials according to the rise and fall of demand. When immigration to Argentina was relatively limited (since the early 1930s), they appeared much less frequently. However, in 1923, the year when Jewish immigration from Poland to Argentina peaked at more than thirteen thousand people, there was a significant increase in the number of ads.

Advertisements of steamship companies appeared precisely in the same newspapers that published articles about Jewish immigration to Argentina. Thus, the Yiddish dailies constituted an unusual combination of commercial and semipublic media representations of the country. On the one hand, the newspapers included articles containing specific and helpful information about immigration laws, wages, and other information (quite often negatively assessing the possibility of a Jewish settlement). On the other hand, the first pages of *Haynt* and *Der Moment* were occupied by commercial and attractive advertisements of international liners that offered a service of transporting Jews from Europe to Argentina, with no investment in their lives after disembarking. The readers of Warsaw's Yiddish dailies were influenced by both forms of portraying Argentina. Thus, the media discourse was instrumental in shaping readers' views on Argentine matters, particularly the possibility of emigration. By informing, encouraging, and warning against Argentina, *Haynt* and *Der Moment* had a powerful influence on individual decisions of migrating Jews.

Vicious Argentina: Jewish Female Trafficking as a Social Challenge

The main spheres of Argentine Jewish life reflected through Warsaw's Yiddish press of the interwar period included Jewish prostitution and sex-related criminality. Sensational, often criminal, news about sex work constituted the core of information about Argentina that appeared in Poland's Yiddish dailies. Sex-related content was found in "lighter" *Hayntige Nayes* but also in the influential sociopolitical dailies like *Haynt* and *Der Moment*. Reports about the underground sex economy in Argentina were based on existing phenomena, but its scale was rather exaggerated. During the interwar years and before, international criminal groups were responsible for the widespread trafficking of women (young Jewish females from eastern Europe were one of the largest victim groups). In the first decades of the twentieth century, Jewish prostitution was a burning social problem, and Argentina became its symbol both in Jewish and gentile imagery. In the 1920s, Russian and Polish women made up 46.8 percent of prostitutes in Buenos Aires.[45] Donna Guy wrote that the atmosphere in Europe then was so tense that women were discouraged from traveling alone to the cities in search of work, as they could be captured and end up in an Argentine bordello. These fears were prevalent even when women did not plan to emigrate.[46] Information about abductions of young Polish Jewesses, about *shtile khupes* ("quiet weddings," a term used to describe weddings quickly arranged by sex traffickers), and the sad plight of girls and women forced into prostitution in Buenos Aires became part and parcel of Warsaw's police chronicles published in the Yiddish newspapers. The conflation of sexual slavery with sex work became the dominant narrative in the prostitution discourse. Neither early feminist activists nor social reformers differentiated between sexual slavery and sex work.[47]

Abductions of eastern European Jewish women must be situated within the broader context of emigration from Poland. The ease with which the Argentine or US Jewish procurers managed to convince women or their parents was a result of the desperate economic situation of many Jews in eastern Europe. Each child was an economic burden, and there was a tendency to encourage girls to marry young. Among the traditional population, marriage was the only available option for Jewish women. Traffickers promised marriage to a respectable American as a strategy to encourage female emigration. Simultaneously, sometimes those women who decided to emigrate alone were regarded as transgressors. However, the portrayal of emigration lands as dangerous for women was not characteristic only for Argentina. Already a few decades earlier, in the 1880s to 1900s, various actors employed propaganda material to discourage emigration. In the interwar years, the Polish nobility and the new industrial tycoons still feared losing their pool of cheap and always available labor. At the same time, religious leaders, both Jewish and Christian, linked emigration to the demise of traditional family structure and encroaching secularization. The immigration of single women to Argentina was considered a danger to the good reputation of Polish Jews. In 1923, the Polish-language Jewish journal *Nasz Przegląd* wrote that "one heard Polish in the bordellos of Buenos Aires" and complained about the ruined reputation of the entire ethnic group.[48] Press reports about coerced Jewish prostitution in Argentina served as a strategy to preserve traditional family structure, while limiting women's autonomy and maintaining communal bonds and a gendered balance of power.

The publication of criminal news from Argentina occurred on two main levels. First, these articles served as a warning for those considering emigration. Criminal news from Buenos Aires, usually related to sexuality, formed a picture of Argentina as a filthy, degenerate land, polluted with the worst elements of Jewish society. Numerous articles describing the tragedy of young girls who fell in love with rich Argentine men of east European Jewish origin served as warnings for women and their families. Second, news about prostitution in Argentina attracted readers interested in "juicy" news from the distant Latin American country. In this context, the publication of articles on this subject was embedded in the process of the exoticization of Argentina in Poland's Yiddish press. In the articles found in *Haynt* or *Hayntige Nayes*, Argentina was often reduced to a place of disproportionate levels of Jewish prostitution. Female trafficking became a symbol of Argentina and its Jewry, determining its image among many Polish Jews. Yiddish dailies likely took interest in Argentine Jewish prostitution because it carried with it an air of exoticism, and tragic inevitability, that could not be extended to the familiar street prostitution of Warsaw. Although some articles primarily aimed to shock readers with detailed descriptions of abductions or with the fact that both pimps and prostitutes were Jewish, they also fulfilled a warning role, discouraging Polish Jews from immigrating to supposedly violent and promiscuous

Argentina. Even though the scale of the phenomena was blown out of proportions by the press, the excessive warning tones influenced the Jewish public, both in terms of migration choices and everyday discussions on Argentina.

Extremely powerful were personal testimonies given by the victims of traffickers. A longer text of this kind, included in a 1924 issue of *Der Moment*, quoted an article published originally in the Buenos Aires-based *Di Yidische Zaitung*.[49] This popular newspaper reported on the tragedy of a young Jewish woman from Poland, who visited the paper's office one evening. The newspaper empathetically described her story, highlighting the pain and humiliation she suffered. The woman was identified as twenty-eight-year-old Dala, who had met a young man by the name of Leybl twelve years earlier in Lwów. He told her about the wonderful and easy life in Argentina and quickly offered to marry her. Her blind love of Leybl deceived her, and she decided to leave her parents and run away with the groom to Argentina. As soon as they had come ashore, the "husband" brought her to a house filled with other young women. After a few minutes, Dala understood where she was. In the brothel, she was stripped of her freedom. The *balebos* (manager) threatened to beat her up with a whip whenever she tried to escape or show any sign of dissatisfaction. After some time, she managed to contact her family, and her parents and brother traveled to Argentina and rescued her.

Although the story had a happy ending, the general message of the article was rather sad. A naive young woman experienced extreme humiliation, was enslaved, and left alone in a foreign country. The article thus served as a direct warning for young Polish Jewish women, as it precisely described the methods of the traffickers (promises of marriage, the wish to marry as soon as possible, wealth in a foreign country, etc.) and showcased the potential consequences of getting acquainted with seemingly single foreigners. As the daily noted, Dala felt in some way responsible for the well-being of eastern European Jewish girls; she made her story public to warn potential victims of the white slave trade. *Der Moment* provided the readers with the exact name of the victim and the trafficker, making the story even more personal and powerful. It reminded the readers that even living among fellow Jews, one was hardly protected from the presumed evils of Argentine prostitution and international Jewish criminality.

It seems that the *froyen-handel* (trafficking in women) was a problem for the whole of Poland, both in big cities and in small towns. Warsaw's Yiddish newspapers reported female victims originating from various Polish regions. Falling victim to the traffickers could happen both in a small town like Wieluń, where a group of traffickers abducted the local beauty, tempting her with a promise of marriage to an American, but also in big cities, such as Vilna.[50] In the latter case, a girl named Sara presumably fell in love with a handsome foreigner she met in a dance hall and decided to marry him against the will of her parents. After the wedding, the couple set off abroad. On the ship, her husband "sold" the Vilna woman to a group of traffickers who brought her to Buenos Aires and forced Sara to work in a brothel.[51] *Hayntige Nayes* from January 1931 described an analogous story of two female residents of Łódź, who, after being seduced by an elegant Argentine Jew, left Poland and immigrated to Argentina where they were forced into prostitution.[52]

All the stories mentioned above emphasized the dramatic situation of young women who, fooled by the traffickers, were forcibly coerced into sex work in Buenos Aires. Despite their suffering, the abducted girls were doubly victimized in the press reports, as journalists tended to ascribe part of the guilt to the victims. They described the women as stupid, naive, disobedient, and materialistic. For the all-male editorial staff of the Yiddish journals, beauty and naiveté were reasonable explanations for abductions and forced prostitution. A picture of binary culpability emerges from their reports on prostitution in Argentina: traffickers and foolish women. Interestingly, prostitution was one of the few areas of social life where Jewish women were allowed to speak out. Yiddish newspapers hardly ever published articles written by women; journalism was a space reserved almost exclusively for men. By quoting the victims of prostitution, the editors of *Der Moment*, *Haynt*, and *Hayntige Nayes* provided women with a unique opportunity to express their humiliation and suffering. This should be seen in the context of some contemporary interpretations that see Jewish prostitutes from early twentieth century as independent actors, consciously deciding to earn money by selling their bodies.[53] Press reports about sex-related criminality were part of a large flashback campaign against independent women. The conservative social milieu disapproved of migration—and the emigration of single women in particular. In that light, the earlier discussed discourse, cautioning against emigration, was part of the same phenomenon as press reports about the supposedly degenerate Buenos Aires.

Argentina's infamous Jewish prostitution problem fit well as a theme for the *shund* (trash) theater that was popular in Poland in the interwar years. Forbidden love, generational conflicts, and mésalliances were the main issues discussed by the Sambation group that played in the Scala Theater in Warsaw or by the Yidishe Bande. An actor and director of Sambation Theater, Izaak Nożyk, wrote a play (together with Abe Lang) that turned Argentina and its Jewish prostitution into a key theme. *Oyfn veg keyn Buenos Aires: Unter der royter lamtern* (On the way to Buenos Aires: Under the red street lamps) was staged for the first time by Zisa Katz, Simcha Rozen, and Nożyk himself in Warsaw's Yiddishn Folks Theater in 1931.[54] In the same year, the play also appeared in Łódź and Vilna (by Morris Lampe). It was probably no accident that *Oyfn veg keyn Buenos Aires* shared its title with a documentary book by Albert Londres, which appeared in Yiddish translation in 1928.[55] Several plays with a similar theme were also performed outside of Poland, but their echoes reached back to Warsaw. *Literarishe Bleter* reported that New York's Odeon played *Dos meydl fun Buenos Aires* (A girl from Buenos Aires) and in Paris *Opgrunt fun Buenos Aires* (Buenos Aires precipice) with Buenos Aires's Yiddish actress Miriam Lerer.

Nożyk's *Oyfn veg keyn Buenos Aires* tells the story of a group of eastern European Jewish immigrants living in Argentina, who become involved in international female trafficking. The play personified the prostitutes and pimps. The characters were far from cold-hearted exploiters and promiscuous fallen women. As in many other shund plays, *Oyfn veg keyn Buenos Aires* featured unhappy loves, unfaithful lovers, intrigues, and murders. An unusually tragic figure is the character of Adela: an aging prostitute in a relationship with a pimp named Frank. In eastern Europe, Frank seduces Adela, and she travels with him to Buenos Aires, where, as she says in a moment of anger, "she became his constantly humiliated slave." As the story develops, Adela pretends to be an aunt of Bela, who just arrived in Argentina to join her father. However, Bela falls into the hands of Frank and becomes an underage prostitute. In the last act of the play, it turns out that Bela is Adela's daughter, whom she left back in Poland, and Abraham, the husband of Adela's fellow prostitute Rosi, is Adela's husband and Bela's father.

Oyfn veg keyn Buenos Aires encompassed a number of popular themes easily recognizable in Jewish American immigrant literature. Abraham longs for the familiarity of the eastern European landscape and believes that he is in Argentina "only for a while." We read about the wealth of the pimps and prostitutes, about the pimps hunting for innocent newcomers in the port of Buenos Aires and about prostitutes who come back to religion in their old age. *Oyfn veg keyn Buenos Aires* defines Argentina as a hotbed of international prostitution, but the drama hardly makes a distinction between Argentina and the United States. The characters throw around English words ("all right," "yes, yes") and talk about dollars. Consequently, Argentina and the United States are blended into one dangerous, promiscuous location but one that still gives hope. The appearance of this play on theater stages of 1930s Warsaw shows how Argentina entered the popular culture and life of ordinary Jews in Poland. The theme of prostitution and the light character of the play made the Argentine debates open to practically everyone.

In addition to news stories about female trafficking, Poland's Yiddish press often covered general information about how the criminality of Buenos Aires affected its Jewish residents. The Warsaw press regularly reported on frauds and murders committed on and by Polish Jews in Argentina. For example, in September 1924 *Der Moment* published a report about twenty-four Jewish immigrants with false passports who were arrested in Buenos Aires.[56] The daily explained that the immigrants were victims of a document forger, who had fooled the ignorant Jews, assuring them that their passports were even valid for entry to the United States. Similar information appeared in *Der Moment* in April 1924.[57] The newspaper, quoting a message by the JCA office in Warsaw, reported that the US State Department informed the Argentine government about many European immigrants heading to Argentina, where they acquired forged passports (using falsified naturalization documents), and subsequently tried to enter North America. Articles that presented emigrants as victims misled by Argentine criminals further stabilized the image of Argentina as a "dangerous" country—where not only women but also Jewish men could become objects of deception.

Argentina appeared in the Yiddish press as a place where new, formerly uncommon problems intruded into the lives of Polish Jews. Jewish immigration to Argentina tremendously influenced the eastern European family structure, and the emigration of young men often led to conflicts between husbands and wives. It is visible in an article from January 1930, published in *Hayntige Nayes*.[58] The journal addressed the problematic issue of marriages that fell apart because of emigration to Argentina or other countries. The evening paper noted that the Warsaw rabbinate had received a letter from one of the Buenos Aires rabbis, describing his meeting with Alexander Perkal, a Warsaw-born hatter who decided to divorce his wife, still residing in Poland. This short article seems to portray the complications connected with emigration that intruded into the lives of eastern European Jews. Although the author never expressed it clearly, the article reads like an accusation against the unfaithful husband, liberated from the obligations of the Old World and enjoying a hedonistic life in Argentina. Yet, the husband indeed contacted a local rabbi, suggesting that he maintained a strong connection to religious and traditional customs. Migration appeared in this article as a family-breaking factor, a hitherto unknown phenomenon that destroyed traditional family relations. *Hayntige Nayes* depicted the couple's problems as part of the unusual and strange "Argentine issues," discouraging readers from emigration by describing Argentina as a seductive and dangerous space that tore families apart. Contrary voices were rare.

Texts describing crime, prostitution, and female trafficking served as a mechanism for limiting emigration. They portrayed Argentina as a country where innocent eastern European Jews were misled by their Argentinized coreligionists, who were only interested in making a profit at the expense of poor and uninformed immigrants. *Haynt* and *Der Moment* seemed determined to convince Polish Jews that Argentina was not only a land of vice and prostitution but also a place where criminality was part of daily life. Whereas Poland's criminal cases and prostitution were also regularly covered, foreign news about female trafficking referred almost exclusively to Argentina. By stressing the vulnerability of new Jewish immigrants to fraud by the local Jewish population of Argentina, the dailies drew a picture of a land where Jewish social networks seemed to be corrupted. Instead of an ethnic support, the more veteran immigrants would betray the new arrivals. While it could be understandable in the context of religiously conservative circles, who feared losing control over the religious community, it is less clear why this type of articles appeared in secular and liberal papers, such as *Haynt* and *Moment*. It may have been the result of a simple snowball effect and the difficulty of crafting a credible counternarrative about Argentina.

Conclusion

In the 1920s and 1930s, the images of Argentina became much more nuanced. Argentina was seen not only as a potential emigration destination but was popularly identified as a hotbed of international Jewish prostitution. In articles published in Poland's Yiddish dailies, we find hope and great expectations regarding immigration to Argentina but also a clear articulation of anxiety and fear. We find competent information about favorable immigration possibilities and, simultaneously, numerous articles describing unsuccessful emigrants who decided to return to Poland and reports on trafficking in Jewish women. Poland's Yiddish press adopted the role of emigration advisor—a channel that helped the impoverished Polish Jews to comfortably settle down in developing Argentina. Simultaneously, by constantly informing readers about the alleged dangers awaiting immigrants in this country (like Jewish female trafficking), the Yiddish press reflected the position of emigration opponents and debated the negative consequences that it could have on Jewish life in Poland. This was reinforced by depictions in popular culture, contributing to the exoticization of Argentina in Jewish Poland. Nevertheless, when conditions were attractive, many Polish Jews followed the advice of Yiddish dailies and boarded steamships departing for Buenos Aires from Danzig (Gdańsk), Hamburg, Trieste, Antwerp, or other European port cities.

At the same time, the fact that Argentina was discussed in the Yiddish daily press marked its absorption into wider debates within the imagined polity of the Yiddishland. Peretz Hirschbein and Hersh Dovid Nomberg, two authors who wrote for *Der Moment* in Warsaw, decided to travel to Argentina to verify the status of Yiddish culture in the new Latin American centers and the general situation of Jewish immigrants. The next two chapters explore their journeys in detail. Chapter 3 analyzes the ways how Argentina was being embedded into the framework of Yiddish culture, whereas chapter 4 portrays how both travel writers strengthened the exoticization of Argentina through Jewish eastern European discourse and society.

3

Argentine Branch

Extending the Yiddishland to Latin America

When Peretz Hirschbein visited Argentina for the second time in 1925, he was already surrounded by an aura as an admirer of and expert on Argentina. The arrival of this Yiddish author and traveler was preceded by the establishment of the Hirschbein Committee that coordinated his visit, organized public meetings, and was responsible for spreading information about the writer's stay.[1] The daily press reported about his every step in the country, printed texts of his talks, and treated him as a guest of honor. Hirschbein himself noted that his arrival in Buenos Aires was a unique experience for him, with hundreds waiting for him curiously at night in the Buenos Aires port and hugging and pushing him from hands to hands.[2]

The same had happened when Hersh Dovid Nomberg arrived in Argentina in 1922. A special committee organized a gala dinner in prestigious Prince George Hall with a performance by the famous Argentine Jewish singer Berta Singerman.[3] During the evening, as *Di Yidishe Zaitung* promised, Nomberg "sent greetings from European Jewry."[4] The Warsaw author was received festively, especially by fellow writers. A. Reziner, in a text written one year after Nomberg's death, recalled that Nomberg felt very well in Buenos Aires. During his visit, local young Yiddish authors "surrounded him with their hot eyes and beating hearts, really almost hugged him," and he felt "like a rabbi between the students."[5] Apart from Hirschbein and Nomberg, other eastern European Jewish writers, such as Shmuel Niger, H. Leivick, Anohi, Melech Ravitch, and others, visited Argentina, where they enjoyed exceptional treatment and were greeted with a genuine enthusiasm. In Argentina, these men were sui generis celebrities of that era: glorified, followed, and cheered.

In this section, I examine the factors that constructed the elevated status given to visiting Yiddish writers in Argentina and what this value system suggests about the identity and belonging of eastern European immigrants in Argentina. These visits informed about Argentine Jewish desire to be involved in transnational networks of high Yiddish culture. Many Argentine Jews wanted to define their new homeland as a vital part of the Yiddishland diaspora. The visits of well-known Yiddish literati gave Argentine Jews an opportunity to publicly express this belonging. Their devotion to global Yiddish culture was manifested in the name of Argentine Jewry and thus was supposed to elevate its status in the global Jewish cultural networks.

Peretz Hirschbein

The ecstatic reception of Hirschbein (fig. 9) in 1925 was primarily an outcome of the special interest he took in Argentine problems. His book *Fun vayte lender*, published in 1916 by New York's daily *Der Tog*, was one of the first comprehensive accounts of Jewish life in Latin America. A book written by an important figure in European and North American Jewish life gave its subjects a sense of recognition. Hirschbein's book elevated the Argentine Jewish experience to a level near to the US diaspora. Argentine Jewry, struggling with marginalization and a dubious reputation, was finally embraced into the ranks of high Jewish culture and its problems resonated in other parts of the Jewish world. Hirschbein's description of both the Jewish urban experience and the agricultural colonies showed that, despite numerous obstacles, the new Argentine diaspora had a strong future ahead, disproving the skepticism of the vitality of Jewish settlements in Argentina.

Hirschbein was born in 1880 in Kleszczele, a shtetl now located in northeastern Poland. Like almost everyone in his generation, Hirschbein initially received an exclusively religious education in a *kheyder* (Jewish religious school). Later he studied the Bible, Hebrew, and Jewish history in various towns of the region, supporting himself through his teens by giving Hebrew and Russian classes.[6] Hirschbein spent a longer time in Vilna, where in 1901 he published his first poem "Ga'aguim" (Longings) in the Hebrew journal *Ha-dor*. He left Vilna in 1904, settling down in Warsaw for a few years. The young author was taken under the wing of a prolific Yiddish author, Yitskhok Leybush Peretz, who introduced him to the city's Jewish literary scene. In 1906, Hirschbein wrote his first Yiddish dramas, *Kvorim-blumen* and *Demerung*. Later in life, Hirschbein became a critic of Hebraism and a supporter of a diasporic Yiddish culture. He admitted that like many in his generation he "left the *beis midrash* [a religious study room] with Hebrew on his lips" but soon understood that the real life of the *yidisher folk* was happening in Yiddish. Writing in 1927, he criticized the "violent disgust" toward Yiddish in Eretz Israel and the local attitude that negated Jewish diasporism. He condemned the Hebraists for "not understanding the *folk*" and "dividing the nation."[7] He also approached Zionism itself in negative terms, describing it as devoid of any content.[8]

In the following years, Hirschbein visited various cities of eastern and western Europe, departing for New York at the end of 1911. In early 1913, believing that the United States was no place for "a revived Jewish life," he returned to Eu-

Figure 9. Peretz Hirschbein, portrait, 1911, from *Peretz Hirschbein. Tsu zayn zekhtsiksten geboyrntog* (New York, 1941)

rope, spending a few months in Vilna.[9] In the summer of 1914, frustrated by the tense situation he encountered in Russia just before the outbreak of the Great War, Hirschbein decided to visit Argentina. Hirschbein noted that he did not see any future in Europe, as he was not allowed to give public talks and felt limited. As his biographer explained, Hirschbein responded to his situation by deciding to go to Argentina to settle in the Jewish agricultural colonies.[10] His decision was clearly influenced by the ongoing debates by the Jewish press in Europe regarding Argentina. In Antwerp Hirschbein boarded *Sierra Nevada*, which took him to Latin America in twenty-two days. His five-month trip began in Buenos Aires, but Hirschbein focused on exploring the Jewish agricultural settlements in the provinces of Entre Rios and Santa Fe. He traveled around numerous Jewish colonies, living for a while with local Jews, trying to formulate his opinions

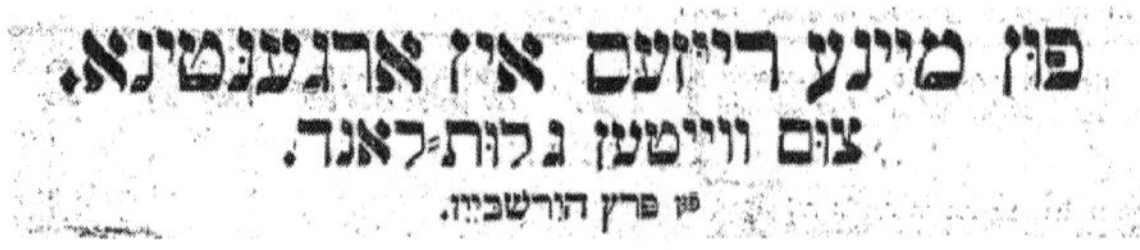
פון מיינע רייזעס אין ארגענטינא.
צום ווייטען גלות-לאנד.
פון פרץ הירשביין.

Figure 10. The title of Hirschbein's article, "Fun mayne rayzes in argentina. Tsum vayten goles-land," *Der Moment*, October 27, 1922. The article was part of *Fun vayte lender*, started in 1916.

of an entire colonization enterprise. While in Argentina, Hirschbein began publishing his travel texts in installments in New York's *Der Tog*. In Poland, his Argentine memoirs were not serialized in *Der Moment* until 1922 (fig. 10).[11] The daily, advertising Hirschbein's travel articles, wrote that the writer was not a party member but a *folks-mensh* (a regular Jew) and poet, who portrayed the countries in a way that was understandable and useful to Jewish readers in Poland.[12]

In 1925, Hirschbein visited Argentina for the second time, reporting on this journey in the Polish and North American Jewish press, as well as writing an unpublished memoir from the trip. Upon returning to Argentina, he noticed the growing progress of the country, though accompanied by new challenges concerning the evolution of Jewish life in Argentina and the local situation of the Yiddishist enterprise.[13] Hirschbein pointed out that Jewish cultural life in Buenos Aires was developing, yet many people lived in poverty, especially those working as peddlers. He warned his readers in Europe not to increase the "army of Jewish peddlers" and to be prepared for a relatively hard life.[14] Hirschbein noticed that the enthusiasm of the agricultural colonists was decreasing and many members of the second generation were leaving for Buenos Aires. In Colonia Mauricio, most settlers presumably left and sold their parcels to non-Jews.[15] Hirschbein dismissed Jewish Argentine accusations of portraying Argentina too pessimistically, arguing for a need of an authentic narrative. At the same time, he admired the bustling *yidishkayt* (Yiddish-centered Jewishness) of Buenos Aires where he felt "as in a Jewish state." He was happy that Jewish libraries served as centers of Yiddish culture.[16] During his second visit to Argentina, Hirschbein was angry about the growing influence of Zionism, mocking Argentine Zionists as those who give a hand to assimilation.[17]

Hirschbein's dramas and travel texts were published in cities with a significant Yiddish-speaking population. His early texts were published in Vilna, or Warsaw, where he lived until 1908. In 1914, Hirschbein published his first text with Vilna-based Vilner Farlag fun B. Kletskin (B. Kletskin Publishing in Vilna) that since then published most of his books for the Polish market. After 1914, the majority of Hirschbein's new books were published both in New York and in eastern Europe. In the United States, he cooperated with the Literarisher Farlag and the publishing house of the daily *Der Tog*, to which he was a regular contributor. Importantly, the travelogues from his trips were published only in Vilna (not in the United States), indicating eastern European target audience of these texts. The following appeared in Vilna, among others: an *Erets Yisroel* travelogue (1929), an India travelogue *Indye. Fun mayn rayze in indye* (1929), and a book on South Africa and Australia, *Felker un lender: Rayze-ayndrukn fun nayzeland, avstralye, doyrem afrike 1920–1922* (1929).

Even though Hirschbein did not live permanently in independent Poland, he remained involved with its local literary scene and Jewish sociocultural issues. In between his numerous journeys around the world, he regularly visited Poland. The reviews of his books often appeared in Warsaw's *Literarishe Bleter*, to which he also contributed numerous travel articles. Thanks to his literary success in the United States, as well as his exceptional inclination for traveling, Hirschbein enjoyed an unusual following in Jewish Poland. When visiting Poland, Hirschbein was welcomed as a guest of honor and a successful ambassador of a global Yiddish culture. In 1932, *Literarishe Bleter* devoted a jubilee volume to him, which praised him as a key creator in Yiddish literature and theater.[18] A Jewish school in his hometown was named after him during his lifetime.[19] Hirschbein visited Poland in 1922 before departing to Argentina and South Africa, stopping by his hometown of Kleszczele where his sister still lived.[20] In Warsaw, Hirschbein was welcomed by the brightest stars of the Yiddish literary scene of the era: Sholem Asch, Melech Ravitch, and Uri Zvi Grinberg. *Haynt* reported that Hirschbein was invited to return to Poland for good and lead the local theater.[21] The author also returned to Poland in 1927, and the Farayn fun yidishe literatn un zhurnalistn (Association of Yiddish Writers and Journalists) organized a festive welcome party for him.[22] *Der Moment* proudly named Hirschbein as its "coworker," and the president of the *Literatn Farayn*, Zusman Segalovitch, welcomed the writer at the train station. In addition, the educational TSYSHO (Tsentrale yidishe shul organizatsye, Central Yiddish School Organization) that Hirschbein supported sent an official welcome delegation.[23]

Hersh Dovid Nomberg

Hersh Dovid Nomberg (fig. 11) was born in 1876 in Mszczonów, a town sixty kilometers from Warsaw. As with Hirschbein and many other contemporary Polish Jewish writers, Nomberg was born to a religious family. He received a traditional religious education but was also exposed to secular writing as he communicated in Polish, Russian, and German. Young Nomberg was influenced by the eastern European Haskalah, which started to develop in the region at the turn of 1850s and 1860s.[24] He questioned the role of religion and tradition in Jewish life and supported Jewish secularization and emancipation. Following the maskilic pattern, Nomberg published initially in Hebrew, writing for the Hebrew journal

Figure 11. Hersh Dovid Nomberg, date unknown, image from the cover of his *Dos bukh felyetonen* (Warsaw 1924)

Ha-tsofeh (between 1903 and 1905). He moved to Warsaw in 1897, where he became a disciple of popular Yiddish writer Yitskhok Leybush Peretz, who persuaded him to write his texts in Yiddish. Probably on his advice and under the influence of his Warsaw flat-mates, Avrom Reyzen and Sholem Asch, themselves aspiring Yiddish authors at the time, Nomberg published his first Yiddish poem "Ha-novi." In subsequent years, he continued writing in Yiddish, including novellas, such as *In der poylisher yeshive* (1901), *Di kursistke* (1908), and the psychoanalytical tale *Fliglman*, depicting an alienated and pessimistic Jewish individual, critical toward contemporary Jewish reality.

After 1910, Nomberg focused on his journalistic and political activism. He was a proclaimed proponent of cultural Yiddishism and underlined the need for a Jewish national renaissance of this language in his belles lettres and journalism. According to Avrom Reyzen, it was Nomberg who coined the term "Yiddishism," which started being used as a description of an entire movement and ideology.[25] Nomberg supported the development of Yiddish art theater, just as Hirschbein criticized the low quality of popular plays. In 1916, Nomberg co-founded the Association of Jewish Writers and Journalists in Warsaw, popularly known as Tłomackie 13, which served as the epicenter of Polish Yiddishism and high Yiddish literature until 1939.

Nomberg was exemplary of the generation of young eastern European Jews who strived for freedom and universal subjects that exceeded the narrow Jewish world. Nomberg rejected both the promises of Zionism and assimilation and searched for other ways to combine Jewishness and modernity. The development of Yiddish culture was for him a basis for the future existence of east European Jewry.[26] He claimed for Yiddish culture a position of a central axis of modern Jewish identity. Jewish literature was for Nomberg a space for reimagining Jewish identities and for approaching the *folk*. Literary critic Nakhmen Mayzel wrote of Nomberg: "He was a child from an era that left one world, but was not fully rooted in the second world. He was disappointed with Haskalah, but was not yet fully convinced engaging in the national and social problems."[27] Both Nomberg's literature and his essay writings suggest a quest for new forms of Jewishness. His travels can also be interpreted as a search for new ways of Jewish existence.

Nomberg's Yiddishism was powerfully visible in his participation at the Czernowitz language conference in 1908.[28] Together with Yitskhok Leybush Peretz, Ester Frumkin, Sholem Asch, Chaim Zhitlowsky, Avrom Reyzen, Nathan Birnbaum, Noyekh Prilutski, and other cultural activists, he debated the future of Yiddish as a Jewish national language. Nomberg, Asch, and Reyzen belonged to the militant Yiddishist monolinguists, who wanted to define Yiddish as "the" (one and only) Jewish national language.[29] Others, including Y. L. Peretz, defended the rights of Hebrew and supported the bilingualist stand.[30] Opening the conference, Nomberg stated that its objective was to bring a revolution to Jewish life and to Yiddish literature: "Our goal is to bring about a social development of the Yiddish language. . . . The nation expects from us to deliver a clear message concerning our new national and cultural values."[31] After the conference, Nomberg wrote: "We have finally articulated the brave words that for so long were waiting on our tongues and we believe that these words will find their repercussions among thousands and millions of our folk. We say: in the midst of the chaos of our life was laid a strong cornerstone on which will raise a beautiful and dignified edifice of our national life."[32] The conference argued that the problems of Jewish culture and Yiddish language were immanently linked with Jewish national and social questions and demanded "political, social and cultural equality and recognition."[33] The Czernowitz conference in 1908 gave an impulse for intensifying Yiddish cultural life. In the same year, Warsaw's daily *Haynt* was established, Shmuel Niger cofounded the first journal of Yiddish literary criticism *Literarishe Monatsshriftn*, and Hirschbein launched his avant-garde theater group.

Throughout his entire journalistic and literary career, Nomberg grappled with the questions of Jewish identity, nationalism, and the Jewish future in eastern Europe. In 1916, during the convention establishing the Folkist Party in Poland, Nomberg said that unlike the Zionists who give "long-term exchange bills," the folkists would focus on the Jewish situation in the short run, in countries where Jews lived. He saw Jewish political and cultural autonomy as his (and the folkists') main objective.[34] In one of his essays, Nomberg developed a concept of a "nationalism of the weak," in which he warned Jewish nationalists of falling into the same loopholes as the Russians, Germans, or Poles. Even as he considered national feelings as natural and obvious, he feared the ways that nationalists built their capital on these values. He warned of nationalism's reliance on animosities, superiority, exclusion, and a return to the "aggressive psychology of wild animals." The revisionist Zionism of Vladimir Ze'ev Jabotynsky was for Nomberg as ugly and dangerous as its German or Polish variants.[35] What he supported instead was a focus on Yiddish cultural work for the folk.

Nomberg was a passionate traveler. Between 1905 and 1907, he visited western Europe (France, Germany, Switzerland) and spent some time in Riga. In 1912, he traveled to the United States, visiting New York, where he observed Jewish life in the city and focused on the Jewish working-class movement. In 1924, Nomberg traveled to Palestine, visiting Tel Aviv, Galilee, and the Negev desert.[36] After returning from his journeys, Nomberg often gave public lectures about the lands that he visited. In 1922, Nomberg departed for Argentina, visiting Buenos Aires and Jewish farming colonies in other provinces. En route to Latin America, he sent travel texts to be published in Warsaw's *Der Moment* (fig. 12).[37] News about his trip also reached the United States. *Foverts* informed read-

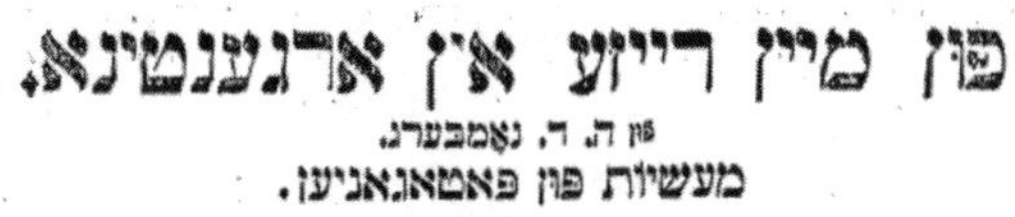

פון מיין רייזע אין ארגענטינא.

פון ה. ד. נאמבערג.

מעשיות פון פאטאגאניען.

Figure 12. The title of Nomberg's article on Argentina published in *Der Moment*. "Fun mayn rayze keyn argentina. Mayses fun patagonyen," March 30, 1923, no. 77, 5

ers that Nomberg visited Argentina as an envoy of the Workers' Emigration Committee and an investigator of local immigration possibilities.[38] A handful of his travel essays were also published in the Buenos Aires *Di Yidische Zaitung*.[39] Like Hirschbein, Nomberg also supported the TSYSHO Yiddishist-secular schooling project during his visit. Even though his trip was planned as a research trip, as Samuel Rollansky put it, "the writer won with an envoy."[40] Nomberg's travel memoirs were published in 1924 by the Farlag Kultur-Lige, together with other essays covering his travels around post–World War I Europe and texts about famous Jewish personalities.[41]

The Travel Writer as a Celebrity: Argentina Welcomes the Guests from the Old Home

Journalist M. N. Shpirnberg of Buenos Aires's Yiddish journal *Penimer un penimlekh* claimed that in 1925 Hirschbein was received as a guest of honor by the entirety of Argentine Jewry.[42] He underlined Hirschbein's interest in the problems of Jewish migrations. Shpirnberg's text presented him as an unusual figure representing both the Old World and the United States, which were then the centers of Jewish life and Jewish creativity. Shpirnberg identified the work of Hirschbein in Argentina as quasi-ethnographic. He described him as one who unveiled Jewish Argentina to a broader public. It was appreciated that Hirschbein decided to focus on a diaspora country that many regarded as less important or marginal. His texts on the Latin American diaspora served, in Shpirnberg's opinion, as a showcase that displayed Argentina to the unfamiliar Jewish public of Europe and North America.

The journalist perceived Hirschbein's second visit to Argentina as a chance to present to the Jewish world the recent achievements of Argentine Jews. He emphasized that during his second stay Hirschbein "would see a different Jewish Argentina: more stable, stronger rooted in local society and finally playing some role on the scene of the Jewish world."[43] Shpirnberg believed that Argentina finally became *mit laytn glaykh*,[44] was "normalized," and had begun to be perceived as any other Jewish diaspora. He hoped that Hirschbein would notice the changes and appreciate the efforts and progress of the local community. Shpirnberg expected that during his second visit the traveler "would have much more study material" and probably would present Argentina in a better light than in *Fun vayte lender*, which some regarded as overly critical and pessimistic. The first visit of Hirschbein in Argentina in 1914 (and a book based on it) was a permanent point of reference in articles covering his second trip in 1925. The attention he devoted back then to the problems and challenges that Jews faced in Argentina transformed him into an expert on Argentine issues and a friend of local Jewry. Especially cordial were the reactions of the Yiddish media, which shared the progressive and Jewish ethnonational agenda of the writer. The leftist *Di Presse* described Hirschbein's arrival in Buenos Aires as a comeback of an old, long unseen friend.[45]

During both visits, Hirschbein traveled widely, visiting Buenos Aires, provincial cities such as Córdoba and Santa Fe, and Jewish agricultural colonies of the interior. His 1914 visit had a less festive character and was focused on examining the situation of developing Jewish farms. The Argentine Jewish press was scarce during this time, making it nearly impossible to locate any printed reports. During his visit in 1925, Hirschbein visited not only Buenos Aires and the colonies but also big regional capitals, including Santa Fe, Córdoba, Mendoza, Parana, and Rosario. This time his arrival was noticed not only by the Yiddish press but also by Spanish-language Jewish periodicals that appreciated his interest in Argentina.[46] In every visited locality, Hirschbein was welcomed as a genuine celebrity (fig. 13). Local Jewish leaders established so-called Hirschbein's Committees that coordinated preparations for the writer's visit: they spread information about the meeting, arranged a venue for the event, printed posters, and taught children poems that they would recite for Hirschbein in Yiddish. Some newspaper reports were quite emotional and full of excitement. Rosario's local journal described the writer as "our Hirschbein." His interest in the problems of the Argentine diaspora granted him intimate access to the local community. As the author of the article wrote, "no one will ever forget the beautiful moments that we spent with Hirschbein."[47] Rosario Jews needed to cooperate with each other to comfortably welcome the guest. As reported by *Penimer un penimlekh*, the Music Society played songs to impress their special guest, Y. Groysman offered a moving welcome speech, while N. Pukhovitch organized a banquet at the headquarters of the Jewish Bank that was later followed by an afternoon *tasa de chocolate* (cup of chocolate) meeting prepared by the Ladies' Union.

The evening in honor of Hirschbein greatly resembled similar events of the aspiring Argentine middle class. The social gatherings revealed how people perceived their socioeconomic status and ways in which they chose to demonstrate their identities.[48] Those events were not insider meetings of a local elite with the visitor but public meetings broadly covered by the Jewish press. Participating in a Yiddish-language event in honor of a Yiddish writer was a sign that eastern

Figure 13. Peretz Hirschbein and his welcome committee in Córdoba, 1925

Europe, Yiddishland, and its culture were relevant for many Argentine Jews at the time. They were confident and conscious manifestations of one's linguistic and cultural identity and belonging. A meeting with Hirschbein was not a reenactment of *alter heym* (old home) nostalgia. The author symbolized a new, modern, secular, ethnonational Jewish identity. By participating in the meetings with Hirschbein, the Jewish immigrants underscored their desire to be part of the modernizing project of the Yiddishland that Hirschbein embodied. Their growing Argentine patriotism, and a sense of already being Argentine Jews, was reflected in their will to represent Argentina in the modernizing debates about Jewish peoplehood and its future in times of a global diasporism.

The attachment to Yiddish culture that some Argentine Jews wished to express is visible in an article in *Rosarier Wochenblatt*, which covered Hirschbein's visit in this city. His stay in Rosario was described as a day of "joy, Jewish happiness and moral pleasure."[49] Hirschbein and his wife were perceived as emissaries of high Yiddish culture that Rosario Jews seemed to adore. Their visit united often conflicted groups: Zionists and socialists, shopkeepers and members of the local elite. Many eastern European Jews living in the town gathered together to celebrate the Yiddish culture that Hirschbein embodied. In a town with a small number of Jews, there was a need and longing for Yiddish cultural contact. The Yiddish language and a common past in eastern Europe were one of the few things shared by Argentine Jews, who were often separated along lines of gender, class, or politics. A meeting with a popular and beloved author was one of the few opportunities that brought such a diverse crowd together. Hirschbein's intellect was not all that drew people to him, but also his social agenda, which underlined the importance of Yiddish-centered ethnicity, secular Yiddishist schooling, and globally entangled Jewish life.

Similar welcome ceremonies took place in other locations. Hirschbein's visit in Santa Fe was covered in *Di Tribune*. His stay was described as a holiday "that made any other issue unimportant." The writer's visit was celebrated festively: Hirschbein and the local organizers began it, as the newspaper reported, "with a beautifully served lunch that was followed by a moving welcome speech of Peretz Hirschbein."[50] Usually the visiting authors did not spend much time in town. In Santa Fe, it lasted only three days. However, the Yiddish press covering the writer's visits often expressed the conviction that "the honorable guest would soon arrive again." It was stressed that the travelers were surprised by the warm welcome they received, by the high level of local Jewish cultural life, and the community's vitality. Argentine Jews were interested in securing the interest and support of those who wrote about Argentine Jewish life for the public abroad. To this end, they presented to Hirschbein and Nomberg their plan to develop the Yiddish press, schooling, and literature and by showing their attachment to eastern Europe and their strong interest in the problems of the alter heym. Although these efforts might have been temporal, they underlined the relevance of transnational belonging in the immigrants' value system. Choosing what to present to the travelers was an ethnocultural process, far from a mere desire to show how the traditional ethnic identity was maintained. Hirschbein was an advocate of change, and the Argentine Jewish life that was then in the process of defining its character was a field where the new ehtnonational Yiddishist project was taking root. Choosing to present to travelers the trappings of progressive Argentine Yiddish culture revealed the values and ethnic emblems that the immigrant Jews were proud of or supported.

Public talks given by the travelers were key points on their Argentine itineraries. The so-called *lektsyes* or *konferentsyes* (speeches, lectures) were effectively advertised in the Jewish press, which usually described them as the great success of local ethnic leaders and organizers. As the Jewish press reported, hotels and theaters that hosted the events were usually almost completely packed. Journalists described the talks delivered by the guests as moving, interesting, or meaningful. The newspapers, often with a certain pathos, expressed the hope and the conviction that the words of the speakers "will remain forever in the memory of the public." The conferences were meticulously prepared shows. The literati performed on the stage so as to be visible and audible to the audience. To some extent, the lektsyes resembled contemporary talks given by celebrity academics or music concerts. Also, the press articles covering the lektsyes were close to the reviews or follow-up texts about art shows. The authors were "performing" (*oystreten*) on the stage and were enthusiastically received by the spectators (*publikum*).

The speeches of Hirschbein usually included fragments of his works read aloud by the author.

The problems discussed during the conferences pertained to a variety of contemporary social and literary issues. In 1935, Shmuel Niger, a Vilna-experienced, New York–based literary critic, presented the situation of Jewish immigrants in North America to the Buenos Aires Jewish public. Speaking at the Yidisher Teater at Avenida Corrientes, he offered a wittingly titled speech, "A Jew in America: Who He Was, Who He Is and Whom He Could Have Been?" On another occasion, in Teatro Albeniz, he entertained the public with a talk, "Humor and Satire in Jewish Literature," later speaking about writers like Sholem Asch and H. Leivick.[51] Despite the captivating character of the lektsyes, the Yiddish press emphasized their educative function. Meetings with literary celebrities were supposed to help Argentine Jews to familiarize them with contemporary Yiddish culture and its transnational challenges and to ground their identities in modern Yiddish cultural nationalism.

Hirschbein and other traveling writers, like H. Leivick or Shmuel Niger, did not come to Argentina only because of their fondness of Argentine Jews. Their visits were also economically motivated. Numerous meetings held by Niger and Hirschbein in Argentina allowed them to improve their often precarious financial situation. Lektsyes or konferentsyes were usually against offering payment. Describing preparations for Hirschbein's visit in Rosario, the *Di Yidische Zaitung* noted that the local "organization committee" was in charge not only of renting a *salon* to host the writer's meeting but also printing and managing the tickets.[52] Yet, there were voices, for instance in *Mundo Israelita*, that strongly rejected any financial incentive on the part of Hirschbein or the organizers.[53] Ticketing and charging for the lektsyes had the effect of lowering the popular character of the events. With only those who could afford it participating in the lectures, the public meetings ultimately turned into arenas for manifesting not only yidishkayt and an interest in letters but a better-off social and economic status.

The visits of eastern European authors were especially cherished by Argentine Yiddishist circles. In the years between 1914 and 1925, when Hirschbein and Nomberg visited Argentina, it was among first-generation immigrant Jews that the character of Jewish life in Argentina was defined. Among them was a group of cultural leaders, who desired to mobilize the broader population for the Yiddishist cause. Importantly, the visits of both travelers coincided with the main wave of post–World War I Jewish migration from Poland that brought a renewed Yiddishization to Argentine Jewish life. Most of those who arrived after the war were already versed in Yiddish literature and in Poland experienced the rise of the Yiddish press and Jewish political movements. A cultural ideology that stressed the importance of the Yiddish language for the Jewish people served as the basis for building their Jewish life in Argentina. Yet, also among those who arrived to Argentina before the Great War was a sizeable group of secular progressive Jews, who were aware of the new tendencies developing in Europe. Those Jews who personally experienced the beginnings of a Jewish social evolution in Poland were most interested in manifesting their connection to the modernizing change reshaping eastern European Jewishness (and often left-wing political positions). The visits of writers who shared a similar worldview were an opportunity to manifest their beliefs and ethnic belonging. This was especially true for the recent Jewish Polish arrivals. As the Yiddishist Pinie Katz noted, almost every Yiddish author who visited Argentina was also invited to the Poylisher Farband, an organization that united immigrants from Poland.[54]

In order to increase the number of spectators, the lektsyes were sometimes offered alongside Spanish translation. This practice became quite common in the 1930s when the number of Argentina-born Jews increased. In 1935, when Shmuel Niger spoke about humor and satire in Yiddish literature, a simultaneous Spanish translation was offered. In the mid-1920s, when Hirschbein was in Argentina for the second time, the organizers did not feel a need to provide a translation. This suggests that in the 1920s, the Argentine Jewish community was still relatively new and consisted mostly of Yiddish-speaking immigrants. In the mid-1930s, the Spanish-speaking children of the immigrants gained a stronger foothold on the Buenos Aires Jewish cultural scene but remained interested in Yiddish subjects from the alter heym. That underscores my argument concerning the simultaneous Argentinazation and renewed Yiddishization among Argentine Jews. While acculturation was on the rise in the 1930s, interest in global agents of Yiddish culture did not decrease. The Jewish Argentines adopted new methods (simultaneous translation) that combined their Argentineness and belonging to the Yiddish people.

In order to support his like-minded Argentine proponents of Yiddish culture, Hirschbein visited a number of secular Yiddish cultural establishments. His support was especially important in the 1920s when new left-wing Jewish school networks were formed in Argentina, modeled on Poland's TSYSHO schools. Support from a prominent Yiddish writer justified the efforts of the local Yiddishists and presented their cause as a part of a global project. During his second visit in Argentina, Hirschbein visited the Yiddish-language Workers' School Ber Borokhov, where he was festively greeted by the students. As a part of the preparation for his visit, the teachers familiarized the students with the writer's persona and creativity. Children drew pictures for Hirschbein and wrote poems that featured, among others, his time in Vilna. One of the Borokhov children wrote in his *kompozitsye* (essay) that the visit of Hirschbein and his wife was a great holiday for the entire school. Another student recalled that the writer was interested if children truly understood the sociopolitical stand of the school they attended.[55] The visit to the Yiddish school showed the crucial importance of Jewish secular schooling for Hirschbein. His visits in these establishments were a clear sign of his ideological preferences.

The involvement of Hirschbein with the progressive schools in Argentina was closely related to his worldview and the situation in Poland. A visit to the Borokhov school, known for its left-leaning position, was not surprising. Hirschbein had repeatedly underlined the importance of secular Yiddish schooling and was its fervent defender both in Poland and in Argentina. He was a supporter of a secular Jewish national awareness and Jewish culture in the Yiddish language in the entire Yiddishland. The income from his 1927 lectures in Warsaw and Vilna was donated to TSYSHO schools.[56] His devotion to Yiddishism was also manifested in his support for the activities of the Jewish Scientific Institute in Vilna, which not only carried out research on the Yiddish language but coordinated the entire Yiddishist enterprise. In 1928, Hirschbein traveled specially to Vilna in order to participate in the third anniversary of the YIVO Institute and offered a public lecture in the local Palace Theater.[57]

The Globetrotters: Hirschbein and Nomberg in Argentina

The Argentine expeditions of Hirschbein and Nomberg were not merely ethnographic. Both writers were public intellectuals of the era, aware of the challenges that Jews faced and the changes that migration, modernity, and assimilation brought to Jewish life. Nomberg was a folkist and an advocate of Jewish Diaspora Nationalism in eastern Europe but, later in life, supported Jewish emigration from Poland. Both intellectuals were aware of the growing poverty and anti-Semitism in their homeland. Like many ordinary Jews, they debated whether migration was the answer to the challenges of Jewish life. Both Nomberg and Hirschbein supported secular Yiddishist educational initiatives that aimed to mirror changing global Jewish life. As they welcomed emigration as a possible solution to the problems in eastern Europe, they also saw migration as a chance building moment for Yiddish life within new diasporic regions. Their travelogues examined the factors influencing the development of a Jewish life in Argentina and the chance of seeing Argentina not only as a refuge but a laboratory for building a modern diasporic Jewish peoplehood.

Consequently, their texts constructed Argentina as a Jewish space and explored the possibility of a stable Yiddish-run diaspora. Nomberg's and Hirschbein's narratives were written in Yiddish. Most of the problems they discussed were Jewish problems and most of the described individuals were Jews. Yet, the travelers drew a complex picture of immigrant Jewish life in Argentina, which was largely influenced by the local setting. Their books documented the formative years when the hyphen between Jewish and Argentine was being drawn. Importantly, Nomberg and Hirschbein demanded from the immigrant Jews to acculturate, to Argentinize themselves, to learn Spanish, not to live in ethnic enclaves, and to give their Jewishness a uniquely Argentine dimension. They mocked those who were unable to acculturate, held back by nostalgia and memories. As Yiddishists, they praised the development of the Argentine Yiddish press, theaters, and other cultural establishments. Hirschbein's and Nomberg's travelogues combined praising both the Yiddish and the Argentine, signaling that the migrants could combine both.

The Argentine travels of Hirschbein (in 1914 and 1925) and Nomberg (in 1922) expressed their individual exploration of the transatlantic evolution of Jewish life. Both personally experienced the ongoing demise of the shtetl and understood that Jewish life was entering a new period. Their travels to Argentina expressed their search for new options for Jews and for Jewish culture. Both Nomberg and Hirschbein, as well as an entire literary generation that had their debut shortly before World War I, were rooted in the experiences of ordinary Jews but questioned the tradition and searched for ways to combine Jewishness with modernity.[58] They were formed by eastern European visions of a new modern Jewish culture born out of anti-Jewish discrimination, surrounding nationalisms, and Jewish linguistic alterity, which at the same time sought answers to the internal changes of Jewish life. Hirschbein, Nomberg, and other Jewish culturists in the East and West grappled with the problem of "modern Jewish culture." They feared that Jewish culture would reach a point of collapse, if emerging new questions were not addressed properly.[59]

Hirschbein and Nomberg wanted their writing and activism to offer an alternative identity policy that mirrored the new social and cultural reality. The progressive Yiddishist ideology shared by both authors suggested a similar direction for Jews living in Argentina. Travel accounts by the prominent personas of Yiddish letters included Argentina in the Yiddishland and defined it as a legitimate Latin American branch, wherein Argentine Jewish cultural policies leaned toward a progressive Yiddish culture. Nomberg and Hirschbein saw Argentina as a laboratory where a new secular Yiddish and self-asserted Jewish ethnic identity could grow strong roots. In many places, Hirschbein repeated that Argentina was a country of Jewish hope.[60] The travelers' vision of Jewish future was both ethnonational and diasporic, as it suggested the possibility of a deterritorialized national Yiddish culture that could flourish both in eastern Europe and in Argentina. Rather than a replica of the Old World, Argentina was to become a place where the new ethnonational project would be employed. Visiting Argentina in 1925, Hirschbein reflected on the national Jewish contents that could be adopted in Argentina and other diasporas. He dismissed "digging in the fog of the past" and rejected the Zionist attachment to the land of Israel. During his second visit to Argentina, Hirschbein was troubled with questions of Jewish ethnicity and diasporization, which compelled him to think if and how the new Yiddish culture could be grounded and stabilized.[61]

The travelogues of Nomberg and Hirschbein give accounts of the development of Jewish-Argentine identities. The travelers derided the homesickness and nostalgia of the Jewish immigrants and understood and supported selected aspects of Argentinization. Whereas the first-generation immigrants were often pictured as a part of the eastern European diaspora, their Argentina-born children were portrayed as a sign of ongoing Argentinization and Jewish rootedness in Argentina. Nomberg welcomed the fact that the children of the colonists adapted to the life in the wilderness of Argentine pampa. As he wrote, little Yankele and Sorele galloping on horseback was the most beautiful sight in Argentina.[62] Not less than their health and bravery, Nomberg cherished the fact that the mouths of Jewish children "were full of Yiddish words." Although their appearance and habits—especially the darker complexion and the sight of riding bareback, unusual for eastern Europe—might have turned them into foreign figures to Jewish audiences in Poland, by speaking Yiddish they managed to preserve the main marker of Ashkenazi Jewishness. The children that Nomberg marveled at were an example of the embryonic Jewish Argentineness: perfectly Argentine at first sight but rooted in Yiddishness. Similar observations were made by Hirschbein in 1925: "In this Jewish life, in Argentine life . . . Jewish children came to me, those born in Argentina, Argentinely slim and with Argentine pride in their eyes, and they spoke with me in Yiddish."[63] Both travelers understood the Yiddish language as the beating heart of the modern Jewish culture they envisioned. Yiddish-speaking, Argentine-born children were proof that Nomberg's and Hirschbein's ethnocultural project could be successful in Argentina, that Jewish migration was not a hindrance but a chance for the development of Yiddish-centered identities.

The progressive Yiddishist approach of the travelers was shared by some of their Jewish Argentine hosts. Most of them were Polish, Russian, or Bessarabian newcomers who settled in Argentina just a decade or two earlier and thus, to a great extent, were influenced by the eastern European Jewish debates. Their ethnonational belonging was fluid and ever evolving, largely shaped by Jewish diasporism. Both eastern European Jewishness and newly emerging Jewish argentinidad were in the process of undergoing unprecedented social turmoil. New Jewish ethnonational identities were shaped predominantly by secularization, urbanization, changing family relations, and, most significantly, migration. At the same time in Argentina, as in the case of other immigrant groups, Jews negotiated a desire to become an organic part of Argentine society, while sustaining their distinctive ethnonational Jewish identity. The travel writers observed the development of Jewish-Argentine identities and the inclusion of Jews into the

Argentine nation, all while they attempted to advance their progressive Yiddishist cultural agenda. Alluding to this process, Argentine Yiddishist Samuel Rollansky wrote that the literary visitors did not realize what an immense influence they exercised on Argentine-Jewish life.[64]

Jewish emigration from Poland to Argentina is a good lens for viewing the development of ethnonational identities, as it highlights the multiple influential factors and possibilities. In the 1920s and 1930s, some of the immigrants imagined themselves as citizens of a transnational Yiddishland and wanted to be defined as a vital branch of a diasporic Yiddish nation. The visits of the Old World literati gave them an opportunity to imagine themselves as connected with the eastern European center of Jewish life, with the Yiddish language and literature. Many of the fresh arrivals, facing exclusion, poverty, and other challenges of immigrant life, longed for their homeland in eastern Europe, which they nostalgically remembered as familiar and filled with emotions. Welcoming famous Yiddish authors in Argentina was also a marker of an emerging Jewish-Argentine identity. The guests were welcomed in the name of Argentina, and the immigrant hosts saw themselves as representatives of their new country. Argentina was responsible for both the successes and the deficiencies of local Jewish life. These approaches were far from exclusive and without clear boundaries. Appreciation for the freedoms of Argentina could be linked with a Yiddishist agenda, and nostalgia might in fact have signified growing rootedness in the new country rather than an actual desire to return to Europe. Argentine Jewish identities were fluid, changing, and hardly ever fixed. Independently of these diverse identifications, a visit by a well-known Yiddish author was a highlight for the entire ethnic community. These encounters allowed the immigrants to symbolically reconnect with eastern Europe, to claim Argentina as an important locale within the Yiddishland, and to boast about their success and progress as Jewish Argentines.

Jewish literary travels to Argentina, travel writing based on these experiences, and its reception in Poland and Argentina formed a space that connected Polish Jews across the Atlantic. The travelogues of Hirschbein and Nomberg offer a chance to observe the trajectories of migrants in the new country and the emergence of a new diasporic community, while negotiating rootedness on both sides of the ocean.[65] As Hirschbein noted in his Argentine travelogue, the migrations paradoxically made the world seem smaller and more familiar. The Jewish presence in Latin America and elsewhere created a new sense of proximity between Jews scattered around the world:

> When we were young, in our imagination the world was much bigger. . . . The farthest travel was to go to visit an uncle or an aunt. . . . There every tree looked different, each stone seemed foreign. . . . Now there is no this pleasure that the shortest trip evoked in childhood. . . . Who knows

> maybe it is the fault of the Jewish people that the world has shrunk before my eyes? The Jewish people had dispersed around the wide world; wherever you go you meet your friends from the *kheyder*, the children of your shtetl. . . . You travel for weeks on the land and across the sea, you reach the shores of the remote country, and your people come to meet you and the weeks-long distance between you and them, shrinks suddenly. You start to think that the journey is not that long, that only the captain chose a wrong route, turning around in the same place all the time.[66]

For the Jews living in Poland, Argentina travel journals allowed them to envision their own image of this country, independent of their desire to immigrate to Latin America. Consequently, the Argentine travels and travel writing of Hirschbein and Nomberg bridged the Polish Jewish community in Argentina and Poland, marking its new transatlantic character. Both travelers seemed to be aware of the transformation of eastern European Jewry that was entering a new dispersed and diasporic period. Following the mass Jewish migrations, Poland became a sui generis archetypical Jewish homeland, and the new communities in the Americas modeled and positioned themselves in relation to it rather than the mythical Zion. By the early twentieth century, diaspora was not a purely religious concept but also a cultural and ethnonational one. Hirschbein and Nomberg not only studied new Jewish diasporization but also partook in its development. Their travels and travel writing were a clear manifestation of a diasporic change experienced by eastern European Jews. Although located in North and South America, a number of Polish Jews—especially those embedded in the progressive Yiddish culture prior to emigration—defined themselves by their relationship to the old European homeland in a Jewish ethnonational life of diaspora.[67] In time, the hyphenated Jewish-Argentine identities became dominant, but for about two decades, Jewish immigrant life in Argentina was influenced both by the local setting and the increasingly ideological, modernizing Yiddish culture, largely imported by the immigrants from Jewish Poland. Travel writers perceived this temporary stage (the experience of the immigrant generation) as a transitory transnational form of eastern European diasporism. Hirschbein and Nomberg and their travelogues let us take a glimpse into the emerging Jewish-Argentine space inhabited by the migrating Polish Jews.

The Polish Center and Its Latin American Colony: Argentina in *Literarishe Bleter*

When exploring the Polish-Jewish debates on Argentina, it is crucial to understand the dynamics of center-periphery relations between both countries. Despite devoting some interest to Argentine developments, from the perspective of Warsaw highbrow Yiddish journal *Literarishe Bleter*, Argentine Jewry never ceased to be peripheral. What is more, Argentine cultural leaders acknowledged these inequalities and lack of parallelism. In 1932, Lazaro Zhitnitsky, an Argentine Yiddishist and YIVO activist, wrote that Poland was a "metropolis" and Argentina its "colony."[68] In another article (for *Literarishe Bleter*), Zhitnitsky described Argentina as "a younger brother" of Jewish Poland: "In the European Jewish literature, it has already become a tradition to give very little attention to the young Argentine-Jewish kibbutz. Only rarely does the local press mention their work and life. Very little attention is being paid to Argentine Yiddish literature. Yet, this is a big mistake towards a younger brother, who struggles to achieve something that would also be useful for the older brothers."[69]

By describing Argentina as a "younger brother," Zhitnitsky stressed the immaturity of Argentine Jewry, though first and foremost he criticized the low attention that Europe gave to Argentine Yiddish authors. For Zhitnitsky, it was clear that in Argentina "grows a new, powerful Yiddish *yishev* [settlement] . . . that with time will have a lot of influence on the Jewish communities around the world."[70] He appreciated the proletarian background of many Argentine Jewish literati, their quality of "self-madeness." Zhitnitsky advised his Jewish Polish readers to carefully observe their creativity. As the journalist argued, Argentine authors promised to be citizens of the Yiddishland, who would immediately react to everything that happened in Jewish Europe. Within the broader Jewish diaspora, Zhitnitsky argued, the Polish and Argentine worlds would inevitably grow closer.

The geographic distance between Poland and Argentina was perceived as a key obstacle to an intensified cultural exchange, which was later interpreted as a source of cultural discrepancies. The remoteness of Argentina was not sensed only from an eastern European point of view. Jewish Argentines themselves underlined their distance, peripherality, and mother-child relationship with the eastern European center of the Yiddish world. Even after many years in Argentina, some authors perceived themselves, and Argentine Jewry at large, as distant (from the eastern European centers). The poet Jacobo Straijer, who arrived in Argentina in 1908, still sensed it in 1944 when he titled his poetry volume *Fun vaytn land* (From a distant country).[71] A few decades earlier, in the first anthology of Argentine Yiddish literature *Oyf di bregn fun plata* (On the shores of La Plata River), Yosef (José) Mendelson wrote: "Argentina is distant, distant from the great Jewish world, from the grand Jewish centers of Europe and North America. This is a distance that can be felt in a way that they imagine us, and in the way that we think about ourselves."[72]

The efforts at including Argentina in the topography of a Yiddish ethnocultural program of modernization happened also in eastern Europe. Throughout the interwar years, the presence of Argentina grew in Jewish Poland, particularly within spheres of local high culture. The highbrow Yiddishist *Literarishe Bleter* approached Argentina with a much detailed interest than the popular or yellow dailies. *Haynt* and *Der Moment* sporadically published articles that could neither be categorized as anti-immigration and female-trafficking-linked warnings nor as calls for emigration. There were barely a few longer articles that dealt with Argentine cultural life. In 1924, Hersh Dovid Nomberg evaluated *Zeglen* (Sails), one of the first literary journals edited by Jewish authors active in Buenos Aires.[73] In 1931, *Haynt* also published an article on Argentine Yiddish literature, mentioning the already relatively well-known authors in Poland—Guiser, Botoshansky, and Zhitnitsky—but also a number of lesser-known writers.[74] The almost complete absence of texts dealing with Jewish social and cultural life in Argentina was based on the fact that in the Polish context Argentine culture was neither immediately relevant for potential immigrants nor exciting on the "Jewish street." More important was the information about wages, immigration laws, and the usual rumors and sexual scandals.

The renowned Warsaw literary journal *Literarishe Bleter* took upon itself the task of presenting Argentine Yiddish literary creativity to eastern European readers and critics. *Literarishe Bleter* attempted to reduce the presumed distance between Jewish Poland and Jewish Argentina. It was the only space in Poland that presented Argentina in a more complex and sophisticated way. The weekly found a place for discussing Argentine-Jewish culture and Argentina's social problems and invited Argentine Jews to publish regular pieces. Attempting to reach not only Polish Jews but a broader public of the citizens of Yiddishland, *Literarishe Bleter* reported about Jewish life in Argentina no less than it did concerning other new diasporas. Its readership basis included around twenty thousand people around the world, including in Argentina.[75] The weekly's regular section "Naye bikher" (new books) informed readers about Argentine book novelties: *Ibergus* by Leib Malach (1926), *Groteskn un bilder fun yidishn aktiorn lebn* by Yankev Botoshansky (1926), *Tsu der geshikhte yidisher zhurnalistik in argentine* (1929) by Pinie Katz, and a new volume by a Poland-born Argentine poet Moisés David Guiser (1933). *Literarishe Bleter* also mentioned and reviewed books written originally in Spanish, though a Yiddish translation became available for the Yiddish-reading public. In addition, non-Jewish aspects of culture were sometimes featured.[76] The weekly played the role of a showcase, in which well-known persona of the Yiddishist scene presented young and promising authors. These articles introduced not only the emerging authors but by including writers from less-known centers, they also broadened the borders of the Yiddishland. When Melech Ravitch visited Argentina in 1938, he wrote a series of articles on local life to the Polish Jewish press. In *Literarishe Bleter*, he presented Berl Grinberg, who "thanks to his Argentine experiences brought new content to Yiddish fiction." Ravitch praised his "new motives, styles, landscapes, unusual people and original approach."[77] A few years earlier, Grinberg himself contributed to *Literarishe Bleter*.[78]

The editors of *Literarishe Bleter* considered Argentina a significant branch of the Ashkenazi diaspora and a promising site of global Yiddish culture. The well-traveled writers and journalists like Melech Ravitch, Nakhmen Mayzel, and Israel Joshua Singer, who edited the weekly, were perfectly aware of the "new diasporization" of eastern European Jewry. In the late 1920s, the Jewish community in the United States was larger than the Polish one by more than half a million and its influence on global Jewish culture, politics, and social life was tremendous.[79] The situation in Argentina was similar. At the turn of the 1920s and 1930s, for the Yiddishist elite in Poland Argentina was already normalized as a Jewish center. The country's Jewry successfully claimed recognition as a well-based and creative part of world Jewry. *Literarishe Bleter* gladly gave it this recognition. First of all, the weekly welcomed the fact that Yiddish culture thrived in Argentina, with regular daily newspapers, Yiddish schools, theaters, and other institutions. For instance, when the Buenos Aires Kaplianski Publishing House celebrated its tenth anniversary, *Literarishe Bleter* published a warm article in appreciation of Kaplianski's role in popularizing Yiddish literature in Argentina.[80] Moreover, a number of projects backed by the weekly, such as the TSYSHO schools or the YIVO Institute in Vilna, relied heavily on foreign aid, including from Argentina.[81] In that sense, writing about Argentina was a way of expressing gratitude for this support—a sign of appreciation from the "Jewish center" in eastern Europe.

In February 1933, *Literarishe Bleter* published an entirely Argentine issue.[82] Dr. H. Gold wrote about Yiddish literature, N. Kriczmer about Jewish colonization, Yankev Botoshansky about Yiddish theater, Yosef (José) Mendelson about the Jewish contribution to scientific and literary advancements in Argentina. In April of the same year, *Literarishe Bleter* offered its readers a panoramic and detailed overview of the Yiddish book scene in Argentina.[83] The Argentine issue was both a presentation of recent accomplishments of Argentine Jewry and a sign of welcome to the expansion of the Yiddishland's literature. *Literarishe Bleter*, although edited in Warsaw, had a clearly transnational character. Its columnists lived in numerous countries of the new diaspora, including Argentina. Both readers and editors belonged rather to the higher strata of the Yiddishland citizens and were probably aware of the dominant exoticizing narrative of Argentina to be found in Poland's daily press. *Literarishe Bleter* challenged this simplistic and reductive approach. Argentina, as represented in the weekly publication, was portrayed as one of the many branches of the Yiddish-speaking world, a place with a bustling cultural and social life, steadily becoming of greater importance in Yiddishland's microcosm.

When visiting Poland, Argentine Jewish ethnic leaders attempted to push their pro-Argentina agenda. They were aware that the hierarchies within the Yiddishland were far from flat, yet they attempted to reshape the way in which Jewish Argentina was discussed in Poland. In 1929, when the Argentine Yiddishist Pinie Katz was on his way back from the Soviet Union, he gave an interview about the Argentine Yiddish cultural scene to *Literarishe Bleter*. Katz described the scene as bustling, dropped references to dozens of names of authors and journalists, and presented Argentina as a prominent center of Jewish life, with a population with a steadily improving cultural level that was cognizant of international developments.[84] Another Argentine Yiddishist leader, Yankev Botoshansky, was straightforward in arguing in *Literarishe Bleter* that Argentine Yiddish journalism and literature needed recognition outside of Argentina.[85] Botoshansky, who traveled to Poland a few times, considered informing the European public about the situation in Argentina as part of his task as an Argentine Jew. He believed that the Jews of Poland should be familiar with the works of prominent Argentine Jews, including Pinie Wald, Pinie Katz, and Israel Helfman.[86] In 1935, Botoshansky represented Argentina at the YIVO congress in Vilna, and his visit marked the global scope of the Yiddishist worldview and Argentine-Jewish claims for visibility and influence.[87] In Vilna, he met with the students of the local Yiddish gymnasiums and held a lecture on Argentina for them.[88] During his stay in Poland, Botoshansky preferred to engage in discussions about Yiddish literature in general and did not want to limit his interviews to Argentine anecdotes. In his talk at the Association of Jewish Writers and Journalists at Tłomackie in Warsaw, he discussed the "diverse cultural territories" of Yiddish culture.[89] As a citizen of the Yiddishland, Botoshanky believed that he could and should be involved in Poland's Yiddish life.[90] Following his visit in Poland, he became a regular Argentine correspondent of *Literarishe Bleter*.

The cultural links between the Polish center and the Argentine colony of the Yiddishland were personified by the emissaries who traveled from Poland to Argentina. Their travels offered the Argentine community a sense of relevance and importance from the eastern European perspective. As the Argentine Jewish leaders successfully anticipated, the travel writers and emissaries reported about their trips in Poland's Jewish press. When Poaley Tsiyon–left activist and publisher Yaakov Zerubavel returned from his trip to Argentina in 1927 (he traveled to raise funds for the secular Yiddishist schools in Poland), *Literarishe Bleter* did not hesitate to ask him about Jewish life in Argentina.[91] He told about the success of his campaign at length, mentioning numerous localities he visited and the Argentine press titles that wrote about his campaign. He presented his Argentine impressions not only in the highbrow *Literarishe Bleter* but also during a lecture in the provincial town of Łuków.[92]

Zerubavel's comments about Zionists protesting against his school campaign assured the readers of *Literarishe Bleter* that political and social problems in Poland and Argentina were largely the same. Zionists and Jewish socialists struggled for control of the "Jewish street"; in both Poland and Argentina, problems of language, schooling, and acculturation stood at the center of debates on Jewish identity and ethnicity. Zerubavel noted that his visit had also invigorated local discussions concerning secular Yiddish schooling. "Our campaign became a center of Argentine Jewish life," the activist said. Underlining the warm welcome in Argentina, Zerubavel portrayed Jewish Argentina as very welcoming and responsibly and permanently connected with the Old Country.

Yiddish theater was an important field of exchange between the Jewish cultural worlds of Poland and Argentina covered in *Literarishe Bleter*. According to theater critic and journalist Nakhmen Mayzel, Yiddish theaters in Rio de Janeiro or Buenos Aires could not exist without commissioning artists from abroad.[93] In 1934, Zygmunt Turkow, a famous actor and director from Poland, went to Argentina with a fifteen-piece theater tour.[94] Turkow, who was then associated with modernist Varshever Yidisher Kunst Teater (VYKT), was warmly received in Buenos Aires. Turkow's plays "proved that high theater could exist in Buenos Aires, a theater that refers to something, that demands something."[95] Even when Warsaw Yiddish and Hebrew actor Rudolf Zasławski settled down in Argentina, *Literarishe Bleter* continued to cover his shows abroad.[96] He spent most of his life performing in Poland's Yiddish theaters (in Warsaw, Vilna, and Łódź), gained fame as a star of Kaminska Theater, immigrated to Argentina probably during World War I, but continued his guest tours in North America, Brazil, and Poland.[97] His appearance in 1925 and 1926 in Buenos Aires, starring in *Tevye der milkhiker* (Tevye the dairyman), brought him fame. He subsequently became an important figure in the struggle against the female traffickers, which then exercised a big influence on Argentine theater life. In writing about Zasławski's success, or about the tour of Turkow, *Literarishe Bleter* acknowledged the new diasporic era of Yiddish theater that was unfolding in Argentina.[98] The actors and theater ceased to be site specific and moved about the Yiddishland relatively freely. *Literarishe Bleter*, the key tribune of Yiddish cultural transnationalism, believed in its responsibility about globalizing Yiddish culture.

The contributions by Argentine authors to *Literarishe Bleter* brought global exposure to the issues faced by Jews in Argentina. They presented Argentine Jewry as very involved in global Jewish debates and as universal in their approach to the questions that Jewish people faced. For instance, H. Gold wrote about Argentine debates concerning Yiddish orthography.[99] The issue was a source of heated debates among the Yiddishists, as some argued for the need to "naturalize" Yiddish and redefine the orthography of Hebraisms. Others opposed this move. Gold wrote that the issue resulted in a heated debate in Buenos Aires, and one of the leading dailies, *Di Presse*, simplified the orthography. Moreover, a number of Argentine Yiddish schools adopted the "naturalized" spelling of

Hebrew words. Consequently, as Gold argued, the children were supposed to learn Yiddish quicker and with greater pleasure. Gold, referring to his Polish readers, summarized his view: "Everyone can learn from the Argentine case that naturalization is needed."[100] A year later, Warsaw's *Literarishe Bleter* elevated the challenges ahead of Argentine Jewish schooling to a transnational scale. Yosef Mendelson criticized the JCA, which had closed more than thirty Jewish afternoon schools in the colonies. Mendelson complained angrily that "the world Jewish community needs to know what is going on in Argentina." By writing to the *Literarishe Bleter*, Mendelson referred to the center-periphery relations, believing that criticism from Poland might influence the situation in Argentina.[101]

The transnational cultural involvement of Argentine Jews in global Jewish problems was also visible during the 1936 PEN Club Congress that took place in Buenos Aires.[102] Both the Argentine-Jewish press and *Literarishe Bleter* broadly discussed the talk given by H. Leivick in Buenos Aires. The Warsaw weekly commissioned their regular Argentine correspondent Yankev Botoshansky for a panoramic, three-page article. The PEN Club meeting was considered a major opportunity for raising not only a literary but broader social and cultural demands and complaints. Leivick arrived there as a representative of the homeless but vital Yiddish literature. Botoshansky assured Polish readers that Leivick was warmly and festively welcomed in Latin America. Whereas other writers were officially greeted by the embassy delegations, Leivick was cherished by hundreds of Jews who "expressed their love for Yiddish culture." The arrival of the author was celebrated with a performance of his newest play *Der poet iz blind gevorn*, directed by Ben Ami and Jacob Mestel. Public meetings with Leivick were attended by thousands of fans.[103] Leivick's speech to the PEN Club was printed in *Literarishe Bleter* in its entirety with Botoshansky reporting in detail about the ovations that the writer received from the public. Leivick's talk fit the general atmosphere of the congress that positioned itself against fascism, war, and discrimination. Further, Spanish dailies printed the translation of Leivick's talk, which, in the words of the *Haynt* reporter, "made a great impression."[104]

The international meeting in Buenos Aires raised the importance of Argentina both in the Jewish and non-Jewish cultural arena. As Yosef Horn recalled, "Jewish Buenos Aires was burning in these months."[105] The fact that Argentina was chosen to host the prestigious meeting, as well as the powerful speech by the representative of the Yiddishland, informed Polish Jewish readers about the growing importance of Argentina in the global politics of culture.[106] Leivick's speech was a representation of the broad Jewish world of Yiddish-speaking Jews. Leivick's invitation (next to Shaul Tchernichovsky, who spoke for Hebrew literature) was a symbolic recognition of the transnational community of the Yiddishland. From the Jewish perspective, the literary meeting turned into a space that marked Argentina as a focal point of discussions about the future of Yiddish civilization. Botoshansky's reports in *Literarishe Bleter* lifted provincial Argentina to a key place for discussing general and Yiddish culture. The talk by the Yiddish writer about the role of literature adamantly defended the languages of a "repressed minority." Leivick proclaimed the diasporism of Yiddish literature and described the Yiddish language as a symbol of universalism. He criticized the lack of the world's interest in Jewish culture and its exoticizing gaze on Yiddish literature: "The European novelists who look deep inside the human soul, searching there for a secret, the last secret of life, what do they see when they come closer to us [Jews]? They see exotics in us. Nothing more." Leivick stood up against the objectification of literature in the service of violence, nationalism and discrimination. He referred specifically to Polish writers, who "kept silent concerning anti-Jewish incidents." For Leivick, all of European literature was "sick and dying," as it did not answer the true problems of humanity: injustice, the suffering of the innocent, and exploitation.[107]

Conclusion

After 1918, the immigration of Polish Jews to Argentina contributed to the globalization and expansion of Yiddish cultural nationalism and to a symbolic inclusion of Argentina into the imagined Yiddishland. Polish-Jewish immigration brought to Argentina a generation of thinkers grappling with the cultural and national implications of Yiddishness. The arrival of new immigrants, among them partisan activists, writers, and journalists, invigorated Jewish Argentine discussions on ethnicity, belonging, and transnational solidarity. These concepts of a modern Yiddish culture developed in eastern Europe at the beginning of the twentieth century, gained a stronger resonance during the post–World War I Yiddish cultural revival, and were brought by immigrants to Argentina. Both new immigrants and more veteran ethnic Argentine-Jewish leaders felt prompted to respond to the new intellectual ferment, be it in the press, literature, or public meetings. Yiddish was the lingua franca of most Ashkenazi Jews around the world and thus a tool that allowed the circulation of cultural contents and ideas, which afterward began to also sprout in Argentina. In Poland, this circulation was performed among others by *Literarishe Bleter*, which wished to include Argentina in the global Yiddish cultural channels.

Simultaneously, eastern European writers Nomberg and Hirschbein not only described Jewish Argentina in their travelogues but they appeared as cultural activists who perceived Argentina as a field for cultural work, especially concerning the Yiddish language and Yiddish schooling. They fit well the Saidian type of intellectual, who actively shapes reality and popular worldview by being personally involved in a certain cause.[108] Their interest in the problems of Jewish immigrants elevated them to the level of celebrities and respected friends of Argentine

Jewry. The special status they achieved was clearly connected with the identitarian and ideological proximity between the political views of many Polish-Jewish immigrants to Argentina and those of the travelers. Their social progressivism and "love for Yiddish" found a liking among many newcomers from Poland. Their travels and travel writing bridged Poland and Argentina, touching upon the issues relevant both in Poland and in Argentina: Jewish education, the relationship to the state, the future of the younger generation, and, most importantly, migration and its repercussions. For some Argentine Jews, the travelers embodied the glorious memory of Jewish eastern Europe and a high Yiddish culture.

Some Argentine Jews, who formed their identities around what they imagined as eastern European Jewish heritage, perceived the visits of Nomberg and Hirschbein as a unique chance of reconnecting with their native land and manifesting their strong attachment to the Old Country. Although in some cases this identification was probably rooted in usual nostalgia, in fact it also marked the emergence of Jewish-Argentine identities. Many saw the visits of these travel writers as a good opportunity to emphasize the vitality of the Argentine Jewish community and a chance to inform European and American Jews that the Argentine diaspora was "normal": that local Jews worked hard for their bread and that Jewish female trafficking and prostitution were already becoming marginal. Boasting in front of foreign visitors about the vitality of progressive Yiddish life in Argentina, immigrant Jews simultaneously claimed their belonging to the imagined polity of Yiddishland and to Argentina, inviting Yiddish culture to flourish in diaspora. Yet, the travel writers were limited by the expectation of entertaining travel reports by their eastern European audience. As the following chapter illustrates, this travel literature ended up exacerbating the exoticization of Argentina within the Polish-Jewish imaginary.

4

Meeting the Gaucho and Searching for Indians

The Trajectories of Exoticization

Sowing the Seeds of Jewish Argentina

While the travels and travelogues of Hirschbein and Nomberg situated Argentina into the global Yiddish culture network, they also perpetuated an exotic and wild, or untamed image of Argentina among their eastern European audience. Nomberg's and Hirschbein's travel books both exoticized and objectified the people of Argentina. As Arjun Appadurai noted, exoticization is a process that constantly underlines the difference between "us" and "them"; this difference becomes the only criteria for comparison.[1] Despite its growing European population, Argentina was commonly portrayed by Nomberg and Hirschbein as strangely different from eastern Europe, as dangerous and unstable. Although the travelers encountered a sense of eastern European Jewish continuity in Argentina, much of their attention was devoted to Argentina's "un-Jewishness" and hazards that awaited the Jews venturing there. Despite being well traveled, both authors were deeply rooted in eastern European realities. As such, these travel writers were constrained by the expectations of their public readership. Although some readers in Poland might have used their texts as an emigration guidebook, others were drawn to them for their sheer entertainment value. Thus, both authors faced a need to strike a balance between providing readers with accurate accounts and offering them an entertaining literary text.

The establishment of a new Jewish center in Argentina raised the interest of Jewish Polish public intellectuals, writers, and journalists who sought to discover Argentina for the curious reading public in Europe. Consequently, the first Jewish immigrants who arrived in Argentina searching for a better life were soon followed by Jewish travelers and travel writers. Their visits and their travelogues written in Yiddish had a profound impact on Jewish life in both eastern Europe and Argentina. First, travel narratives were a tool for imagining Argentina in Jewish Poland. In eastern Europe during the first decades of the twentieth century, Argentina emerged as a desired immigration destination, but migrant networks were still developing and the press transmitted mixed messages about opportunities in Argentina. At the same time, the end of the Great War brought ideological instability to the status of Jews in Europe, in Poland specifically. Both poverty and Polish nationalism, from which Jews were excluded, made them question their very place in the Polish republic and motivated many to emigrate. Responding to a scarcity of in-depth news and information, the Argentine travel accounts of Hirschbein (*Fun vayte lender. Argentine, brazil yuni, november 1914*, 1916) and Nomberg ("Di argentinishe rayze" in *Dos bukh felyetonen*, 1924) appeared as much-needed and well-researched books, sought after by those considering emigration and those for whom it was not a viable option.[2] Their works fueled discussions on Argentina and helped Polish Jews to formulate their own conceptions of the country across the Atlantic.

Nomberg and Hirschbein were personally influenced by the earliest exoticizing depictions of immigration and colonization. For instance, the previously mentioned guidebook to Argentina, written in 1893 by Yaakov Yedvabnik, provided a comprehensive account of colonization, as well as the dynamics between the Jewish colonists and Argentina's indigenous population. Yedvabnik's description of both groups makes clear his partisan commitment to European colonists. He described the local inhabitants as wild and their expulsion from Rio Negro as a logical and necessary step toward a new civilized population.[3] Yedvabnik seemed to share a perspective common among the Argentine elite of that era, during which European immigration was seen as a positive influence capable of civilizing a "barbaric" indigenous population. He pictured the Indians as a barrier to the development of modern Argentina. Indigenous resistance to these European newcomers made the colonization of the interior dangerous and relatively weak.

Several decades later, Nomberg began to grapple with the "indigenous question." He clearly stated that by coming to Argentina he was looking for encounters with the "red Indians."[4] This was probably influenced by the availability of information in Europe regarding the native populations of the United States. Nomberg portrayed as exotic the places in Argentina that were discernibly non-Jewish and non-European and thus "in need" of European exploration. Following the zeitgeist of the era, the writer believed that every corner of the planet should be investigated, described, and thus theorized about from a white, Western perspective. Although he probably did not meet any representatives of the indigenous populations, his travelogue contains numerous descriptions of these people (based probably on Yiddish penny press news and rumors he heard from Argentine Jews). He extensively used the exoticizing stories he heard about Patagonian Indians and the *guarani* tribes in his texts.[5] In a chapter titled "Mayses fun patagonye" (Patagonia stories), he presented Argentina's natives as a quasi-mythical people populating the remote and inaccessible areas of the country. The Andean mountains were allegedly inhabited by a cruel and exceptionally tall Indian tribe, whereas the northern areas, on the border with Paraguay, by shorter people, who Europeans exploited in sugar mills and silver mines.[6] He described both groups as unusual and as fearful of the white man.

The way that Nomberg described both tribes was radically different from the way he referred to the Jews. Nomberg approached the indigenous from a superior position. The indigenous communities appeared only as a homogenous population, without unique and individual subjectivities. Although Nomberg was sympathetic and moved by indigenous suffering during colonial rule, they remained for him only an interesting but inferior group that could be examined as an anthropological subject. Describing the indigenous population, he clearly did not attempt to make his story based on credible facts or to present it as ethnographic. He did not verify the narratives he heard about the indigenous. Instead, he decided to transmit the legends and tales.

Further, describing the population of the interior, the so-called criollos, Nomberg retold the opinions he heard from Jewish colonists. In Argentina, the criollo identity was constructed mainly in opposition to multinational European and urban Buenos Aires populations (*porteños*) rather than an adopted racialized character of mixed white/indigenous ancestry as in other parts of Latin America. Criollos lived in the countryside of the interior provinces, often had Spanish ancestry, cultivated traditional and rural Spanish heritage, and were seen as hardly European. Nomberg depicted them as figures who relied on primordial skills, lived close to nature, and were familiar with its laws and moods. His criollos recognized the beginning of the rain season by observing snakes and shared this knowledge with the Jewish colonists. For Nomberg, they constituted an interesting and attractive group of people. They signified the primordial Argentineness but also the ultimate exotic Other. They belonged to the "native" population of Argentina, inhabited the virgin pampas and mountains, and came to signify for Nomberg the "real Argentina." Descending from the European colonizers, the criollos were certainly different from the indigenous people. Their relative whiteness and European descent placed them closer to the immigrants. Nevertheless, the borders between the Jews and the criollos, who often lived side by side in the Argentine interior, were clearly defined. Nomberg mentioned that in Buenos Aires he was warned of them. The porteños he met described the criollos as goodhearted and "sweet as sugar" but aggressive and dangerous when insulted.[7] In attempting to reflect the popular understanding of the Argentine Other, Nomberg used phrases like "people say" and "some believe." These less personal words significantly weakened his statements that became vague and generalized. Yet by reproducing these stereotypes, he again applied an exoticizing narrative, making his story entertaining for the readers in eastern Europe.

Quite often, the urban Jewish immigrants, those who were on their way to becoming porteños, expressed a sense of superiority over the criollos. Discrimination against the criollo may mark their own sense of exclusion and lack of security in the Argentine ethnic mashup. It might have been related to a sense of European superiority claimed by some of the Jews. Within this framework, immigrant Jews represented the enlightened Europe that challenged the allegedly backward criollo habits. This system of discrimination referred not only to criollos of Spanish ancestry but also to indigenous populations. These hierarchies were visible in criollo-porteño encounters provided by the developing tourism. In the 1930s, middle-class children of European immigrants (including Jews) were increasingly involved with tourism within the country's interior, organizing trips to the Andean villages, Patagonia, and other places inhabited by indigenous populations. This came in the light of the discourse that emphasized the need on the part of porteños to travel to the interior (*internarse*) to establish a bond with the national territory. The discourse of "patriotic travel" saw the rural Argentines as both purveyors of the ancient spirit of the Argentine nation and as exotic others. The tourist movement revealed the hierarchies within Argentine society by "darkening" subaltern classes and strengthened the notion of a homogenously white Argentina. White porteño tourists of European ancestry constructed visualizations of criollos and the indigenous as backward, traditional enclaves among a modern white nation.[8] These attitudes toward presumed criollo inferiority were perfectly visible in the interviews conducted with Polish Jewish immigrants by Rosana Gruber in the 1980s. One of her interviewees said: "The Jews have more culture because they come from Europe and bring with them all their knowledge, their past. A criollo, on the contrary, what does he know? He is born and dies in a village. The Jews live in the cities, and in the cities, culture is created. And the criollo lives in a village, and even when he comes to the city, he won't learn [the culture] as the young children do." Another added: "The immigrants were important here, they taught [the locals] how to work. The criollo liked the grilled meats, mate. . . . [The Jews] taught him how to work."[9]

The local Jews helped Nomberg to familiarize himself with the Argentine imaginary of the Other. Jewish immigrants informed the travel writer about local conflicts and politics. They were the intermediaries and cultural translators, who linked the eastern European visitor with the popular opinions circulating in Argentina. The years spent in Latin America influenced their perception of local conflicts and dynamics. As foreigners and outsiders, the eastern European immigrants sought to understand the Argentine hierarchies and were quick to realize that indigenous peoples (and to a lesser extent also criollos) were from a Buenos Aires perspective at the bottom of the social ladder. Aspiring to join the Argentine mainstream, many Jews adopted the local attitudes toward nonwhites. As May E. Bletz put it, "European immigrants discovered all too soon they could benefit from local racial policies and often only acquired an 'ethnic consciousness' and a 'white' skin color after coming to their host country."[10] Although Hirschbein and Nomberg were bothered by negative opinions about the eastern European Jews circulating in Argentina, they did not have a major problem with Eurocentric stereotyping and stigmatizing of the indigenous or the criollos.

Both travelers had a desire to experience the travel of an average immigrant. Their descriptions of ship travel were an attempt to reenact a typical immigrant journey. It included departing on a vessel from a European port, spontaneous interactions with various ethnic groups, traveling together and making contact with often unpleasant or disrespectful ship staff. Nevertheless, the travel conditions experienced by Hirschbein and Nomberg differed significantly from the journeys of third-class passengers, who spent around three weeks in dark and poorly ventilated *tsvishendek*, or steerage. However, in order to give at least a partially reliable account of the situation of poorer migrating Jews, both writers descended from their comfortable cabins to the overcrowded third-class area. The passengers who traveled in the tsvishendek could hardly recognize Hirschbein as a fellow Jew. Yet, in the role of ethnographer, Hirschbein approached other Jewish families, talked with them in Yiddish, and documented their fears and hopes. He conversed with the passengers and tried to understand what they knew about Argentina and how they reflected on their emigration from eastern Europe.[11] Nomberg also broke the rules of the ship by conversing with a third-class Jewish worker, despite the dirty looks shot at him from the staff, which kept the social classes separated on the ship.[12]

Both authors used literary techniques to increase the "authenticity" and vividness of the depictions that they transmitted. In order to raise the level of authenticity of their narratives, Hirschbein and Nomberg included the voices of Jewish migrants. As autoethnographers, the travelers conducted interviews that, paraphrased later, served as a canvas for their travel texts. In discussing the early years of the colony Moisés Ville, Hirschbein quoted one of the first settlers at length. On another occasion, he incorporated the personal story of an immigrant disenchanted with his life in Argentina. Nomberg broadly retold the narrative of one of the madams he met on the ship.[13] Hirschbein also wrote that he was aware that his Argentine hosts wanted to show him the better side of their lives. Still, he decided to leave the bubble prepared for him by the welcome committees. He wrote: "I know how poorly you live in Argentina. I know how much you get for your jobs. I know how all your hard work allows you to rent the smallest flats with no windows. You did not take me to your houses. But I looked into your houses when you did not notice. Together with the rest of the Argentines, you drink from a cup of poverty and need."[14]

Both Jewish travelers tasted local foods and aspired to follow some of the regional traditions. Participation in unusual practices and ceremonies emphasized their direct contact with foreign peoples and their immersion in the local context. In an attempt to make his story more "authentic" and entertaining, Nomberg joined the colonists for a *mate* drinking ceremony; mate is the national drink of Argentina. He not only enjoyed it but even claimed that it "made him feel healthier."[15] Here, Nomberg showed his readiness to explore the unfamiliar customs and support the social changes that immigrant Jews were undergoing. They began to drink mate like the locals, and this cultural practice symbolized their becoming Jewish Argentines.

The travelers straddled a thin line between an "insider" and "outsider" perspective. Nomberg often presented himself as part of the local Jewry. He frequently used the pronoun "we" in order to describe the situation of the Jewish colonists in Montefiore (in the province of Santa Fe). For example, a Spanish teacher working in this colony became "our teacher" in his narrative.[16] It appears that the few weeks he spent among the settlers in Montefiore sensitized him to their opinions, complaints, and demands. Nomberg also took sides in local Argentine conflicts. He supported the Jewish actors in their dispute with the theater managers and set up an organization tasked with protecting the rights of the colonists.[17] Although his position as guest was clear to both him and his hosts, Nomberg decided to pose as a semilocal Argentine in the story told to the readers in eastern Europe. Further, alluding to the situation of Jewish farmers, Hirschbein presented himself as an expert on the subject, as a person who, thanks to his eastern European background, understood the psychology of Jewish immigrants and the problems of ordinary people. His interest and expertise in Jewish colonization supposedly eliminated the class and cultural distinctions between the man of letters and the agricultural laborer.[18] The writer had firm views on Jewish agricultural settlements and their demographic and economic problems. Argentine Jewish problems were understood as "ours," pertaining to the Yiddishland and by extension to Hirschbein.

The Jewish colonies in Argentina gave the visiting authors a sense of ethnic pride. Unsurprisingly, their depictions of Jewish farming settlements emphasized the exceptional nature of the project. The way that the beginning of Jewish colonization was depicted in *Fun vayte lender* and "Argentinishe rayze" was similar to the imaginaries of the Zionist project of building a new, strapping Jewish class of agricultural workers. Immigration to Argentina was born from the same narrative of altering the Jewish professional structure and making Jews "productive." Nomberg and Hirschbein portrayed the future colonists as brave people, who arrived to a virgin land and subdued local nature, turning it into a fruitful space serving man and his needs. Describing the establishment of the colony of Moisés Ville, Hirschbein presented Pinchas Glazberg, Yosef Ludmer, and Leyzer Koyfman (originating from Podolia, then the Russian Empire) as the founding fathers of the Argentine yishev. Despite being ordinary village Jews, they not only managed to make their way to Argentina but also personally coorganized the emigration of the first groups of settlers.[19] Hirschbein was thrilled to see that despite the problems in gaining the mere support of the JCA and the lack of agricultural experience, his fellow eastern European Jews were able to create and maintain a thriving community that he described as a miracle and the best thing ever built by the "Jewish hand" in Argentina.[20]

The travelers stressed the exceptionally hard conditions that awaited the Jewish immigrants, the conflicts and misunderstandings with the presumably unprofessional staff of the JCA, or a lack of agricultural experience among the new colonists. Describing the development of Moisés Ville, Hirschbein mentioned numerous hardships and obstacles that the colonists had to endure for the years: the destruction of crops by locusts and floods and JCA's attempts to close down the colony and resettle its residents.[21] Against all odds, the Jewish colonists continued their struggle with Argentine nature and poverty.[22] Hirschbein pictured the early years of Moisés Ville as a heroic battle for dignity and independence. In his view, the suffering and effort only strengthened the colonists and helped them to form a close and intimate bond with the land they worked. He pointed out that the hardships the colonists went through only emphasized their subsequent success. Despite numerous problems and initial failures, both Nomberg and Hirschbein seemed to regard the Jewish colonies as an excellent project that could at least partially solve the problems of eastern European Jewry. They clearly expressed their support for this initiative. Moisés Ville was for both Nomberg and Hirschbein the best sign of successful Jewish colonization. Nomberg described it as the "crown" of the Jewish colonies and portrayed it as an idyllic land of green fields and strong, happy people working and resting under the beautiful blue sky.[23]

Initially, nature was stronger than humans. The newcomers got lost in the pampa, the farm animals ran away, and pouring rains made work impossible. The underprepared settlers were losing the "battle" against Argentine nature: they had no shelter, and their children were dying of hunger. Despite all the hardships and obstacles, the settlers continued to struggle with the wild nature of the Argentine interior. They started to build houses, plant first crops, and burn out the overgrown grass. The civilization personified by the Jewish colonists began step by step to win over the mighty and perilous Argentine nature. Hirschbein was proud of the settlers' accomplishments. He appreciated their devotion and strong belief that they could create a better future in Argentina. The author perceived their sacrifices as a warranty that the Jewish Argentine diaspora would become strong and stable. He wrote that their suffering helped to create "a bond between the weak Jews and young, wild Argentine nature."[24] Thus, struggling with Argentine nature, the Jewish colonists passed an entry exam to Argentine society and laid the foundations for a future Jewish Argentine life.

The Argentine pampa was rumored to have been particularly unwelcoming. Nomberg pictured it as a dangerous and deserted space. The pampa was portrayed as an infertile land covered with a thin layer of soil, making it virtually unsuitable for farming. The trees of the pampa were short and sick. The land always thirsted for rain, was full of snakes, and was regularly flooded by tropical rainfalls. The climate portrayed by Nomberg was far from mild: it was aggressive, there were no rains, except heavy storms with thunder and lighting. It was not charming, it did not enchant the traveler, who could even become quite bored with the monotonous view from the train window.[25] The strong pampa wind, known as the *pampero*, was angry and "no one should try to fight with it."[26] In addition, the Latin American jungle, which Nomberg saw along the Brazilian coast, looked like a living creature to the traveler, moving and shining with different colors, almost "like a peacock."[27]

Traveling through the pampa in 1922, Nomberg portrayed a country hit by an economic crisis. He described neglected cows pasturing on the pampa without any interest of their owners. As the locals told him, "in current times a cow is not worth anything." Europe was no longer interested in importing Argentine meat. Neglected animals died in the fields, while carnivorous birds feasted on their bodies.[28] Nomberg noticed numerous shining white skeletons of fallen cows. In this section, he portrayed the pampa and thus Argentina as a land of death and misery. Underlining the difficult situation of Argentine farmers, he seemed to convey a message that although Argentina might have potential for farming, the current situation was not inviting at all. At the same time, he was convinced that while Argentine might be wild and perilous, it still could develop into a safe harbor for eastern European Jews. As the dry sands of the pampa through the hard work of Jewish settlers might turn into a fertile land, also Argentina might become a firm new branch of the Jewish diaspora.

For Hirschbein, struggling with an unwelcoming climate was part of the initiation into the life of Argentina. To emphasize this narrative, the author told the story of one of the first Jews to settle in the sparsely populated interior.[29] The settler described a number of obstacles faced by the colonists since their arrival in Argentina: administrative problems with the authorities, a lack of knowledge about the local conditions of life, and poverty. But it was wild and mighty nature that was his toughest enemy. Only by subduing nature would Jewish newcomers be able to take advantage of the rich Argentine soil. The wild grass had to be cut with an axe to make passage for the colonists; wild bovines had to be domesticated. In the eyes of the writer, the first settlers were like the early modern conquistadores, who came to the wilderness of Latin America and struggled with the fearsome powers of nature. The depopulated Argentine interior became a space of exploration that justified the civilizing mission of the Jewish settlers.

The heroic struggle of the Jewish colonists endowed them with a symbolic right to claim a sense of belonging to Argentina. The clash of Jewish newcomers with the unwelcoming nature proved their determination and heroism. Crossing the Atlantic, they did not arrive to a *goldene medine* (golden land), where

Figure 14. Jewish colonists in the province of Entrie Rios, 1930s, reproduced in *50 Años de colonización judía en la Argentina* (Buenos Aires, 1939)

life was pleasant and easy, but rather to a demanding environment characterized by a struggle for survival against numerous obstacles. The clash with Argentine nature appeared here as a rite of passage and a right of entry for belonging in the new country. The travelers depicted the Argentine climate as capricious, with unusually strong winds and too heavy rains. The picture of the country that emerges from their travel texts is an unbearable one. Nevertheless, Jews continued to settle there and managed to establish the foundations of Jewish life (fig. 14).

A Laboratory of Diversity: Jews and Other Argentines

Hirschbein and Nomberg devoted a lot of space to the ethnic heterogeneity of Argentina. Although their native Poland was filled with national minorities, the Spanish, Italian, and criollo population was something new and exotic for them. In the travelers' narratives, not only were the indigenous described as exotic others but so were southern Europeans, Moroccan Jews, or western European Jewish leaders of the JCA. The linguistic and cultural differences between eastern European Jews and members of ethnic groups unknown in Poland were used as the fabric of an exoticizing narrative. The travel writers also reproduced the real or imagined tensions between Jewish immigrants and other ethnic groups. They often repeated the opinions and stories they heard from the Argentine Jews hosting them. The brief period of their stay and the difficulties in communicating in Romance languages did not allow them to interact with the local Spanish or Italian-speaking population. For Hirschbein, this was a major problem. He described himself as "a man without a tongue," who could not chat with anyone.

On the main streets of the Argentine capital, he felt foreign and detached from the familiar surroundings.[30]

Describing the non-Jewish aspects of Argentina, Hirschbein and Nomberg familiarized readers with the local ethnic structure, pointing out that the ethnic groups surrounding the Jewish immigrants in Argentina were different from the local eastern European *goyim*. Nomberg was amazed at the ethnic diversity of Rio de Janeiro, where he stopped before arriving in Buenos Aires.[31] Hirschbein made several mentions of encounters with Italians. He did not interact with them but solely described their appearance and behavior. Arriving in the colony of Lucienville, not knowing the topography of the locality, he decided to stop at a hotel named Italia. The Jewish writer and Italian hotel manager did not even have a way to conduct small talk. Curiously, but not entirely surprisingly, the Jewish presence in the province of Entre Rios seemed to have an influence on the younger generation of non-Jewish immigrants. Hirschbein's communication with the hotel owner was made possible by a teenage Italian immigrant who, through intensive contact with the local Jews, had learned basic Yiddish.[32] This linguistic exchange was also confirmed by Maximo Yagupsky, who grew up in a Jewish colony in Entre Rios. A number of local criollo women learned to speak Bessarabian Yiddish from neighboring colonists.[33] Lea Literat-Golombek remembered that criollos imitated Jewish prayers, tasted Jewish foods, and even said blessings in Hebrew before drinking wine. For Literat-Golombek the mutual cultural exchange was smooth and never forced.[34]

The travelers portrayed the Jewish colonies as arenas of interaction between the Jewish and criollo populations and thus both Jewish and Argentine spaces. Criollos taught Jewish immigrants how to speak Spanish and how to survive in the pampa. The Jewish presence in the colonies also influenced the native population. The criollo Spanish teacher whom Nomberg met in Colonia Montefiore was initially full of prejudice against the Jews but came to realize that in fact the Jews "stood on a higher social level" than his countrymen from the interior. Only among the immigrant Jews could he find partners for intellectual socialist discussions. These were the Jews who introduced him to anarchist theories. While visiting the Moisés Ville, Nomberg was surprised to see a gentile traveling salesman and a Jewish colonist, who answered him coldly and impolitely. In Argentina, the typical eastern Europe role of Jewish salesman and Christian farmer was turned around.[35] The Jewish colony became here not only a space of Argentinization for the immigrants but an arena that allowed mutual exchange and transformation.

Hirschbein and Nomberg recycled common stereotypes and painted Argentines and Spaniards as exotic. Analyzing the influence of Spanish immigrants on Argentine society, Hirschbein noted that Spaniards had a hot and impulsive character that was "even strengthened by mixing with the indigenous blood." He noted that most of the Spaniards were Catholic and had a "Latin" temperament accompanied, in his view, by "shades of the Middle Ages."[36] For Hirschbein, a Spaniard might have been as foreign as the indigenous people. Temperamental and outspoken, in his perception they differed significantly from the Poles, Germans, and Russians he knew from Vilna or Warsaw. Nomberg made similar observations after seeing Spanish beggars, whom he regarded as talking in an angry tone and having evil eyes. The dancing of Spanish villagers was for him wild yet full of true happiness.[37]

Both travelers marked a clear border for Argentinization: the process should not lead to abandoning Yiddishness, which they understood in a linguistic and ethnocultural context. Instead of condemning the adaptation to local conditions and the transfer of local customs, they saw it as rather natural. For instance, drinking mate was a positive sign of Argentinization that Polish and Russian Jews underwent in Argentina. In addition, both Hirschbein and Nomberg argued that knowledge of Spanish was essential in a Spanish-speaking country. Nevertheless, they believed that Yiddish should remain the main language of communication of Argentine Jews. This attitude toward language was especially apparent during Hirschbein's visit to a JCA-administered Jewish school in Moisés Ville. The traveler was disappointed by the low level of Jewish curriculum in the local school. Hirschbein noticed that a poorly prepared teacher was not able to attract the children's attention or interest them in Jewish subjects, leaving him deeply dissatisfied with the fact that the professor was unable to transmit to the children "a sense of Jewish pride and belonging to a broader Jewish world." The traveler confronted the Jewish teacher, as well as the Moroccan-Jewish school director.[38] According to Hirschbein, the principal looked upon eastern European Jewry and described the students of Russian origin in the following manner: "The Jews of Russia are indeed wild and uneducated. There is no chance [of integration] for the fathers, but the children must be rescued. True, they need to know that they come from Abraham, that their forefathers were enslaved in Egypt, but now they must see the light."[39]

Hirschbein saw the Moroccan Jewish director as an enemy of Yiddish schooling and an obedient servant of the Argentine government that promoted the Argentinization of immigrant children through national Spanish-language education.[40] Although Hirschbein understood the need to speak the local language, he was equally sure about the need for competent and enriching Yiddish schooling. He wanted to see the future generations of Argentine Jews as a part of the Yiddish-speaking world, aware of their ethnonational yidishkayt. The supplementary Jewish schooling offered in Moisés Ville was for him counterproductive. During his next visit to Argentina in 1925, Hirschbein advocated for a modern Yiddishist schooling, based on the model of TSYSHO schools in Poland. Then, in a much less proacculturation approach, Hirschbein saw the Argentine atmosphere as "sick and foreign," hence dangerous for the existence of Yiddish culture.[41]

In discussing the socioeconomic situation in Buenos Aires, Nomberg was relatively pessimistic. Due to the time of his visit in 1922, the travel writer did not have a chance to experience the future industrial boom that redefined the entire district of Buenos Aires. Nomberg devoted a lot of attention to the poverty of immigrant workers and their precarious living conditions. He criticized Argentines for not being able to save and invest their money, presumably spending significant sums on lotteries or horse races. The traveler criticized the Jews for their increasing fondness for gambling. His accusations were directed at the emerging Jewish-Argentine identity. By embracing horse races, or *la lotería*, immigrant Jews claimed their belonging to the sociocultural world of Argentina.[42] At the same time, it was hard for many immigrants to save any money when one lived from hand to mouth. Eight years earlier, when Hirschbein walked the streets of the Once area in Buenos Aires, he noticed lots of Jewish poverty. Children were dressed poorly, and on their faces, he saw "all the despair that puzzled their parents."[43] The immigrant poverty of Buenos Aires in the early 1920s was confirmed years later in an interview with Lazaro Pinchuk. Pinchuk recalled that when he arrived in Argentina in 1923, he could barely earn a living. He was unable to send any money to his family back in Włodzimierz Wołyński (Volodymir-Volynskyi) in Poland. Working as a *cuentenik* (a peddler), he had enough money for a *puchero* (a stew) but needed to share a room with four other single men.[44] Pinchuk described his early years in Argentina as sad and full of suffering.

Nomberg noticed the porteño customs that immigrant Jews observed and were exposed to. He noted that life in Buenos Aires was much more public than in Poland. Men spent much of their time outdoors, conversing either on the plazas or in the cafes. Working-class Argentine homes, so-called *conventillos* (multistory houses with a shared courtyard in the middle), were crowded and dark and encouraged residents to spend as little time as possible inside. Consequently, as Nomberg lamented, family life deteriorated: women spent their days alone in claustrophobic homes, whereas men went gaming or enjoyed their time at the plaza. The writer described these situations as significantly different from the Polish reality, as foreign and pathological. "These are not our houses, where one is immersed in a homey atmosphere," Nomberg wrote.[45] Eastern Europe appeared in his narrative as a world of traditional values and Argentina as its negation. For Hirschbein, not only were the living conditions in poor and crowded conventillos problematic but so was the "exaggerated luxury of the main streets." Hirschbein considered the expansive and well-kept entrance halls and gilded doorbells not truly Argentine but rather "imported and exaggerated" or "without a soul."[46] The city looked to him as "a palace from which the royals left and only the servants remained."[47] He saw Buenos Aires as nouveau riche and chaotic, attempting to follow the European example, yet resulting in childish mimicry. Exploring Buenos Aires in 1914, he noticed a sharp divide between the rich minority and the poor masses. He saw an impoverished multiethnic crowd that "lives outside the city, in houses covered by rotten metal and surrounded by mud."[48]

Both authors expressed criticism of the situation of women in Argentina, especially concerning their discrimination. Nomberg was deeply bothered by the uneasy situation of women in Argentina. He believed that Jewish men excluded women from participating in public life by following the example set by Spanish and Italian immigrants. In the early twentieth century, women in Argentina were confined to the private sphere of child rearing, cooking, cleaning, and other house chores.[49] Similar conclusions were drawn by Martin Grinstein, who in his memoires of Colonia San Antonio described the male colonists as "highly *machista* men."[50] In the eyes of the travelers, the discrimination of women was an example of the negative influence that acculturation with Argentine society had on immigrant Jews. By the same token, they constructed Argentina as unprogressive and backward, a place where discrimination against women was inscribed into the system of national values.

Although at the beginning of the twentieth century, women's rights in Poland were a far cry from the rights of the male citizens, the situation in Argentina was worse. In Poland or the United States, Jewish women were often actively engaged in supporting their families working as merchants or in factories. Women who belonged to the urban middle class in Poland often socialized both with boyfriends and girlfriends, strolling around the city, going for picnics or sunbathing in the summer. Already in the first decade of the twentieth century, cafés had become popular on Warsaw's Jewish streets, attracting both men and women. In the Polish-Jewish context, cafés quite often functioned as a nexus between secularism and progressive politics that advanced the position of women.[51] In Argentina, the problem of female trafficking influenced the freedoms of ordinary Jewish women. Nomberg pointed out that in Argentina, going out with boyfriends was unthinkable.[52] This was also the experience of Raquel Minces, who arrived in Argentina from Poland at the age of twenty in 1930. She recalled that it was impossible for her to enter a restaurant alone and eat lunch by herself. Answering a question of a researcher who was interviewing her, she said: "You don't know the Argentina of sixty years ago [in the1930s]. A woman could not walk alone in the street." Raquel's neighbors complained to her mother if she went out alone.

Hirschbein, who also noticed the underprivileged situation of women in Argentina, criticized it in the following words:

> When a girl comes to Argentina wanting to work in a factory or to be independent in any other way, instead of looking for a groom who would

> rescue her—no, Argentina is a swamp for these kinds of girls. It is already a tradition in this country that a girl should sit and wait for a future husband. The daughter waits, parents wait. A woman is helpless here. And should the girl transgress the borders and just go out to look for a job, she will be treated with suspicion. After work she cannot spend any moment hanging outside. In North America, I see Jewish daughters who go out with whomever they want. This is natural. But the local ethics in Argentina do not allow it.[53]

Responding to such developments in Argentina, Hirschbein made his critique against Argentine moralists. He mentioned that most of the young immigrant girls from eastern Europe were accustomed to different standards and had much more personal freedom there than in Argentina.[54] Hirschbein was saddened by the fact that the Jews began to look down upon each and every girl who wanted to live as she lived in the alter heym. Hirschbein's narrative stressed that women's voices and interests could not be overlooked. The author reminded his readers that those considering immigration to Argentina should also keep in mind the widespread discrimination against women and their underprivileged situation.[55] Hirschbein, as an advocate of modern, secular Jewishness, associated the conservative backlash in Argentina with a traditional, Orthodox approach to Jewish women. He was disappointed as he wanted to see the new diasporas in the Americas as a better world, where oppressive traditional practices would no longer carry the same weight. The discrimination of women collided with his perception of liberal and free Argentina.

Presenting the Argentine Jewish immigrant reality, both travel writers often compared Argentina with other diasporas. They made references not only to the eastern European society and landscape but also to other emigration lands. Due to the dominant exodus to the United States, Polish Jews had a relatively well-grounded picture of this country, and North America emerged as the classic model of Jewish emigration. As a result, the Argentina that appeared as a destination for Jewish immigrants some twenty years later was often compared to the United States. Hirschbein wrote that Argentina's laws were as liberal and democratic as in the United States.[56] Nomberg, though sympathetic toward those struggling to establish Jewish life in Argentina, was aware that Argentine Jewish life was far behind its American counterpart. Life in Argentina was no match in terms of modernization, as was the case with narratives of the United States of the early twentieth century.[57] Argentina did offer possibilities and was a refuge for many immigrants, but industry and modernization hardly appeared in Hirschbein's and Nomberg's texts. Although some markers of modernity were included—trains that took settlers to colonies and Buenos Aires's trams or electric street lamps, for example. However, these aspects were not featured as key issues in their narrative. Rather, Nomberg and Hirschbein centered the development of the agricultural colonies and underlined contrasts between Argentina's underdevelopment and the modern, urban experience of immigrants in the United States.

Jewish Travelers in Latin America and the (East) European Context

To a degree, the tours of Hirschbein and Nomberg through Argentina resembled the journeys of western European explorers who traveled to South America, Africa, or the Middle East at the turn of the nineteenth century. Both Jewish and non-Jewish travel writers had a desire to uncover the lives of peoples little known in Europe and to succeed as the ones to offer firsthand accounts of remote lands. However, the meaning of travel by eastern European Jews and travel by western European nationals of colonial empires were evidently different. As numerous studies have shown, western European travelers served as an intellectual and scientific arm of colonization and conquest.[58] Mary Louise Pratt argued that travel writing served as a form of legitimization of the expansion of empire.[59] Nineteenth-century cartographers, geographers, and biologists were the forerunners or supporters of a military takeover of non-European lands. Whereas female travelers such as Isabella Bird or Jelena Dimitrijević might not have been personally involved in the subordination and control over the areas they studied, other geographers and explorers often partook or organized the state-commissioned expeditions.[60] This was the case with the Russian exploration of Siberia, where the state's financial support clearly suggests political, not scientific, motivations.[61]

During the late nineteenth and early twentieth centuries, many Europeans traveled to Latin America, Asia, or Africa with a desire to examine local peoples, explore nature, and to experience exotic lands. Many perceived their expeditions as semiscientific, believing that their travels could reveal what was previously hidden and unreachable, manifesting the power of the White Man, armed with modern European science. Many of these explorers left written memoirs or published travel accounts. In that era, traveling was also a part of European elite formation. Young upper-middle-class Europeans and up-and-coming members of the intelligentsia traveled around major European cities, with a few visiting the United States. This was also true of more established European Jews. In recent decades, the travel writing of the nineteenth and early twentieth centuries has become a popular topic of study. Inspired by the studies of Said and Foucault, through an analysis of travel narratives, scholars exposed the complexities of colonial discourse and criticized the Eurocentric understanding of world history.[62] In their rereadings of European travel writing, researchers have focused largely on Asian, African, and Middle Eastern territories under colonial rule. The texts describing travel and exploration of Latin America (which had gained independence from Spain in the early nineteenth century) were less examined. While Amazonian South America emerged as a significant travel writing theme, and later an important subject of literary criticism, Argentina was regarded as more European, less "exotic" and thus, not a frequent destination for travel writers.[63]

It is problematic to place the work of Jewish travelers to Argentina in the category of colonial travel writing. Using Edward Said's framework of Orientalism, it might be tempting to perceive the non-European people of Argentina in a similar way to the indigenous people of Middle East. In this case, the European authors traveling to Argentina would fit into the shoes of Western explorers, objectifying and exoticizing the lives of Argentines, while underlining the positive influence of European immigration. Jewish colonial discourse (including Zionism) indeed often saw Jews as a civilizing force for the local population.[64] However, the situation in Nomberg's and Hirschbein's Argentine travelogues was much more complex. First of all, they focused on Jewish immigrants rather than on the non-Jews. The power imbalance between Jewish travel writers and their Jewish subjects was much smaller than there was between a British explorer and their indigenous subjects in central Africa. Jewish travel writers and their subjects shared a common language, an eastern European background, and the experience of travel or migration. Some contemporaries even questioned the possibility of a real Yiddish travel literature. The Warsaw-based historian and journalist Bernard Mark noted that "adventurous travel literature was unthinkable in Yiddish."[65] In his view, Jewish diasporization forced travelers to focus on the real Jewish problems that appeared together with migration, rather than to write heroic stories of geographic exploration. Likewise, the Yiddish writer and traveler Melech Ravitch argued that Jewish migration was counterproductive for Yiddish travel literature.[66]

Jewish travel writers were similar to the female authors whose texts did not expose the same clear-cut qualities of colonial discourse as did male writing. As Sara Mills stated, female travel writing is not Orientalist in the way described by Said.[67] She noticed that although female travel writing featured colonialist statements, we also find numerous passages that undermine the assumption of colonial superiority. The situation of eastern European Jewish travelers in Argentina was largely analogous. They also did not fit precisely in the Saidian discourse on colonialism and were only partially located within the European male travel discourse. The cultural, social, and political contexts of Jewishness placed Jewish travelers on the margins of the classic travel discourse of the era. Hirschbein and Nomberg were white males and belonged to a cultural elite, but their Jewishness made them weaker and "abnormal" when compared with the Western travelers.[68]

Jewish voyagers did not have a symbolic or real support of a colonial power that could potentially benefit from their exploration or use their narration as a tool of domination. Furthermore, as numerous scholars argue, Jews were not "entirely white."[69] Although their skin might be pale white, Jews were not Christian and were not nationals of a powerful European nation-state but lived in dispersion, which often excluded them from the "white" category. Centuries of European discrimination and persecution against the Jews placed them in a position of weak subjects and victims, rather than powerful hegemons who narrated supremacy and conquest through travel writing. Hirschbein noted that other nations usually had one "national home," whereas the "Jewish home" was scattered around the world. He envied the presumed stability of other nations, noticing that their nation-states represented the interests of their citizens. The Jewish diasporization following the Great Migrations evoked in him ambiguous feelings. He underscored a sense of being a "homeless Jew" but also appreciated the opportunities that multiple rootedness offered.[70] Although Nomberg's and Hirschbein's approach to Argentina was not colonialist, it was Eurocentric. Eurocentrism, defined by Shohat and Stam as a discursive "residue" or "precipitate" of colonialism, exerts its powers even in the absence of colonialism, as it normalizes power-relations by taking them for granted and rendering them as inevitable or progressive.[71] Nomberg's and Hirschbein's gaze was Eurocentric as they looked on Argentina from the perspective of representatives of an eastern European cultural tradition that was in their eyes natural and obvious. The Argentine reality that contradicted their approach, or did not fit within their worldview, was exoticized and imagined as disordered, unprogressive, or inferior.

Traditional travel writing relied on the existence of a group of readers who shared the traveler's worldview, language, and values, and groups of "the others," who were described as foreign, different, and strange.[72] In the case of eastern European Jewish travelers describing Argentina, the difference between the readers and the described was vague, as in both cases these were Yiddish-speaking Ashkenazi Jews. Yet, whereas the interaction between Jewish travelers and Jewish immigrants was an intercommunal experience, their portrayal of non-Jewish Argentina served a different agenda. Nomberg and Hirschbein constructed a distinct type of "otherness" in their texts that pertained to non-Jewish Argentines and hardly Judaized spaces, such as the pampa and the mountains. Consequently, the Argentina they portrayed was a mixed space: both Jewish and gentile, both familiar and foreign.

Jewish travelers concentrated on their own countrymen who immigrated to Argentina from Poland and other corners of eastern Europe. Their approach was autoethnographic or, as Tamar Lewinsky put it, "national ethnographic."[73] They analyzed their own situation as traveling Jews among Jewish immigrants. This fits the definition of autoethnography that can be analyzed as either an approach that seeks to understand cultural phenomena through the examination of personal experiences of the ethnographer or as a methodology that pertains to the study of the researcher's own ethnic group.[74] In a number of western European travel accounts of that time, the narrators excluded themselves from the described reality by underlining differences between themselves and the examined people. In the case of Nomberg and Hirschbein, the narrators were insiders to the ethnic group they described. Their texts are marked by the frequent use of the pronouns *we* and *ours* when talking about Jewish or Yiddish aspects.

Yiddish travel writing about Argentina needs to be seen in the context of social and cultural transformations related to Jewish mobility in the early twentieth century. It is easy to fall into a trap by reducing eastern European Jewish movement to forced emigration and displacement. Jewish mobility included frequent short-distance business trips between neighboring towns and villages, permanent relocation between localities of the same region or educational migration to bigger urban centers. At the end of the nineteenth century, the industrializing cities of Łódź and Białystok in Poland attracted thousands of internal Jewish migrants.[75] Following the pogroms of 1881 and 1882, thousands of Jews from the Pale of Settlement moved to the Kingdom of Poland, where anti-Jewish incidents were less violent.[76] Whereas Jewish movement within the Russian Pale of Settlement was limited, the situation in Habsburg Galicia and initially in the Kingdom of Poland was different. Jews from Galician towns could travel freely around the Austro-Hungarian Empire, and those who lived in the Kingdom of Poland could relocate within the area and cross into the Pale of Settlement.[77] Additionally, in the first decades of the twentieth century, a number of central and eastern European Jews engaged in new forms of mobility and travel. Leah Garrett was right to note that most Jewish travelers were often excluded from the "good forms of travel," as their movements were often a matter of necessity instead of free will.[78] Yet, this did not reflect the situation of an entire Jewish population. At the beginning of the twentieth century, new travel-centered types of mobility, such as trekking or sightseeing, became increasingly popular in Jewish Poland and were not limited only to the secularizing middle class.[79] These forms of movement accompanied migration in influencing the character of Jewish mobility at the turn of the century.

The travel writings of Hirschbein and Nomberg were an answer to and an additional facet of increased Jewish mobility of the early twentieth century. Nomberg and Hirschbein were not forced to go to Argentina; they were not economic or political emigrants. It was their personal interest in the new Jewish diasporas, the Yiddishist agenda, and a certain passion for traveling that encouraged them to travel around the world. The expeditions of both Jewish writers to Argentina had the same historical and social background as the development of tourism in interwar Poland and the emigration. Both stemmed from secularization, industrialization, and the demise of the shtetl. Jewish emigration from eastern Europe expanded the Jewish world both geographically and psychologically. Geographical relocation became physically possible and psychologically comprehensible for more and more people. As the new diasporic Jewish identities evolved, travel and migration became increasingly connected. Nomberg's and Hirschbein's texts exemplify the close relationship of both phenomena. Their books connected the worlds of east European Jewish immigrants in Argentina with the reality of those who planned to emigrate but also with the experience of this group of Polish Jews who preferred to look at distant Argentina from the safe and comfortable position of a reader of a travel report. Through the travelogues, Jews explored the non-Jewish worlds lying beyond the well-known un-Jewishness of their Polish gentile neighbors. These books promoted interest in the nonlocal and non-Jewish aspects of life.

This interest in narratives of life in other countries was expressed by an impressive number of travel accounts published in Poland in the interwar years. This can be traced both in Yiddish literature and in books written in Polish. Nomberg, apart from his Argentine travelogue, also published a book about Palestine and North America.[80] Hirschbein wrote about India, Palestine, Soviet Russia, Australia, New Zealand, and South Africa. Other travel writers included Elimelech Neufeld, Schulim Gottlieb, Bentsiyon Hoffman, Shemarya Gorelik, and Boruch Glazman.[81] Apart from written travel accounts, Polish Jews eagerly participated in evening lectures given by the travelers. In 1925 in Radom, a theater poster invited audiences for a meeting with B. Jesurowicz, who was supposed to talk about his trip to India.[82] Also in Radom, in 1927, a famous Yiddish poet Zusman Segalovitch shared his impressions of a trip to Paris and London with the public.[83] In 1924, G. Zybert, who "traveled around the entire America," spoke in Lublin, Radom, and Biała Podlaska.[84] Yiddish-language travel journals were also available.[85] When Nomberg returned from Palestine, he delivered several lectures in provincial cities. In the 1930s, Leib Malach gave public talks on life in Brazil and Argentina.

The travels of Hirschbein and Nomberg were regularly reviewed in Poland's Jewish journals, opening new debates about Argentina and the intersection of migration and travel. In 1929, *Literarishe Bleter* published a review of Hirschbein's Eretz Israel travelogue.[86] When visiting Poland, Hirschbein met not only with fellow writers from the Association of Yiddish Writers and Journalists but also took part in public meetings. Returning from Asia in December 1927, he gave a lecture titled "Iber indyen, yapan un khina" (Through India, Japan, and China) in Nowości Theater at Bielańska Street.[87] Another lecture, "Di velt vi ikh ze zi" (The world as I see it), took place in Kamińska Theater.[88] Similar lectures were organized in Białystok and Vilna.[89] The prices were very cheap in order to enable the participation of the poor. A year earlier, Hirschbein published regular travel articles from Asia in Warsaw's *Literarishe Bleter.*[90] Travel articles from his Eretz Israel expedition were printed in *Der Moment.*[91] The daily published Hirschbein's texts every Friday and presented him as a unique voice among Jewish travel writers. Upon returning from a trip to Soviet Russia,

Hirschbein gave another series of public lectures in Poland, and a few articles were printed in the Warsaw Yiddish press.[92]

The emigration debates and the new interest in tourism were experienced not only by the Jews but were a part of broader non-Jewish reality in Poland during the interwar period. Around 1.8 million people left Poland in the interwar years, most of them non-Jews.[93] Jewish and non-Jewish emigration and colonization societies fueled discussions about the possibilities of emigrating from Poland. At the same time, Christian Poles were also more and more interested in traveling. There were a few Polish-language journals that featured columns on travel and tourism. A good example was *Świat* (World), an illustrated weekly edited by gentile authors but published by the Jewish publishing house of the Orgelbrand family. *Świat* published a book series called Biblioteka Podróży Egzotycznych (Library of exotic travels) that, next to Argentina, also featured Borneo, Angola, and Ethiopia. In 1929, traveler, emigration activist, and researcher of tourism Mieczysław Fularski published a travelogue from Bolivia, Paraguay, and Argentina.[94] Fularski, a gentile, similarly to Nomberg and Hirschbein, focused foremost on his own ethnic group: non-Jewish Poles. Yet, he noticed the increasing presence of eastern European Jews in Argentina, both in Buenos Aires and in the agricultural interior. He mentioned the economic success of Max Glücksman, a Czernowitz-born Jew who became an owner of a cinema chain, and the activities of the Poylisher Farband. Fularski also transmitted accounts about Jewish colonists and concluded that the colonies produced "a new type of brave, Jewish farmer." Like their Yiddish counterparts, Polish-language fiction writers (Konrad Wrzos, Zbigniew Uniłowski, and Antoni Słonimski) traveled to Latin America to investigate and give accounts of the experience of Polish immigrants.[95]

The Argentine journeys and travel writing of Hirschbein and Nomberg did not exist in a cultural and historical void but were part and parcel of the Jewish experiences of the 1920s and 1930s in Poland and Argentina. The interwar years witnessed a shared reality in which traveling and migration played an increasingly prominent role. Emigration from eastern Europe created a new diasporic Jewish world and diasporic Yiddish literature, while the Yiddish press evolved to a major platform linking the communities in Europe and the Americas. Social changes in the Jewish heartland of eastern Europe increased the interest of Polish Jews in the non-European world. The Argentine travel narratives of Hirschbein and Nomberg serve as a lens for exploring the writing territory that stretched between eastern Europe and Argentina.

Conclusion

Yiddish travel writing and travel to Argentina was a space that both fostered and reflected a cultural, social, and national interconnectedness between Jewish Poland and Argentina. Hirschbein and Nomberg acted as cultural mediators, who translated Argentina to Polish-Jewish readers seeking accurate information on emigration, or as entertainers in the form of a good travel book. Knowing both eastern Europe and Argentina, they showed that the distance between the exoticism and familiarity was narrower than commonly believed. Their Argentine travelogues responded to the needs of eastern European Jews, who searched for firsthand accounts about Jewish life in the new centers of Ashkenazi diaspora, but at the same time, they nurtured the very development of these needs. The fact that *Fun vayte lender* and "Argentinishe rayze" were read and known both in Poland and Argentina (as well as other Jewish centers) defined travel writing as a new and important transatlantic platform that allowed dispersed Polish Jews to reconnect and join a discussion.

Narratives of Hirschbein and Nomberg showcased Argentina as an exotic space with a difficult climate and a population that was unpredictable and diverse. Unlike travel writing by western Europeans, Hirschbein and Nomberg analyzed their fellow Jews. They inscribed their accounts in emergent discourse on Jewish sociology and migration and reflected a general growing interest in areas outside of the geographic Jewish core in eastern Europe. Both travel writers noticed how the new surroundings influenced eastern European Jewish immigrants: the immigrants started speaking Spanish, interacting with other ethnic groups, and working the land. Whereas the immigrant generation continued to be influenced both by eastern Europe and Argentina, their children were usually a product of Argentina. The next chapter observes how the offspring of the immigrants voiced their belonging to Argentina. It follows how Spanish and Yiddish cultural expressions were deployed in order to manifest the belonging to Argentina.

5

Israelita Argentino or *Argentiner Yid?*

Cultural Choices, National Belonging, and the Weight of European Baggage

The Place of Jews in the Argentine Nation

As Warsaw-born Argentine Yiddish culturist Samuel Rollansky once put it, the years of interwar Jewish immigration to Argentina were "a time of storm and stress." Those who came after 1918 brought new problems to Jewish Argentina: "Hard feelings from the *alte heymen*, war and occupation experiences, hunger, revolution, class struggle, anti-Semitism."[1] The post–World War I immigration of Yiddish-speaking, largely secular, and nationally mobilized Polish Jews shaped the way that Yiddish culture, Argentineness, and being a Polish Jew were conceptualized in Argentina. These immigrants invigorated Argentine Jewish life with new ideas, and their arrival shook up previously held assumptions and attitudes. The issues of ethnic identity and national belonging appeared at the center of social and cultural debates. In the 1920s and 1930s, Argentina became a space where Argentine policies of nationalizing immigrants competed with other national visions of the Jewish future imported from Europe. The relationship between Yiddish heritage and cultural integration informed the debates about the meaning of the eastern European past, the new Argentine homeland, and the divisions within the emerging Argentine Jewry. This chapter provides the Argentine context to the transatlantic networks in which the Polish Jews engaged. It shows how Jews in Argentina searched for ways to combine Jewishness with argentinidad and how Polish-Jewish immigration of the 1920s complicated Argentine Jewish cultural life.

The veteran immigrants and those who arrived in early 1920s often differed in terms of their orientation toward their old home and the new Latin American homeland. For most veteran and established Jewish Argentines, Poland was an alter heym, still visible on the Argentine horizon, but definitely not a central axis of their lives and debates. To this group belonged largely second-generation immigrants, children of those who arrived at the very end of the nineteenth century or those who immigrated at a very young age, in short, those "formed" in Argentina. Many of them abandoned Yiddish for Spanish in search of integration and success in Argentine society or looked for a language that would not remind them of their immigrant parents.[2] In a 1923 editorial, the Argentine acculturalist-leaning journal *Mundo Israelita* proclaimed, "We are different," demanding recognition and respect from the new immigrant generation. The editor pointed out that Jews who were socialized in Argentina were influenced by the surrounding society and obviously differed from new immigrants. Rejecting any notion of cultural superiority, Jewish Argentines demanded that immigrant Jews recognize the sociocultural differences between them and not decry natural cultural and linguistic changes.[3]

In the 1910s and 1920s, Argentina witnessed the linguistic acculturation of second-generation children.[4] Russian envoy Nikolai Abramovich Krukov, who visited Argentina in 1903, wrote that Jews "change quickly in Argentina, they wear the same clothes as the Argentines, do not have side locks anymore, their faces are brave and honest, especially among the youth who graduated from local schools and speak Spanish."[5] Children of Jewish colonists often received public education in Spanish and only a limited course of Hebrew and Yiddish organized by the so-called Cursos Religiosos (established in 1911).[6] Some ethnic activists in the capital and in the colonies criticized this situation. In 1901, Yankev Liachovitzky complained in a letter sent to Poland that "they [young Jews in Argentina] wear the same clothing as the Argentines, go shopping on Saturday, and play a local game *bollas*." He lamented the fact that "those under twenty do not have any connection to their people."[7]

For the post–World War I generation of immigrants, Poland remained an important reference point, a center of the imagined Yiddishland and a place from where Jewish social, political, and cultural trends resonated on smaller diasporas. Many of the Polish-Jewish newcomers of the 1920s were familiar with or were involved in the recent ethnonational and political revival in Jewish Poland. Their bond with the alter heym was a malleable state of mind and a relation to a past left behind, or as Frank Wolff put it, a "mythscape filled with emotions, experiences and expectations."[8] Polish politics attracted their attention and opinions held by fellow Jews in Poland regarding their new home were of a big importance.

To a certain extent, this challenged and redirected the ongoing acculturation processes in which the older generation of immigrants was involved. In the 1920s and 1930s, discussions about the place of Jews in Argentina and the meaning of Yiddish culture were led on multiple fronts. These included the Spanish and Yiddish general press, landsman debates, Yiddish literature, but also in communal institutions.[9] At the very beginning, relations between the *gele* acculturationists and the *grine* Yiddish-speakers were far from smooth. The Yiddish word *gel*, or yellow, referred to immigrants who already spent a longer time in Argentina, whereas *grin*, or green, denoted the newly arrived. Many of the veteran Jews, following Argentine cultural nationalism that dominated the intellectual discourse of the era, accused the newcomers of not being or not wanting to be fully Argentine. Yet, there was no clear division between the attitudes of old and new Jewish immigrants. The lines were blurred. Some of the Spanish-oriented Jews noticed their own distancing from Judaism and Jewishness and saw the newly arrived as more authentic and found a growing interest in Yiddish culture and the Jewish ethnonational revival in eastern Europe and beyond. For instance, in Yiddish theater that was "a school of *yidishkayt*" for already Argentinized Jewish porteños.[10]

Samuel Rollansky noticed that those Jews who were very distant from traditional Jewish life, quite often already very high within the Argentine social hierarchy, were filling up Yiddish theaters, especially for the low-brow entertaining plays, the so-called *tshulent-pieses*. Rollansky wrote that some Buenos Aires Jews did not speak Yiddish, did not read any books or newspapers in Yiddish, and the theater was their only connection with yidishkayt.[11] Yiddish theaters in Argentina mostly staged foreign works, usually those composed in Poland or the United States. Theaters served as a space that extended the borders of Yiddish life and included those who felt more comfortable in Spanish-speaking circles. Also, gentile theater critics visited Yiddish stages, especially in the 1920s, when Spanish theater was still not well developed. Especially attractive were the guest plays by foreign directors. Zygmunt Turkow from Poland or Maurice Schwartz from the United States were always received as stars. Despite performing a more challenging literary theater, the venues seemed to be packed with theater aficionados.[12] Yiddish-speaking and Argentinized Jews mingled in the same cultural institutions, foremost in Yiddish theaters.

The generational differences did not always go together with linguistic and broader changes in identity. In order to grasp these complexities, it might be useful to adopt Raanan Rein's notions of "Argentine Jews" and "Jewish Argentines," with the former emphasizing Argentina as a place of residence while at the same time identifying with world Jewry or the Yiddishland, and the latter stressing a stronger cultural and national connection to Argentina as a factual or adopted homeland.[13] In thinking about the new Polish immigrants in the 1920s and 1930s, I prefer to use the term *Argentine Jews*, or *argentiner yidn*, as a cultural rootedness in the Yiddish culture was often a dominant identity factor in their progressive ethnonational vision of new Jewishness. They were of course simultaneously Argentine, but their Argentineness was a specific cultural idiosyncrasy of their Jewishness. I see being an Argentine Jew as a temporal stage that led to becoming a Jewish Argentine, or *israelita argentino*, later in life. In the Argentina of the 1920s and 1930s, both groups lived side by side: more veteran Argentinized, Jewish Argentines and Argentine Jews, who were relatively recent arrivals. Although using different argumentation, both groups claimed their belonging to Argentina. Whereas some saw themselves as Argentine patriots and underlined the cultural-religious basis of their Jewishness, the Yiddish-speaking immigrant majority described themselves as argentiner yidn, an ethnonational diaspora of those who belonged to a *yidisher folk* and formed an Argentine part of a global Yiddish ethnocultural network.[14] The Argentine Yiddish culturist Samuel Rollansky believed that a common Yiddish language and eastern European past marked Jews in Argentina as a "national group."[15] Yet, as time passed, more and more Jews saw themselves as Jewish Argentines, citizens and members of the republic, not as Jews in a national sense.

Jews in Argentina and the Politics of Language and Culture

Argentine Yiddishist journalist Pinie Katz noticed that in the 1920s some Jewish merchants perceived the linguistic conversion into Spanish as a social upgrade.[16] The need to speak Spanish with non-Jewish customers often transformed into a worldview, and Yiddish began to be perceived as a ballast. Some Jews pretended not to speak Yiddish, which turned them into tragicomic figures, in the eyes of Katz. Others, like Jewish doctors or lawyers working with Jews, were forced to use Yiddish, but sometimes they perceived it as questioning their integration and progress within the Spanish-speaking world. Katz claimed that linguistic acculturation was often superficial and was reduced merely to speaking Spanish without being involved in the Spanish-language culture. Likewise, the Polish Jewish writer and journalist Marek Turkow, who traveled around the Jewish colonies in the late 1930s, bemoaned the linguistic Argentinization of Moisés Ville.[17] He criticized the Argentina-born generation of degrading "the sounds of juicy Lithuanian Yiddish by blending in Spanish words."[18] Argentine Yiddishist Yankev Botoshansky was analogously skeptical about acculturation and saw linguistic transformation as a danger.[19] David Ajzensztat of the Poylisher Farband had similar views and wrote in 1941: "Our children are naked. Without Jewish contents, without Jewish hope. Without a Jewish environment."[20] An anonymous landsman writing in the journal of the Poylisher Farband was convinced that linguistic acculturation was dangerous as it "alienated the youth from the Jewish language, culture, and their own parents."[21]

Language was a key sphere through which immigrants manifested their identity and ethnic background. Whereas, in the interwar years, the majority (both new and old immigrants) were Yiddish-speaking proletarian families, the number of acculturated, Spanish-speaking, Jewish middle-class families was on the rise. Sociologist Jacob Shatzky estimated that at the beginning of the 1950s 40 percent of Argentine Jewish press readers read only Yiddish journals, while another 40 percent read only in Spanish.[22] Although in the 1920s and 1930s the number of those who read only in Spanish was certainly lower, the linguistic evolution into Spanish was already visible. Economic progress moved Jews closer to the Spanish-speaking sphere.[23] There was a clear tendency among the Argentina-born generation to perceive Spanish as a language of communal and national belonging. The Argentine regime allowed and wanted Jews to be and feel Argentine, yet simultaneously demanded that they define their Jewish ethnic identities as private or semiprivate and operated within family or civic society.[24]

This was noticed by Isaias Lerner, who grew up in the 1930s in Buenos Aires. Lerner identified two clearly separate spheres: Argentine public and Jewish private. He wrote: "Jewish life was never led in public and consisted of minimal religious practices that were hardly visible. Thus, we led a double life. . . . We were Jews within the walls of our homes and citizens whose religion became imperceptible in the life that began only when we stepped out into the street."[25] Recalling his childhood in Buenos Aires, Lerner wrote that his parents decided to look for a private Jewish teacher instead of sending him to a Jewish school, at home they read Yiddish literature with him and celebrated Jewish holidays in a secular way as a "folkloric-gastronomic practice." At the same time, the Lerners mingled within the circle of liberal Argentine Catholics and Isaias went to a public school.[26] I am hesitant to extrapolate Lerner's experience and to argue that a clear-cut separation between "a private Jewish" and "public Argentine" arena existed in Argentina. Mobilized by nationalizing influences of the state, immigrant Jews indeed claimed Argentine national belonging. Public schooling raised the new generation of Jews with a common Argentine national memory, mythology, and vernacular language.[27] At the same time, there was a broad Jewish public sphere, encompassing both Spanish and Yiddish expressions.

The Argentinization of the Argentina-born or socialized generation of Jews was strongly interconnected with Argentina's state policies concerning nation building. The beginning of the twentieth century was an era of national positivism that underlined values such as patriotism, hard work, and aspiration for social progress. The sociobiological discourse of the turn from the nineteenth to the twentieth century saw Argentina as a living organism that should progress in a way that mirrored natural evolution. Argentina was supposed to aggrandize and to become powerful, and immigration was primarily seen as a source of population increase that would guarantee Argentina's bright future. The immigrants were to be turned into Argentine subjects, while Argentineness, or national belonging, would neutralize class differences in society.[28] National education was conceived as tool for creating a "governable" nation that favored the interests of the *patria* over the individual. The educational system, designed by José M. Ramos Mejia (head of Consejo Nacional de Educación, 1908–12), established practices of *culto de la patria* and shaping the "patriotic spirit," a key mechanism in "making" Argentines. It was designed to counter both the presumed immigrant isolationism and a sense of proletarian (versus national) identity.[29] The generation of immigrant Jews that grew up in Argentina around the *centenario* (1910) was to a great extent influenced by these visions of national belonging and Argentineness.

The cultural and political attitudes of Argentinized Jewish Argentines were inspired by a number of gentile politicians and intellectuals, the zeitgeist of that era, and a desire common to all immigrants to be accepted by the majority. The Argentine attitude toward European immigration evolved with time, and the immigrants' place in the nation was a subject of constant political and social debate. The Argentine liberals of the nineteenth century considered European immigration as a chief way of developing Argentina. Statesman and politician Juan Bautista Alberdi argued that European immigration would elevate the economic and cultural level of Argentina. His views were largely incorporated into the 1853 constitution and Ley de Inmigración y Colonización N° 817. The phrase *gobernar es poblar* (to govern is to populate) became the motto of an "open door policy" that reigned in Argentina until 1930.[30] Alberdi's views were later shared by future president Domingo Faustino Sarmiento, who, drawing on the famous dichotomy of *civilización* versus *barbarie*, called for reshaping Argentina into a modern European-styled state by promoting European immigration. For Sarmiento, the Argentine countryside was a hotbed of barbarism that produced *caudillos* and dictators like the "infamous" Juan Manuel de Rosas. Europe, for him, was an example of an advanced civilization, and European immigrants would serve as the material for remodeling the society and politics of Argentina in the desired direction.[31] Sarmiento's views reflected Argentine racial explanations that ascribed certain characteristics to the European and indigenous populations.

At the very beginning of the twentieth century, around the centenario of Argentine independence, new voices of cultural nationalism began to gain in power. Intellectuals and politicians, such as Manuel Gálvez, Ricardo Rojas, and Emilio Bécher, feared that the flocking of a foreign population endangered the essence and traditions of Argentina.[32] Parliamentarian Estanislao Zeballos suspected that Buenos Aires would become "like Montevideo, a city without features, [and] one day we will find ourselves transformed into a nation without language, traditions, character or flag."[33] The nationalist slogan of "coming back to the roots" of Argentina emphasized the symbolic value of soil and *gaucho*, which with the influence of immigration would produce a genuinely Argentine nation. For instance, the sociologist Carlos Octavio Bunge believed in the superiority of the Argentine criollo race, due to its "relatively homogenous racial character" when compared with other countries of the region. As a Social Darwinist, he relied on the category of race and imagined that a new argentinidad could be constructed, as the positivists believed.[34] In his vision, immigrants and criollos would become subjects that unified Argentine nationalism. The visions of the intellectuals were transferred both to natives and immigrants via the very popular so-called *literatura criollista*.[35]

Around 1910, the settlement of the land and agropastoralism came to be imagined as an embodiment of authenticity and national ethos. Discursive associations between the new immigrant and the gaucho served the former as a claim for belonging to the national body. The de Hirsch Jewish agricultural project at the turn of the century fit with this paradigm. It allowed Jews to imagine themselves and be imagined as primordial Argentine land-laborers. This was visible in the speech given by Juan Montovani, the Minister of Education and Development of Provincia Santa Fe, on the fiftieth anniversary of the Jewish colony of Moisés Ville: "The Jewish colonies reflect the economic effort and the effort of the irreversible assimilation with our soil. . . . Although they preserve their religion, the Jewish colonies are villages filled with the national spirit."[36] Next to the Jews, access to the nation via land labor was also true of other immigrant groups in Argentina, including Germans, Danes, Poles, and Ukrainians.[37]

The *crisol de razas* (melting pot) ideology that was dominant in Argentina from the end of the nineteenth century often demanded from the immigrants the abandonment of the old country customs and loyalties and integration into a newly formed Argentine ethnonational community. This was intensified by the cultural nationalists, who around 1900 to 1910 began to downgrade the positive influence of immigration and feared a "disorder" that the intermingling of peoples and races could bring about.[38] Józef Włodek, the first consul of Poland in Argentina, wrote in 1923 that "Argentines do not like the phrase *colonia* [colony, settlement] or *colectividad extranjera* [a foreign community] . . . and prefer to see only Argentine citizens or at least Argentine residents. Argentine society, especially the nationalists, demand that all immigrants quickly adopt the essence of Argentine national life."[39] The process of embracing Argentine nationality by immigrants, and its effectiveness, was viewed ambiguously. Sarmiento, for instance, believed that whereas immigrants in the United States quickly became Americans, in Argentina "the immigrant preferred to remain a foreigner forever."[40] The beginning of the twentieth century marked an intensified patriotic nationalization of immigrants. Argentineness was defined as something that can be constructed and formed, and the state apparatus engaged intensively in "making Argentines."[41]

Fears of constructing an overly segmented and inauthentic Argentine society were also voiced in response to Jewish immigration. In 1917, Carlos Ibarguren, a historian and a former Minister of Justice and Education, argued in the acculturalist-leaning Jewish weekly *Vida Nuestra* that "the sons of the Hebrew immigrants should above all be Argentine."[42] On another occasion, Ibarguren convinced the readers of *Vida Nuestra* that "your homeland is where you live well" and supported the amalgamation of immigrants into a "great Argentine nation."[43] Further, Alberto Gerchunoff, a canonic Jewish-Argentine writer, endorsed the acculturation of Jews into the Spanish-speaking world. His 1910 novel *Los gauchos judíos* was a manifesto of the Jewish contribution and devotion to Argentina. As May E. Bletz put it, Gerchunoff's book transferred the Jewish immigrant culture to the nationalist nostalgia of the early 1900s. Gerchunoff, as an immigrant, but also a member of the Argentine pronationalist avant-garde circles, attempted to bridge the chasm between upper-class and immigrant formulations of Argentineness.[44] By cultivating the Argentine land, returning to pastoral, quasi-biblical activities, and interacting with the gauchos, the first immigrant Jewish colonists pictured by him claimed a place in the national imaginary. On the land, they were not corrupt city cosmopolitans but a truly Argentine creation. Gerchunoff's book transformed Jewish colonists into a part of the Argentine nation. Writing the book in perfect Spanish, using no Yiddishisms, Gerchunoff established the linguistic code for Jewish inclusion in the nation.[45]

Even limited Jewish schooling was perceived as a danger by state educational institutions and by Argentine nationalists.[46] In 1914, Cursos Religiosos had only sixteen schools in Buenos Aires (out of a network of around one hundred in Argentina), and most Jewish children in the capital studied only in the obligatory state schools.[47] In 1929 in Buenos Aires, only a third of Jewish children received any Jewish education, which corresponded to 8,493 students at all levels of instruction.[48] Governmental *Monitor de la Educación Común* complained in 1908 that "it is insulting and depressing that there are schools where the education that children receive is exclusively foreign."[49] In 1919, the national authorities took over schools run by Cursos Religiosos. Throughout the entire pre–World War II period, the quality of Jewish schooling was considered a major problem and schooling was an arena where conflicting visions of Jewishness and Argentineness met.

Contrary to the fears of Argentine nationalists, the children of Jewish immigrants were increasingly fluent in Spanish and proud Argentines. This was the case in provincial cities, where, in the words of Poland's consul Józef Włodek, "parents did everything so that no one would recognize they were Jews and even sent their children to Jesuit schools."[50] Włodek noted that state schooling was a channel for nationalizing immigrant children in the spirit of Argentine patriotism. In public schools "patriotism was a prayer, learning, entertainment, morality, an ideal and even a god."[51] Włodek noticed that the Argentine government gave special attention to the nationalizing function of schooling, which primarily emphasized love for the new homeland. Włodek's observations were very accurate. Since the end of the nineteenth century, "school patriotism" became a key tool of Argentinization. Nationalist schoolbooks (like Carlos Octavio Bunge's 1910 *Nuestra Patria*), patriotic youth associations, and celebrations of national holidays were designed to create Argentines devoted to their homeland. School patriotism was supposed to differentiate between good and bad Argentines or between Argentines and non-Argentines.[52] At the same time, public schooling offered the promise of a university education, often had better infrastructure, and was considered to be on a higher educational level than complementary ethnic schools.[53]

In a multinational country, with hundreds of thousands of new immigrants, it was impossible to impose ethnic and linguistic uniformity. Argentine discourse on nationality and citizenship, to a certain extent, allowed immigrants to maintain emotional connections to former homelands. As Desmond King argued in the US context, the Americanization (and in our case, Argentinization) did not conform to the melting pot ideal as immigrants did not abandon ethnic traditions. In fact, much more powerful was a gradual "bottom-up" or "organic" acculturation of immigrants. For instance, spontaneous immigrant associations constituted a medium of socialization into the new society.[54] The Argentinization expectations of policy makers did not always coincide with the practice on the ground and the social reality. In Argentina, Juan A. Alsina, director of the Migration Department, already in 1910 acknowledged the existence of multiple immigrant belongings:

> We do not force the new homeland upon an immigrant, but we expected that arriving under the protection of our flag, of his own free will, he would quickly want to acquire Argentine nationality in order to fulfill the obligations of a citizen and enjoy the rights of a citizen. We expected that he would cut off contact with the *madre patria*, with the school that shaped him, with family, friends and national memories. But the reality turned out differently. Immigrants not only did not erase the image of the homeland from their heads, but some are trying to oppose his family and descendants becoming Argentine. . . . The immigrant does not stop to love his homeland, the immigrant seems to love two homelands, the one where he was born and the one whose welfare he enjoys.[55]

The establishment of Jewish agricultural settlements and nationalization of immigrant children did not relinquish the fears associated with Jewish immigration to Argentina. Some Catholic nationalists feared an intensified Jewish immigration. One of the earliest voices was *La Bolsa* (1891) by Julián Martel, which served as an anti-Semitic tirade against foreigners in general.[56] Using the theme of Jewish involvement in female trafficking, Martel portrayed Jews as prone to crime and promiscuity, and as a group actively destroying traditional Argentine morality.[57] Importantly, his book was published precisely during the first years of the Jewish agricultural settlement in the Argentine interior. The tendencies against Jewish immigration continued throughout subsequent decades. Following the coup d'etat of 1930, the nationalist author and journalist Gustavo Adolfo Martinez Zuvirría gained popularity for his anti-Semitic novel *El Kahal* (1935).

The political situation raised him to the position of director of the Argentine National Library and Minister of Education in the early 1940s. Zuvirría's racial anti-Semitism was nurtured by Argentine nationalism and Catholic militancy that dominated Argentine public life of the 1930s. Under the pseudonym of Hugo Wast, Zuvirría produced a number of pulp novels that posited the existence of a world Jewish lobby and played on anti-Jewish race rhetoric popular in that era.[58] Isaias Lerner recalled that *The Protocols of the Elders of Zion* were openly sold on newsstands in the 1930s and Wast's pamphlets were frequently read at public Argentine schools.[59]

Unlike the US context, the experience of being an ingredient in the Argentine melting pot that mixed immigrants of diverse patrias into a homogenous Argentine nation was not explicitly attractive. Citizenship was not granted to immigrants that quickly, and for many years, Jews struggled for economic and social inclusion, rather than actively participating in Argentine politics.[60] Whereas the first years of the twentieth century were marked by intensive communist and anarchist Jewish political activity, following World War I the partisan left-wing problems never regained their prewar importance. In the 1920s and 1930s, other issues stood at the center, chiefly the social and economic progress, Jewish education, and the status of Yiddish culture.[61] Consequently, the naturalization and political identifications of immigrants were not at the core of the Argentine Jewish debates of the era.[62] Many Jewish Polish immigrants who arrived after 1918 could not vote and were mostly excluded from the political process. Edgardo Bilsky concluded that foreigners were marginalized and could not find ways of expression in a traditional political process.[63] However, the children of the more veteran immigrants were granted citizenship by birth and placed many hopes with the Union Civíca Radical (UCR) in the 1920s, especially during the governments of Marcelo Torcuato de Alvear and Hipólito Yrigoyen. The UCR opened channels that incorporated immigrant children into Argentina's political life and was indeed supported by Jews aspiring to the middle class.[64] The coup d'etat of 1930 ended this period of relative tolerance and inclusion and brought about an "oligarchic restoration" that lasted until 1943.[65] In 1931, the government of José Félix Uriburu limited immigration possibilities and reinstalled an alliance between conservative ruling elite and the Catholic Church.

We Are Argentines, Not European Guests! The Paths of Jewish Inclusion

The second generation of *colonias*-born Jews, many of whom later left for Buenos Aires, were key figures in the Argentinization of Argentine Jewish cultural and social life.[66] For this group, reading a journal in Spanish or belonging to a Spanish-speaking Jewish ethnic club was marking their actual self-perception as Argentines but also their desire not to be considered outsiders, holding on to old-country traditions. Lazaro Zhitnitsky, a *Di Presse* contributor and later president of Argentine IWO (Jewish Scientific Institute), argued that the colonists' children had "creolized" by choosing a path between Jewish *natsyonalkayt* (a Jewish ehtnonational identity) and assimilation.[67] The Centro Juventud Israelita Argentina, established as early as 1909, grouped sons of colonists who left for Buenos Aires. Many of them felt themselves first and foremost Argentine rather than Jewish in an ethnonational sense, yet wished to stress their Jewishness.[68] The acculturalist-leaning journal *Juventud* proclaimed in 1916 that: "Israelites . . . have found a profound sense of belonging and look at this adopted land as their own. . . . We are convinced that respect to [our] tradition and origin does not decrease [our] love to the adopted nation."[69]

Argentinized Jews sought out inclusion into the local national discourse. For some, it was an expression of devotion and belonging to Argentina. For instance, in 1924 *Semanario Hebreo* proclaimed: "If Argentina wouldn't have conquered liberty we celebrate on May 25th, Jews wouldn't have this generous land, and wouldn't have conquered the new Canaan, a new land of promise, a new blessing from God."[70] In 1939, a son of first-generation colonists in Moisés Ville proclaimed his belonging and gratitude to Argentina: "I am a son of those immigrants full of belief and hope, love of work and a cult of this land of promise. I am a native son of this colony that celebrates today its fiftieth anniversary. . . . I proclaim with pride to be profoundly Argentine, I am blessing my parents thousands of times for coming to this land."[71]

In 1923, the Asociación Juventud Israelita Argentina (AJIA, Association of Argentine Jewish Youth) was founded, which apart from diffusing Jewish culture, argued for a need for strengthening the ties between Jewish and gentile cultural circles. In 1928, Sociedad Hebraica Argentina (SHA), established after the unification of AJIA with Asociacion Hebraica in 1926, had 1,400 members and exercised influence over an important but small fraction of Argentine Jewry.[72] In the 1920s and 1930s, SHA and its circle became a center for the formation of a new Argentine-Jewish cultural elite. Secularism, liberalism, and the Spanish language formed the ideological framework of SHA. The fact that most of its members were middle-class citizens, who had already proven their success in Argentina, made this group credible and marked them as "good Jews" in the eyes of the Argentine political elite. Membership in SHA included young engineers, lawyers, and doctors, as well as individuals who shaped Jewish life in Argentina in subsequent years: Matías (Mordechai) Stoliar, Alberto Gerchunoff, and León Dujovne.

Soon after the formation of the first Argentinized Jewish Argentine societies, they began publishing their own journals that voiced their acculturalist-leaning agenda. For Jewish Argentines, Jewish journals in Spanish were an attempt to feel at home and to claim their right to Argentina. The sense of belonging to Argentina among Jews was often emphasized by frequent references to a *marrano* heritage, a Spanish Jewish Golden Age, and a meticulous use of the language of Cervantes.[73] *Juventud* (1911–17) and *Vida Nuestra* (1917–23) were followed in the 1920s by *Mundo Israelita* (1923) and *Semanario Hebreo* (1923). *Vida Nuestra* invited gentile Argentine intellectuals to comment on Jewish problems, especially after the Russian Revolution and the Balfour Declaration in 1917. The contributors included among others Leopoldo Lugones (a nationalist author), Alfredo Palacios (a socialist politician and professor), Juan E. Carulla (a nationalist politician), and Ricardo Rojas (a nationalist historian). *Vida Nuestra* created a space of discussion on Jewish and non-Jewish issues that included both the gentile and Jewish-Argentine cultural elite. Around the same time, *Liga Israelita Pro-Argentinidad* was established in Buenos Aires. It endorsed an overly patriotic form of Argentinization that regarded knowing one's new country, its laws, culture, and language as a requirement for Jews. *Liga* was formed by a group of Jewish businessmen connected with Argentine political and economic elite. The organization quickly associated itself with the gentile nationalist *Liga Patriótica Argentina* and backed anti-immigration policies aimed against the Yiddish-speaking proletariat.[74]

Salomón Resnick was a perfect example of Jewish-Argentines. He belonged to the first wave of Jewish immigrants to Argentina who arrived before World War I. In 1902, he emigrated from southern Ukraine as a six-year-old boy and was socialized in Argentina, after his father was commissioned to become a rabbi of a Jewish agricultural colony. Like many second-generation colonists, Resnick left for Buenos Aires. He began working for the journal *Juventud*, and from 1917, he was translating literary works from Yiddish to Spanish and cofounded both Yiddishist *Di Presse* (1918) and the acculturalist-leaning *Mundo Israelita* (1923). In 1929, he gave classes on Yiddish literature in the Spanish-language Colegio Secundario Israelita that he also helped to create. In 1933, Resnick founded the Spanish-language Jewish journal *Judaica* and until his premature death in 1946 was a key promoter of making Yiddish literature available for Spanish speakers. *Judaica* was largely based on translations from Yiddish to Spanish. An issue from September 1934, published to commemorate the 75th birthday of Sholem Aleichem, included almost in its entirety the translated texts of Shmuel Niger or Baal Mahshoyves. Among Resnick's translations from Yiddish was Sholem Aleichem's *The Travels of Benjamin III*, which Resnick coupled with a new subtitle: "The Jewish Don Quijote." Many others belonged to the same group of Spanish-writing Jewish Argentines, such as Alberto Gerchunoff (writing for *La Nación)*, Gregorio Fingermann (*La Nación*), César Tiempo (*La Columna*, later *La Prensa*), Enrique Lippschutz (*La Prensa*), and Enrique Dickman, the first Jew to become a member of the Argentine parliament. Many Jewish immigrants were also active in non-Jewish publishing. Samuel Glusberg was an editor of the Babel publishing house and of a literary journal under the same name. Manuel Gleizer was a successful publisher in the gentile world and until 1937 did not focus on Jewish subjects.[75]

Answering the needs of a growing community that socialized in Spanish, a part of the ethnic leadership preferred to deliver the Jewish contents in more accessible Spanish, rather than to bemoan the decreasing importance of Yiddish among second-generation immigrants. This phenomenon was visible not only concerning journalism but also in book publishing. The founders of the Spanish-language daily *Mundo Israelita*, León Kibrick and Salomón Resnick, took up a project of translating the key works of Yiddish literature into Spanish. The transmission of Jewish culture to the younger generation born in Argentina was a major concern of community activists. Some argued that the lack of interest in Jewish issues was related to linguistic deficiencies, as the young rarely read Yiddish or Hebrew. In this context, the translation of Jewish works into Spanish seemed to many a reasonable solution.[76] The Jewish writer and journalist Yosef Mendelson described the Spanish publications on Jewish themes as "spiritual nourishment for Jewish youth" and "a tool for informing the gentiles about the Jews and thus a way of combating anti-Semitism."[77] Resnick's translation projects were supported by the left-wing and starkly Yiddishist daily *Di Presse*, which saw in Resnick "a true lover of Yiddish" and understood his desire to make Yiddish literature more available.[78] Resnick's translation project not only informed Argentine Jewish readers about the richness of Yiddish literature but helped immigrant Jews to formulate their belonging to a high Jewish culture and defined the Yiddish tradition as not inferior or less progressive than Argentine or western European traditions.[79]

Jewish Argentines rejected accusations of assimilation hurled at them by some Yiddishist groups in Argentina and abroad. When Yiddish-speaking Labor Zionists raised the issue of the linguistic assimilation of Jewish youth in Argentina, *Mundo Israelita* fiercely defended its position.[80] The situation in Argentina was depicted by the journal not as assimilation but as "involuntary distancing" (*alejamiento*). Argentine youth were described as close to Jewish ethnonational life; they were interested in Jewish history and culture; yet not knowing Yiddish well enough, they searched for ways of expressing their interest in Jewish topics using Spanish. As *Mundo Israelita* summed it up, "the essential lies in the feelings, not in the exterior," while critics who demanded Jewish culture only in Yiddish and Hebrew were described as archaic. The voices about the intermixed and diverse character of Argentine Jewry were articulated already in 1919 by Yosef Mendelson. Mendelson wrote that Jewish life in Argentina was an amalgam of the old life in Russia with new La Plata influences.[81] Years later, Samuel Rollansky wrote that apart from the obvious local impact, Argentine Yiddish writing was inspired by multiple sources: by modernist Yiddish from the United States and by the unrest of Polish Yiddish poetry and social themes characteristic of Soviet writers.[82] Jewish-Argentine cultural leaders argued that Spanish could be a way of manifesting Jewishness and that, in Argentina, Jewishness and transnational links with eastern European Jewry were legitimately articulated in various linguistic ways and constructed in relation to belonging to Argentina.

For the Case of Progress: Jewish Argentines, Argentiner Yidn, and Cultural Alliances

For many Polish Jewish immigrants who arrived after World War I, the cultural and socioeconomic identities of Argentina-socialized Jews were initially quite foreign. On arrival in Latin America, those who grew up and formed their worldview in Poland needed to formulate it anew in Argentina. Although the embrace of Argentina as a safe haven that offered economic opportunities was relatively easy, the sociocultural aspects of integration were much more complex. The obvious aspects desired by veteran generations of Jewish Argentines included embracing Argentina as a caring and generous homeland and being fluent in the majority language, which might have been difficult for the new immigrants. Especially complex was the question of language and ethnicity.

The more veteran Jewish Argentines often differed culturally from the new immigrants arriving from Poland in the 1920s. For many Polish Jews who arrived after 1918, it was Yiddish and Yiddishness that defined their hybrid Argentine Jewish life. Some perceived the maintenance of Yiddish as a guarantee of not only safeguarding the Jewish ethnicity but also as a tool for Argentine Jews to participate in global Jewish ethnonational projects. The Argentine Yiddish journalist Yankev Botoshansky said in 1931 that "Yiddish is the best security belt. Yiddish isolates and concentrates, Yiddish is a substitute for territory, for land. This is also acknowledged by the non-Yiddishists."[83] Botoshansky was proud of the development of secular Yiddish life in Argentina. In another interview, he described Yiddish as the "ground under the feet," a cultural space that promised a certain identity stability to Jews.[84] In the 1920s and 1930s, the new immigrant Jewish population of Buenos Aires was not overly enthusiastic about the acculturalist-leaning position of the veteran generation. Some immigrant intellectuals began to imagine Argentina as a branch of a transnational Yiddishland. Although many new immigrants quickly learned Spanish in order to function in the multinational city, the linguistic evolution from Yiddish to Spanish gave rise to opposition well into the 1940s.

The relative vitality of Yiddish in Argentina in the 1920s and 1930s had to do not only with a "hanging on" to migrant language and culture but was embedded in the transnational ethnonational Yiddishland project that resonated from eastern Europe to Argentina. Many of the post-1918 immigrant Jews from Poland brought with them a sense of Yiddish-centered cultural pride and did not deem Yiddish culture as inferior to the surrounding Spanish Argentine culture. This reasoning came in the wake of the revival of Yiddish cultural life in interwar Poland, the United States, and the Soviet Union. In the interwar period, Poland was a center of innovation, ideas, and publications that were transferred to the Americas by migrating Jews. Consequently, these developments in Jewish Poland partly defined Argentine goals, conflicts, and structures when it came to Yiddish culture.[85]

Yiddish conveyed not only the traditional ethnoreligious culture of Ashkenazi Jews, but also a newly envisioned, ethnonational project of a diasporic *yidisher folk* (Yiddish nation) inhabiting an imagined Yiddishland. European Diaspora Nationalist intellectuals, such as Nokhem Shtif, desired to build a modern, secular Jewish national culture, with the Yiddish language as a linguistic national principle. In the interwar period, this was realized by forming the YIVO Institute in Vilna, establishing Yiddishist educational institutions, supporting a blossoming Yiddish literature, and including Yiddish in the agenda of Jewish political parties.[86] These developments of the interwar years also reached Argentina. The freshness and attraction of the Yiddish ethnonational project to some extent temporarily tempered the desire to embrace Argentine nationalism represented by the veteran immigrants. Although other European ethnonationalisms crossed the Atlantic and put down roots in Argentina (like Basque or Irish), the grassroots, diasporic, and transnational character of Yiddishist ethnic, cultural, and national belonging gave it a special status. Consequently, the re-Yiddishization of Argentine Jewish life following the 1920s immigration had few parallels among other immigrant groups.

In the 1930s, the separation between the veteran Jewish-Argentine cultural circles and the propagators of Yiddish culture might have been becoming very vague. Yiddishism, especially after the foundation of Vilna's YIVO Institute, was an important factor in global Jewish life, including Argentina, and did not automatically contradict acculturation. A 1925 editorial of *Mundo Israelita* encapsulated the diversity of possible Jewish allegiances in Argentina. The daily claimed that only "narrow minds" would think about the exclusive duality between being Argentine and being involved in global Jewish problems. Being an Argentine and an active Jew standing up "for the rights of his brothers" elsewhere in the world was seen as complementary.[87] The Argentine reality proved that Yiddish could at times be employed as a tool for claiming belonging to Argentina, as in the case of Yiddish tales about the childhood of President Sarmiento.[88] A number of Argentine ethnic leaders moved smoothly between the pastimes of the Spanish-speaking middle class, the Zionist cause, support for Yiddishist schooling, and defending the rights of the Jewish minority in Poland. When Matías Stoliar, the editor of *Yidische Zaitung*, went to the United States in 1935, the proacculturation publication *Mundo Israelita* praised him for informing the world about the progressive character of the Argentine yishev and appreciated Stoliar's organizational talents and intellectual curiosity.[89] His trip to the United States was seen as strengthening the ties within the *familia judía*, a synonym for global Jewry. For *Mundo Israelita*, it was important that Stoliar properly represented Jewish Argentina abroad. When Yiddishist Stoliar contributed to elevating the status of Argentina in other diasporas, the proacculturation community also backed it. His personal linguistic and cultural choices were then irrelevant.

When Marcos Regalsky, a contributor of *Yidische Zaitung*, traveled to Europe in 1935, he not only represented Argentina in a Zionist congress but also went to Vilna for a conference of YIVO.[90] The proacculturation publication *Mundo Israelita* expressed satisfaction that a representative of Argentine Jewry would be there, keeping the Argentine Jewish public updated about developments in the Old World. As *Mundo Israelia* remarked that, even though the partisan Yiddishists had founded YIVO, with time the institution focused on Yiddishism in a cultural sense, making it acceptable for the Zionists too.[91] At the same time, to a certain extent Zionism accepted multiple visions of a Jewish future, including both a Hebrew-speaking settlement in Palestine and Yiddish revival in the diaspora. Consequently, even the Zionist-leaning *Mundo Israelita* appreciated the advancement of Yiddish culture. A fitting example can be found in the warm welcome offered by the Spanish-language weekly to the Yiddish literary critic Shmuel Niger, who was described as "our illustrious guest" during a visit in Argentina.[92]

Although *Mundo Israelita,* SHA, and their circle might have seen Argentina as their physical and spiritual home, they were not indifferent to the problems of Jews in the Old World. Although the numerous fund-raising initiatives for the Jews of Poland were managed chiefly by the Yiddishist wing of Argentine Jewry, we do find its repercussions in the Spanish-language news. Here, the linguistic context helps to understand the broader identity-related phenomena. The Yiddish newspapers wrote about "brothers in Poland" and "having national responsibilities," whereas in *Mundo Israelita* they dealt with "coreligionists." This wording tells us something about the ethnic and religious identities of Jewish Argentines. Some of the Jewish Argentines might have considered themselves as "Argentines of the Mosaic faith," with their Jewishness reduced to cultural and religious aspects. Proacculturation institutions usually preferred to use the neutral and quasi-religious word *israelita* (Israelite), instead of the ethnically loaded word *judío* (Jew). Yet, it would be misleading to draw a dichotomy of Yiddish-speaking masses that saw themselves as Jews by nationality, language, and religion and Jewish Argentines, who were first and foremost Argentine patriots and Jews second. The divisions were hardly ever clear-cut and changed over time.

Despite linguistic and cultural discrepancies, both the Jewish Argentines and the newly arrived immigrants from Poland found a common language and spaces for cooperation. For instance, the proacculturation daily *Mundo Israelita* backed some causes that were clearly Yiddishist. The committee founding the Argentine section of Vilna's Yiddish Scientific Institute YIVO (IWO in Argentine spelling) included not only Yiddishist leaders such as Pinie Wald or Yankev Botoshansky but also Salomón Resnick, who bridged Yiddish and Spanish Jewish cultural circles. When Yaakov Zerubavel arrived in Argentina in 1928 to raise money for the TSYSHO schools, he was warmly welcomed by the Spanish-language newspaper.[93] *Mundo Israelita* expressed sympathy for his efforts and wished him lots of success.[94] The figure of Zerubavel, who was both a Yiddishist and a Zionist, attracted the support of the more veteran, middle-class circles of Argentine Jewry. Despite ideological differences, the secular Yiddish schools were seen by many as a symbol of "Jewish modernization" in Poland, consistent with the modern cultural values of editors and readers of *Mundo Israelita*. It was appreciated that Zerubavel wanted to "liberate the new generation of Jews in Poland from the disgraceful influence of religious fanaticism." The newspaper even praised his "clear and elegant" Yiddish.[95]

The formation of Jewish-Argentine identity was present in the fusion of Yiddish and gentile Argentine cultural subjects. The most prominent example might have been Hevl Katz, a popular Yiddish performer, singer, and comedian in Argentina in the 1930s. Katz, born in Vilna in 1902, immigrated to Argentina in 1930 and quickly became a key figure that reflected the experiences of thousands of other immigrants. His songs brimmed with Argentine subjects, parodied the challenges of life in Argentina, and consequently helped to anchor immigrants in their new surroundings.[96] His satirical songs allowed the immigrants to laugh about their problems, like poverty or imperfect Spanish. At the same time, his songs focused on the Argentine reality, often with a tango-melody and spiced up with Argentinized Yiddish, exemplifying the formation of Jewish-Argentine ethnic identity. The figure of Katz shows how popular culture became an arena of negotiating the inclusion of immigrant Jews and their children into Argentine society. A fellow Polish-Jewish immigrant journalist, Yosef Horn, wrote that Katz's success was a natural development. Polish Jews slowly forgot the words and melodies of the songs they knew from Poland, and Katz's music fit their new situation in Argentina.[97]

One of the intellectual imports from Poland was a project of secular Yiddishist schooling. Although a number of educational establishments related to various left-wing movements existed in Argentina already prior to the 1920s wave of Polish Jewish immigration, the crystallization and strengthening of the movement happened only later, largely thanks to the transnational networks of the Bund.[98] In 1924, Guitl Zak de Kanutsky immigrated to Argentina. She had been engaged in Bundist schooling in Polish Białystok, where she worked as a tailor.[99] Two years later, Zalman Orensztein, who was active in leftist Labor Zionism in his shtetl of Sokołów, arrived. After them came thousands of other Jews inspired by secular progressive Jewish movements in Poland. In 1931, Kantusky, together with Samuel Rollansky and Pinie Wald, established the Society for Secular Yiddish Schools in Argentina (*Gezelshaft far yidishe veltlekhe shuln in argentine*), which was linked to the Argentine chapter of the Bund.[100] Orensztein was a crucial figure behind a competitive network of Central Secular Yiddish School Organization (TSVYSHO) schools.[101] The new organizations were supposed to "bring to Argentina the spirit of TSYSHO schools in Poland."[102] In Argentina in the 1930s, the blossoming of secular schooling manifested a desire to build a new Yiddish life in the diaspora. Between 1934 and 1938, around 40 percent of Jewish children in Buenos Aires also went to supplementary secular-Yiddish schools.[103] In that era, Yiddish schools were multidimensional cultural institutions that attracted not only children but also served as a basis for the development of a progressive Yiddishist agenda also among adults. They offered afternoon programs for the parents and demanded that they would actively take care of Yiddish education of their offspring.

The attitude toward religion and social modernization made the Spanish-speaking proacculturation community a key ally to the Yiddishist cause. Jewish Argentines saw the TSYSHO schools as a good example of modern Jewish education, much better than the one offered locally in Argentina. Although emphasis on Yiddish and Jewish nationhood might have been controversial, a modern Jewish curriculum was aspirational. As *Mundo Israelita* commented, Argentine Jewry also needed to "end the period of infancy and dependency" and develop its own modern Jewish schools that would raise Argentine and Jewish children.[104] The daily complained that traditional Jewish education led to a distancing of Jewish youth from the Yiddish language and culture.[105] The focus on religion in regular Jewish educational establishments did not reflect the conditions of life in Argentina and a growing interest of the youth in broader universal problems. The TSYSHO was a good example of modern Jewish schooling that the acculturated Jews found a liking for. The attitude toward TSYSHO in Jewish Argentine circles exemplified a cultural re-Yiddishization of the Argentinized segments of Argentina's Jewish society. The progressive charm of Yiddishism proved to be also attractive to the acculturated Jewish Argentines.

Salomón Resnick was a person capable of uniting Yiddish and Spanish-speaking Jews, without antagonizing them or quarreling about cultural supremacy. He was deeply convinced about the vitality of Yiddish literature, welcomed its heterogeneity, and appreciated its "literary citizenship" when Yiddish received a formal recognition by the PEN Club.[106] His journal *Judaica* was a most successful attempt at drawing both back to Jewish tradition, as well as to a secular Yiddish heritage. As Leonardo Senkman wrote, Resnick helped to creatively transform the tradition of eastern European Jewry into Latin American modernity.[107] His support for Yiddish was noticed by Yiddishist establishments, who entrusted him with various tasks. In 1936, Salomón Resnick was sent by Vilna's YIVO on a research trip to Colombia, Chile, and Peru. For this purpose, YIVO, a Yiddishist authority, needed a middleman who was equally immersed in Yiddish as in Latin American culture. The nomination of Resnick was warmly welcomed by the Yiddish periodicals *Yidische Zaitung* and *Morgnzaitung*.[108] Two years later, Resnick was nominated president of Buenos Aires YIVO (IWO), which he headed until 1940.[109] Similarly, Resnick became a defender of Yiddish as a Jewish national language in his dispute with philologist Teofilo Wechsler. Wechsler argued that *castellano* (Spanish) should become the national language of Argentine Jews and accused Yiddish of being a "yellow rag decorating the attire."[110] Resnick strongly criticized Wechsler's aversion to Yiddish, named him an "outdated *maskil*," who failed to notice the development of modernist Yiddish literature in Europe and North America. For Resnick, Yiddish, as a language of the people, contributed to the cultural diversity of the world.[111]

Resnick was the editor of the journal *Judaica* (fig. 15), which, despite its Jewish-Argentine character, took part in the cultural Jewish life of the global Yiddishland.[112] *Judaica* was not only a platform that popularized translated Yiddish classics within the Spanish-speaking population but at times took a stand on Yiddishland debates. For instance, its February 1937 issue was entirely devoted to the Yiddish writer Yosef Opatoshu, and the list of contributors included Yiddish intellectuals Jacob Shatzky, H. Leivick, Osher Finkelstein, Rokhl Korn, and Kadia Molodowsky. *Judaica* welcomed Jewish culture in all its linguistic forms and was motivated to keep Argentine Jews updated about developments in Poland, the United States, and other countries. This broad geographic focus referred not only to Jewish problems. For instance, in a universalist approach, *Judaica* called on Jews to support the Spanish Republicans during the Spanish Civil War in the late 1930s. Salomón Resnick was the main contributor to Argentine-Jewish transculturation.

Further, in terms of Jewish Poland, *Judaica* kept its finger on the pulse. In 1937, the journal discussed Meier Balaban as a pioneer of Jewish historiography in Poland.[113] Another article by Moses Merkin discussed the social challenges of Polish Jewry and called upon the Jews of Argentina to extend a helping hand in a gesture of Jewish brotherhood.[114] In July of the same year, Jacob Lestschinsky, a renowned sociologist, published a detailed report about the economic crisis hitting the Jews of Poland.[115] A report written and sent from Warsaw was first-hand evidence proving that Spanish-speaking Jewish-Argentines also took an interest in Polish problems. In the same issue, Yosef Horn, a member of Argentine Poylisher Farband and a writer, informed the readers of *Judaica* about the most recent Yiddish literature in Poland. Another article discussed medieval and

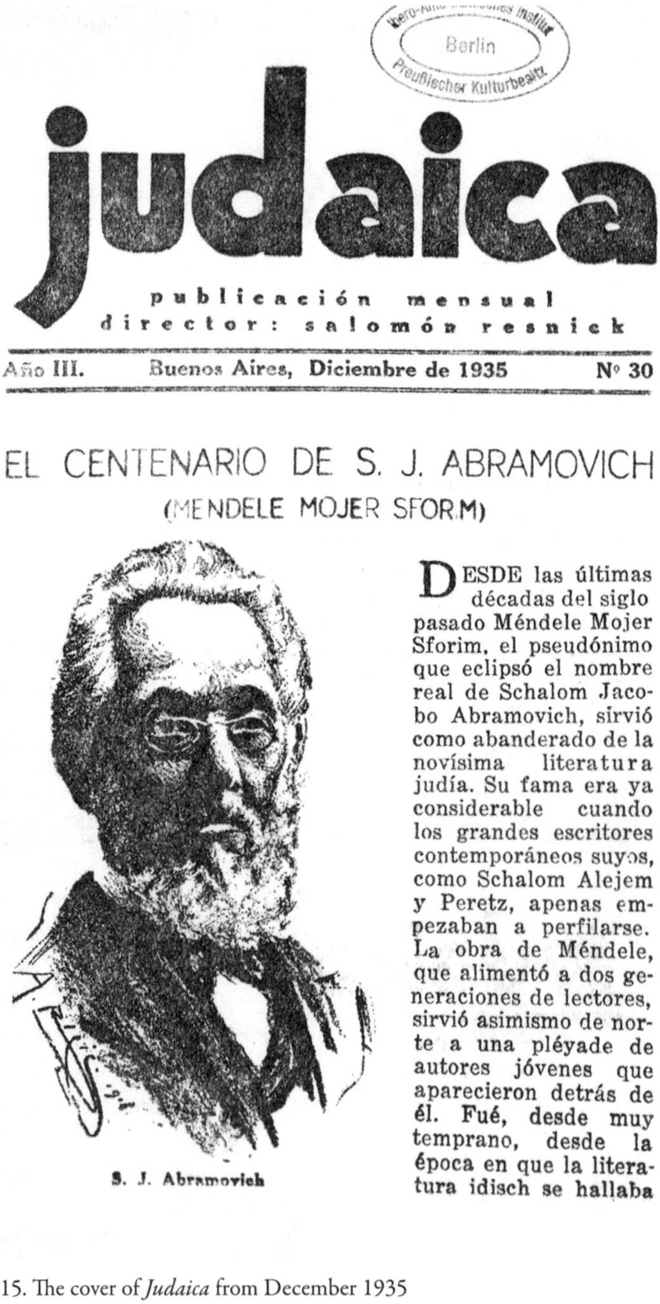

judaica

publicación mensual
director: salomón resnick

Año III. Buenos Aires, Diciembre de 1935 Nº 30

EL CENTENARIO DE S. J. ABRAMOVICH
(MENDELE MOJER SFORIM)

S. J. Abramovich

DESDE las últimas décadas del siglo pasado Méndele Mojer Sforim, el pseudónimo que eclipsó el nombre real de Schalom Jacobo Abramovich, sirvió como abanderado de la novísima literatura judía. Su fama era ya considerable cuando los grandes escritores contemporáneos suyos, como Schalom Alejem y Peretz, apenas empezaban a perfilarse. La obra de Méndele, que alimentó a dos generaciones de lectores, sirvió asimismo de norte a una pléyade de autores jóvenes que aparecieron detrás de él. Fué, desde muy temprano, desde la época en que la literatura idisch se hallaba

Figure 15. The cover of *Judaica* from December 1935

modern history of the Jews in Poland.[116] In the mid-1930s, following the sharp rise of anti-Semitism in Poland, *Mundo Israelita* also published frequent reports about the worsening situation.

The Jewish cultural sphere in Argentina was not an immigrant insular space, but a hybrid place where Argentine Jews voiced their Argentineness and yidishkayt. Their self-perception as both Argentines and Jews was not exclusive. There was no "either this or that." Salomón Resnick wrote that his journal, apart from being Jewish focused, was open to non-Jewish readers and contributors.[117] The weekly and many of its contributors and readers lived between two cultures and did not feel a need for exclusivist ethnolinguistic choices. The Jewish and the Argentine were cofertilizing each other, creating an especially interesting mixture of insights. As in other diaspora countries, the first-generation migrants derived inputs and inspiration both from their Polish-Jewish and local (here Argentine) experiences. This is articulated clearly in a pioneering essay on Jewish cultural diversity written for *Judaica* by Melech Ravitch, a Polish Jewish writer and intellectual, during his visit in Argentina in 1938.[118]

The text entitled "Bigamia cultural" explored the possibility of Jewish belonging in more than one culture and is a fine source for exploring the situation of Polish Jews living in Argentina. Explaining the phenomenon from his own example, the writer claimed his belonging to Jewish, Polish, and German cultural spaces. Ravitch clearly approached the transcultural exchange in positive terms. He wrote: "I feel richer than the cultural exclusivists. And in this aspect, I am not an exception. There are millions of individuals like me within the Jewish people and tens of millions in other nations of the planet."[119] Ravitch rejected both the concept of absolute Jewish cultural autonomy and those who endorsed "cultural assimilation." In an era of growing nationalism and biological reasoning concerning ethnicity and race, Ravitch's views brought a spirit of imminent multiculturalism in the postwar era. His article seemed to convince the newcomers that they did not need to decide whether to be Jewish or Argentine. He was sure that mixed identities were possible and that Polish, Jewish, and Spanish influences could be smoothly integrated. In that respect, Ravitch endorsed the positions of Salomón Resnick, Yosef Mendelson, and the sociocultural profile of *Judaica.*

The views of Ravitch were to some extent shared by the Argentine Yiddishist Pinie Katz, who explicitly argued in the *Judaica* that the linguistic preference that Jewish youth lately gave to Spanish did not pose a danger to Yiddish. Conversely, believing in the possibility of a coexistence of two linguistic spaces, Katz argued that the Jewish youth of Argentina were anyway connected to modern, global Jewish life and the flock of new migrants from Europe would further strengthen the local Yiddish culture. For Katz, of much greater importance were the progressive, secular, and democratic values conveyed by Yiddishism.[120] On another occasion, he rejected the presumed Yiddishist isolationism and wrote that "Jewish culture cannot remain untouched from the Argentine ambience and Argentine spirit." In an integrationist appeal, he concluded that the Argentine climate and environment influenced Jewish thoughts and feelings. Katz believed that there was a huge difference between Argentine-influenced Jewish culture (that he supported) and consciously chosen assimilation. Noticing the emergence of Jewish Argentines in place of eastern European Jewish immigrants, Katz said: "Our interests are connected with this country; and everything cultural that we brought with us, everything we get every day from the general Jewish world, and all things Jewish that we ourselves create here and in Yiddish . . . need to be imbued with local tones, different from analogous Jewish creations in Russia, Poland, North America, etc. Otherwise it would mean that we don't live in Argentina, that we breathe another air, that we don't have a clue about what's going on around us, that we have closed ourselves in an economic and spiritual ghetto."[121]

Narratives of Success/Narratives of Disillusionment and the Ethnic Visibility

Many Argentine culture makers glorified and idealized Argentina as a new Jewish safe haven. The devotion expressed toward the new homeland was part of a broader process of negotiating the nation and language in the ever-diversifying immigrant society. Writings about beauty, justice, and freedom were supposedly so prevalent in Argentina were embedded within debates about the place of Jewish immigrants in Argentina. It was a way of claiming the right to call Argentina a homeland. The attitude toward immigrant languages and immigrant literatures informed the discussion about the place that the voice of the immigrant had in the society and about what was Argentina and who were the Argentines. The minority literatures, such as Yiddish, were often accepted and endorsed by the hegemonic cultural circles if they fulfilled a goal of building a new Argentine Jewish literature and proclaimed a belonging and gratitude to the republic.[122]

Despite the often overlapping agendas, there were several observable differences between the Yiddish and Spanish-speaking Jewish Argentine cultural scenes. In Argentina in the 1920s and 1930s, Jewish literature and journalism was mostly in Yiddish, which defined it as an intragroup experience often unavailable to the outside Spanish-speaking word.[123] Those who wrote in Yiddish felt more comfortable with criticizing life in Argentina. As Alan Astro correctly noted, in Yiddish writers rarely had to engage in apologetics, whereas in gentile languages they often had to negotiate with specific agendas.[124] The texts in Spanish never catered only to Jews but always had a utilitarian agenda of "showing who we are" to non-Jewish Argentines.[125] Writing in Yiddish, the writers enjoyed the comfort zone of an intracommunal debate. Using Yiddish permitted internal Jewish discussions without the fear of being accused of a lack of gratitude to Argentina for its liberties and the chances it offered. Simultaneously, the public use of Yiddish, with its foreign alphabet, marked Jews as others, holding on to their old-country belonging. That, together with common racism, antireligious prejudice, and resentment toward the success of a ruso or a *turco*, often ranked the Jews at the bottom of Argentine society.[126]

The embrace of Argentina as a homeland was visible in the creativity of those Jewish authors who mastered Spanish enough and those who still lived in the Argentine nationalist agenda of the 1910s. In a collection of short stories (in Spanish), the writer and editor Samuel Glusberg pictured the arrival of Jewish immigrants to Argentina and their inclusion into the nation. In "Mate Amagro," a greenhorn immigrant named Petacovsky, after a short time as a peddler, decides to establish a copperplate company, together with the sons of his criollo landlord. At the beginning, Petacovsky's family fears interactions with gentiles and his wife cannot imagine cooking in the same kitchen as *goyish* women. Yet, working together with the Bermudez family, Petacovsky begins to eat *galletas* and drink mate. The Bermudez brothers give him lessons on Argentina's history, and he moves from a conventillo on calle Corales into a beautiful house on avenida Almirante Brown. His daughter receives a Christian name of Elisa, enrolls in Escuela Nacional, and when she is big enough to play, the father purchases her a piano. Glusberg's "Mate Amagro" was a story of Argentinization, of progress, and success in the new land. By writing it in Spanish, Glusberg presented the Jewish narrative to the gentile public. Jews were portrayed here as good entrepreneurs, who were eager to interact with criollos and to embrace Argentina as a homeland.[127]

Jewish belonging to Argentina was made visible in the canonical *Los gauchos judíos* (1910) by Alberto Gerchunoff. The book portrays immigrant Jews as turning into Argentines by cultivating the land and subsequently becoming like the archetypical gaucho. Gerchunoff, alluding to religious concepts, depicted the travel of Jews from oppressive Russia to generous Argentina. In this narrative, Russia appears as biblical Egypt enslaving the Jews, and Argentina as the Promised Land of Zion. By incorporating the biblical element, Gerchunoff referred to widespread Christian concepts in Argentina. The archetypical virtues of a Jew as a farmer corresponded with the virtues of a gaucho: by cultivating the pampa, immigrant Jews found appreciation in the eyes of centennial intellectuals. The Jews in *Los gauchos judíos* do not speak any Yiddish, but perfect Castilian Spanish, and seem to already be linguistically Argentine.[128] *Los gauchos judíos* functioned as a claim or request for Jewish naturalization in the country, allowing Jews to argue for their incorporation into Argentine culture.[129] As one of the best "gerchunoffians," as Edna Aizenberg put it, *Los gauchos judíos* is a story of negotiating the breach between the demands of homogeneity and the need to sustain ethnic identity.[130]

A part of immigrant Jewish cultural production and discourses directed at the non-Jews was bound to suffer from a problem characteristic of ethnic history: the overrepresentation of success and the tendency to reduce the meaning of experienced hardships, tensions, and hostilities. As Michael Humphrey put it, ethnic history has been written and forged by the successful in the context of exclusionary discourses.[131] Also, much of the scholarship on Jews in Latin America portrayed them as a homogenous, unstratified group that rapidly and exclusively moved to the middle class.[132] In that context, Yiddish literature written by immigrants is a great complementary source for uncovering the stories that ethnic leaders preferred to hide. Some Yiddish writers and cultural leaders took up the task of complicating the narrative of migration and Jewish life in Argentina in a way that would include disillusionment, misery, nostalgia, and a sense of displacement. Among others, we can mention here Pinie Wald, Moshe Granitstein, Moshe Kaufman, Hirsh Blostein, and Moisés David Guiser.

The story of agricultural colonists building Argentina and the economic and social progress of Buenos Aires did not tell the complete story of immigration. New immigrants (after 1918) belonging mostly to the working class did not share the same experiences as the successful businessmen, who in the 1920s were already sending their children to universities and well-paid professions. The division between the history of the middle class and the history of proletarian Jews was clearly visible in the days of the *Semana Trágica* in 1919, a labor unrest that transformed into an anti-Jewish pogrom in which the nationalist volunteer squads of Guardia Blanca raided the homes of numerous Jews.[133]

The attitude towards the Semana Trágica offered an interesting perspective on Jewish identities and belonging, and attitudes toward Argentina and Eastern Europe. For those who feared for their economic and social status, the strikes and unrest endangered their vital interests. At the same time, the underprivileged, new immigrant blue-collar workers saw it as a heyday of socialist struggle that ended in typical anti-Jewish violence that they knew so well from Eastern Europe. The former even asked the Argentine gentile public for forgiveness regarding "the crimes of a minority" that "could not have developed in the womb of [our] community," but were rather based in "the negation of God, *la patria* and law."[134] The acculturated leaders continued saying that Argentina was their adopted homeland and that they were loyal to the Constitution and were ready to defend the interests of the Nation. Soon afterwards, the pro-acculturation publication, *Vida Nuestra*, asked the prominent personalities of the Argentine gentile elite to answer their questionnaire about the situation of Jews in the country. As they expected, the popular figures rejected the responsibility of Jews for the recent violence and stated that the Jews were loyal and useful residents.[135] Some prominent pro-acculturation actors, such as Alberto Gerchunoff, remained silent about the events.[136]

The Poland-born proletarian leader and journalist Pinie Wald, who himself was imprisoned during the Semana Trágica, slammed the Jewish elite for presenting the Jews only as "desirable guests" without a claim of belonging to Argentina. For Wald, Jews were already rooted in Argentina as citizens with the rights guaranteed by the democratic constitution.[137] The controversies aroused in Argentina after the Semana Trágica showed how class and ideology divided the Jewish population. Wald feared for his life, did not know what the Argentine authorities planned to do with him, and felt deprived of his rights as in tsarist Russia.[138] The Argentina that appeared in Wald's narrative was violent, reactionary, and far from the ideals of freedom that brought Wald from Polish Tomaszów to Buenos Aires. The observations of Wald were very apt. The postwar economic crisis, the disarmament of the proletarian movement, and the conservative ideological transformation of the Argentine liberal elite increased the power of nationalism in Argentina. The immigrant population began to be considered a risk to the unity of the nation, for many nationalist organizations, such as *Liga Patriótica Argentina*, regarded them as a source of the presumed "dangers of the social disorder."[139]

The proletarian narratives of disillusionment often did not become a part of official history written by the burgeoning Jewish leadership. It became especially visible in the emphasis given to the mythological founding ethos of Jewish colonization and omission of narratives of poverty, conflict, and lost dreams. The process of "whitening" the history of Jewish immigration to Argentina became visible in the first decade of the twentieth century but strengthened in the 1930s. This was visible in the efforts at pushing away the memory of Jewish involvement in female trafficking. A desire not be perceived as a yishev of prostitutes and *froyen-hendler* (women trafficker) was not shared exclusively by the wealthier veteran community members. But those who were already successful particularly feared losing their good name. Tarring the entire Jewish population with female trafficking endangered their reputation as good citizens, good immigrants, and good Argentines. The same held true for reflections on the failure of Jewish colonization. The colonist enterprise was imagined as a glamorous founding of Jewish Argentina and a negation of the anti-Semitic narrative about "unproductive" Jews. The frustration of many colonists with the administration of JCA, the debts they had, or sometimes the forced immigration to the city were hardly visible in official Spanish-language channels. In contrast, criticism of colonization is visible in many Yiddish sources, including the narratives of Chasanovitch, Alpersohn, and Vital. Nonetheless, for many Yiddish-speaking poorer Jews, colonization also served as an anchor that justified the Jewish contribution to building Argentina, which balanced the negative narrative of Jews as froyen-hendler.[140]

In the 1920s and 1930s, the official, often proacculturation Jewish institutions and individuals at times attempted to ignore or disguise the surrounding immigrant misery. The leaders of Hevra Kadisha Ashkenazi (Buenos Aires elected Jewish representation) worried about the respectability and reputation of the Jews as such and opted not to focus on narratives of poverty, frustration, exploitation, and fear when constructing their ethnic history. Consequently, the ethnic narrative about early twentieth-century Argentina centered around hardworking colonists and rapidly progressing urban entrepreneurs. The 1920s immigration from Poland was often pictured as a challenge to which the veteran community responded with sympathy and assistance. In Argentina existed many middle-class-run Jewish ethnic bodies, which openly dealt with difficult and unpleasant problems like prostitution or poverty, but they performed their activities from the position of respectable, acculturated, rich *israelitas argentinos*, who feared for the reputation of Jews as a whole. Ethnic charity and welfare institutions became an arena for raising ethnic claims to an acknowledged presence in the city.

A vivid example can be found in charities like Sociedad de Socorros de Damas Israelitas de Beneficencia (Rescue Society of Israelite Ladies), Sociedad de Beneficencia "Ezrah" ("Ezrah" Charity Society), or Liga Contra Tuberculosis (League against Tuberculosis). Those standing behind these institutions were proud of their involvement in the cause of poor immigrants, but at the same time, they drew borders of separation along lines of social class, immigration, generation, and status. The Yiddish weekly *Penimer un penimlekh* regularly printed photos depicting those involved in the case of the poor, as in 1926 when journalists visited the Beis Yetoymim (orphanage). The visitors were impressed by the magnificent building of the orphanage that was a "pride for the entire Argentine Jewry."[141] Journalist Marcos Regalsky wrote that "charities and their facilities are witnesses of the creative impetus of the Jewish community."[142] The praising articles served the interest of the rich benefactors, portraying them as economically and socially successful Argentines, yet generous and devoted Jews.

Minorities claimed social respect and ethnic visibility in Argentina via economic and charitable accomplishments. For example, this was visible within "architectural ethnic expansion." In the early twentieth-century, architecture and urban planning became a space for presenting the ethnic visibility of the community within the city's architectural landscape. It was certainly true for Spanish and Italian immigrants, who wanted to mark their city apartment houses with what they perceived as their national flavor, chiefly an Art Nouveau style. The Jewish story was similar. It was made visible by landmark edifices built by Jewish architects and businessmen. For example, the Passage Teubal was built by Jaques Braguinsky and commissioned by the textile kings Teubal brothers.[143] Many communities, including German and Italian, wanted to build their own hospitals, orphanages, and the like, which was often supported by rich patrons.[144] Similarly, Jews opened their Hospital Israelita in 1921, and soon, it became the apple of the community's eye and a symbol of ethnic pride.[145]

By means of these public edifices, Jews built their sense of belonging in Buenos Aires and played the same ethnic card as other immigrant groups. Whereas the iconic big-scale endeavors were organized by upper-class organizations like Sociedad de Beneficencia de Damas Israelitas or SOPROTIMIS (Society for the Protection of Jewish Immigrants), the borders between them and the subethnic associations (such as Poylisher Farband) were not always clear.[146] As the members of smaller immigrant associations grew in wealth, many of them became involved with larger Jewish ethnic institutions and imagined themselves as Jewish Argentines. Pedro Chapov from Vengrover Faryan (from the town of Węgrów in Poland) served as head of Moshev Zkeynim, an old-age home, from 1933 to 1936, and of Beis Yetoymim, an orphanage. Poylisher Farband, which could not fund its own hospital, was very proud of its *consultorio medico*, or drop-in clinic. The welfare institutions and public edifices were rooted in a desire for ethnic visibility and respect.

The degree of actual assistance of Jewish charities and Hevra Kadisha to the poor was at times questionable. Even though between 1922 and 1926 around 25,000 immigrants arrived in Argentina from Poland, SOPROTIMIS offered its assistance to barely 3,343 souls.[147] Hevra Kadisha (AMIA from 1949) saw its role mostly in providing religiously motivated aid; yet in the 1920s and 1930s, it also focused on ethnic community assistance. Thus, it financed Moshev Zkeynim, Beis Yetoymim, and the hospital Yidisher Shpital and perceived these institutions as the "jewels" of the community. At the same time, the challenges of daily life were often neglected or pushed aside. The Jewish working poor or unemployed were supported only with symbolic amounts of money, and Hevra Kadisha hoped that other institutions would take care of the problem of Jewish poverty.[148] The mere help that the charity institutions offered did not correspond with the actual needs. It was especially visible in the early 1930s, following the economic crisis. *Dos Naye Vort* reported that both Ezrah and Hevra Kadisha reduced their assistance to the poor.[149] Charities were in constant argument, passing tasks onto each other. A *vengrover* landsman wrote that many communal leaders only searched for "tumults, noise and pomp."[150]

Silencing the narrative that included the shady side of Jewish immigration to Argentina was especially visible in anniversary publications in Spanish, which were supposed to underline the Jewish contribution to Argentina and the success stories of individuals and community. A good example is *50 años de colonización judía en la Argentina*, a 1939 volume celebrating fifty years of Jewish agricultural colonies in Argentina. The book does not mention at all the challenges faced by colonist children and their problems with making ends meet. The book, written in Spanish, opens with a quote from the Argentine constitution and serves as evidence of Jewish usefulness, productivity, and belonging to Argentina. The prologue highlights the "assimilation" of Jewish immigrants into Argentina. The Jews are euphemistically named *pueblo de la Biblia* (people of the Bible), instead of the more accurate, but sometimes negatively emotionally charged word *judío* (Jew). Argentina appears in the book as an "immaculate blue and white pavilion," whose doors were opened wide to migrants by the 1853 constitution.[151] *50 Años* quotes a full list of names of the first immigrant contingent that arrived in Buenos Aires in 1889. It establishes the internal hierarchies within the immigrant community: the heroic early agricultural pioneers versus the difficult, complaining later arrivals of the 1920s. A similarly praising and sycophantic characterization can be found in publication unsurprisingly edited by the JCA itself.[152] Interestingly, *50 Años* was based on the much longer Yiddish original *50 yor yidishe kolonizatsye in argentine*. The Yiddish version underlined the Jewish contribution to Argentina and was much less ecstatic about the situation in the country.

Similar patterns are visible in a volume commemorating twenty-five years of the existence of Poylisher Farband. The Spanish foreword to this book is full of expressions of gratitude and devotion to Argentina.[153] We read in them of Argentine hospitality, "breathing an air of liberty and equality" and a desire to see Argentina "great and powerful." It assured readers that members of the Farband faithfully celebrate Argentine national holidays on May 25 and July 9. The Yiddish foreword bore an entirely different message and emphasized the progress of the Jewish Polish community in Argentina, providing a historical summary of the last twenty-five years. The Yiddish texts praised Polish Jews as those who, as the book authors saw it, in fact built Jewish life in Argentina, starting from agricultural colonization, via the proletarian movement, to Yiddish theater. In the Yiddish introduction, there was no word about privileges that Argentina offered or any mention of proclaiming Jewish loyalty to the republic. This showed that Polish Jews adopted specific (but complementary) strategies when it came to appearances in a gentile public sphere and in an internal Jewish world. Spanish was a language of a public appearances and a channel of Jewish inclusion to the Argentine nation, as well as a way of arguing for Jewish belonging in Argentina. Yiddish, on the other hand, was an intimate language that permitted articulating what was probably deemed inappropriate in Spanish, or what was meant for the Jewish public. The immigrants needed to learn how to navigate between languages, belongings, and norms.

Conclusion

In Argentina in the 1920s and 1930s, two groups of Jews lived side by side: acculturated Jewish Argentines and Yiddish-speaking Argentine Jews. Both Spanish speakers and those who preferred Yiddish expressed their sense of belonging to Argentina, yet often had distinct views concerning the importance of the European past. The differences between both groups were not clear-cut; yet, their approaches to the questions of language, performing ethnicity, and relation to new and old homeland often differed. Those who grew up in Argentina felt comfortable in speaking Spanish, and Argentine environment was their major point of cultural reference. Interwar immigration of Polish Jews transferred national and cultural dilemmas of eastern Europe to Argentina to a certain extent. This referred foremost to language politics and Yiddish cultural nationalism—in the 1920s, Argentina experienced a certain Yiddish revival with new press titles and theaters being opened. New bonds of intellectual, cultural, and discursive exchange and dialogue made the connection between both diasporas even stronger. This change was visible in the heated intellectual discussions about the place of Jews in Argentina and their relations with the Old World. Interbellum Argentina experienced both the development of Yiddish print culture and schooling, while witnessing the growing inclusion of Jews into the nation. Argentine Jews sought ways of combining Jewishness with Argentineness. In sum, the 1920s and 1930s proved a compatibility of Jewish diasporic and Argentine belonging. In those years, discussions on the future character of Argentine Jewishness were shaped by a variety of actors with diverse positions (liberal, pro-acculturation, Yiddishist, Zionist), who searched for ways of building a foundational identity of their liking. Whereas this chapter explored how these issues were approached on the level of intellectual discussions, press debates, and literature, the next chapter focuses on the practices of merging Argentine and eastern European belonging. Looking at the activities of the Poylisher Farband, I explore how the landslayt searched for ways for voicing their interests on the local Argentine and transatlantic levels.

6

Being a "Good Polish Jew" in Buenos Aires

Landsmanshaftn and Jewish-Polish Ethnicity

The Children of Jewish Poland and of Jewish Argentina

Following the immigration of around sixty thousand Polish Jews to Argentina during the interwar years (1918–39), Buenos Aires became a home for a multitude of Polish Jewish landsmanshaftn. In 1916, Poylish yidisher farband in argentine (Polish Jewish Union in Argentina, later abbreviated as Poylisher Farband), which aspired to represent all Polish-Jewish immigrants in Argentina, was established. Landsmanshaftn were voluntary organizations that united Jewish immigrants originating from specific localities in eastern Europe. They appeared in every country to which eastern European Jews immigrated: The United States, Argentina, Canada, France, South Africa, Australia, Brazil, and so on. Unfamiliar with local customs and often initially finding it difficult to comfortably socialize with the dominant population, some immigrants preferred to build their social life within a community of their countrymen. "Hometown societies" were a product of this need, as they allowed the newcomers to communicate in their native language, discuss problems with fellow immigrants, and, no less importantly, to preserve a linkage to their homeland "on the other side of the sea."

Poylisher Farband was one of many Jewish Polish landsmanshaftn active in Argentina, and along with Bessaraber Farband (established in 1916) and Galitsianer Farband (established in 1913), one of a few with a broader regional character. Poylisher Farband wished to represent all Polish Jews in Argentina and temporarily managed to establish a federation of smaller, city-focused lansdsmanshaftn. Of all landsmanshaftn in Argentina, Poylisher Farband developed the most extensive structures and activities involved in both the process of building Argentine Jewish life and being engaged in dialogue with and about Jews in Poland. Argentine Yiddishist Pinie Katz praised Poylisher Farband as a key player in strengthening the Yiddish culture in Argentina, though in its adapted Argentine version.[1] The number of landsmanshaftn varied, making it virtually impossible to talk about their membership rates.[2] It is impossible to track if there were individuals who belonged to diverse landsmanshaftn. One of the few available sources mentions that in 1942 twenty-six landsmanshaftn operated in Buenos Aires with around

8,000 members.[3] The data presented in Zhitnitsky's article was far from complete. Only a few landsmanshaftn participated in the survey conducted by IWO Institute. Another source stated that more than a hundred landsmanshaftn were in existence in the 1930s.[4] Poylisher Farband reported that it had 1,075 male members, while emphasizing that this number was imprecise (fig. 16). Varshever Yidisher Klub (Warsaw Jewish Club) alone reported 500 members in 1939. Landmanshaft statistics become even more complicated when we check the data provided by other sources. In a letter to the Ministry of Foreign Affairs in Warsaw, the Polish Embassy in Buenos Aires claimed that in 1937 the membership in Poylisher Farband was as low as 120 persons,[5] whereas *Dos Naye Vort* wrote that in 1932 Poylisher Farband had around 2,000 members, and in 1933, the journal by then wrote about a "few thousand members."[6] Farband's 1924 almanac listed 232 members; the 1928 issue spoke of more than 400 members.

Writing about New York landsmanshaftn, Michael Weisser noted that the landsman societies "were viewed as relics of the past," claiming that the people who joined them were at the same time "rejecting the larger society and resisted the opportunities of assimilation."[7] The insularity and backwardness that Weisser ascribed to landsmanshaftn are problematic arguments. This rather erroneous vision had little to do with Argentine reality. Polish-Jewish landsmanshaftn in Buenos Aires were not afraid of Argentina and its Spanish-speaking population. What is more, the societies themselves eagerly adopted several practices and customs characteristic of Spanish-speaking society. Argentine Jews of Polish origin tried to find ways that allowed them to be self-aware Polish Jews and successful Argentines. When Poylisher Farband inaugurated their Mutual Help Committee in 1933, Rene Weksman appeared as a star singer of the gala, described as a queen of "Spanish-Jewish recitation."[8] To the applause of the gathered public, Weksman recited a Spanish poem by Rubén Darío, "Los motivos del lobo." Weksman, who appeared at numerous Jewish events, was a member of the women's section of Poylisher Farband, but at the same time was successful in broader Argentine society and was fluent in Spanish literature. Her appearance linguistically represented the diverse and inclusive Jewish-Argentineness that many *poylishe* (Polish Jews) envisioned for themselves or their children. Another example of Argentine-Jewish spaces can be found in the regular picnics organized by landsmanshaftn, usually in the forests of the Olivos neighborhood. At the time, this pastime was increasingly common among all segments of Argentine society.[9] However, by organizing exclusively Jewish landsman picnics, immigrant Jews marked the boundaries of their own subethnic community and took care of fostering intracommunal bonds. The picnics allowed them to present themselves as middle-class Argentines, who simultaneously acknowledged the importance of a shared past in Poland and a shared ethnonational belonging.

The development of the landsman movement was not always welcomed in

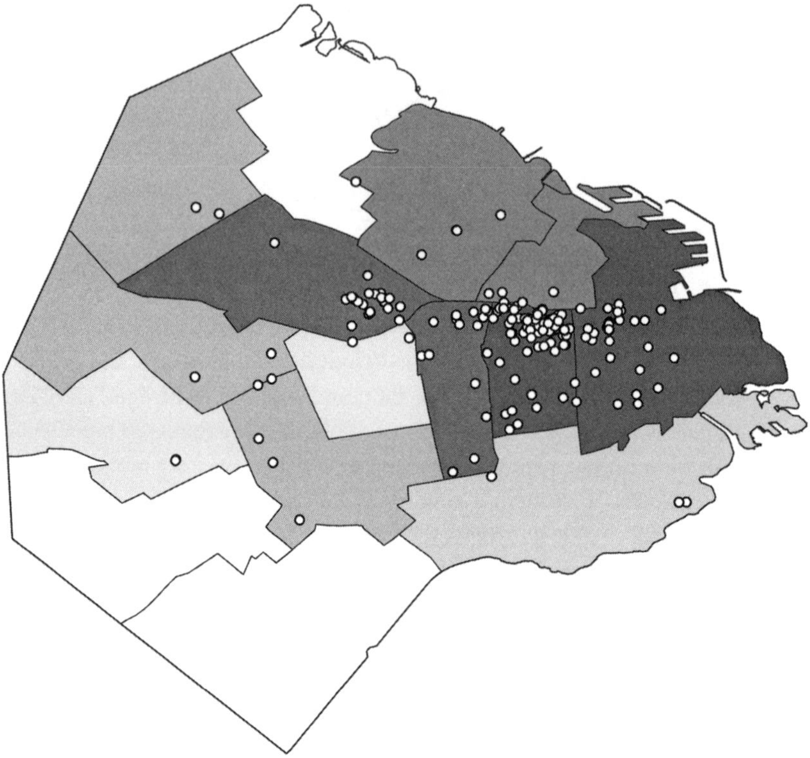

Figure 16. Members of Poylisher Farband according to their place of residence in Buenos Aires, 1928. Based on the addresses published in the 1928 almanac of the Farband. The map shows the concentration of the landslayt in Once, a growing new center in the west in Villa Crespo, as well as some successful individuals who lived in the old core of the city.

Jewish Argentina, especially by the proacculturation Jews and left-wing internationalist Jewish circles. Founding a specifically Jewish Polish institution was regarded by some of its adversaries as endangering the project of building a new, specifically Argentine Jewry. Both those who opted for quick Jewish inclusion in the Argentine nation and those who supported internationalist positions often saw landsmanshaftn as reactionary and isolationists. In 1928, the proacculturation daily *Mundo Israelita* published an article against the presumed *espiritu localista*, a localist spirit of the landslayt, an allusion to Polish Jews.[10] Its author rejected any significant differences between immigrants from various European countries and referred to the infeasibility of conducting big scale projects by landsmanshaftn. He supported the engagement with specific Jewish communities abroad, but only united, as Argentine Jews, rather than as separate Polish Jewish groupings. He saw the fragmentation as an obstacle in institutional development and as a challenge endangering the formation of Argentine Jewry. This critical voice was typical for representatives of an earlier immigration wave, who arrived in Argentina as small children or were born there. From their perspective, the Polish Jews arriving in the 1920s were reminders of the eastern European roots among proacculturation Jews and of their unstable position in Argentine society. For many veteran immigrant Jews, the landsmanshaftn embodied the ethnic separatism that could hinder their efforts of being seen as part and parcel of the Argentine nation.

Of course, hometown societies were not a particularly Jewish phenomenon but were characteristic of a majority of newly established immigrant communities. Similar ethnic organizations were formed by other groups of European immigrants: Poles had their *ziomkostwa*, Germans their *Vereine*, and Spaniards their *uniones de residentes*. In Argentina, Germans and Frenchmen, who arrived in the first half of the nineteenth century, established their fraternal organization several decades earlier than the Jews, whereas Spaniards and Italians numerically outnumbered any other European immigrant group. The principles guiding the establishment and management of these associations were largely the same. Primarily, they united mostly immigrant males, offering them various benefits such as financial support in case of unemployment or need, medical assistance, or assistance in issuing immigration invitations for family members. Second, ethnic organizations helped their members to progress economically by establishing credit institutions and cooperatives that offered financial support and security often unavailable elsewhere. Finally, the hometown societies nurtured and enforced the subethnic identification of the immigrants. Their homey atmosphere and feeling of being among kin were key arguments that hometown societies used to attract new members.

The fraternal immigrant societies around the world were based on the same principle of solidarity, and their initial activities concentrated on helping the sick, the poor, and the new immigrants. During the first years of their existence, immigrant societies functioned largely like an insurance company, or "safety networks" as Tobias Brinkman called them, and provided their members with a sense of security in case of emergency.[11] They emerged from the developing proletarian culture, represented the interests of artisans and workers who made up the Argentine working class, and "aspired to be a space without the control of the powerful and rich."[12] Mutualist immigrant societies aimed to prove that popular organizations could provide immigrants with what the Argentine state failed to offer them: security in case of accident, poverty, or sickness.[13] The security and financial support they offered allowed members to make their life easier. Even small Jewish hometown societies decided very early to found their own credit institutions, so-called *lay-kases*, that offered members low or noncommission loans. The lay-kases helped immigrant Jews to establish their own shops and factories and consequently to leave the urban proletariat and move into the middle class.

With time, the lay-kases also evolved into proper banks, like Banco Israelita Polaco, reflecting the general burgeoning of Jewish immigrants.

The paradigms of a melting pot, as in the United States, or Argentine crisol de razas, which saw immigrants as rather passive objects of assimilation, did not reflect the landslayt's multiple commitments and belongings. Most of the studies on the landsman movement were reduced to a dichotomy between assimilation and cultural retention.[14] This study goes beyond this and includes the transatlantic aspect of ethnic and political mobilization. Throughout the interwar period, the "looking back to Europe" landsmanshaftn members (and their families) did form one of the many components of American and Argentine Jewish identities. Reducing immigrant Jewish experiences to the desire of embracing and succeeding in a new country is an oversimplification of this complex story. Interwar Jewish Argentina was an extremely diverse and heterogeneous collective. This country, although often attractive and promising individual liberties and rights, was at the periphery of the Jewish world.[15] In that context, the immigrants from Poland often related to their European homeland, which until 1939 remained the key vibrant center of Jewish life. Landsman organizations, underlining the importance of a common origin, which was supposed to function as a binding thread bringing together people of different class backgrounds, marked the central role of the Yiddish language and the eastern European past.[16] Also, for those who already acculturated and preferred reading *Mundo Israelita* over the Yiddish dailies, Poland remained a significant reference point. Integration within Argentine society, while maintaining a transnational conversation with Jewish Poland, was, despite the tensions, compatible and possible.[17] Poylisher Farband could both raise money for the Yiddish schools in Poland and at the same time buy the actions of Fomento Agrario to develop Argentine "national agriculture." This chapter sheds light on the experiences of Jewish immigrants who did not separate themselves from their Polish past with a thick line of oblivion but rather drew new lines of connection that linked Jewish realities in Poland and in Argentina.

A global transnational network of landsman institutions often directly connected the members of Jewish landsmanshaftn. This was visible both on the level of the local "hometown" and a broader Polish Jewish level. The Białystok landslayt analyzed by Rebecca Kobrin had a common "Białystok agenda" that transcended political and geographical borders.[18] The conviction about common interests and responsibilities of Polish Jews was also shared by delegates of the Polish-Jewish diasporas who congregated in international conferences, such as the World Congress of Polish Jews in London in 1935. Consequently, the activities and functioning of the landsmanshaftn were often influenced externally and embraced the transnational character of a worldwide Polish-Jewish diaspora. The interwar years were the heyday of transnational Jewish networking, whether it concerned emigration policies, combating anti-Semitism, or financial aid. A shared Yiddish language facilitated this. In Argentina, Yiddish remained the key language of discussions and publications, marking the involvement of Argentine Jews in the world of a transnational Yiddishland and their stronger rootedness in the Yiddish-speaking world. The language chosen by the landslayt (at least in their publications and minutes) emphasized the relevance of ethnonational Yiddish culture to landslayt identities and their embeddedness in the progressive Yiddish-centered cultural projects.

Even though most of the Jewish immigrants from Poland did not join the landsmanshaftn and chose different ways of being Jewish and Argentine, landsmanshaftn were still an important component that shaped the character of the emerging Argentine Jewry in the 1920s and 1930s. The interwar landslayt history has largely been forgotten, as their engagement with the European old countries, Yiddish language, and culture was overshadowed by the postwar supremacy of Zionism in the organized Argentine Jewish community of the post–World War II years. In this regard, landsmanshaften shared the fate of non-Zionist Jewish forms of ethnonationalism that were analogically marginalized in the historiography.[19] At the same time, after 1945 the landsmanshaftn often limited their activities to commemorating the Old World destroyed by the Holocaust and were consequently later remembered mainly as "commemoration clubs."[20] Their prewar ethnic discourses, engagement in Argentine place-making, and transnational networking were covered by oblivion or were undermined as nostalgic and marginal.

The Argentine landsmanshaftn were spaces where new "dual" or "hyphenated" identities were formed. The landsmanshaftn allowed their members to smoothly integrate into the society of the new country with respect to the old country habits and the new diasporic belongings. Landsmanshaftn were not insular spaces where the old country was fanatically worshiped but a space for defining and formulating new kinds of identities, adjusted to the life of the new country. As Daniel Soyer emphasized, both continuation and transformation defined the immigrant experience in the New World.[21] Landsmanshaftn helped Jewish immigrants to find themselves in the new country, without renouncing their eastern European heritage. The democratic character of the landsmanshaftn helped their members to feel more secure in social and political activism. The landsmanshaftn served as an "ethnic training room" for social engagement that was later, or simultaneously, performed outside of lansdmanshaft sphere. While they nurtured subethnic identities, they also enhanced the wider Jewish and Argentine identities of their members.

Polish Brothers—Poylisher Farband in Argentina

Poylisher Farband evolved from previously formed ethnic organizations of Polish Jews. The Vengrover Landslayt Farayn (from Węgrów, Poland), together with a dozen young immigrants from Łódź, founded Agudas Ahim (Union of Brothers), the first strictly Polish-Jewish organization in Argentina. The landslayt, narrating the 1916 establishment of Agudas Ahim, wrote that the organization was established as a consequence of the outbreak of World War I, which limited contacts with their hometowns and families in Europe.[22] Well aware of the dire situation in war-torn Europe, the landslayt wanted to find ways of helping their families and communities in Poland. However, the establishment of a distinct Polish-Jewish relief subcommittee within the general Tsentral komitet far di yidishe milkhome laydende (Central Committee for Jewish War Victims) had additional motivations. As Rebecca Kobrin suggested, many Polish Jews aspired "to carve a niche" for themselves within Argentine Jewish society.[23] They did not want to be labeled as rusos (Russians), a popular moniker for all Ashkenazi immigrants, who were popularly linked with anarchism and revolutionary rhetoric.[24] The same happened in Palestine when Russian Jews also occupied a dominant position in the Yishuv, defining its society and concepts of Jewish "nationhood."[25] By emphasizing their distinct Polish-Jewish origins, the founders of Agudas Ahim began an emancipatory discussion about subethnic Polish-Jewish immigrant identities. My examination of Polish-Jewish subethnicity questions the often falsely monolithic visions of Argentine Ashkenazi Jews.

After 1918, Jews in Poland ceased to be one of the many minorities merged together within multinational empires and found themselves in a new nation-state. In that context, the independence of Poland shattered the old geographies and belongings, while new questions appeared: What does it mean to be a Jew from Poland in Argentina? Are Polish Jews different from other eastern European Jewish newcomers? What is and what should be the relation between those who left Polish lands and the new Polish authorities? After emigration, the common origin assumed more significance, and Polish-Jewish subethnicity became more pronounced.[26] The 1916 establishment of Poylisher Farband was an outcome of ethnic mobilization brought about by the outbreak of war into the world of Polish-Jewish immigrants in Argentina. The same happened among Polish-Jewish immigrants in Palestine. Prior to 1918, Abraham Polak argued, Polish Jews in the Land of Israel were not even considered Polish, and Polish-Jewish associations were established only after Poland regained its independence in 1918.[27] The fall of the European empires raised new questions about Jewish identities and loyalties. It all came together with the development of Zionism (and non-Zionist Jewish national movements) and revived debates about Jewish nationality and the place of Jews in the new nation-states. The establishment of the Argentine Agudas Ahim was one of the answers for these new questions and challenges.

The Hebrew name of the newly founded organization connected it to traditional Jewish charitable institutions like Hevra Kadisha, Linat Hatsedek, and Bikur Holim. Agudas Ahim was, however, far removed from Jewish orthodoxy. In a photo showing its founders, we see a group of young, fashionably dressed,

Figure 17. The founders of Poylisher Farband in 1916 (the photo shows members of Farband's relief committee for Jewish war victims). Photo from *Poylishe yidn in doyrem amerike* (Buenos Aires, 1941), 53.

smoothly shaven men (except for one) (fig. 17). Even though no one wore traditional Jewish garb, the members chose to emphasize the religious background of Jewish charity. The organization's name was quickly lengthened to Poylish Yidisher Farayn Agudas Ahim (Polish Jewish Union of Brothers).[28] Marking the rising aspirations of association's leaders, the name was changed to Poylish Yidisher Farband in Argentine (in 1925).[29] What might seem like an unimportant change of labels was in fact a sign of a meaningful transformation within the organization. First of all, some progressive *poylishe* hesitated to join an institution with a quasi-religious name.[30] Secondly, it signified that an organization that was previously a classic landsmanshaft, assisting needy members and new immigrants, now sought to become the representative ethnic body of all Polish Jews in Argentina. Farband leaders saw the Poylisher Farband and Argentina's Polish-Jewish community as branches of a worldwide Polish-Jewish diaspora, and the organization was increasingly interested in underlining its transnational engagement and permanent contact with Jewish Poland and other parts of the Yiddishland. A landsman leader, David Aizenberg, used the term "Argentine part of Polish Jewry" to describe the Polish-Jewish community in Argentina.[31]

The founders of the landsmanshaftn, including those of Poylisher Farband, were usually young males who had arrived in Argentina five to ten years prior, in the wake of Russia's revolution of 1905. They and many other immigrants belonged to a generation of young blue-collar workers from industrial centers, such as Łódź or Białystok, usually with some partisan and union experience.[32] Emblematic of this generation of immigrants was Abraham Fridman. He was born in 1877 in Lublin, Poland, but as a young man left for industrializing Łódź, where he worked in the textile industry. Fridman, who was close to left-wing party Poaley Tsiyon, immigrated to Argentina in 1907. In 1916, he was one of the leading figures behind the establishment of Agudas Ahim and the landsmanshaft's president of many years.[33] More left-wing immigrants, often convinced of internationalism and the inevitable decline of nationalism, stood aside from the landsman movement.[34] Pinie (Pinye or Pedro) Wald (1886–1966) was a good example of this trend. Born in Tomaszów in central Poland, he moved to Łódź at the age of thirteen and became a Bundist activist (the party was then illegal in Russian Poland). In 1906, following the persecution of the 1905 revolutionaries, Wald left for Argentina. Wald quickly and easily engaged in leftist Jewish politics in Buenos Aires, cofounding the socialist workers' organization Vanguardia and writing for the movement's paper *Der Avangard*. In the 1920s, he helped to establish the Argentine branch of YIVO (IWO) and for the rest of his life served as editor of the left-wing Yiddish daily *Di Presse*. Wald never joined the Poylisher Farband, declaring that he felt more Argentine than Polish, yet his journalistic texts often dealt with Polish-Jewish issues and he engaged in help campaigns for Bundist schools in Poland.[35]

The post-1918 immigration wave catalyzed the development of the landsman movement. The Węgrów landslayt recalled that the sociocultural changes in Poland also had an influence in Argentina. Migrants to Argentina imported the new secular Yiddish culture, shaping the way that landsmanshaft functioned. Whereas in New York many landsmanshaftn were initially centered around synagogues and prayer houses, from the very beginning, landsmanshaftn had a more ethnic than religious character in Argentina. The vengrover landsman Leizer Kochan wrote: "Religious sentiments and Hassidic fanaticism have characterized the life of our town [Węgrów]. But the war [World War I] came, and afterwards a new refreshing breath of cultural activities that transformed the *shuln* and Hassidic *shtetls* into libraries and secular schools. The traditional lifestyle of a shtetl got a new rhythm, one felt a new air. The youth grew in the spirit of secular culture, with interest in Yiddish literature and with social awareness. This new generation, which for various reasons, but mostly due to economic factors, was forced to emigrate, brought to Argentina cultural and social baggage that had a strong influence on the activities of your Farayn."[36]

At the same time, the founding of an ethnic organization of Polish Jews was prompted by local Argentine phenomena. The establishment of formal Polish-Jewish representation was also an attempt to free the Polish-Jewish community from what they regarded as a shameful link between the community and Argentina's pimps and prostitutes, many of whom came from Poland. Meir Lerner remembered that when he came to Buenos Aires in 1921, he immediately felt like the "other" and that he was "looked down from above" when he told people he came from Poland. Although Lerner was convinced that there should be no geographical divisions between Jews, he believed that these were the internal dynamics of Buenos Aires Jewry that forced the poylishe to form a separate institution.[37] Although the immigrants from Poland constituted only a portion of Buenos Aires's paid-sex underworld, Polish Jews became popularly associated with female trafficking.[38] It might only be a slight exaggeration to say that in early twentieth-century Buenos Aires, to be a *polaca* meant to be a prostitute, and to be a *polaco* meant to be a pimp. Sometimes the derogatory vocabulary was used to refer to Jews as such in general. Isaias Lerner recalled that in the late 1930s this manner of referring to Jews was often transformed into an insult when a ruso or polaco was embellished with adjectives like *sucio* (dirty).[39] These evoked concerns about the ethnic respectability of Polish Jews that the Poylisher Farband sought to address.

Also, according to its president Abraham Fridman, the Poylisher Farband was established in order to separate the respectable Polish Jewry from the *shvartse mishpokhe* ("black family," a Yiddish label for the sex underworld). Fridman lamented that the Jewish-Polish "families of honor" were insulted by other Argentines because of their Polish descent. In this situation, many Buenos Aires Polish Jews welcomed the establishment of Poylisher Farband. It was, as Fridman said, "the first attempt to get rid of the dirt thrown on Polish Jews."[40] Another Polish-Jewish landsman, Jacobo Pukach, recalled that the landsmanshaftn isolated the pimps and did not allow them to join the landsmanshaft.[41] The statute of the Poylisher Farband precisely required a good moral standing, and "unmoral occupation" led to exclusion from the association.[42] At the beginning of the century, membership in a landsman organization was imagined as a guarantee of honesty and a symbolic defense shield of Polish Jews in Argentina.[43]

The foundation of the Poylisher Farband was, to an extent, successful in establishing a barrier between those involved in the sex underworld and the presumably honest rest of the immigrants. Félix Hershkovich, Farband's president in 1928, wrote that it was absurd to continue repeating the same story of Polish Jews involved in female trafficking.[44] Hershkovich saw more than a decade of benevolent and honest activities of the Farband as sufficient proof of the virtue and integrity of Jewish Polish immigrants. In 1933, an unnamed poylisher landsman argued that it was Jews from other regions who in his view formed racist stereotypes about the moral deficiencies of Polish Jews. Anti-Polish sentiments from the side of Bessarabian, Lithuanian, or Russian Jews apparently regarded Polish immigrants to be of lower status and devoid of morality. The angry author counterpunched by stating that Polish Jews should be proud of their achievements in

Argentina and use them as the basis for developing a positive Polish-Jewish identity in Argentina.[45] A Polish Jewish immigrant Meir Lerner believed that in the mid-1930 the discrimination of Polish Jews decreased, but it was still noticeable.

The landsmanshaftn aspired to provide the greenhorns, especially the poor ones, with a sense of communal empowerment, allowing those serving as ethnic communal leaders to present themselves as functionaries of powerful institutions. Argentine landsmanshaftn, even those who brought together fewer than fifty members, had an extended structure, with a president, several deputy presidents, an executive commission, a culture commission, an audit commission, a women's section, and so on. Numerous posts allowed the landslayt to envision themselves as important figures, who could influence not only the situation of their landslayt in Argentina but also generously help their hometowns in eastern Europe. Although the official goals of the landsmanshaftn were community oriented, the outcome also fostered a place for self-declared ethnic leaders, who used social welfare as a space to claim individual agendas.[46]

Natan Fruchter, writing in 1929 for the almanac of Galitsianer Farband, pointed out that although most of its members were workers, *petit* merchants or artisans, the more well-to-do members were also increasingly present. The situation in the Poylisher Farband was similar (table 5).[47] To the complaint and dismay of Fruchter, the successful landslayt, such as business and factory owners, did not support the landsmanshaftn enough.[48] The Yiddishist leader Pinie Katz added that the same was also true for Jewish professionals (doctors, lawyers, engineers).[49] For this group of people, the landsmanshaftn ceased to have the function of a mutual help society but was rather a framework for showing their middle-class aspirations when serving in top landsman positions. This was perfectly visible in the greetings from the landslayt printed in the 1941 jubilee publication of Poylisher Farband, where we see the landsmanshaft members photographed as successful businessmen in their factories or stock houses. Similar patterns were characteristic of other immigrant groups: the Japanese and Danish ethnic leaders in Latin America were often those who achieved financial fortune and social standing.[50]

In the 1930s, immigrants increasingly played important roles and the landsmanshaftn adopted a more middle-class character. The 1930s witnessed the economic progress of Jewish immigrants and the subsequent evolution of their status in Argentina and their self-perception as new Jewish Argentines. Many members were rich merchants or even worked in the free professions. Farband's president in the 1920s, Abraham Hersh Fridman, was a successful entrepreneur, an owner of a large hat factory named Varsovia on Avenida Boedo in Buenos Aires.[51] His son Jacobo was a well-known doctor and head of department in Hospital Ramos Mejía.[52] Abraham Yitskhok Bal, one of the founders of Poylisher Farband in 1916 and an ex-Farband president, co-owned a textile business and worked in Nuevo

Table. 5. The Professional Structure of Poylisher Farband in 1924

Number of members	Profession
118	artisans (tailors, shoemakers, jewelers, etc.)
39	workers (proletariat)
39	*cuenteniks*—peddlers
25	merchants
12	free professions (clerks, teachers, writers)

Source: Prepared by Pinie Katz for *Almanakh 1928. Ferter zamlbukh aroysgegeben fun poylish yidishn farband in argentine*, ed. Moisés David Guiser, 57 (Buenos Aires: Poylish Yidisher Farband in Argentine, 1928) (Buenos Aires, 1928).
Note: Only half of the members answered Katz's questionnaire. The table includes Katz's calculation for entire membership.

Banco Argentino in the 1930s. Abraham Feuerman, who was active in the Poylisher Farband for years, at the same time owned a shoe factory employing more than 160 people. Landsman Gustavo Zielony owned a company importing and selling wool and other fabrics.[53] Boris Knobel was a head of Banco Israelita Polaco de Buenos Aires and later of Banco Israelita de Credito de Beunos Aires.[54] Their economic prosperity as immigrant Jews in Argentina was unquestionable. They led comfortable lives in Argentina, probably spoke good Spanish, and could see themselves as a part of an aspiring Buenos Aires entrepreneurial middle class. At the same time, Fridman, Bal, Zielony, and Knobel stressed their Jewish Polish origins and their commitment to less fortunate immigrants. For some landsman activists, their success in Argentina also meant a sense of obligation to the social and cultural work of the local Polish-Jewish community. Their personas, and the landsman movement as such, embodied "the Jewish" and "the Argentine" that combined almost seamlessly.

The immigrant societies reinforced and channeled existing solidarity among national, regional, and religious groups. As the immigrants were often in a weaker socioeconomic position than the Argentine born, the intracommunal solidarity proved to be a useful strategy. For instance, Fayvel Gross, who owned a restaurant on Guardia Vieja St. in Buenos Aires called on fellow Polish landslayt to dine and organize family parties at his venue.[55] In a joking way, Gross suggested that by visiting his restaurant the poylishe helped a landsman "to stand on his own feet." Eating Polish food at a landsman-owned restaurant was presented by Gross as a landsman obligation similar to publishing souvenir almanacs or joining a farayn. Banco Israelita-Polaco, for its part, promised to be the most reliable institution for all Polish-Jewish *komertsiantes, industrieln*, and *talleristn* (merchants, industrialists, and workshop owners).[56] Consequently, the shared ethnic background was translated into a discourse and practice of ethnic solidarity.

The establishment of landsmanshaftn was not an easy endeavor. Although it might seem natural that immigrants from the same town decided to join forces and establish an institution of mutual help, the reality in early twentieth-century Argentina was more complex. Immigrants from big urban centers found it hard to start their institutions. Pre-1918 initiatives to form a landsmanshaft by former residents of Warsaw, Łódź, Lublin, and Lemberg (Lwów after 1918) were unsuccessful. Some landsmanshaftn often functioned for only a few years, then went defunct, and sometimes reappeared. The relatively late appearance of the landsmanshaftn uniting ex-residents of big Polish cities could be explained by the fact that the newcomers from big urban centers had rarely known each other before coming to Argentina. The situation was different in the case of shtetls and small towns of a few thousand residents. The premigration networks might have helped to build the communal, often informal, networks in Argentina. This was the case with Vengrover Landslayt Farayn, apparently the first hometown society established in Argentina.[57] Spatially broader countrywide landsmanshaftn were funded on the eve or during World War I: Austro-Hungarian in 1913 (transformed into Galitsianer Farband in 1925), Polish in 1916, and Bessarabian in 1916.[58]

According to the landslayt, the emphasis given to a distinct Polish origin was not intended to exclude non-Polish Jews. As Argentine landsman Meier Iagodinsky put it in 1941, "highlighting *Polishness* was not meant to draw borders, but to emphasize our contribution to the new land."[59] According to Marek Turkow, a writer and Yiddish activist, the Jews in Poland expected the involvement of Jewish Polish diasporas in Poland's internal problems. In Turkow's view, the landsmanshaftn needed to adjust to new conditions and reality. He suggested that they reinvent themselves from networks of immigrants to subethnic associations with a transnational agenda.[60] Writing in 1937, before his emigration from Poland to Argentina, Turkow stressed that in a period of growing anti-Semitism in Poland, Polish Jews abroad were obliged to build strong and popular organizations that would support Poland's Jewish community. Turkow demanded both financial and "moral" support, which he understood as exercising external pressure on Polish authorities directly or via local governments. Turkow attempted to bring forward his concepts during his later service in top positions of Argentine Jewish institutions. The landsmanshaftn served as an important space where the connection between urban regionalism and Jewish identity was debated and imagined.[61] These organizations were a space where the self-understanding of the Polish-Jewish immigrants in Argentina was being negotiated. Behind the facade of landsman nostalgias and seemingly unimportant and repetitious community events, the landsmanshaftn sources allow to dig for traces of transnational Jewish engagement and the fluctuating collective and individual identities of the migrants.

Landsman Sociability and Making Home in Argentina

Although the landsman organizations might have presented themselves as official and structured bodies, they were also a place for intimate discussions and interactions. Polish Jewishness in Argentina was articulated not only through congresses and journals but also during landsman family parties and picnics that brought together a community that believed in the ethnic importance of time spent with fellow Polish Jews. As numerous press articles, memoirs, and landsman publications stated, the landsmanshaftn were designed as a space of intimacy and inclusion, where Yiddish could be spoken and the problems of the immigrant Jewish community were central to discussions. The landslayt argued that one of their chief goals was to maintain traditional and comfortable social relations in the Old World milieu. In that sense, landsmanshaftn were an important space for Jewish immigrants in their Argentine place making.[62]

The landsmanshaftn developed an extended system of libraries, youth clubs, women's sections, social and family events, and periodicals, which served lansdlayt social and cultural needs or interests. They promoted intragroup interactions and served as venues offering specific cultural contents unavailable in gentile establishments, but with time became spaces where hyphenated Jewish Argentineness was negotiated. Following landsman terminology, landsman "salons," libraries, and clubs allowed the patrons to immerse themselves in what was called a *heymishe svive*, a homey environment.[63] Landsman Borekh Ismach claimed that the atmosphere of familiarity and security that the landsmanshaftn offered helped immigrants to find their place in Argentina and to earn a living independently.[64] A landsman from Ostróg recalled that after a day of hard work, the immigrants felt miserable and meeting a countryman at a landsmanshaft club was their biggest happiness.[65]

Heymishe svive is a key term for discussing the emotional meaning of the landsmanshaft for their members. It appeared over and over again in the landsmanshaft brochures inviting guests to events and in texts on Farband's history written by its members. Heymishe svive was also used as a slogan for recruiting new members. The term defined landsmanshaftn as a space of intimacy and a sui generis extension of the eastern European home. David Szyszacki, a secretary of IWO in the postwar period, recalled that new immigrants often turned to landsmanshaftn in order to talk about people and stories that the landslayt coming from the same town knew.[66] In addition, Abraham Milberg remembered that even though he almost did not know anyone when he first came to the Vengrover Farayn, the conversations about his hometown created an atmosphere of intimacy and "heymishkayt" that allowed him to forget his economic problems.[67] Some opted to come first to the small town *faraynen*, rather than to associate with bigger institutions like Poylisher Farband or Galitsianer Farband.

For example, heymishe svive could be found in the headquarters of Poylisher Farband at Junin Street in the Once neighborhood in Buenos Aires. The organization repeatedly invited new members with a promise of a "homey environment and warm relations."[68] By homey, the landslayt probably understood the possibility of spending time chatting in Yiddish with countrymen, playing chess, or reading books and newspapers. The first almanac of Poylisher Farband in 1924 clearly pointed out that "every Polish Jew in Argentina should become a member of the Farband," and those who would not help to establish the Farband "should feel ashamed."[69] In the Ostrog-Voliner Farayn, everyone contributed something to the landsmanshaft club: some brought cakes, other renovation equipment. An *ostroger* landsman, Haim Glaizer, often gave musical performances.[70] The landsmanshaft "salon" was supposedly especially important for the new immigrants who longed for a "Jewish book, a Jewish word, a Jewish song."[71]

Another landsmanshaft, the Varshever Yidisher Klub, described its salon in the following way: "Everyone who visited the Varshever Yiddisher Klub would confirm that the Klub is one big social home, where the members find an intimate, friendly, homey environment. Every evening the club is full of people. Old and young. Everyone finds something for himself. The young ones enjoy their sport games or just chat, others play board games like domino, chess or damka. Dozens of people occupy the reading room, immersed in interesting articles or books."[72]

In order to provide their members with cultural subjects, almost every landsmanshaft aspired to have its own *lokal* (landsmanshaft headquarters or club) that would host landsman meetings and serve as a substitute for their eastern European hometown. Possessing one's own lokal was also a sign of the community's prosperity, stability, and prestige within the landsman microcosm. Poylisher Farband had its first seat at Junin 447, but the lokal turned out to be insufficient for the growing needs and functions of the organizations. Raising money for the new lokal for Poylisher Farband in 1924, its leaders called upon all Polish Jews to buy the so-called bricks to help build Farband's headquarters. The contribution was seen as a communal and ethnic obligation, and those who refused to support the call were supposed to, again, "feel ashamed."[73] The lokaln were usually rented in areas densely populated by Jews, like Once or Villa Crespo in Buenos Aires. For bigger events, more spacious venues needed to be acquired: in 1937 Galitsianer Farband rented a salon of the Unión de Tramvíarios to host its dance party.[74] Some of the events were held in theaters, such as Ombú or Excelsior. Cinema Cataluña at Corrientes Street even offered discounts for Jewish events.[75]

The landslayt lokal needed to be filled with cultural material. The landsmanshaft leaders highly praised both Jewish high culture and popular cultural events. Poylisher Farband claimed to be the "first on the Jewish street" to sport a bar that quickly became a popular venue. The farband also had a library and a read-

Figure 18. The reading room of Poylisher Farband in 1928, *Dos Naye Vort*, November 23, 1928

ing room with newspapers and magazines from Poland, the United States, and Palestine (fig. 18). The library included books by Jewish authors, as well as general European literature. The library was supposed to elevate the cultural level of the immigrants but also to allow them to remain up-to-date with cultural and social life in the alter heym, with which, as the landslayt claimed, every member was strongly connected.[76] The libraries also had a local, Argentine focus. The recently arrived immigrants could learn Spanish in evening courses, and everyone could find advice about migration and naturalization problems.[77] Galitsianer Farband had its own drama section that organized private performances of classic Yiddish theater pieces. The Galitsianers regularly organized picnics, *matinées danzantes* (dancing parties for the youth), and attracted their members with an extended cultural offer.[78]

Proud of the recent cultural accomplishments of Jews in Poland, Polish-Jewish immigrants in Argentina aspired to continue this cultural tradition. In 1939, the construction of Central Yiddish Library (Tsentrale Yidishe Biblyotek, coordinated by IWO) was initiated. Yosef Horn, a recent Yiddish journalist newcomer from Poland, calling for financial support for this initiative, wrote that "the Polish Jews in Argentina will not insult the honor of the cultural traditions of the Old Home."[79] Access to books and newspapers in Yiddish was especially important for those who did not read Spanish. The functions of the libraries were then broad and were part of a process of the "social progress" and "enlightenment" of the working class.[80] As Alejandro Dujovne showed, prior to 1939 most of the books available in Buenos Aires Yiddish libraries and bookstores were published in Poland.[81] For instance, the available books included those by renowned publishers like Kletskin Farlag from Vilna (later Warsaw) or Gitlin (Warsaw).[82] By reading the books imported from Poland, the landslayt participated in the circulation of Yiddish cultural contents between Poland and Argentina. This practice speaks to the deficiencies of the Argentine Yiddish book market, the domination of Old World cultural production in the "colonies of Yiddishland," and the interests and preferences of the landslayt. In landsmanshaftn reading rooms, the international Jewish press was also available. With time, the landsman libraries came to include books in Spanish, and Spanish translations of classic Yiddish texts began to be more available.[83]

Throughout the 1930s, Kultur-tsenter "Moritz Minkovsky" (or Centro Minkovsky in Spanish) was the main establishment of Poylisher Farband that served landsman social and cultural needs.[84] The earlier *kultur-sektsye* (culture section) was transformed into a separate institution named after the famous Jewish Polish painter Maurycy (Mauricio, Moritz) Minkowski (Minkovsky). In the mid-1920s, future Argentine Yiddishist leader Samuel Rollansky coordinated the cultural program of Poylisher Farband.[85] Centro Minkovsky organized diverse cultural events that expressed the Argentine needs and preferences of the landslayt and their families. On September 25, 1937, the centro hosted a Gran Velada Danzante, where both younger and older members could dance to "continental jazz" and live music performed by a saxophone quartet. In the same year, the centro purchased ping-pong tables that were "enthusiastically welcomed" by members and associates. The centro was also a venue where smaller banquets were hosted. Kultur-tsenter also coordinated the library of the Farband that in 1933 had around three hundred regular readers.[86] In the late 1930s, the centro was farband's branch that reached out to the Argentina-born generation. In a 1938 issue of *Dos Naye Vort*, the text about the centro was the only one written in Spanish, the first names of its activists were already typically Argentine rather than Jewish and those in charge much younger than the Farband authorities.[87]

Throughout the 1930s, landsmanshaftn played the role of ethnic social clubs rather than mutual help organizations. Most of their leadership achieved relative economic prosperity and belonged or aspired to a middle-class status. Jewish social and cultural life of the landslayt was born out of these middle-class aspirations. Samuel Blutrajt, who in the early 1930s was a simple truck driver but in a few years became a *fabricante* (factory owner), remembered going for regular picnics in a *quinta* (suburban mansion) in Vicente Lopez.[88] As one landsman remembered, the public in Yiddish theaters was composed of butchers, grocers, and other merchants, who aspired to economic and cultural progress. The evolution of their cultural interests went hand in hand with a higher economic position. The members of the Lemberger Farayn believed that the organization was responsible for "raising the cultural level" of its members.[89] In most cases, the landslayt intended to raise their own cultural level by popularizing the high Yiddish culture. As many of the Farband members preferred to communicate in Yiddish and were proud of the revival of Yiddish culture, the cultural offer of the landsmanshaftn was seen as a *geystiker heym* (spiritual home) for the immigrants.[90] This home was supposed to be filled with a high-quality Yiddishness, be it imported from the Old World or created in Argentina.

The luncheons, tea parties, and dance balls organized by landsman organizations were one of the few occasions where Jewish women and men could interact freely, as the moral ethic of the early twentieth century usually forbade casual interactions between men and women. Working-class women participated in the job market in Argentina, but middle-class Jewish women were usually confined to the home sphere. The landsman events were for them often one of the few spaces where they could socialize. Female middle-class Jews gladly attended these social gatherings and became their chief organizers and coordinators. The children and youth clubs, regular *té danzantes* (dance tea parties) were the domain of women.[91] Similar developments occurred in broader Argentine society. *Bibliotecas populares*, with their courses and lectures, were geared principally at the women of the neighborhood.[92] In the mid-1930s, Polish-Jewish women began to claim a more prominent role in the Farband. Ofelia Targovnik wrote that both men and women falsely believed that women had less interest in social activism, pointing out that numerous Argentine institutions had women's sections and claimed that Poylisher Farband should also establish one. She suggested that women could take care of the drop-in clinic and assured that Polish-Jewish women were talented, hard-working, and willing to contribute to the Polish-Jewish community.[93] Farband's president Félix Hershkovich later openly supported her call for democratization and inclusiveness, and a women's section was indeed created and presided over by Ofelia Targovnik.[94] The relative ease with which a women's section was established is somewhat surprising, considering the patriarchal structure of other immigrant societies.[95] Poylisher Farband's attempts to reflect tendencies present in other Argentine associations testify how general Argentine customs and innovations were adopted and expressed in immigrant unions.

Big landsmanshaftn, such as Poylisher Farband, or Galitsianer Farband, organized regular family dance balls in the winter and picnics in the summer. These regular events were followed by a number of "welcome" or "goodbye" *bailés* organized for visitors from Europe and by banquets organized within the framework of one of the *aktsyes* (fund-raising campaigns). In 1938, Galitsianer Farband organized a *gran camping* in suburban Vicente López. The participants ate beef grilled on *gran parrilla criolla*, danced, and sang Jewish songs together with a singer named Genia Pasternak. In attempts to attract children to the landsman events, the Galitsianer prepared children's games and an athletic show, organized by its youngest members.[96] Fancying Argentine foods and adopting essentially Argentine forms of leisure marked the growing sense of argentinidad of Jewish immigrants. The landsman outings were both Jewish and Argentine in their form and content and reflected the changes in identity that the immigrant population experienced.

Dance parties organized by the Poylisher Farband and smaller landsmanshaftn easily combined the Argentine entertainment needs of an aspiring middle class with a building sense of Polish-Jewish subethnicity and their Jewish *madre patria* of eastern Europe. Argentina, similar to Poland, was experiencing a transition to new forms of tourism and leisure. Since the end of the nineteenth century, horse races were very popular and porteños searched for refuge in the green quintas on the outskirts of the city or on the beaches of Mar de Plata.[97] Often the outings and entertainment merged with ethnic activism. In 1931, the local fund-raising committee in Villa Crespo published a flyer inviting guests to a "big family party" (*groysn familien bal*) to raise money for the Yiddishist TSYSHO schools in Poland. The party that took place on October 24, 1931, in Salon Nordau featured games, a beauty contest, and a concert of "the best Buenos Aires orchestra."[98] On August 22, 1931, La Plata organized a similar program on behalf of the same cause. After the welcome speech of the TSYSHO emissary Borys (Beniamin) Tabachinski, the patrons enjoyed an evening featuring stand-up comedy by M. Auerbach, a show by Misha Schwartz, a violin concert by E. Novarra, and songs performed by opera singer Estela Budman.[99] The program of the La Plata event shows that in the world of Polish Jews in Argentina there was little contradiction between living an Argentine life and remaining committed to Jewish Poland. By raising money for the TSYSHO schools, they acknowledged their responsibility for the alter heym, whereas choosing an Argentine, probably of a Spanish origin, violin player to perform on the TSYSHO event, La Plata Jews manifested their involvement in the gentile cultural world of Argentina. The same was also true for the events held by Poylisher Farband. The Gran Velada Danzante of 1937 featured both the Italian saxophone quartet of Vincente Tagliacozzo and the Jewish jazz quartet of Leo Feidman.[100] The combination of Jewish and non-Jewish artists, of European and Yiddishist goals of the TSYSHO action with Argentine entertainment practices, was proof of the heterogeneous and transnational lives of Polish Jews in Argentina.

The landsman entertainment events were always meticulously featured in the landsman publications. Reporting about banquets and picnics, the landslayt highlighted their middle-class aspirations, if not belonging. In the 1930s, when most of the landsmanshaftn were already far away from the initial mutual help associations, they functioned as Jewish ethnic social clubs, frequented mostly

Figure 19. The kinder-klub of Poylisher Farband in Argentina

by the members of the middle class. This is clearly visible in the photos found in the landsman souvenir journals, where we see fashionably dressed men and women in elegant outfits and hats. In that era, landsman events became an arena for manifesting one's economic success, belonging to the middle class, and recognizing one's (sub)ethnicity. However, not everyone appreciated the cultural goods on offer at the landsmanshaftn. In 1939, an anonymous contributor to *Dos Naye Vort* denounced the low level of Jewish culture in Argentina. Complaining about the unwillingness of Argentina's Polish Jews to invest and participate in high culture, he wrote that he envied the Jews in the alter heym. According to him, Polish Jews in Argentina had "bread, meat and wine" but were unable to support Jewish cultural establishments.[101] The cultural activities of the Poylisher Farband and smaller landsmanshaftn remained controversial and disputed for most of the interwar years.

In order to attract younger members, Jewish Polish landsmanshaftn founded youth and/or children's sections (fig. 19). The Galitsianer Farband opened its *yugent-krayz* (Youth Circle) in 1932.[102] The establishment invited young galitsianers to regular concerts and dance parties with cotillions or to sing together. By attracting young people to the landsmanshaftn, the older generation hoped to guarantee the continuation of eastern European Jewishness. Further, a part of the Jewish youth seemed to support the idea of ethnic youth clubs. I. Singer, a member of Galitsianer yugent-krayz, wrote that young galitsianers were in a good situation because their parents "took care of the cultural needs of the youth" and opened the landsmanshaft.[103] For young Singer, the landsmanshaft was a cultural home "that we missed so much in this country." The activities offered by the farband were supposedly so attractive that nongalitsianers also joined the Youth Circle. According to Singer, the circle's offer was much better than the activities in the political youth movements. Another young landsman, Marcos Gottdenker, appreciated the newly formed sport section, which included tennis, dance, and football subgroups.[104]

However, as A. Pinsker of Poylisher Farband lamented in 1932, Jewish youth were already "on the path of foreign [meaning Argentine] culture." He complained that through public schooling young Jews were losing their connection with Jewishness and the Yiddish language and culture. Pinsker thought that the landsman initiatives to attract the youth were doomed to fail. The youngsters were establishing their own Argentinized organizations and cared only for "horse races, football or tango."[105] These forms of entertainment were becoming typical for Argentine youth in general. The fact that young Jews shared these passions suggests that second-generation migrants saw themselves as firmly embedded in Argentine national culture. The landsmanshaftn that incorporated typical Argentine forms of entertainment and leisure, such as dances, picnics, or beauty contests, tried to attract the Argentine-born generation to the ethnic Polish Jewish events. Some landslayt argued that the efforts to attract the youth were inappropriate because, for example, the program of the events did not fit the interests of the young ones.[106]

The youth clubs of the landsmanshaftn were spaces where Jewish Argentineness was created and where the new hyphenated identities were conceived. Time has shown that the tango could also be danced in the salon of a landsmanshaft. Leon Menin recalled that before the football games of Racing, around three hundred to four hundred Jewish youth came for the *kabalat shabbat* ceremony in Avallaneda.[107] The older landslayt of Poylisher Farband and Galitisianer Farayn largely acknowledged these new developments and adjusted the landsman activities to the new times but still looked with hope toward the recently arrived Polish teenage immigrants, who could in their opinion revive and "re-Yiddishize" the community.[108] Yet, for some new immigrants who arrived in the 1920s or 1930s, the landsman picnics and dance parties were seen as activities for the Argentinized *señoritas* and their middle-class parents, certainly not for the grine immigrants who struggled with making ends meet.

A Jewish Word: The Landsman Publications and Their Agendas

Publishing a journal pointed to the landslayt's ethnic success and was a testament to their high "cultural level." Following the influx of new Jewish immigrants from Poland in the 1920s, including a number of professional journalists and writers,

Polish-Jewish landsmanshaftn in Argentina began to publish souvenir journals and semiregular periodicals. These publications featured classic landsman pieces in which the landslayt expressed their longing for their hometown left behind in eastern Europe, reprints of texts by famous Yiddish writers, and social and political articles about Polish-Jewish problems. By keeping a pulse on the economic and political situation of Jews in Poland, the articles published in landsman periodicals signaled the transatlantic character of Polish Jewry. The landslayt insisted that one remained a Polish Jew even after immigration to Argentina. The landsman publications nurtured a reading public that sought to navigate a new, diasporic relationship to Poland and to other Polish Yiddish-speaking Jews scattered around the world.[109]

The landsman publications proclaimed the landslayt to be a tight-knit and supportive community. Both regular and ephemeral publications allowed Polish Jews in Argentina to come closer to each other, to cooperate, and to imagine themselves as a subethnic community with shared goals and problems. The memory of a home shared by the landslayt was an imaginative repository of otherness that helped to maintain a distinct identity in the new country.[110] The members of the landsmanshaftn themselves edited their publications. The process of collective writing, selecting, and editing articles was also a way of defining the Farband's priorities and marking the community borders. These periodicals stressed the existence and vitality of the landsmanshaftn within Argentina's immigrant population. Polish-Jewish ethnic publications focused primarily on community issues and the situation in Poland. Landslayt's Argentine lives were portrayed in the economic and advertisement section of the journals, where the landsman promoted their businesses and boasted of their financial success. The landsman journals barely touched on general Argentine problems: those were rather covered by the daily press in Spanish and Yiddish.

The first publication of the Poylisher Farband was the 1924 almanac edited by Leib Malach. This Yiddish poet, playwright, and novelist was not a typical Jewish immigrant but rather a transnational citizen of the Yiddishland. He fit in the category of interwar Jewish globetrotters, such as Hirschbein and Nomberg. His literary career started in Poland, and later, he traveled widely around western Europe and the Middle East, settled for a longer period in Argentina, lived in the United States for a few years, returned to Poland (probably in 1933), and died young in Paris in 1936. In Argentina, Malach served as a coeditor of a popular Yiddish weekly *Far grois un klein* (associated with *Di Presse*).[111] It is unclear why Malach decided to edit the *Almanakh*. It is likely that his fellow Polish landslayt were searching for experienced authors to coordinate the editorial effort. Malach brought with him the charm of success from the Old Country and years of a promising literary career. The same was true with the 1928 almanac of Poylisher Farband, edited by another famous immigrant poet, Moisés David Guiser.

The almanacs were a first attempt at writing an ethnic history of the Polish Jews in Argentina. The 1924 almanac included a broad historical section describing the beginning of the Poylisher Farband. The almanacs celebrated the Argentine reality in which the contributors and readers lived and marked the ethnic presence of Polish Jews. These publications included a number of commercial advertisements, another mechanism for showcasing the economic progress of Polish Jews, which invited the landslayt to support each other economically. Yiddish culturist Pinie Katz praised the *Almanakh* as a source for exposing the Argentine-Yiddish writing.[112] Also, Guiser, the editor of the 1928 issue, took pride in the fact that most of the included literary texts were written by Argentina-based authors. This showed that Polish Jews in Argentina were a creative spirit in Jewish Argentina, involved in Yiddish culture and not dependent on imports from eastern Europe.

The farband published the annual almanacs from 1924 through 1928. Each issue included a wide selection of articles on social problems, the farband's activities, and literary pieces written by the landslayt or reprinted texts by famous Polish Jewish writers. The 1926 issue included "Poyln," a narrative poem by Efraim Kleinman that pertained to the dilemmas of a young Polish Jew and Poland's independence, a biographical article about the popular Polish writer Stefan Żeromski, and an article praising the Polish political leader Józef Piłsudski.[113] Some of the texts were expressions of landsman nostalgia about eastern Europe and their rootedness in the Polish social and political context. The 1924 almanac featured a poem entitled "Copernicus" written by Y. L. Kalushiner and "Varshe" (Warsaw) by Moisés David Guiser. Both texts expressed a longing for Warsaw, but their authors had different backgrounds. Guiser was not a simple landsman, but a well-known member of the Buenos Aires's literary scene. He immigrated to Argentina in 1923, and prior to that, he was a member of Yiddish avant-garde literary circles of Warsaw. Kalushiner was probably one of numerous landslayt who contributed nonprofessional pieces. Kalushiner nostalgically recalled the monument of the great astronomer Copernicus located in downtown Warsaw, whereas Guiser discussed the centuries-long history of the city, mentioned its emblem (the mermaid), and proudly discussed the city's heroism and suffering during numerous wars.

By including both professional and amateur authors, the landsman almanacs formed a mix of popular and high culture in that they shared the same sources: devotion to Yiddish and nostalgia for the eastern European heym. Publishing not only amateur texts written by the *amkho* (common people) but also pieces by popular Yiddish authors from Poland, the landslayt emphasized their pride of the descendants of Jewish Poland, which they imagined as a key center of modern Yiddish culture. Texts by Nomberg, Schneiderman, or Warszawski presented farband members as a "high society" well-read in Yiddish literature and remaining in permanent cultural dialogue with its Polish creators. By reprinting texts by successful Yiddish writers, the landslayt argued that geographical borders and migration did not separate Polish Jews scattered around the world. The printed word was a space that allowed them to reconnect with their native country. Writing, publishing, and reading landsman publications served as a collective reaffirmation of memory. They used their past in Jewish Poland as a basis for building an ethnic community in Argentina and imagining it as a part of a global community of Polish Jews.

In October 1928, the role of the official press channel of the Poylisher Farband was taken over by a newly established weekly (from March 1931, a monthly) journal *Dos Naye Vort*. The periodical, which appeared for roughly ten years (with breaks), sold around 1,500 copies a month and was the main tribune for articulating Polish-Jewish interests at the end of the 1920s and into the 1930s (fig. 20).[114] *Dos Naye Vort* was a key tool for uniting and forming a self-aware Polish-Jewish community. The journal published articles about political, social, and cultural life of Jews in Poland and aspired to defend their interests even from Argentina.[115] Its authors believed that a regular publication would help to develop a strong Polish-Jewish identity among the immigrants or, as they would phrase it, would facilitate in "organizing" them. For many years, left-wing leader Mendel Pschepiurka, also active in the Vengrover Farayn, edited *Dos Naye Vort*. In the second half of the 1930s, journalist Yosef Horn, recently arrived from Poland, edited the journal. Horn incorporated many issues of general Jewish interest into the journal and attempted to also attract nonmembers.[116] In the 1920s, the editorial board included engaged and veteran farband members, like Leybush Weisblat or David Hirsch. In Argentina in the 1930s, next to *Dos Naye Vort*, there were other more or less regular landsman publications. Most of them began to appear at the end of the 1920s and early 1930s, when the Białystoker and Lemberger landsmanshaftn were established.[117] In the texts of the smaller hometown societies, we notice fewer political texts than in *Dos Naye Vort*. Town-related landsmanshaftn did not share the cultural-political agenda of Poylisher Farband, which aspired to play a role in the transnational networks of Polish Jewry. The Lubliner or Bialystoker landsmanshaftn shared many commonalities with their North American counterparts. Organizing landslayt parties and publishing often nostalgic texts written by their members, the smaller landsmanshaftn focused on comforting their members, who sometimes felt like outsiders in Argentine society.

In their publications, the former hometowns were idealized, and as Rebecca Kobrin argued, were imagined as organic Jewish polities and as comforting alternatives to their often-unpleasant Argentine present. Through their publications, the landslayt not only expressed their yearning for a "more authentic" and "more Jewish" eastern European hometown but primarily articulated their sense of shared experience of "exile" in Argentina. In the landsman texts, Poland was

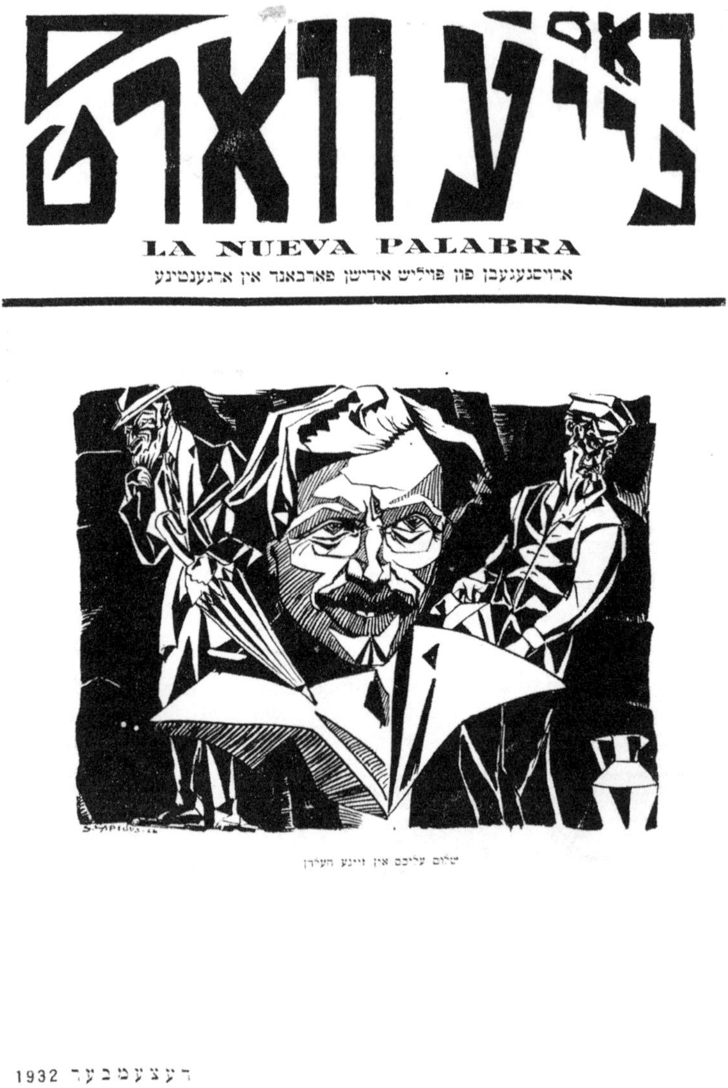

דאס נייע ווארט

LA NUEVA PALABRA

ארויסגעגעבן פון פויליש אידישן פארבאנד אין ארגענטינע

שלום עליכם און זיינע העלדן

דעצעמבער 1932

Figure 20. The cover of *Dos Naye Vort* from December 1932

often portrayed as very Jewish. Landsman writer Pinchas Bizberg claimed that "Jewishness grew into Polish nature, into the Polish climate."[118] As eastern Europe was becoming more and more distant, landsman organizations embraced a new diasporic identity with Poland as "eastern European Zion." The passage of time had overshadowed the motivations that pushed the immigrants to Argentina, while disillusionment with the local conditions of life often mobilized immigrants to imagine Jewish Poland as a better Ashkenazi Zion.

Conclusion

The Argentine landsman movement, chiefly the Poylisher Farband, played a crucial role in forming a Polish-Jewish diasporic subethnicity. The experience of emigration, the prevalent role of Poland as a post-1918 successor of the tradition of eastern European Jewry, the transnational Yiddish culturism, as well as the multiethnic character of Buenos Aires, all contributed to the emergence of a specific Polish-Jewish self-identification. Initially, by forming an ethnic organization, immigrant Jews initiated a certain kind of security network that helped them in the event of sickness or unemployment. Yet, as the Poylisher Farband adopted a more middle-class character, issues of communal prestige and ethnic respectability gained in importance. The landslayt cared about their Polishness as a function in their Argentine lives. At this later stage, shared ethnic goals and memory of home, rather than an actual need for mutual assistance, united the landsmanshaft members and their families. Even though the new immigrants still sought assistance, the ethnocultural manifestations became a key arena for Poylisher Farband.

The national or ethnic kinship that connected the immigrants through their engagement in landsman organizations transformed into a sense of unity and around common goals, both in the Argentine and Old Country contexts. Consequently, landsmanshaftn functioned as spaces and mechanisms of ethnic and regional empowerment. Landslayt cultural activities, and attempts to attract the younger generations, were part and parcel of what the activists described as "organizing oneself." In the eyes of the landslayt, it was only by being organized and by joining and participating in landsman activities that the heritage of eastern European Jewry could continue in Argentina. The landslayt believed that they could achieve their economic, social, and cultural goals in the new country only if they organized and united. A formal membership in landsmanshaftn was less important than active membership via participation.

Belonging to a Polish-Jewish landsmanshaft and highlighting one's ethnic background did not signify voluntary exclusion from Argentine society, ethnic isolationism, or refusal to acculturate. As Raanan Rein argued, the dichotomy "to assimilate, or to separate from surrounding world" was simply false in the

Argentine context.[119] Yiddishist Pinie Wald wrote that no one could question the Argentineness of the Jewish generations born in Argentina and that their rootedness in Argentina did not contradict the need for Yiddishness.[120] A wide "in-between" space existed. For many Jewish immigrants from Poland, their belongingness to Argentina was as clear as their real or desired commitment to their alter heym. In fact, the landsmanshaftn became a space that facilitated the social integration into the Argentine mainstream. In the multiethnic and immigrant society that Argentina undoubtedly was during the interwar years, immigrant experiences defined the mainstream. Articulating one's (sub)ethnicity was thus a channel, not an obstacle, for inclusion into what was understood as Argentine. As Ben Gidley aptly put it, the relationship between home roots and rootedness in the new land was the main defining feature of the landsmanshaftn.[121] Although it was Polish-Jewish ethnicity that the Poylisher Farband emphasized, in the long-term it was their Argentine Jewishness that the landsmanshaft demarcated. The sense of commitment to the alter heym was undeniably visible during Argentine Jewish campaigns of help to Jews in Poland; the next chapter will explore this subject in greater detail.

7

Aktsyes, Protest-aktn, and Helping the Old Home

Argentine Children of Jewish Poland Respond to a Changing Europe

Poland's independence and the Great War in Europe were factors that prompted pre-1918 Polish émigrés to question their relationship with a new independent Poland. The developments in the home country probably troubled Yankel Piotrovski, a tailor, an ex-resident of the industrial city of Łódź, and founder of Agudas Ahim, the first Polish-Jewish organization in Argentina. Although it is hard to speculate about the exact motives of Piotrovski and his partners when they founded Agudas Ahim, it seems that the chaos of the Great War and the new stabilization of the postwar period transformed the self-understanding of Jewish immigrants in Argentina.[1] They needed to reconceptualize their attitude to their new old homeland. The approaches were ambiguous. For many Polish Jews in Argentina, it was obvious that they needed to develop a transatlantic structure of ethnic support for devastated and persecuted Jews in Poland. Writing the history of the farband in 1941, its members stressed that Poylisher Farband was founded in order to reestablish contact with family members who remained in Europe, to acquire information about developments in war-torn Poland, and to examine the possibilities of help. A few months earlier, in April 1916, they established a Polish-Jewish Help-Committee for the War Victims.[2] Polish Agudas Ahim was also one of the most active money raisers for the Argentine Jewish Central Committee for the Jewish War Victims (Tsentral komitet far di yidishe milkhome laydende).

The development of the landsmanshaft movement was influenced not only by the needs of immigrants in Argentina but also by their attachment and sense of obligation toward the alter heym.[3] It was through Europe's Great War, the transition from great empires to new nation-states, and the dire situation of the civil population that the immigrants from Polish lands were able to enter into a discussion about what it means to be a Polish Jew in Argentina. Forming a landsmanshaft was only one of many options available. Some immigrant Jews devoted themselves to economic activities, working in or opening workshops and factories, some quickly acculturated and became involved outside of the Jewish immigrant community. Others contributed to the development of "organized Polish Jewry in Argentina." To be organized meant to be a part of a landsmanshaft or of any other immigrant institutions. It meant adopting an active stand concerning Polish-Jewish problems and being an ethnically active Polish Jew. Whereas the nonorganized probably did not consider their Polish Jewishness as a decisive element, the organized Polish Jews shared a belief that only by building an ethnic structure could one truly express one's distinct ethnic identity and ethnic interests.

The system of communal engagement and mutual support that the landsmanshaftn previously developed on a mutual help level (help to the members) was exercised on a transnational level in their "Poland campaigns" in the 1930s. Throughout the 1920s and 1930s, Polish Jews in Argentina organized or co-organized diverse campaigns of help for Jews in Poland. This was based both on shared ideological stands (as in cases of secular Yiddish schools) or a general empathy for fellow Polish Jews. Poylisher Farband aspired to be the main voice of the organized Polish Jewry in Argentina, as well as concerning the situation of Jews in Poland. The Argentine landslayt demanded international recognition for the Jewish diaspora in Argentina and presented themselves as ready to get involved in improving the Jewish situation in Poland. This was clearly visible, for instance, in the Poylisher Farband report summarizing the 1935 World Congress of Polish Jews. Their delegate, David Hirsch, argued there that the new Polish-Jewish *yishevim* are willing and ready to invest all their strength to help "our brothers in Poland."[4]

The outbreak of the Great War in 1914 brought insecurity to the Jewish towns and cities of partitioned Poland. As military conflicts in that part of Europe hardly ever left civilian populations intact, Jews correctly linked the impending war with the danger of pogroms, death, and famine. These fears were shared not only by those residing in Russian or Austrian Poland but also by the dispersed Jewish Polish community worldwide. Those Jewish individuals, who left Poland between the 1890s and 1910s, looked at the developments in their native land with no lesser anxiety. The Great War led to a political reconfiguration in Central Europe. The Austro-Hungarian and Russian empires fell apart, the German Keiserreich was over, and new nation-states appeared or reappeared on the continent's map. Newly drawn geographical borders signified numerous changes for the former subjects of the fallen empires. In 1918, Poland reemerged in its largely prepartition borders, becoming a home to almost three million Jews.[5] The rebirth of Poland was accompanied by violent pogroms in the country's eastern borderlands. The Polish-Soviet (1919–21) and Polish-Ukrainian (1918–19) wars did not make the situation any easier. In the following years, many Jews decided to leave. Between 1920 and 1925, around 184,000 Jews left Poland; this accounted for approximately 40 percent of the overall emigration from Poland and corresponded to a quadrupled Jewish share of the overall population.[6]

At the same time, some Polish Jews in Poland and abroad were hopeful about the newly independent Polish state. During the war in 1916, the Warsaw rabbinate supported the independence of Poland symbolically by taking part in the first legal celebration of the anniversary of the first Polish constitution of 1791.[7] A number of Polish Jews fought on the battlefield for the independence of Poland.[8] After the Polish-Soviet War of 1919–21, the Jews of East Galicia openly called for remaining in Poland versus land swapping with Soviet Russia.[9] Some Jews believed that the national state of the Poles would be inclusive and respectful of minorities. When in June 1919 Poland signed the so-called Minority Treaty in Versailles, Jewish hopes for a better life in a democratic and liberal country reached their peak. The first months after the Great War were a time of enthusiasm, and some believed that even those who left would return to Poland.[10] Many dreamed of a free Jewish press, unrestricted Jewish political parties and unions, equality for all the citizens of the republic, or even state support for Jewish cultural and educational establishments. A day after the declaration of independence, Marshal Józef Piłsudski met a Jewish delegation that shared their hopes, fears, and demands with him. Żagiew, the Union of Polish Youth of Jewish Origin, wrote in November 1918: "Polish Jews! We believe that from this day you will be able to prove with your deeds that you possess undeterred feelings of gratitude and affection to the land that for many centuries nurtured your ancestors."[11] Three months later, during the so-called Jewish debate on February 24, 1919, rabbi Perlmutter declared the loyalty of orthodox Jews to the new Polish state and demanded full equality of rights, Jewish religious-cultural autonomy, and state support for Jewish establishments.[12] Other Jewish leaders were already more concerned. Noyekh Prilutsky from the Folkist Party accused the government of not combating anti-Semitism and opposed the perception of Jews as a religious minority, demanding a recognition of their national minority status.[13]

These developments in Poland were followed with great interest in Argentina. Buenos Aires's *Yidische Zaitung* enthusiastically reported about the December 1918 conference of Polish Jews that channeled the future actions of Jewish activists in independent Poland.[14] Matías Stoliar of the same daily argued that in terms of equal status for the Jews of Poland, Jewish national awareness and the democratization of Europe were more important than legal provisions.[15] Some Argentine Poland-born Jews had great expectations regarding the status of Jews in independent Poland. Some Jews imagined that the shared experience of living under tsarist and German oppression was guarantee that Jews would be treated well in Poland.[16] Others saw the independence of Poland as a success of Polish nationalism and an example for Jewish national claims. A member of Poylisher Farband remembered these days in the following way: "The independence of Poland brought to each of us an internal happiness. We feel and all the time have felt, in spite of all the pain that separates us from Poland, the love of children for their home, from which they were torn away, and all the time are attracted to it."[17]

In 1919, Buenos Aires newspapers reported on the horrendous pogrom in Lwów with seventy-three victims, where the Polish military assisted (or did not oppose) anti-Jewish violence. On another occasion, the Argentine Yiddish press reported on a pogrom in Vilna, where Polish soldiers murdered more than sixty Jews.[18] *Yidische Zaitung* also wrote about hundreds of hungering Jews.[19] In May 1919, during the Polish-Soviet War, the newspaper wrote about ongoing anti-Semitic agitation in Poland and accused the Polish government of anti-Semitic policies. The daily reported on the pogrom in Pińsk, where the military shot thirty-five Jews, and asked rhetorically: "Is it culture that Poland is bringing to Lithuania? It is a series of pogroms and mass murders that Poland introduces wherever it comes."[20] The reports on pogroms conveyed a message of distrust and disappointment toward independent Poland. In July 1919, *Yidische Zaitung* wrote bluntly: "Jews live in fear of the Poles."[21] The Argentine Jewish Committee of Help for War Victims wrote that independent Poland was "a studious disciple of tsarism," explaining that pogroms against the Jews proved that Poland did not deserve its independence for which many Jewish fighters devoted their lives.[22]

The majority of Argentine Jews feared for Jews in independent Poland. David Szyszacki of IWO pointed out that after 1918 many Galitsianer Jews in Buenos Aires did not welcome the fall of the Austro-Hungarian empire, especially after the pogrom in Lwów. Many Galitsianers preferred to see their native Galicia as a part of a multinational empire rather than subordinate to a Polish republic.[23] The disappointment with the first months of Polish independence was visible in the letters the immigrants received from Poland. The mother of Buenos Aires–based Józef Śpiewak wrote a letter full of despair and hopelessness to him and his brother about the situation in her shtetl, Działoszyce: "My dear children . . . with all my heart I would love for you to come home for Passover, to find your brides here. But the life of every Jew here is now in danger, I am forced to wish that you will be happy there [in Argentina] and that your eyes will never see this bloody land again."[24]

The painful events in Poland and the Ukraine moved Jews in Argentina. As the situation in eastern Europe was supposedly a "thousand times worse than a decade ago," emigration was often seen as the only solution to improve the situation of the Jews in Poland.[25] In nearly every issue, Jewish journals in Buenos Aires debated emigration possibilities and expected an intensified immigration stream to Argentina. Yet, Argentine Jews were aware that wide segments of the Argentine conservative ruling class were against receiving war refugees, seeing them as carriers of revolutionary thought. The dramatic situation in Europe and the outbreak of the Russian Revolution in 1917 only strengthened these attitudes.[26]

With few options for active help, on July 29, 1919, Argentine Jews organized a mourning and protest ceremony in Buenos Aires.

Polish-Jewish Interests and Landsman Relations with the Polish Embassy

The activists of Poylisher Farband often manifested their belief that a good relationship with Polish authorities was more beneficial to the Jewish community both in Poland and in Argentina than outward criticism of government policies. The leaders of the landsmanshaft often underlined their close and positive relations with the Polish ambassador to Argentina, Władysław Mazurkiewicz. The embassy in Buenos Aires opened in 1922, and Poylisher Farband quickly began regular working meetings with its officials. As the farband claimed, the embassy appreciated that the farband represented the entire (as the landslayt claimed in exaggeration) Polish-Jewish community in Argentina and was a reliable partner. Thanks to that, the farband was supposed to be effective in providing immigrant Polish Jews with much-needed assistance from the embassy.[27] Since its establishment, *Dos Naye Vort*, the official journal of the farband, was known for its positive attitude toward the Polish state and taking pride in the shared past of Polish Jews and Christians.[28] This stand was proclaimed by Aharon Leyb Schussheim, the first chief editor of *Dos Naye Vort*. In 1928, Schussheim argued that any "anti-Polish" actions would be harmful to the Jews of Poland and would make it more difficult for the Argentine diaspora to be involved in Polish-Jewish matters: "As an organization of Polish Jews in Argentina that wants to be in a close relationship with its brothers in the *alter heym*, our Farband . . . is fully loyal to the Polish state and its legal representation [in Argentina]. We don't turn our eyes away from the political situation experienced by our brothers in the alter heym. . . . Yet, we don't want to stop believing that Poland is a country of religious tolerance and that, in the end, the reborn Polish Republic will find a way out of all political and economic hardships, and that Poland will fulfill its stately mission of being a home for all its citizens, regardless of differences of religion and nationality."[29]

The main points of this declaration were true for the official policy of the Poylisher Farband for the entire interwar period. The Poylisher Farband kept warm relations with the Polish diplomatic mission in Argentina and Polish officials visiting the country. The organization was proud of its attitude. The anniversary publications featured photos from the festive banquets organized for its guests by the farband.[30] In 1933, the farband organized a gala dinner for the marshal of the Polish senate, Władysław Raczkiewicz, who visited Argentina during his research trip.[31] Since the 1930s, the farband used a trilingual name: in Yiddish, Spanish, and Polish. The adoption of a Polish name, Centralny Związek Żydów Polskich w Argentynie, emphasized the specifically Polish character of the institution and its good relations with the Polish embassy and served as a possible sign of openness to cooperation with the Polish Catholic community in Argentina. It was also the ability to speak Polish that allowed the farband's leaders to strengthen friendly ties with the Polish ambassador. Speaking Polish and referring to one's Polish background was a strategy used by the farband for defending and articulating Jewish interests in Poland and abroad.

The representatives of Poylisher Farband were in regular contact with the veteran Polish ambassador in Buenos Aires, Władysław Mazurkiewicz. Through these meetings, they not only manifested their connection with the representatives of the Polish state but also tried to defend the interests of Polish Jews in Argentina and in Poland. Farband members discussed with the ambassador problems of re-emigration to Poland and the issue of citizenship of those individuals who left Polish lands before 1918.[32] As *Dos Naye Vort* reported, the meetings were usually very friendly and the ambassador "heard their demands with interest and understanding."[33] Direct relations with Polish officials gave the organization top-level recognition and allowed it to imagine itself as a quasi-embassy of Polish Jewry in Argentina. This echoed the "social prestige hunger" that was prevalent among many landslayt. Both in Poland and in Argentina, there was a number of Jews that saw more benefits to be gained from friendly relations with the Polish state than in straightforward criticism and accusations of anti-Semitism and discriminatory practices.[34] On the other hand, Poylisher Farband was preoccupied with anti-Jewish policies and incidents in Poland and the growing Jewish poverty and issues with educational and cultural establishments. During the 1930s, the farband organized help actions for Poland's Jews and protested against the growing anti-Semitism in Poland.[35]

Extending a Helping Hand: Poylisher Farband and Poland Help Campaigns

In the 1930s, Argentine Jews engaged in a number of causes in Jewish Poland, including educational projects, protesting against anti-Semitism, and direct financial assistance. It quickly proved unrealistic that the Polish state would support Jewish educational and cultural institutions. Although interwar Jewish Poland did experience a period of journalistic, social, cultural, and political efflorescence, most of the Jewish population struggled with poverty and economic instability. Even landmark institutions like YIVO in Vilna relied heavily on foreign aid. The Argentine Jewish press and landsmanshaftn kept Polish-Jewish immigrants up-to-date about the challenges that faced their *brider in poyln* (brothers in Poland). The activists of the Poylisher Farband regularly called for solidarity with the unfortunate and the discriminated, both in the form of financial help (*aktsyes*, actions or fund-raising campaigns) and moral support (public expressions of empathy, open letters).[36]

The support for the Jews of Poland was based on a system of individual and collective solidarity. The work of the landslayt was exclusively voluntary and not remunerated. The members built their sense of pride on ethnic involvement and working for the cause. The benevolent functionaries of the landsmanshaftn were praised in the landsman journals and at cultural or social events. This was true both for internal engagement in Argentina and for the assistance offered the Jews in Poland. For instance, the landslayt from Węgrów were proud both of their help for the Jews in their hometown and of the fact that many of their members served in top positions or founded the key general Jewish institutions.[37] After every aktsye, a detailed report was published (fig. 21). It specified not only the overall incomes and outcomes but even provided information about specific donors or fund-raisers. The supporters liked to picture themselves as devoted, generous, and altruistic. The *barikhtn* (reports) published by the fund-raisers and also jubilee publications of the landsmanshaftn narrated a story of social ascent and Polish-Jewish and Argentine Jewish ethnic triumph. They served the immigrants as a platform, showing both their Argentine success and transnational responsibility for their Polish brethren.

Individual and institutional fund-raising support was no less important than the financial outcome. The words of gratitude for those who financially supported the acquisition of new books for a Yiddish library, or co-organized a picnic raising money for Jewish Poland, were almost obligatory. The "celebration of achievement," as Michael Humphrey put it, that was performed during the campaigns was not just a question of personal pride for a fund-raiser but a demand for the social recognition of these achievements.[38] Consequently, a remuneration for community involvement was communal prestige. This mechanism was not without its critics. Pinie Katz argued that Jewish merchants and professionals treated their social activities within the Jewish realm as an addition to their career and were not motivated by the importance of the cause or by benevolence.[39]

These transnational solidarity campaigns had clear ethnic goals, but they also served to defend the Jewish position in Argentina. The campaigns voiced the economic success of Jewish Argentines (and consequently their economic contribution to Argentina). Simultaneously, the campaigns focused on combating anti-Semitism in Poland showed that Jews stood up for democracy and pluralism both in Poland and in their new Argentine home. For instance, a Warsaw help fund organized two picnics and a dance party where money was gathered for poor Jewish Varsovians and a "fight with Polish fascism." The organizers declared that "there should be no family event or a party where money is not raised for

הילפס קאָמיטעט פאַר די יידיש וועלטלעכע שולן אין פוילן

באריכט

פון דער אַקציע, דורכגעפירט אין ארגענטינע פון סאָף מאַי

ביז סאָף נאָוועמבער 1931

בוענאָס אירעס

Figure 21. A report summarizing the 1931 Argentine-Uruguayan campaign for the Yiddish secular schools in Poland

the victims in Europe."[40] Oftentimes, the organizers of charity campaigns applied pressure to individuals and Jewish institutions. Insufficient financial support or low turnout at events, such as anniversaries of famous Yiddish writers and farewell dinners for those departing to Europe, were often publicly condemned in the community press. When only a small number of landslayt joined an event commemorating the sixtieth birthday of Yiddish writer Peretz Hirschbein, Natan Fruchter blatantly condemned the landsman leaders who ignored the celebration.[41] Public expressions of dissatisfaction were supposed to invoke a feeling of shame and boost the campaign. No one wanted to be publicly condemned and singled out as uninvolved or unengaged with the community.

The assistance offered to hometowns or institutions in Poland was organized twofold: small landsmanshaftn often were in direct contact with specific institutions in their hometown and sent money directly. Węgrów Farayn supported local Gmilat Hased (benevolence society), a children's summer camp and evening school run by the Bund and Poaley Tsiyon.[42] Big events, so-called aktsyes, were considered more prestigious and required a lot of logistical work and a months-long collection of money throughout all of Argentina. This was visible particularly, but not exclusively, in fund-raising for Poland, including campaigns in support of secular Jewish schools in Poland or an event benefitting the YIVO Yiddish Scientific Institute in Vilna. Some campaigns, like the campaign for the victims of floods, were organized individually by Poylisher Farband. In this case, Abraham Shimshelevich, Yankev Vengrover, and Boris Knobel coordinated the fund-raising.[43] Other campaigns were often organized by a broader coalition of Jewish institutions, not only by Polish Jews. Then their activities were marked as "Argentine help" and served as a manifestation of generosity of the entire Argentine Jewry.[44] Yet, the leaders of Poylisher Farband were usually key personas behind the help campaigns. In the late 1930s, Gezelshaftlikher hilfs-komitet le-toyves di yidn in poyln (Jewish Argentine Social Committee of Help for the Jews in Poland) was headed by Moisés Elisabetsky, a president of Poylisher Farband, and administrated by Boris Knobel and Guillermo (Volf) Orzech, who were also active members of the landsmanshaft.[45]

The joint efforts to help the Jews in Europe were initiated during World War I. The Tsentral komitet far di yidishe milkhome laydende (Central Committee for the Jewish War Victims) grouped together a number of institutions. A later example of an Argentina-wide campaign was the One Million Campaign of 1938. The campaign was supposed to raise one million pesos for the needs of refugees from Germany and Austria, as well as investments in Palestine. The goal was not met (851,000 pesos was raised), but the money was indeed distributed among different organizations involved abroad (a quarter for Keren Hayesod).[46] The One Million Campaign allowed the often-divided groups—Polish

Jews (Poylisher Farband), German Jews (Hilfsverein Deutsch-sprechender Juden), and Zionists—to cooperate in a shared cause and underlined the unity of Argentine Jewry. The executive committee included members of Poylisher Farband (Gregorio Pachter, Moisés Elisabetsky, and Boris Knobel) but also well-known personas, such as film pioneer Max Glüksman and Yiddish journalist Marcos Regalsky. Mrs. Schussheim, wife of a former president of the Poylisher Farband, coordinated the collection by the women's committee.

The aktsyes were usually organized by a relatively narrow group but targeted the larger Polish-Jewish community in Argentina. People who stood behind them were often landsmanshaft members but many others were Jewish journalists or cultural activists (*kultur-tuers*). Some Yiddishists, like Marcos Regalsky, saw international cooperation "of national-progressive Jews" as the only option, rejecting cooperation with what he regarded as "assimilationist-bourgeois" charities.[47] Whereas the monthly dues paid by members funded the regular activities of the landsmanshaftn, the external involvement, such as organizing help actions for Jews in Poland, required special strategies and additional funding. In order to gain public support, the aktsyes were broadly advertised in the Yiddish press, especially in the landsman periodicals. Fund-raising events often took the form of parties and luncheons, which sometimes included artistic or musical performances. For instance, a 1927 letter from the Hilfs-komitet far di yidish veltlekhe shuln in poyln (Help Committee for the Jewish Secular Schools in Poland) expressed gratitude to the famous actor Morris Schwartz, who organized a morning show and donated his income to the TSYSHO schools in Poland.[48]

Throughout the 1920s, prior to the global economic crisis, Polish Jews in Argentina did not perceive the situation in Poland as desperate, and aid initiatives were less present in community activities. Poylisher Farband was not that involved in assisting Jews in Poland until anti-Semitism became more poignant in the late 1930s.[49] The first half of the 1920s was largely a period of mass immigration, and assistance to Poland did not reach the importance that it would gain in the coming years. In 1920, the farband debated sending an envoy to Poland, who would bring the gathered funds and packages to the needy and letters to families.[50] The issue was controversial and some community members criticized the need for such travel.[51] *Di Presse* editors suggested that it was cheaper and wiser to do it via US relief institutions. Yet, the delegation of the Folks-komitet far folks-hilf (Popular Committee for National Help) and delegations from Polish and Ukrainian farayns had additional goals: to mark their responsibility for the welfare of the Jews in the alter heym and to boast about their Argentine success. The same was visible during the TSYSHO campaign at the turn of 1927/28. Polisher Farband argued that the money they gathered placed them in the first place among the collaborating institutions, including those with much bigger budgets.[52]

In the 1930s, despite the fact that poverty and unemployment also grew in Argentina, the situation in Poland was perceived as urgent and necessitating help from Jewish Polish diasporas abroad.[53] Landsman Borekh Ismach recalled that the 1930s were a period of stabilization and a "blooming" of the landsmanshaftn, and the associations were crucial for bringing help to the families living in Poland.[54] The help actions for the Jews in Poland had various specific goals. At the turn of the 1920s and 1930s, money was collected several times for the TSYSHO schools, which were Poland's secular Yiddishist schools. In 1932, Zalmen Reyzen, special envoy from Vilna, helped to develop a fund-raising campaign for the YIVO Institute.[55] In 1934, the farband organized a fund-raising campaign for those who suffered as a result of flooding in eastern Poland. In 1937, the farband co-organized a "campaign of constructive help for the Jews of Poland," when money was raised for establishing artisan and industrial Jewish cooperatives, a future solution to the increasing problem of the boycott of Jewish labor in Poland.[56] In the mid-1930s many landsmanshaftn established *hilfsfonds*, help-funds, that regularly raised money for their hometowns. In 1935, Jewish Lithuanian *patronato* (charitable institution) was opened and in 1937 its Łódź counterpart, while numerous others cooperated within a general Argentine Jewish task-force.

In Argentina during the 1930s, supporting an aktsye was equivalent to supporting Jews in Poland. Local social and cultural leaders worked to establish a sense of responsibility among Polish Jews for the situation of Jews in Poland. It was poignantly visible during the campaigns, when in highly emotional calls the *tuers* (activists) linked financial support for the campaign with being a good Polish Jew. Arguments about shared responsibility for the well-being of Jews in Poland were especially used during the campaigns but also on a daily basis. Poland's problems were often described as "our Argentine Jewish problems." For instance, the campaign for the "Polish Jewish child" was presented as a "holy and brotherly obligation of all Polish Jews in Argentina."[57] The campaigners argued for the existence of "closeness" and unity between Polish Jewry worldwide. Emphasizing the diasporic ties between them, campaigners cut across the power of the nation-state.[58] In its propaganda materials, Jews in Poland were called "our brothers and sisters" and these "familial relations" supposedly obliged Polish Jews in Argentina to answer the calls of their impoverished "family members" in Poland.

This was evident in 1937, in the Argentiner yidisher kampeyn le-toyves di yidn in poyln (Argentine Jewish Campaign for the Jews in Poland). The language used in this campaign by Poylisher Farband was full of emotions. The key argument used by numerous contributors to the special issue of *Dos Naye Vort* concerned the "national debt" that the Argentine Polish-Jewish community was obliged to pay through their financial support for impoverished Jews in Poland. Moisés Elisabetsky declared that "Argentine Jews need to repay their national debt." Chaim Brusilovsky, a landsman and an owner of a catering business, had a similar attitude: "Helping Jews in Poland is now a national obligation!"[59] Gregorio Pachter, a landsman and successful cashmere merchant, was sure that the "national debt" of Polish Jews in Argentina toward their fellow Polish Jews would be paid off. Wolf Bressler wrote about "our brotherly help for Polish Jewry."[60]

This argument was based on a sense of belonging to the same subethnic category of Polish Jews in diaspora. Within this paradigm, Poland functioned as a Jewish madre patria for Argentine Jews of Polish ancestry. Independently of whether or not they were born there, they were imagined as the symbolic children of Jewish Poland, belonging to the same transnational extended family. Following this reasoning, living in Argentina, a country with broader democratic liberties and relative economic stability, Polish Jews should be responsible for taking care of their "old and weakly mother" (Jewish Poland), torn by the diseases of popular anti-Semitism, economic crisis, and state discrimination.[61] Even though the 1930s in Argentina were a time of short-lived fascist-like upheavals, the Jews of Argentina still enjoyed more freedoms and privileges than those living in Poland. During the One Million Campaign in 1938, a similar rhetoric was used. The campaigners talked about the fear and hunger that were prevalent in Europe, about the happy situation of Argentine Jews, who "are not in the hell that Europe recently turned into," about German Jewry whom "Nazi barbarians want to turn into ashes." Argentine Jews were called to express their brotherly solidarity as they were morally responsible "before history and Judaism."[62]

The TSYSHO Campaigns and Transnational Solidarity Networks

The TSYSHO campaigns were emblematic of the transatlantic engagement of Polish Jews from Argentina. The campaigns were embedded in a vision of a global, committed Jewishness, imagined with the aim of linking together a community of secular, progressive Jews from major diaspora centers, who supported a cultural and ethnonational revival in Yiddish. Bundists and other secular left-wing Jews believed that only Yiddish secular schooling could secure the rights of Jews as a nation and form the basis of modern national and cultural revival in Yiddish. This vision of the world rejected both the complete assimilation and abstract internationalism by linking progressive and ethnonational messages. The Central Jewish School Organization TSYSHO was founded in Poland in 1921 by Bund and Poaley Tsiyon activists who wished to strengthen secular Jewish schooling in the Yiddish language and combine it with a socialist ideology. TSYSHO leaders, such as Beynish Mihalevitch or education theoretician Malka Frumkin, saw their school network as a tool for promoting ethnonational Jewish revival, symbolized by the YIVO Institute in Vilna and high Yiddish literary culture.[63] The Argentine TSYSHO campaigns reflected the political and social choices of many Yiddish-speaking, secular, and usually left-wing Argentine Polish Jews. The intellectual foundation of Poland's TSYSHO schools was similar to the educational system that secularist Argentine-Jewish leaders of Polish origin, such as Pinie Wald or Samuel Rollansky, tried to push forward in Argentina.[64] As Rollansky put it, the schools "transmitted secular-Jewish culture in Eastern European form."[65]

A number of Polish-Jewish landsman leaders in Argentina shared Yiddishist and Bundist values. Bundism, as Frank Wolff claimed, developed into a transnational network of socialist activism.[66] Jewish migrants and emissaries visiting Argentina were messengers of Bundist thought into new diaspora countries.[67] Some of them perceived the TSYSHO campaigns as a momentum to start talking about Jewish secular schooling also in Argentina.[68] In the mid-1930s, secular schools modeled on TSYSHO in Poland were established in Argentina. The schools were a place of "lived Yiddishness" and cultural centers rather than simple educational institutions.[69] Supporting TSYSHO campaigns did not only mean backing the cause but was also a space of experiencing a secular Jewishness that the Bund and other progressive Yiddishist movements envisioned.[70] The campaigns helped to organize Polish Jews in Argentina as a subethnic community, yet allowed those living in Argentina to emancipate as an independent part of Yiddishland. By extending a helping hand to Jews in Poland, those residing in Argentina labeled themselves a *folks-kibets*, a national Jewish subgroup that maintained transnational ties with the Jewish communities in the Old World.[71] The campaigns centered around the Yiddishist enterprise emphasized the "national unity of a diasporic Jewish nation."[72] By supporting TSYSHO schools or the YIVO Institute, Argentine Jews inscribed themselves into a "Yiddish nation" and perceived their help as an entry criterion to collective prestige within Yiddishland hierarchies.

In November 1929, Buenos Aires's *Di Presse* published an article by Vilna Yiddishist culturist Zalmen Reyzen. Reyzen described the economic crisis in Vilna, pointing out the recent changes that challenged the traditional Jewish economy.[73] Zalmen Reyzen saw the pauperization of Jewish Vilna as a threat to Yiddish cultural life in the city, as many authors, teachers, and activists, unable to make ends meet in Vilna, left for other places in Poland and abroad. Reyzen described the overfilled classes and children who wanted their education in Yiddish. By writing about the problems relevant for Jews both in Poland and Argentina, Reyzen imagined them as cocitizens of a diasporic Yiddishland. Despite the geographical distance, the problems centered around the Yiddish language and progressive Yiddish schooling seemed to be similar everywhere.

S. Freilach (Freilaj) is a prime example of a Polish Jew who transmitted Bundist ideals directly to Argentina. Born as Litman Geltman in Międzyrzec (Mezrich) in Podlasie, Poland, Freilach served in the Polish army during the Polish-Soviet War. Afterward, he finished the TSYSHO teachers' course in Warsaw and taught in TSYSHO schools. After immigrating to Argentina in 1924, he continued to be active in the cause of Jewish secular schools. When the Zionists and *Haynt* launched a campaign against TSYSHO in Poland, he wrote for Buenos Aires's *Di Presse* a sharp article denouncing the Zionists as provocateurs and crazy. Freilach argued that the Zionists always wanted to destroy the very concept of Yiddish secular schooling and described Warsaw's Zionist-backing *Haynt* as reactionary chauvinists. The heated debate concerning TSYSHO schools epitomized the fact that education always stood at the very center of political and cultural struggles in interwar Jewish Poland. Through messengers like Freilach, the issue was globalized, and also Zionism was forced to compete with the Yiddishist progressive movement in Argentina.[74]

Freilach's calls were quickly followed by a *proklarmirungs-akt* in support of TSYSHO schools in Poland. On November 5, 1929, various renowned Argentine Jewish figures spoke in Salon Italia Unida on Congallo Street in Buenos Aires: poet Moisés David Guiser, journalists and activists Lazaro Zhitnitsky and Marcos Regalsky, the Polish-Jewish veteran of the proletarian movement Pinie Wald, while Rita Kiten sang. Regalsky said that despite being a Zionist, he believed that Yiddish Bundist schools were the foundation of Yiddish culture and deserved support and protection.[75] Participants of the event had to pay entrance fees, and the income was devoted to the schools in Poland.[76] *Di Presse* wrote that financial support for the secular schools was "ammunition" to defend the Yiddishist cultural space and to defeat the Zionist enemy.[77] The anti-TSYSHO campaign was depicted as a campaign of "assimilators, nationalist Zionists, enemies of the Yiddish national language and Yiddish culture."

Volf (Guillermo) Orzech, future secretary of the Poylisher Farband, argued that the responsibility of Argentine Jewry for Jewish schooling in Poland was part of a broader program of solidarity between secular Yiddishists worldwide. Orzech was one of the most prominent figures to provide financial assistance to Jews in Poland. He served as secretary of Gezelshaftlikher hilfs-komitet le-toyves di yidn in poyln (Social Help-Committee to Help the Jews in Poland) and later as the secretary of Poylisher Farband's cultural center. In a September 1931 article, Orzech wrote that TSYSHO schools were "a bright point on the clouded horizons" of Jews in Poland. He praised the schools that "continue the fight for a better tomorrow" and "prepared a new generation of physically and spiritually fit Jewish children."[78] Orzech and other progressive Jewish ethnic leaders feared that the financial collapse of TSYSHO in Poland would endanger the Yiddish national project in eastern Europe, Argentina, and elsewhere. Orzech called upon Polish Jews in Argentina to "save the educational edifice that we built with our blood and sweat," arguing that learning in Polish state-run schools would lead to Polonization and would be "an insult" to the national culture of Polish Jews.[79] Orzech stressed that in a situation when the Polish government limited the subsidies for Jewish educational institutions, Polish Jews living abroad must take upon themselves the responsibility of financially supporting the TSYSHO schools in Poland.

Poland as a common place of origin was often not enough to secure stable relations between the immigrant community in the Americas and their compatriots in Poland. Consequently, strong and permanent links and alliances were often built both around ethnicity and common political outlooks. Jewish institutions in Poland often searched for financial help from the branches of a given party or movement in other parts of the world. The Yiddishist ethnonationalism of TSYSHO fell close to the ideals of many Polish Jews in Argentina. Many left-wing Jews who supported Bundist goals lived in Buenos Aires. Thousands of Jewish blue-collar workers were members of trade unions and backed the local Partido Socialista and Unión Cívica Radical, while others supported the illegal Communist Party. Also, TSYSHO found numerous supporters in organizations more removed from left-wing politics. Although in the 1930s landsmanshaftn had convened social elements of the rising middle class, proletarian traditions were well remembered. In the language used by landslayt in their publications, one sees clear socialist influences. Thus, we read about "Jewish working masses," about "blood and sweat" and class struggle. Poylisher Farband, which still contained many laborers, underlined the importance of Yiddish and secular schooling in Yiddish on numerous occasions, debating even opening its own educational institutions. Jewish left wingers in Argentina were largely centered around Yiddish institutions and media. *Di Presse*, a leading Argentine Yiddish daily, had a clear leftist stand.

The fund-raising efforts for the TSYSHO schools in Poland were coordinated since the mid-1920s by the Argentine Help Committee for the Yiddish Secular Schools in Poland (Hilfs-komitet far di yidish veltlekhe shuln in poyln). The Hilfs-komitet included a number of activists of workers' libraries, workers' associations, and a few landsmanshaftn (Bialystoker Farband, Vengrover Farayn, Poylisher Farband, Galitsianer Farband). The committee organized meetings informed about the situation of secular Yiddish schools in Poland and began the fund-raising. The authorities of the Yidishe shul-organizatsye in Warsaw were in permanent contact with Argentine campaigners, and Warsaw-based activists Jacob Lestschinsky and Yaakov Zerubavel sent regular telegrams to the editors of *Di Presse*. In November 1929, they thanked fund-raisers "in the name of 25 thousand children" for a recent money transfer. A month later, a telegram warned about the increasing financial difficulties of the TSYSHO schools in Poland and urged the Argentine supporters to send more money.

The left-wing *Di Presse* did the propaganda work for the campaign. The daily published numerous articles discussing the work of TSYSHO schools in Poland and presented its modern methods and commitment to educating a generation of secular, Yiddish-speaking, nationally conscious Jews. The landsmanshaftn determined the specific financial goals of the aid campaign. In a letter from August 15, 1931, Poylisher Farband informed the Folks-komitet that they had already collected 414 pesos of the planned 1,000.[80] The Peretz Hirschbein Biblyotek of Buenos Aires allowed the Hilfs-komitet to use its premises for the entire month of November 1929.[81] The Poylisher Farband assigned a room in its headquarters for use by the TSYSHO committee.[82] The Farband's paper, *Dos Naye Vort*, partook in the campaign, offering its readers overviews about the situation of Jewish schooling in Poland, reporting about its financial misery, and encouraged support for the campaign. The Farband also took part in a *protest-akt* against the persecution of TSYSHO schools organized in Buenos Aires on September 20, 1931.[83] Yet, not every institution answered positively. The Galitisianer Farband informed that due to a financial deficit and a high number of other campaigns conducted in the previous weeks, they were unable to offer more than twenty pesos.[84] Unión Israelita de Residentes de Polonia from Tucumán replied that currently no campaign could be conducted because support would be weak.[85] Yet, they stated that they passed a resolution condemning the measures against the TSYSHO schools taken by the Polish government.[86]

Understanding that often women oversaw the education of their children, Poylisher Farband specifically approached immigrant women during the 1931 TSYSHO campaign. A poster, announcing a women-only meeting, wrote that in Poland thousands of Jewish parents "lead a brave fight in order to save their children from moral enslavement and assimilation." It suggested that Jewish women in Poland and Argentina shared (or should share) similar attitudes about the national meaning of Yiddish and progressive schooling. Those living in Buenos Aires were prompted to express their solidarity with fellow Jewish mothers in Poland. One poster read: "Could Jewish mothers and sisters remain passive and distant? Not contribute to this holy work? To remain indifferent when thousands of our brothers and sisters are desperately fighting for the maintenance of schools, when they are sacrificing themselves?"[87]

As in the case of other campaigns, the TSYSHO campaigners presented their fund-raising activities as a noble and difficult task. Their charity involvement was presented as a virtue that demanded coping with numerous disadvantages or hardships. When Pinie Wald reported about the TSYSHO action, he began by describing the difficult life of Argentine Jewish workers, who lost their jobs and other sources of income due to the world financial crisis of 1929.[88] Wald drew a picture of impoverished Argentine Jews, who not only were hardly in the position of helping their Polish compatriots but were also unable to financially support their own families. The journalist added that numerous "elements" of the Argentine Jewish public decided to fight against the TSYSHO campaign. The fact that the beneficiaries were linked to the Bund supposedly made it a goal of Zionist and communist defamation campaigns. The obstacles presented by Wald, combined with the financial support that the Jews of Argentina did offer despite their own poverty, presented the fund-raising campaign and its participants as exceptionally committed and devoted. The report summarizing the 1931 TSYSHO campaign primarily emphasized those who supported the cause though volunteer work.[89] On the first page of the brochure, the bold text emphasized the names of respected Buenos Aires Yiddishist activists: Pinie Wald, Pinie Katz, and Samuel Rollansky. The backing of the ethnic leaders helped to gain popular support for the cause and increased the prestige of the action. The organizers appreciated not only the big personalities who "donated" their name for the campaign but also those who had less prestigious, though no less important, tasks, including children's and women's committees that also raised funds for the aktsye. The TSYSHO campaign was defined as a popular effort, and each contribution and sacrifice were appreciated and praised.

The strategy of engaging respected personalities from Argentina's Jewish world, which was used in the TSYSHO aktsye in 1931, was also applied in the following campaign in 1937. The special issue of *Dos Naye Vort* featured articles of personalities such as Pinie Katz, Yankev Botoshansky, Lazaro Zhitnitsky, Leyb Schussheim. Each of these personalities supported the campaign not only by writing a text for the special issue of *Dos Naye Vort*, but also in the big Jewish dailies they edited. Schussheim, himself a Polish Jew born in Galicia in 1879, immigrated to Argentina at the age of forty-seven, after a successful journalistic career in Kraków and Poaley Tsiyon activism. In Buenos Aires, he worked for the Yiddish daily *Di Yidische Zaitung*. In his text in *Dos Naye Vort*, he specifically turned to Jewish elites. Appealing to their generosity, he argued that the wealthier members of the community had a bigger obligation and that one expected more from them when it came to social engagement like the TSYSHO campaign. Rich Argentine Jews who did not support the help action were supposed to "stain their name." For Schussheim, those who refused to help were simply "bad Jews." The journalist equated their success in Argentina with an obligation of substantial financial involvement in helping the Jews of Poland.[90]

The TSYSHO campaigns were supported by emissaries sent from Poland. The Bundist activists from Poland were "cart-horses" of these campaigns.[91] In Argentina, they represented both the traditions of the alter heym and the charm of a new progressive Jewish life developing in eastern Europe. This dual character of the emissaries facilitated gaining the support both from those who felt obliged to take care of the well-being of their brothers in the alter heym and also those who looked to the future, living a new secular, progressive Jewishness. In 1931, Borys (Beniamin) Tabachinski arrived in Argentina from Białystok. He stayed in Argentina for several months and gave numerous public talks in hotels or salons. Although the financial success of Tabachinski's visit might have been limited, the campaign brought the problems of Yiddishness and Yiddish schooling to the center of Jewish debates in Argentina. Soon after Tabaczyński's visit, Marcos Regalsky, Samuel Rollansky, and Guitl Kanutsky formed Gezelshaft far yidishe veltlekhe shuln in argentine (Society for the Yiddish Secular Schools in Argentina) largely based on Poland's TSYSHO concepts and pedagogical methods.[92] In 1936, the TSYSHO head office sent to Argentina a well-known writer and journalist, Borekh Schefner, head of the Union of Jewish Writers and Journalists in Warsaw. Schefner spoke in numerous venues in Buenos Aires and in the provinces. Also, this time the campaign was a joint effort of various groups that labeled themselves as the "progressive elements" of Argentine Jewry. Among the most active leaders were Yankev Botoshansky and Pinie Wald, and both socialist and Zionists groups joined the campaign. Collecting money for TSYSHO schools in Poland combined transnational Yiddishist progressive activism with a local *kultur-arbet* (cultural work) in Argentina. As Frank Wolff wrote, TSYSHO campaigns were *Vergemeintschaftungsprozessen* (processes of community building) that constructed a secular, progressive Argentine Jewry.[93] The campaigns allowed Argentine Jews to unite around a certain goal and were an opportunity for creating Jewish-Argentine identifications. By uniting diverse groups, the campaigns helped to define the shared goals and priorities on the local Argentine level. The impulse that the campaigns gave to the Argentine Yiddishist schooling broke the dichotomy that saw the Old World as the destination of help efforts and the new diasporas as a base of resources. TSYSHO campaigns constructed a new transnational space centered around the ethnonational importance of secular Yiddish schooling. Progressive Jewishness was imagined as a global phenomenon that needed to be developed on the local level. In the 1930s, the transnational solidarity networks were focused not only on material help but witnessed new transatlantic Jewish cultural transfers and the emergence of imagined global Yiddishland society: a secular diaspora Jewry that lived in a reality of a transnational *doikait* (hereness).

We Condemn! Protesting Anti-Semitism in Poland

Another aspect of transnational outreach and interest of Poylisher Farband (and of many nonaffiliated immigrants) were protest gatherings against anti-Semitism in Poland, conducted throughout the entire interwar period. Solidarity with the "brothers in Poland" in the context of anti-Semitism can be traced to the very beginning of Poylisher Farband's existence. The first protests against anti-Semitism were organized in Argentina after a wave of pogroms that occurred in Poland and Ukraine between 1918 and 1921. A Jewish protest committee against the pogroms in Poland (Comité Israelita de Protesta contra los Pogroms de Polonia) was established in 1919, and Poylisher Farband was affiliated with this committee from the very beginning.[94] Following a bloody pogrom in the Polish-Ukrainian borderlands, the committee organized in Buenos Aires a day of mourning on July 29, 1919, and Poylisher Farband sent delegates to the event, including its president Abraham Fridman.[95]

The committee's activists understood the pogroms in Poland largely as a contradiction of Argentine liberal values that Jewish immigrants often quickly internalized. The situation in eastern Europe was seen as the negation of a civilized world. A 1919, a Spanish-language poster condemned Poland as ungrateful for its new independence. It said: "The new nations that emerged after the peace treaty, inaugurated their existence with massacres of Jews. . . . Thousands of people were murdered or buried alive, women were raped and children tortured, thousands of houses are destroyed. This is what Europe's East looks like in this hour of universal joy. . . . In order to understand what is happening in Poland, one would need to return to the most barbaric era of persecution."[96]

Some Jews in Argentina expected that a country, partitioned for more than a century, would place more value in democratic and liberal standards. The protesters suggested that "the Argentine voice should be heard among the protests of other free nations" and consequently make clear to Poland that the crimes against the Jews would always be met with condemnation. The protests constructed immigrant Jews as Argentines, who used their democratic privileges to condemn the events in their home country. This helped to define the Jews of Poland as the victims of barbarism, and those living in Argentina as preoccupied but lucky to live in a freer world.

In later years, issues concerning the rights of minorities in eastern Europe were carefully followed in Argentina. Polish Jews in Argentina quickly understood that the situation of the Jewish minority in Poland would be far from rosy. In March 1922, *Di Presse* reported on a visit to Poland by L. Maas, a representative of the Comité Central de Socorro a las Victimas Israelitas de los Pogroms y de Protección a los Inmigrantes (Central Committee of Help to the Victims of Pogroms and of Immigrants' Protection). The daily printed his reports from various Polish cities, in which he described the situation of the Jewish population and their economic and social problems. Maas's visit principally focused on the Ukrainian Jews, who suffered from pogroms during the Russo-Ukrainian war of 1917 to 1921 and often fled westward to Poland. Maas himself described his visit and help campaign as a *hilfs-aktsye far ukrainishe yidn* (help actions for Ukrainian Jews), rather than those of Poland. Anti-Semitic incidents in other countries were also followed. In 1928, a protest against pogroms in Romania was organized in Buenos Aires.[97] In the 1930s, numerous protests were organized condemning the anti-Jewish policies of Nazi Germany.

In 1925, Zvi Cohen of the Poylisher Farband complained that Jews in Poland did not enjoy national minority rights as proclaimed by the Versailles treaty and were an object of increasing Polonization.[98] In 1926, *Di Yidische Zaitung* reprinted a speech by Polish-Jewish parliamentarian and journalist Noyekh Prilutsky given at the Minorities' Conference in Geneva.[99] Hundreds of articles described the deteriorating economic situation in Poland and the rise of anti-Semitism in the late 1930s. The issue of Jewish discrimination in Poland was also followed by the Jewish press in Spanish.[100] In 1925, *Mundo Israelita* described the situation in Poland in the following way: "In Europe, there is a half-Asian, half-Balkan country called Poland. It shares so many commonalities with Asia and the Balkans, especially concerning barbarism. . . . The redeemed Poles began to celebrate their independence with Jewish blood. This led to international condemnation, even by those who fought for Poland's independence. . . . Yet later Mr. Grabski [Poland's prime minister] found a bloodless way to strangle the Jews. The excessive taxes hit the Jews only and kill them without spilling their blood. . . . There is no day when we don't hear about aggression against the Jews. . . . The Constitution that provides Jews with equal rights is a fifth wheel in the policies of the Polish government."[101] The article concluded with a desired reaction of Argentine Jews: "We Jews, who have the luck to live outside of this barbaric country, we can't do anything but to voice our protests and condemnations of the recent pogroms again and again. Let the innocent blood remain on the executioners!"

Throughout the 1930s, and particularly following the death of Poland's respected leader Józef Piłsudski post-1935, the anti-Semitic rightwing organizations were increasingly influential in Poland. The nationalist party of the National Democrats (*endecja*) and smaller radical groups emphasized the alleged existence of a "Jewish problem," which claimed that Poland's economic hardships were the result of Jewish "anti-Polish" activities. Anti-Semitic campaigns called for a boycott of Jewish businesses. The already uneasy situation of three million Polish Jews worsened even further. TSYSHO schools were deprived of municipal subsidies. Jewish ritual slaughter was limited in 1936.[102] As a result of anti-Semitic student demands, so-called "bench ghettos" that separated Jews and non-Jews were introduced at many universities. The 1930s were a decade of numerous anti-Jewish incidents, sometimes leading to bloody pogroms. Polish Jews in Argentina were well-aware of the deteriorating economic and political situation of Jews in Poland. Dozens of articles covered the anti-Semitic attacks and pogroms that occurred after 1935. The reports and letters from Poland that described the contemporary reality appeared in the general and landsman press. Columns entitled "Fun der alten heym" (From the Old Home) or "Brif fun poyln" (Letters from Poland) kept Jews in Argentina up-to-date about the most recent developments in their native country.

The growth of fascist anti-Jewish sentiments in Poland in the late 1930s demanded stronger actions from Argentina's Polish Jews. In mid-1935, a number of landsman hilfs-fonds begun to cooperate and opened their own press outlet: *Zaitshrift. In di interesn fun di karbones fun eyrope* (Newspaper for the interests of European victims). *Zaitschrift* regularly called for financial and "moral" help for eastern European and especially Polish Jews. In 1937, Z. Weinfer, an Argentine Jew, visited Poland after not being there for eight years. Weinfer reported about the worsening situation and direct attacks on Jews. He wrote that until 1935 Poland's leader Piłsudski "held a dog muzzle on nationalist's mouths"; yet, after his death, the endecja was "biting the Jewish body with its poisonous teeth."[103] Stone-throwing teenagers attacked Weinfer himself when he was traveling with his old and bearded uncle. In the late 1930s, the aid campaigns were directed primarily toward Polish Jews, who were devastated by boycott-attempts or direct attacks by right-wing organizations. In 1938, the fate of Polish Jews was inscribed in wider anti-Jewish policies in other parts of Europe. Yet, as *Zaitschrift* argued, Argentine Jews were supposed to be best informed about the whereabouts in Poland, whose government they described as fascist. Articles often referred to the persecution of socialists and democrats. The newspaper called to "search for all possible means of help." It underlined that "each Jewish immigrant in our new home needs to support those who stayed in the Old Country and suffer persecution by local military regime."[104]

The newspaper underlined a need to combine financial help with protests against "barbarian policies of Poland's authorities" and growing anti-Semitism. This should give Jews in Poland an impression that they are not left alone in their struggles.[105] Consequently, *Zaitschrift* reported that fifty families in the shtetl of Chmielnik were without any means of existence, as well as about anti-Jewish boycotters not allowing Jewish merchants to sell on the market in the town of Wyszków. Leyb Aronson who was supposed to protest against the *piketnikes* (boycotters) was allegedly sentenced for six months of prison for "insulting the Polish nation." Writing about Aronson's fate, the Argentine newspaper merged his lack of possibilities of earning a living with the ever-violent anti-Semitic attacks of Polish right wingers.[106]

Subethnic solidarity, transnational involvement, and sheer empathy pushed many Argentine Jews to actively protest anti-Semitism in Poland. The leaders of Poylisher Farband believed that even living abroad, they shared a responsibility for the well-being of Jews in Poland, and the fact that they lived in a relatively free and democratic country obliged them to react to injustices against the Jews in their home country.[107] Although it is hard to assess to what extent the protests of the Poylisher Farband had any influence on changing the situation of Jews in Poland, for the landsman, it was clear that they had to respond to the increasing anti-Semitism in Poland. Mordechai Vengrover of the Poylisher Farband argued that it was solidarity and a wish to "internationalize" the problem of anti-Semitic violence that pushed the international Jewish protests further.[108] A librarian of the Farband, Leyzer Stokhammer, writing for the 1924 almanac, argued that presenting the harsh situation of Polish Jews to foreign public opinion was the only way for Poland-born Argentine Jews to influence the situation. As Stokhammer stressed, Poland feared for its good image abroad and was truly interested in reducing the tensions with Jewish Polish diasporas abroad, including the Argentine one. In Stokhammer's opinion, Argentine Jewish protests could indirectly influence the policies of the Polish government. His reasoning shows that for members of the Farband it was of great importance to have a sense of being influential and having agency in Polish-Jewish problems worldwide.[109]

Following the bloody anti-Jewish events of November 1932 (in Vilna, Warsaw, Kraków, Lwów, and other places), a group of Farband members visited the Polish ambassador, Władysław Mazurkiewcz, and handed him a note of protest to be sent through him to the Polish government. As *Dos Naye Vort* reported, Mazurkiewcz, consul Kicki, and migration attaché Pankiewicz "expressed their sadness about the recent anti-Jewish incidents in Poland and joined the protest."[110] Mazurkiewicz, however empathetic with the protests taking place in Argentina, asked the Farband to publish his response, which in a way questioned the harsh accusations of Farband's delegates. Mazurkiewcz wrote that state officials always prosecuted the anti-Jewish attacks and that these incidents were in fact against Polish interests, as they harmed Poland's "good name" abroad.[111] The Federation of Polish-Jewish Landsmanshaftn also sent a telegram to the Polish president (see below) demanding an active stand against the anti-Jewish violence perpetrated by the right wing, again referring to the problems that Poland's reputation would suffer. Telegrams demanding intervention were also sent to the president of the League of Nations and the Human Rights League.[112]

> Démarche [protest note] to the Polish Government:
>
> The Jews grouped in the Poylisher Farband and in other associated organizations, thousands of Jews altogether, are protesting against the recent indescribable hooligan events against our brothers in Poland.
>
> Every other year in Poland attacks are repeated on the peaceful Jewish population, attacks that one politely calls "extsesn" [excesses], that leave hundreds of victims and wounded. . . . This does not bring Poland any honor and harms Poland's reputation abroad. The reputation of a nation that was enslaved for 150 years, a nation that is the cultural wall of the East, a land with a constitution that grants its citizens all freedoms.
>
> The systematic and planned discrimination of the Jewish population in all branches of the country's economy, but also in regard to cultural and political life, is a bloody insult to us, Jews, who are spiritually connected with

> our brothers in Poland. The shameful tools of inquisition, like throwing out of trains or beating innocent citizens, that are not (till now) prosecuted, makes us feel that the government is very passive concerning these incidents, despite the fact that the government has all the means to react. . . .
>
> Deeply saddened, we demand that the government intervene, and in a spirit of human rights, put an end to the shameful hooligan attacks. The hooligans break the constitution that promises "freedom, equality and brotherhood" to all of Poland's citizens.[113]

The protest continued beyond the meeting with the Polish ambassador. The farband members, claiming a "spiritual connection with our brothers in Poland," together with other Polish-Jewish landsmanshaftn, organized public protest gatherings.[114] These meetings allowed a "collective outrage" and were an expression of emotions shared by Polish Jews in Argentina. Protesting against anti-Semitism in Poland en masse, the protesters defined themselves as empathetic, sympathetic, and committed members of a worldwide Polish-Jewish diaspora, as those who react when their "Polish brothers" suffer and are discriminated against. Similar protest gatherings were also organized in other centers of the Polish- Jewish diaspora. In the United States, the Federation of Polish Jews in America issued a formal letter of protest.[115]

On December 15, 1932, an "imposing protest-akt" against the pogroms of Jews in Poland took place in Prince George Hall in Buenos Aires. The Jewish press reported that the hall was "overfilled with thousands of protesters."[116] The recently established Federation of Polish-Jewish Landsmanshaftn in Argentina organized the event, but it attracted broader support from Jewish Buenos Aires. The protest-akt was supported by Sociedad Hebraica, Hevra Kadisha Ashkenazi, IWO Institute, TSVYSHO schools, the Zionist Federation, several landsmanshaftn and Jewish financial institutions. The organizers were proud of the massive mobilization of Argentine Jews, quite uncommon for this highly divided group. *Dos Naye Vort* reported that the president of the committee organizing the ceremony, Dr. Bergman, spoke about how "moved and outraged were the Argentine Jews hearing about the incidents in Poland." Dr. Lazaro Zhitnitsky touched upon the consequences of anti-Semitism for Jewish economic life in Poland. Whereas those two spoke in Yiddish, another member of a protest committee, a lawyer by the name of Steinberg, spoke in Spanish. The language in which Steinberg spoke showed that acculturated Jews, including those who probably belonged to second-generation immigrants and identified primarily as Argentines, likewise maintained a certain commitment to Jewish Poland. The protest-akt served as a way of manifesting the power of Argentine Jewry and its desire to be involved in the problems of the Old World. The identification with the experiences back home were articulated in and impacted Argentine dynamics.[117] The 1932 protests were still remembered in 1941, when they were prominently featured in a jubilee publication.[118]

The protesters, gathered in Prince George Hall, unanimously agreed on the following declaration:

> The Jewish masses of Buenos Aires, together with the delegates of the Argentine Jewish institutions, protest against the constant incidents of violence against the Jews in Poland. Referring to the consciousness of the Polish nation, and to its traditions of freedom, we demand a stop to the hooligan attacks on Jewish citizens, who have lived on Polish lands for generations, and have participated in all fights for Polish national liberation.
>
> We condemn the unjust anti-Jewish economic policy and the passivity of the Polish government in combating the anti-Jewish incidents. We demand that the government fulfill the obligation of the state to protect the Jewish citizens, rescuing the sagging prestige of liberated Poland in the eyes of the honest and civilized world.[119]

The declaration was largely based on Marcos Regalsky's speech given during the ceremony in Price George Hall. He alluded to Jewish support for the independence of Poland, which in his view was too often challenged by anti-Jewish policies and pogroms.[120] The declaration showed that the loyalty of Jews to Poland, as well as their engagement in Poland's struggles for independence, was used as an argument against anti-Jewish policies and incidents. By emphasizing this, the organizers of the protests were touching on a very sensitive point. No one could question the centuries of Jewish life on Polish lands, the Jewish contribution to the development of the Polish economy, and the involvement of Jewish soldiers in World War I and earlier uprisings. This point of view presented Jews as an integral part of Polish society that deserved equal rights and respect.

This logic was also apparent in an editorial of *Dos Naye Vort* from December 1932. Its authors wrote about the shared experiences of Jewish and non-Jewish Poles, who were "connected by the same destiny, same suffering, same happiness" and together struggled for their bread. The landslayt underlined the "love of Polish Jews for Poland," a country where they were born, whose "fruits they ate," and whose character, culture, and life they knew the best. For Poylisher Farband members, loyalty and commitment to Poland was the ultimate argument that proved that Poland's Jews deserved respect, instead of persecution and discrimination.[121] The landslayt dismissed the accusations of making "anti-Polish" propaganda (the way that their protests were often described in Poland). They pointed out that they protested "against anti-Semitic hooligans and *pogromshtchikes*," against the "anti-Jewish intelligentsia that regards anti-Semitism as a virtue," against the "passive and indifferent" Polish government, and not the Polish nation as such. Underlining the shared experiences with Catholic Poles, Polish Jews in Argentina identified anti-Semitism as an exception and a form of anti-Polish activity that destroyed Polish prestige abroad.

Polish Jews in Argentina tried to interest the gentile population in their protest. One of the 1931 posters, shouting "*Argentinos!*" in bold font, tried to attract non-Jewish support for the protests organized by the Buenos Aires Jewish institutions.[122] Underlining the liberalism and freedoms of Argentina and praising the presumed devotion of Argentines to justice and equality, the Jewish protesters called for universal participation in the protest. Even though the 1930s were a time of a right-wing backlash in Argentina, the guiding principles of Argentine democracy were still applied as a rhetorical tool in the case of anti-Semitism in Poland. For the Polish-Jewish community, liberal Argentina appeared as an antithesis of oppressive Poland. The attempt to attract the interest of non-Jewish Argentines was to internationalize the narrative about anti-Semitism in Poland. By spreading the Argentine Jewish position on this issue, the protesters hoped that it would result in official condemnations on the side of Argentine authorities (something the Polish government wanted to avoid).

Conclusion

In Argentina, the landsmanshaftn formed a mesostructure, located somewhere between the official Jewish community and those unaffiliated with major Jewish organizations. It was a semiprivate and semipublic ethnic space, satisfying both the specific cultural needs of the migrants as well as, via local and transatlantic engagement, answering their desire for a collective recognition. During the 1920s and 1930s, Polish Jews in Argentina engaged in a wide range of transatlantic aid campaigns. Raising money for their fellow Jews in Poland, they relied on shared ethnic interests. By organizing help campaigns or protesting against the anti-Semitism in Poland, Argentine Jews underlined that the developments in eastern Europe and the fates of their "brothers in Poland" were for them of high importance. This was especially true for the landsman movement. The landslayt developed a discourse that suggested a "national obligation" that Jews of Polish origin need to pay off by supporting their homeland in Poland. The discourse of the Polish landslayt imagined Polish Jewry as a national body: scattered between new diasporic centers, yet connected by a shared past, a narrative of secular Yiddishist commitment, and networks of transnational solidarity.

Simultaneously, the landslayt did not perceive their involvement in local and transnational diasporic networks of Polish Jews as incongruent with being proud, committed, and successful Argentines. On the contrary, the Argentine society of the 1920s and 1930s was largely a world of recent immigrants. As such, ethnically specific expression among Polish Argentine Jews served as a pathway into the Argentine immigrant mainstream. By referring to the broader Argentine Jewish public living, the organizers defined themselves as argentiner yidn, Argentine Jews. The assistance and support offered to their brothers in Poland was defined as *hilf fun oysland*, foreign help. Precisely by living abroad and enjoying more freedom and better economic chances, Argentine Jews were called upon to help the less fortunate Jews in Poland. In contrast to Tobias Brinkman's argument, that immigrants did not think too much about the world left behind, I believe that many Jewish immigrants "had time to look back."[123] The next chapter focuses on the intricacies of the relationship of Argentine Jews to eastern Europe.

8

All Immigrant Jews Live with Their Soul in Poland?

Debating the Tension between New and Old Home

Argentine Jewish journalist Yosef Mendelson in 1919 in the first anthology of Yiddish writing in Latin America wrote:

> The Jewish Argentina, I want to say, still is—and probably will still be for many years—an unknown land, a *terra ignota* for the broad Jewish public in Russia and America; Argentina is still one of those "distant lands," which the broad Jewish world does not comprehend, or almost does not comprehend.
>
> Argentina is distant, distant from the great Jewish world, from the grand Jewish centers of Europe and North America. This is a distance that can be felt in a way how they imagine us, and in the way how we think about ourselves.[1]

This quote shows that for many Argentine Jews, not only for those of Polish origin, eastern Europe of the interwar years was a major reference point as a bustling center of Ashkenazi civilization. For nearly two decades, many Argentine Jews perceived themselves as a new branch or chapter of eastern European Jewish life. At the same time, the proacculturation actors quickly helped to develop their sense of Argentine belonging. The Argentine yishev attempted to underline its "independence" in cultural and social areas, but relations with eastern Europe were defined by center-periphery dynamics. Even in anthologies that celebrated Argentine-made Yiddish literature, the editors felt obliged to include texts by authors from the eastern European center, who, by visiting and describing Argentina, put a sui generis stamp of approval on the local Yiddish creativity.[2] This chapter looks at the role of the memory of eastern Europe in the development of Argentine Jewish culture. It explores Argentine literary debates concerning the focus of local Yiddish literature and investigates the importance of the eastern European context for Jewish life in Argentina.

The Jews in Argentina, both those who perceived Buenos Aires as a part of the global Yiddishland and those who saw themselves as patriotic Jewish Argentines, were sensitive about European opinions of Argentina. An editorial written in *Mundo Israelita* in 1924 read that the Yiddish dailies were alarmed by any negative opinions about Argentina that appeared in the United States or Poland.[3] The Spanish journal itself also complained about the misinformed European visitors, who were often surprised to find that Buenos Aires did not have a cultural level "lower" than Warsaw or Vilna. *Mundo Israelita* wrote about the lack of cultural reciprocity between Jewish Poland and Jewish Argentina. Whereas in Argentina there were circles that worked to promote eastern European Yiddish culture, there was hardly anyone who would talk in Poland about Jewish-Argentine writer Gerchunoff and local cultural production.

Mundo Israelita advised not to focus on European yellow press reports but to support attentive and objective visitors who were truly interested in Argentine Jewish life. As examples of such professional reports, the journal mentioned those of Nomberg, Anohi, Latzki-Bertoldi, and Yuris. The Argentine narrative of Nomberg was seen as supportive of "Jewish rootedness in Argentina, our attachment to the land and our intellectual progress." The weekly believed that his depictions of Argentina would produce "enlightenment work" in Poland and would balance the "legends originating in ignorance and malevolence." *Mundo Israelita* appreciated the value of Nomberg's book at a time of increased migration to Argentina and saw it as a credible source of information for those "who would settle on these beaches forever."[4]

Argentine Jews themselves attempted to influence the way Jews in Poland looked on Argentina. In October 1929, *Di Presse* editor Pinie Katz visited Vilna.[5] The journalist, who served as one of the key promoters of Yiddishism and progressive Jewishness in Argentina, was welcomed in Vilna as an old comrade. Katz spent a week there and visited numerous Jewish institutions (schools, theaters, editorial offices, etc.) and gave a lecture about Jews in Argentina in the Vilna branch of Farayn fun Yidishe literatn un zhurnalistn (Association of Jewish Writers and Journalists). The local activists of Yiddish PEN Club used Katz's visit in Vilna as an opportunity to talk about opening an Argentine branch of the institution. S. Erzet (probably Vilna-based Leyb Szereszewski), in a report to *Di Presse*, mentioned that Katz was the first guest from Argentina's literary-journalistic circle to come to Vilna.[6] Katz was seen as a representative of all Argentine Jewry and was warmly welcomed by Zalmen Reyzen, one of the most prominent figures of the YIVO Yiddish Scientific Institute. Katz's visit to Vilna and the recognition given to him by YIVO was a symbolic embrace of Argentina into the Yiddishland, no less important in its symbolic capital of Vilna. Welcoming Katz, Reyzen said: "What do we know about this healthy, unique Jewish life on the shores of La Plata, on the endless South American pampa? What do we know about suffering and happiness of those pioneers of Jewish production, liberating the Jews from their humiliating professions? . . . But only in hearing his stories about the builders and activists of the Jewish yishev in Argentina has this land become so close to me, this land of so many fulfilled and broken hopes for a new healthy, productive Jewish life. . . . A land of people who within forty years laid a strong foundation for a yishev of 250,000 souls, a yishev that already began to contribute its part to world Yiddish culture."[7]

Reyzen's speech was a eulogy to Jewish Argentina. The Yiddishist scholar was amazed by the development of Jewish life in Argentina and argued that Argentina was dear and close to him. For Reyzen, Argentina was already a part of the Yiddishland microcosm, unique in certain aspects but also sharing many commonalities with other diasporas. In that way, Katz's visit to the YIVO Institute in Vilna was a symbolic confirmation of Argentina's status as a part of the Yiddishland.[8] The community of interests between Katz's agenda in Argentina and the YIVO sociocultural program was clearly visible and officially voiced during the 1929 meeting. Jewish Argentina received the desired recognition from the Yiddishist heartland, while YIVO leaders could use the example of Argentina to speak about a global and vital Yiddish culture.

Especially painful for Argentine Jews were eastern European reductionist tendencies, which conceived of Jewish Argentina as a space merely for prostitution and female trafficking. At times, they were challenged by Argentine Jews visiting Poland. When journalist and author Yankev Botoshansky visited Grodno in 1931, he complained that Poland's Yiddish newspapers blew sex crimes in Buenos Aires out of proportion: "Just yesterday your newspapers wrote that some Zisa Zaydman murdered some Aba Zonschein, who wanted to snatch a girl to Argentina. I'm not saying you should not describe these events in the newspapers. But do it with proportion: for every thousand Jewish immigrants who go to Argentina to work hard and in bitterness . . . maybe five are female traffickers. The remaining 995 do not murder and do not cause scandals, but the newspapers do not write about them. Yet about those five who do murder, the newspapers do write about them. The result is: no one knows here anything about our honest and hard life and people believe that all of [Argentine Jewish] life consists of female traffickers!"[9]

It bothered Botoshansky that Poland's journalists started their interviews by asking about female trafficking, despite the fact that "there were so many interesting things to talk about, about building, living, creating." For Botoshansky, who spoke in Grodno about idealistic Jewish colonists who had to cut through the jungle in order to work the land, it was important to push a heroic perception of Argentine Jewry in Poland. Botoshansky confirmed that colonization did not have much of a future, but even in this aspect, he criticized the Polish Jewish exoticization of Argentina, saying that it was "formed by the spicy stories of Mordechai Alpersohn" and had little to do with reality.[10] Botoshansky proclaimed that he came to Poland "to fight against the lack of local interest in a meaningful Jewish life in Argentina." As an Argentine Yiddishist, he saw himself as responsible for combating the simplistic portrayals of Jewish Argentina at the heart of the Yiddishland. The problematic reputation of Argentina in eastern Europe challenged Argentine Yiddishists' desire to see Argentina as an equal part of the Yiddishland. Also in the United States, Buenos Aires was a metonym for white slavery. As Argentina loomed large on the international white slave trade map, the struggle for the good name of Argentina abroad was conducted not only by Jews but also by Argentine authorities.[11]

Some Jews in Argentina considered eastern European opinions on Argentina as exaggerated or even dangerous to the formation of Jewish Argentine identities. The issue of maintaining relations with Poland and being perceived as Polish-Jewish was not always met with understanding among Argentinized circles. León Kibrick, one of the cultural leaders of Jewish Argentines, saw argentinidad as a new phenomenon, fresh and uncontaminated by the Old World plagues. Kibrick believed that "Argentina belongs to Jews in the same way that it does to Catholics" and proudly voiced his identification with the Argentine republic.[12] He fiercely opposed linking Jewish prostitution and female trafficking with Argentine Jewry and Argentineness as such. He described it as a clearly Polish-Jewish issue, as most of the pimps and prostitutes originated from Poland. He wrote in 1926: "We deal here with a Polish question, rather than an Argentine problem. We can proudly shout that no Israelite woman born here practices prostitution and no man who saw the light of this country works as a pimp."[13] Kibrick went on to continue that these were the Jews of Poland who accused the Jewish Argentines of vice and a lack of morality, spreading the bad fame of Argentina. "The sons of Polish Jewry come to us, to share with us our freedom and our bread, and as soon as they disembark, they start to preach to us about morality and cast a plague on us that is exclusively theirs," the journalist noted. Kibrick drew lines of separation between the Jews socialized in Argentina and those who immigrated recently. He later argued that "it's high time that we start to see ourselves as Argentine residents, rather than European guests. We should get rid of prejudices and also mentally move to Argentina, as we did physically. Then we would see things in a different light. Our colleagues from the Yiddish press, so badly influenced by the recent immigration wave, should be the first to give example and stop living on a lease. The Argentine Jewish organism is robust enough to emancipate itself [from eastern European influence]."[14]

Kibrick's accusations resulted in a fierce protest by Poylisher Farband that saw the article as besmirching all of Polish Jewry, including those living in Argentina.[15] The Poylisher Farband president argued that in the current situation, when cultural contacts between Jewish Poland and Jewish Argentina grew much stronger (after the new wave of Polish-Jewish immigrants), it was absurd to continue imagining Polish Jews as female traffickers.[16] Moreover, Pinie Katz from the competing *Di Presse* criticized Kibrick by pointing out that their accusations about Polish Jews, including the new immigrants, were just stupid.[17]

The Argentine Yiddish Press and the Polish Question

Yiddish print culture (both literature and periodicals) was the main arena from which to voice the agendas, belonging, and evolving identities of the Yiddish-speaking immigrant public in Argentina. It was an ethnic space, shaped both by the Argentine presence and the Polish past of the immigrants. Due to the outbreak of the Great War in 1914, European journals ceased to arrive in Latin America, and the Jewish immigrants were largely cut off from any Yiddish source of information on developments in their homelands and in Argentina. In order to fill this gap, a group of activists founded *Di Yidische Zaitung (El Diario Israelita)* in 1914.[18] The daily was directed for many years by Matías (Mordechai) Stoliar and with time evolved closer to Labor Zionism. A few years later, in 1918, the procommunist daily *Di Presse* started to be published. *Di Presse*, managed for years by its editor Pinie (also Pinchas, Pedro) Katz, became a platform for voicing the interests of Argentine Yiddish-speaking proletarian Jews (fig. 22).[19] Both dailies featured short news articles from Argentina and abroad and longer political and cultural essays, especially in the more robust weekend editions. Although most of the contributing journalists lived in Argentina, the texts sent by eastern European authors made up a significant share of the *Di Presse* and *Di Yidische Zaitung* columns.

Writing in Yiddish allowed immigrant Argentine Jews to imagine themselves as "citizens" of Yiddishland and to participate in global Jewish discussions, including debates about the challenges faced by the Jews of Poland. Already in 1900, Yankev Liachovitzky was writing in the Argentine *Der Tsionist* about Warsaw-based canonic Yiddish writer Y. L. Peretz.[20] In the 1920s and 1930s, the key figures of Argentine Yiddish cultural life gladly took the opportunity of writing for Poland's or the US Yiddish press. Yankev Botoshansky was a longtime contributor of *Literarishe Bleter* in Warsaw, and in 1933, the weekly managed to publish his *Portretn fun yidishe shrayber*.[21] *Literarishe Bleter* often informed readers about the Argentine careers of Polish Jewish authors, as in the case of Moisés David Guiser.[22] The continuous involvement of Argentine Jewish contributors with Jewish Poland corresponded with a general Jewish Argentine desire for external recognition. Would the Jews in Poland be properly informed about the whereabouts in Argentina, they would start to perceive Argentina as an important brick in the politics of an imagined Yiddishland, believed the Yiddish activists from Buenos Aires.

The Jewish press, both Spanish and Yiddish, was central to informing those living in Argentina about the situation in Poland. We can divide the press articles

Figure 22. Anniversary volume published by *Di Presse daily* in 1928

about Poland into several categories: 1) reprints from Poland's Yiddish press, 2) articles commissioned from authors living in Poland, 3) news agency reports, 4) satiric texts, and 5) articles written by Argentine experts on Jewish Poland. The texts of journalist Yosef Horn belonged to the last category. Horn was a member of Poylisher Farband and a Bundist activist. Typically, he updated the Argentine Jewish public on recent developments in Poland's Yiddish literary scene. In one of his texts, he mentioned Chaim Grade, Avrom Sutzkever, Rokhl Korn, and numerous others, who were described as the new starlets of Yiddish letters in Poland.[23] Yosef Horn (1906–43) was born in Międzyrzec Podlaski in eastern Poland. In 1936, he emigrated to Buenos Aires, where he began to write for the local press and was an editor of *Dos Naye Lebn*, a monthly of Poylisher Farband in Argentina. After his immigration to Buenos Aires, Horn continued writing for Poland's Jewish periodicals and about Poland for the local Argentine titles. Horn embodied the transnational Polish Argentine Jew, living between two geographical centers, yet bound together by the Yiddish word and Yiddishist ideology. In the late 1930s, Horn was an editor of the literary journal *Der Spigl* and, as Samuel Rollansky argued, Horn understood the young Argentine yishev better than those living for a long time in Argentina.

An important section of Buenos Aires Yiddish periodicals were texts reprinted from Poland's Yiddish newspapers. In 1928 and 1929, *Di Presse* published the articles of Melech Ravitch on Yiddish female writing.[24] On other occasions, these were texts about the port cities Gdańsk (Danzig) and Gdynia, about debates in the Literatn un zhurnalistn farayn in Warsaw, or about conflicts concerning the TSYSHO schools in Poland.[25] In November 1929, a text , written by a certain Warsaw-based B. Abramson, appeared about Józef Piłsudski and his relations with the Polish parliament.[26] Another Warsaw journalist, Borekh Schefner, under the nickname of Beit Shin, published regular pieces, including his impressions from his travels in the Polish periphery.[27] Zerubavel wrote regular updates from Warsaw about the worldwide conference of the YIVO Institute in Vilna or about conflicts between Jewish artists in Poland and the United States.[28] In 1928, *Di Presse* reprinted an article by Lazar Kahane about the filming of a novel by Yosef Opatoshu in Warsaw.[29] Some of the commissioned authors had visited Argentina previously, and there established links continued after their return to Poland.

Regular articles written by journalists residing in Poland had a prominent place in shaping Argentine Jewish discussions about the alter heym. A veteran Polish correspondent of Buenos Aires's *Di Yidische Zaitung* was Abraham Goldberg (1891–1933). Commissioning Goldberg as the daily's correspondent signified that the editors were well-informed on Poland's Jewish life. Goldberg was not just a journalist but also one of the leading figures of pre-1939 Jewish Poland. He was the founder of *Haynt*, a liberal Zionist, and fervent defender of Jewish national rights. Like many of his generation, Goldberg believed that Jewishness should be based linguistically in both Hebrew and Yiddish, yet secular in its essence. In 1928, he helped to establish a secularist *Shul-un kulturfarband* that managed a network of schools teaching both in Yiddish and in Hebrew. His articles appeared in Buenos Aires almost every week and featured a broad cultural and political spectrum. For instance, in 1926, Goldberg informed Argentine Jews about developments surrounding the coup d'état of Marshal Józef Piłsudski.[30] On another occasion, Goldberg reported on conflicts between left-wing secularists and the orthodox or commented on news about Poland appointing its first Jewish minister.[31] Goldberg's input to Argentine journalism was recognized by the daily in 1928 when he was invited to contribute to the tenth anniversary jubilee issue of *Di Yidische Zaitung*.[32]

In commissioning texts by Abraham Goldberg, Mendel Menin, I. Goldinger, and other Polish correspondents, the editors of *Di Yidische Zaitung* utilized their network of contacts with Jews in Poland.[33] In the same vein, the proacculturation periodical *Semanario Hebreo* published articles by Warsaw-based N. M. Fregler. By publishing their texts, the Jewish journals brought to Argentina a range of clearly Polish Jewish problems and opinions. These articles answered both the needs of new immigrants for updates from their homeland and manifested the involvement of Argentine Jewry in Polish Jewish affairs and Yiddishland as such. Goldberg writing from Warsaw to *Di Yidishe Zaitung* or Argentina's Yankev Botoshansky writing for *Literarishe Bleter* in Warsaw, as well as thousands of longer and shorter pieces about Jewish Poland, established lines of cultural, literary, and discursive connections between Jewish Argentina and Jewish Poland.

Alongside articles commissioned from Poland and reprints and editorials by local Argentine journalists, *Mundo Israelita*, *Di Yidishe Zaitung*, and *Di Presse* received news from the Associated Press (AP) and the Jewish Telegraphic Agency. The big news agencies had their own correspondents in Poland, Palestine, the United States, and other places, where they served as intermediaries spreading the *yidishe nayes* (Jewish news) around the Jewish world. The articles based on the agency reports were usually political. The AP informed readers about the opening session of the Polish Sejm, the political upheaval of 1926, economic data, and so on.[34] *Mundo Israelita* published regular news from Poland in the section "Información judía del todo el mundo" (Jewish information from around the world), including, for instance, texts on the development of academic anti-Semitism in the late 1930s or Zionist projects in Poland.

Di Presse also published a separate column "Bilder un pasirungen fun der alter heym" (Images and events from the Old Home). It usually contained sensational news, which reflected similar columns in Poland's Yiddish dailies. Whereas in Poland, Argentina was a source of weird stories, in *Di Presse*, the Old World began to function as a place of irrational, strange events, such as an alleged new trend in Galicia, where Jewish weddings were organized without a klezmer orchestra.[35] Other articles featured a transsexual artist traveling through the region of Polesie, a story of man buried alive in Vilna, or a wave of suicides in Warsaw.[36] In 1933, a column titled "Komishe un ernste bilder fun ydishn lebn in Poyln" (Comical and serious images of Jewish life in Poland) received a specifically Polish character. An analogous column was found in *Di Yidische Zaitung*. In it, a certain K. Israel reported from Łódź about a love affair between the wife of a Polish officer and a Jewish doctor.[37] Presenting the Old World as weird and funny marked immigrants' growing sense of belonging to Argentina. As time passed, the Argentine reality, rather than Polish memories, was perceived as standard and normal.

Glorious Memories and Painful Nostalgias

When writer Peretz Hirschbein arrived in Buenos Aires for the first time in 1914, he began his search for signs of Jewishness. Seeing a theater poster that invited theater-goers to a play in Yiddish, he was truly relieved. It was a clear sign that Yiddish life thrived in the capital. Plays like *Lend Me Your Wife* reminded him of analogous cultural productions elsewhere in the Yiddishland.[38] Hirschbein felt at home in Once, "as in any other big Jewish city." The local commercial streets reminded him of the bustling Dzika and Dzielna Streets in Warsaw. The face of a Jewish bookseller looked to him "familiar and Jewish."[39] The populous and newly immigrated Buenos Aires Jewish community was for him a potential basis for building a strong Argentine diaspora. The district of Once was for them a reservoir of yidishkayt that could be channeled in multiple directions.

A few steps farther, the writer noticed the Yiddish bookshop of Matías (Mordechai) Stoliar (who in a short time would establish the daily *Di Yidische Zaitung*). To his surprise the shop window displayed his own books and the newest publications from Warsaw and Vilna. Hirschbein started to comprehend that the local Jewry remained in permanent contact with the Yiddish cultural world in Europe.[40] A visit in a porteño Jewish bookstore showed Hirschbein that Argentine Jewish life was flourishing and preserving its Yiddish character. The traveler was surprised by the perfect Yiddish spoken by the locals. As he wrote, "Spanish seems not to glue itself to Yiddish as happens with Russian or English." The writer frankly said that he did not expect such a "great Jewish youth that is up-to-date with the problems of the Old World." He felt ashamed that "we" (Jews in eastern Europe) knew so little about the life of their countrymen in Argentina. He stressed that Jews in Poland were not aware of the extent to which their Argentine compatriots remained involved with the cultural, social, and political problems of eastern Europe.[41]

Argentine travel texts of Hersh Dovid Nomberg and Peretz Hirschbein reveal that for first-generation immigrants, their eastern European homeland remained a major reference point. For some immigrants, eastern Europe and the shtetl life were transformed into a familiar space of cohesive meanings and values, a stark contrast to the Argentine surrounding that often seemed suspicious and foreign. As Nomberg and Hirschbein pointed out, Polish and Russian Jews often yearned for their homes in eastern Europe, which they associated with warmth, close and authentic family relations, and a sense of security. The ambiguous feelings of the immigrants signified that they lived in an *in-between* space: physically in Argentina but still strongly rooted in an eastern European context. Despite the growing poverty and persecution, leaving the familiarity of eastern Europe was a major social and psychological challenge, not to mention a sign of bravery. Hirschbein sympathized with the immigrants, who felt compelled to "uproot" themselves from everything they knew and "root" themselves anew in the unknown Argentina.[42] As many immigrant Jews faced financial insecurity and anxieties related to their problematic situation in Argentina, eastern Europe seemed to them a simpler and better world. Consequently, as Rebecca Kobrin wrote, eastern European Jews in the Americas often expressed strong dedication and maintained an impressive sense of belonging toward their former homes.[43]

Both Nomberg and Hirschbein noted that the immigrants often idealized Poland or Russia. Hirschbein wrote that those who left Europe were desperately awaiting any news from the old home. When a Jewish newspaper arrived from eastern Europe, readers curious about the news were "falling on every line of the text."[44] Hirschbein wrote that unlike Germans or Englishmen, the immigrant Jews "were pulled out with their roots from Eastern Europe" and only rarely had a chance to return back home.[45] The difficulty or impossibility of returning or traveling to Europe made Argentine Jews even more interested in the cultural Yiddish production of the Old World.[46] The cultural material was able to pass through geographical borders rather easily, becoming relatively available. The memories of poverty disappeared quickly and many desired to imagine their birthplace foremost as a place of strong Jewish culture. The interest and participation in Yiddish cultural production in Argentina did to some extent substitute actual life in eastern Europe.

Hirschbein and Nomberg appreciated the strong interest of Argentine Jews in eastern European literature and theater. Unlike their irrational longing for eastern European foods and landscapes, their involvement in eastern European high culture was a sign of their desired permanent attachment to their homeland. When Nomberg visited Argentina in 1922, he concluded that local Jewish life already had "strong foundations." He was impressed by the number of Jewish libraries, workers' organizations, and political movements of all stripes. For Nomberg, the vitality of the Argentine yishev was strongly interrelated with Jewish life back in Poland. He attributed the relatively high cultural capital of Argentine immigrants to their socialization in eastern Europe. The Jews who immigrated to the United States at the very turn of the century were, as he saw it, "largely uneducated and socially and culturally passive," whereas the immigrants who arrived in Argentina in the 1920s to a large extent had attended schools in eastern Europe and were raised as a generation "aware of the proletarian movement, Yiddish literature, and Yiddish journalism."[47]

When Hersh Dovid Nomberg visited Moisés Ville in 1922, the colonists bombarded him with numerous questions about Jewish life in their native eastern Europe. They asked him about the postwar situation, about anti-Semitism, but also about the newest Yiddish literary developments. Nomberg suggested that the colonists were not only interested in the eastern European reality but in Yiddish culture specifically. When visiting Jewish colonies, the settlers proudly led Nomberg to their library and showed him his own name in the library catalogue. In Moisés Ville, the newest books from Europe were available and, no less important, collectively debated.[48] To his surprise and delight, Jewish farmers seemed to care not only about their economic well-being in Argentina but also about the cultural scene in Vilna or Warsaw.[49] The transfer of social and cultural material between eastern Europe had created new global networks.

Although the travel writers appreciated the engagement of the immigrants in the advancement of Yiddish culture in Argentina, they rejected irrational nostalgias for their Old Home. The nostalgia was experienced especially by those who failed to succeed in Argentina or left behind their nearest and dearest in eastern Europe. One of the immigrants developed a strong longing for eastern Europe only when he realized that life in Argentina was far from easy and comfortable. He was not able to find any job other than that of a street cigarette seller and did not see any chance of improvement. Despite the fact that he was a victim of violent anti-Semitism in Russia, and consequently decided to leave his native Odessa, in Argentina he concluded that his decision was wrong and that he should have never left eastern Europe.[50] Hirschbein was very surprised when he conversed with another immigrant, a young, broad-shouldered Jew, who still longed for his parents in Russia. The young man was jealous that the writer was able to travel or even to return to eastern Europe whenever he pleased. He did not see any chance for a return. The only thing he was left with was his nostalgia.[51] Others who longed for eastern Europe referred to the deficiencies of Jewish life in Argentina. One of them, answering Hirschbein's question about his unwillingness to put down roots in South America and to acknowledge it as his new home, answered him angrily: "How can one forget Russia?! There Jewish life flows as a huge river, and here I'm suffocating. I was born there and it is my country. I would consider myself a beggar if I stopped thinking that this big country named Russia is not my home."[52]

As in the case of many other diasporas, it is certain that Jewish émigrés quite often idealized and sugarcoated their homeland and perceived it much more positively than prior to their departure. As numerous studies have shown, many immigrants developed a strong homesickness, at least at a certain stage of their lives. Immigrants face an increased level of stress that is related to the difficulties of immigration and acculturation, based on four major factors: social isolation, cultural shock, goal-striving stress, and cultural change.[53] Eugene Tartakovsky, referring specifically to Jewish adolescents immigrating to Israel, differentiated three stages that immigrants go through: the devaluation of the homeland and idealization of the country of immigration in the premigration period, the disillusionment with the host country and strengthening of the cultural identity of the homeland in the first years after the emigration, and the formation of an inconsistent bicultural identity in the later postmigration period.[54]

Were the Jews encountered by Nomberg and Hirschbein in Argentina experiencing a prolonged second stage of Tartakovsky's typology? Were they in the period when the homeland seemed like the only good place and the immigration country was becoming increasingly overwhelming and hostile? When memories of pogroms disappeared, wiped out by fresher impressions of obstacles experienced every day on the Argentine street, not infrequently eastern Europe emerged as better and friendlier than Argentina in their eyes. For some of the newcomers disillusioned with Argentina, even Polish food seemed to be much tastier and fresher than the food available in South America. Nomberg viewed these nostalgias as pointless. To the complaints of an older immigrant about the weak aromas of Argentine food, Nomberg commented angrily: "Getting old, the man did not notice that his senses had become dysfunctional."[55] Here, the writer adopted an authoritative position: the subjective feelings of the immigrant were incorrect and only he, an outsider, was able to honestly and independently judge the situation.

For Hirschbein, the pain associated with putting down roots in Argentina was a sign of the stability of the Jewish settlement in Argentina. Longing and homesickness were for him a sign that the immigrants considered a return impossible.[56] Despite all the obstacles they experienced, Hirschbein underlined the potential and the strength of Argentine Jews. In a chapter titled "Di yidishe gas benkt" (The Jewish street longs), he repeats several times "un dokh es iz a yidisher yishev" (but still, there is a Jewish settlement), repetitively reassuring the reader about the "miraculous" development and stability of the Argentine diaspora.[57] Although the Jews encountered by both travelers often mentioned the temporality of their stay in Argentina, Hersh Dovid Nomberg was convinced that immigrants used these voices as strategies to silence their longing and sense of disorientation that they experienced in Argentina. Not acknowledging that they would stay in Argentina forever, eastern European Jews convinced themselves that they were in Latin America only for a short period (*far dervayl*). Nomberg commented jokingly: "They opened their workshops for a while, they married for a while, they even died for a while."[58] Aharon Leib Schussheim, once president of Poylisher Farband, made similar observations, noting that while living in Argentina "for a while," the immigrant Jews built up a bustling Jewish social infrastructure and experienced professional progress. Sons and grandsons of the peddlers were already journalists, architects, lawyers, and doctors.[59]

Both Hirschbein and Nomberg noticed that many Jews who missed eastern Europe did so because of the low position that Jews enjoyed within Argentine society. The arrival of a guest from Europe was an outlet for "a storm of emotions."[60] One of the immigrants stated that "Argentina is not a country for the Jews," arguing that there it was a disgrace to admit that one was Jewish.[61] Another commented that in Argentina "people forgot that they once had souls," likely alluding to selfishness and individualism that in his opinion dominated communal values. These voices stressed that internal Argentine Jewish dynamics were also a factor influencing longing and homesickness. Lonely eastern Europeans, often let down by their fellow Jews, might have developed frustrations and longing for the familiarity and predictability of life in Poland or Russia. According to Nomberg, these were the Polish Jews who missed eastern Europe the most. As he wrote: "No one is so connected to the *heymish* forest, river, nature, as the Polish Jew." He described it as a specific weakness of Polish Jews that made it harder for them to accept their new country.[62] Nomberg explained the desire expressed by some immigrants to return to eastern Europe with the fact that only rarely did they arrive in Argentina by their own free will. Some of them immigrated in fear of continuing pogroms, others were brought to Argentina as a "contingent" of the Jewish Colonization Association or chose Argentina because of an inability to afford a ticket to New York.[63] This was the case with the Blutrajt family. Samuel Blutrajt recalled that his father wanted to immigrate to Argentina only in order to later move on to the United States. In the end, the entire family stayed in Latin America.[64] The "randomness" of immigration to Argentina made some question their future in the new country.

Although the homesick Polish Jews who yearned for eastern Europe bothered and surprised the writers, they were altogether impressed by the vitality of Argentine Jewish life. The Yiddish-speaking children of Polish and Russian immigrants in particular symbolized for them the stability and rootedness of yidishkayt in Argentina. Hirschbein often used a botanical metaphor that described the firm basis of Argentine Jewry and its permanent linkage with eastern Europe. In this vision, Argentina appeared as a branch of eastern European Jewry that experienced a new diasporic period. In the eyes of the travelers, eastern Europe functioned like a trunk of an "Eastern European Jewish tree" with new green branches growing out in Argentina, the United States, Canada, and France. Hirschbein developed this metaphor, attributing the weaknesses and problems of Argentine yishev to its relative youth and to the significant distance that divided it from the nurturing "trunk" of eastern Europe. He commented that the Argentine Jewish settlement was as unstable as a thin and fragile branch that "can be broken by every rush of air."[65] Elsewhere, Hirschbein compared the immigrant Jews to seeds that are thrown from land to land, hardly able to strike roots anywhere. As a result, to the welcome of Hirschbein, a transnational Yiddishland was on the rise: "The borders were wiped out, all cities seem to become one, all countries become one land."[66] Despite initial "groaning and longing," the immigrants struck deep roots in the Argentine soil. These passages on the relationship between Europe and Argentina reveals that Hirschbein believed in a double rootedness. For him, no contradiction existed between being a citizen of the Yiddishland and a confident Argentine Jew.

Looking across the Ocean or Doing It Argentine Style? Ethnic Belonging and Immigrant Literary Expression

Similar to Hirschbein, Argentine Yiddishist Pinie Katz also saw the Jewish immigrants (and specifically their literary expression) as a tree that had roots from both eastern Europe and Argentina. As he believed, creating in Yiddish meant being a part of the transnational cultural space of Yiddishland, but discussing Argentine problems and expressing the "Argentine fever" enriched global Yiddish writing with a specific Argentine Jewish character.[67] With time, many Yiddish-speaking and Yiddish-reading Jews, who immigrated to Argentina after 1918, also began to consider themselves clearly Argentine. Whereas their primordial eastern European subethnic identifications played an important role, many immigrant Jews felt a sense of community as an Argentine chapter of the world Jewry. Being an Argentine Jew also meant for some representing Argentina within the Yiddishland, at times "defending" the new homeland in internal and international Jewish debates. The argentinidad of the immigrant Jews was an amalgam of eastern European and Argentine experiences, manifested in the transformation of language, new pastimes, and communal and family life. For instance, Argentine Yiddish incorporated words such as *taller*, *conventillo*, and also a number of Latinisms. Eliahu Toker described the Yiddish spoken in Argentina as *ídishñol* or *castidish*.[68]

The relations and discussions that some immigrant writers wished to maintain with Jewish Poland, eastern Europe, and the broader Yiddishland world were at times met with sharp criticism. The accusations of not willing to become truly Argentine were often heard not only from acculturated, Argentinized veterans but also from fellow immigrant greenhorns. Poland-born journalist Gershon Henekh Zakhak (Zajak, Zając) claimed in 1926 that the argentinidad of the immigrant population was only external and a wide gap existed between immigrant and Argentina-born Jews. Although many new immigrants changed their names to sound more Hispanic (Yankel became Jacobo and Fayvel Federico), Zakhak argued that "they were spiritually fed with what they brought in their baggage." He claimed that the immigrant Jews had barely anything in common with the Argentine reality, and "there was nothing new, nothing that would mark their Argentine character." According to the contributor of *Di Yidische Zaitung*, only the immigrants' bodies were in Argentina, whereas their minds were "wandering around the world, through the *heymish* cities and shtetels." Zakhak correctly noted that immigrants arrived in Argentina with many preconceptions and prejudices. Poland's Jewish discourse on Argentina to a great extent *exoticized* Argentina, marking it as a mixture of vice and economic failure. Zakhak criticized the importance that immigrant Jews placed on opinions in eastern Europe. He complained that instead of gratitude for financial help, the only thing that the alter heym offered was "a condemnation and a stupid pride."[69]

As Zakhak argued, the children of the postwar immigrants could overcome the gap between Jewish Argentines and immigrant Jews. They were free from nostalgia and liberated from the Old World views. Although Zakhak wrote that he did not want to force acculturation and did not believe in the "superiority of Argentinized Jews," his observations clearly downgraded the way of life and priorities of the new immigrants. He suggested that all Argentine Jews should develop a sense of self-pride, independence, and agency and cease being dependent on Jewish communities in Europe. He called for ending discussion with the *oysland* (foreign lands) about the condition of Argentine Jewry and its reputation. Zakhak believed that newcomers should be incorporated into the Argentine environment instead of continuing to live in the "style of Nalewki Street in Warsaw."[70]

Zakhak categorically rejected any notion of identifying with the Old World homelands. He refused immigrants the right to define themselves as "Polish, Bessarabian or Romanian Jews" and encouraged Argentinization. This process, as imagined by Zakhak, was far from linguistic acculturation in Spanish. Zakhak saw it as a development of a specifically Argentine Jewry—proud and free of Old World belongings. Actually, the fury of Zakhak in criticizing the multiple transnational belongings, exemplified the powerful dominance of immigrant-shaped cultural and social phenomena in 1920s Argentina. To his frustration, many immigrant Polish Jews, including writers, remained connected with eastern European life. For many, what acculturation afforded was hardly attractive or unavailable during the first years. Those who grew up in Poland, together with the development of Jewish ethnonational movements, experiencing poverty and harsh life in Argentina, noticing the sociocultural deficiencies of a local Jewry (concerning Yiddish culture), rarely aspired to become exclusively Argentine. Conversely, many post-1918 immigrants participated in influencing Argentine Jewish life in a direction they desired: a strong Yiddish-speaking diaspora, with

Yiddish culture and schooling, involved in the issues of the Old World and in a sociocultural dialogue with it. While for some immigrant Jews, Poland came to be imagined as a romantic cultural home, for the Yiddishists it was a progressive heart of their movement.[71]

Zakhak seemed not to acknowledge that the Yiddish world entered a new era and that immigration did not automatically create strong links between immigrants and their new country. Even acculturated Jewish ethnic leaders never voiced such radical and militant criticism toward Yiddish and transnational Jewish belonging. Within the global Yiddishland of the 1920s and 1930s, it was possible to be physically in Argentina and *mit nefushe in Poyln* (with a soul in Poland). The Jewish worlds of Poland and Argentina began to interfuse and "Argentine-only" separation and exclusivity ceased to be an option. In an era of developing transnational Yiddish cultural networking, with Yiddish books from Poland regularly on sale in Buenos Aires, with Yiddish theaters traveling around the world, with newspaper reports keeping immigrants updated about eastern Europe, no one could expect from the immigrants that they would choose a blindfolded love and belonging to the new home.

Whereas Zakhak complained that the new Yiddish-speaking immigrants did not Argentinize as quickly as he wished, Yiddishist journalist and literary critic Pinie Katz interpreted developments in Argentina rather positively. For Katz, being Argentines and Yiddishness-spirited Jews was compatible. Speaking in the name of Argentine Jewry, he offered a sui generis manifesto of argentinidad: "We call ourselves Argentine Jews with full awareness and conviction that we are Argentine Jews [argentiner yidn], and that we desire to be Argentine Jews. Both those of us who were born in Argentina and those who immigrated, who settled here and linked their destiny and future with this country, we love this country as one loves a thing that one had made himself or one has helped to create, as one loves a *heym* that one has built with one's own hands."[72]

In his essay, Katz chose to describe Argentina with the intimate word *heym* (home), usually reserved for the Old Home, the alter heym. His 1940 text showed an emotional appreciation for the liberal policies of Argentina that allowed thousands of Jews to build new lives in the Southern Cone. Katz emphasized the need for coexistence with other immigrant groups and the willingness of Jews to contribute to the development of Argentina. His essay was an expression of Jewish gratitude to Argentina and a way of envisioning the immigrant Argentine Jews as Jewish Argentines, already a part of the republic's society. For Katz, the post-1918 boom of Yiddish culture in Argentina and elsewhere in the world was a sign of blooming Jewish ethnonational life. This life was also being transplanted together with the migrating Jews to Argentina and precisely thanks to Argentine liberties was able to flourish and evolve. Katz did not see any contradiction between being Jewish and Argentine and endorsed the existence of a vital, Yiddish cultural-ethnic life, combined with love and praise for Argentina.[73]

Katz's text, published in an anthology of Argentine-Yiddish writing, established a connection between the immigrant biographies and Yiddish literature written in Argentina. Yiddish literature, according to Katz, was supposed to be a product and a report of Argentine experiences and a contribution to the transnational Yiddish culture. Katz wished that Buenos Aires would become the fourth world center of Yiddish literature, in constant cultural dialogue with those in New York, Moscow, and Warsaw.[74] The embodiment of his efforts was the tenth anniversary volume published by *Di Presse*. The 1928 book was filled with texts by Yiddish authors from all over the world, yet Argentina was also presented as a Yiddish literary center. The dialogue and cultural exchange between Argentina and other parts of the Yiddishland was constantly developing in the 1920s and 1930s, but Buenos Aires reached a more prominent place within the Yiddishland only when the Polish center was destroyed.

Katz was convinced that while the roots of Yiddish literature of Argentina were indeed located in eastern Europe and should not be forgotten, he was equally sure that the immigrant writers should be dealing with local problems and themes.[75] Creating in Yiddish meant being a part of the transnational community of Yiddishland, but discussing Argentine problems and expressing the "Argentine fever" enriched global Yiddish writing with a specific Argentine-Jewish character.[76] Katz argued that Argentina needed its own "Argentine-Yiddish literature" versus "Yiddish literature written in Argentina." Katz called for Yiddish literature to be written "*itst und do*," "here and now." In a jubilee edition celebrating the twentieth anniversary of his daily *Di Presse*, Katz wrote that the journal was "first and foremost a product of *argentinidad*."[77] Katz ironically pointed out that immigrants "did not leave the shtetl" in order to deal with this theme in their writing. For him Argentina was a new yishev, grouping Jews together from all around the world, and a local Yiddish literature should express their Argentine experiences. For Katz, only those authors who dealt with current problems were regarded as "good servants of the Jewish nation."[78] This came in the context of immigration from Poland in the 1920s, when some veteran Jewish Argentine writers and literary critics felt that the journals were "flooded" with the "green" newcomers and Old World topics.[79]

The decades Katz spent in Argentina influenced the way he perceived his new country and the Yiddishland. Even though he was a convinced Yiddishist, he did not share the experience of Yiddish revival in eastern Europe. He emigrated from Russia to Argentina in 1906, prior to the development of new Yiddish social, political, and cultural frameworks. The situation was different among those who arrived from Poland around the 1920s. For the newcomers, Argentina was not familiar enough to be reflected in their works. It was the Polish past and the experience of migrating that found expression in the literary creativity of this generation. A key opponent of Katz's Argentine localism was Moyshe Granitstein, a young immigrant author from Kowel in eastern Poland.[80] Granitstein underlined the immaturity of the Argentine yishev and advocated for the right of authors to deal with eastern European problems in an Argentine context. Granitstein believed that due to the migration experiences, Argentine Yiddish literature was *nisht do gedakht un nisht itst gedakht* (not conceptualized here and not conceptualized now). Granitstein argued that immigrant Jewish authors should also touch on Old World topics in their work. He criticized Katz's desire for localism and expression of Argentine life and style (*shtayger*). As Granitstein noted, no national literature started from a local style. Conversely, it originated in the life of the folk and was an "extract of its essence." Granitstein, responding to Katz's critique, wrote: "When Argentine Jewry is chaotic and unstable, when it is based on transformation and adaptation, when everyone is still overloaded with the baggage from the alter heym, when everyone still sucks from the breast of the alter heym, . . . when no sign of a local style is to be seen, . . . where should I get you [a local] style from?"[81]

Granitstein believed that the European experiences of immigrants could not be "unloaded" and left aside. He claimed that the whole Jewish experience in Europe, starting from life in the shtetl through the experience of World War I, would also resonate in Argentina. Granitstein criticized the older Argentine authors, who "were so busy with avoiding the 'old [world]' that they were left with barely anything new."[82] Granitstein believed that it was precisely by referring to the Old World that writers were joining and mirroring the experiences of the immigrant masses. In that sense, he thought that a construction of a Jewish identity in a new country was possible only by referring to eastern Europe. Granitstein claimed that refusing to write about the alter heym made Argentine literature "culturally empty and *bodenloz*" (without a basis).[83] The views of Granitstein were also formulated in his novel *Avantures fun haver hamerl*, in which he portrayed the literary circles of Buenos Aires, including his opponent Katz. Granitstein's novel describes an immigrant Jewish writer, who suffers a creative breakdown following demands for "localism." The protagonist writer is not local, he is not yet Argentine and cannot not find a way to express argentinidad in his writing.

Granitstein gave voice to the fluidity of Jewish experiences that stretched between the continents and not bound exclusively to the current place of residence. For Granitstein's generation, it was obvious that Yiddish cultural life had multiple centers and that the experience of migration was one of the key factors shaping their literary creativity. Katz's positions during the debate in the 1920s should be defined as supportive of an old paradigm and characteristic of his own generation, which saw migration as a transformative point that signified a complete immersion in the New World. These two standpoints, although both voiced in Yiddish, reflected to a certain extent the debates between Argentinized veterans and the newcomers. With time, Katz largely accepted the arguments of Granitstein, and his opposition toward Old World links became less radical. In the anthology published in 1944, Katz argued that Jewish life in Argentina had two roots, one eastern European and one Argentine, but the crown of the tree was already a fully Argentine cultural product. The conciliatory change of Katz's opinions might have been influenced by the ongoing destruction of eastern European Jewish life and the transformations it brought to world Jewry.[84]

What to Do with These Greenhorns? Argentine Yiddish Immigrant Writing

The Yiddish poetry and prose written by immigrants from Poland contained not only artistic aspects but was a medium for negotiating everyday Argentine problems and thus a firsthand subsidiary source for historical research. As Stuart Hall and Claudia Furman noted, literary representations did not only reflect but also constituted cultural identities.[85] Yiddish literature was a witness of the social and cultural changes that immigrants from Poland experienced: generational conflicts, rise into the ranks of the middle class, and acculturation within the Argentine nation. Argentine Yiddish fiction was rooted in everyday experiences of the immigrants and bridged their Polish past and Argentine present. The following section offer insights into Argentine Yiddish literature written by Jewish Polish immigrants up to 1939. It reconstructs the literary narratives marginalized in the dominant popular discourse that saw Argentina as a promised land for the persecuted and an idealized version of a Jewish pastoral paradise. Discussions focused on Argentine Yiddish literature were in fact a conversation that reflected various options available for the Jews of Argentina. Some stressed their growing rootedness in Argentina, marking the beginnings of becoming Jewish Argentines, whereas others, including many freshly arrived authors from Poland (after 1918), claimed a right to focus on Old World themes and asserted that Argentina was not yet familiar enough for them. Similar time-space developments can be traced in immigrant literatures of other immigrant groups.

Liliana Ruth Feierstein described the Argentine Jewish writing as a "writing territory" (*Schriftserritorium*) that stretched between the Jewish settlements in Argentina and the European homelands. She coined a very apt notion of a "paper bridge," a literary-journalistic passage that immigrant authors used for combining their European pasts and Argentine presents.[86] The immigrant literature written in Argentina quite often referred to the pre-emigration experiences. Also, widely discussed problems, such as Jewish poverty, lack of hope, generational and cultural changes, attracted attention on both sides of the Atlantic. The immigrant authors brought their cultural baggage and their European motifs and themes. Consequently, Argentine Yiddish literature and literary criticism became a transcultural arena for discussing the tensions between the challenges of new Argentine life and the memories of Jewish Poland, which, although physically left behind, still resonated in texts by migrant writers. Sometimes unprofessional, sometimes highly praised, Argentine Yiddish writing was a community-building practice and a space for discussing the tensions between Jewish ethnonational identity and belonging to Argentina. Yiddish literature acted as a field for discussing the meaning of language, the future of the youth, the relationship to Poland and, as such, served not only as an artistic expression but also a position in social and political debates.

Most of the Jewish literature written in Argentina in the 1920s and 1930s was written in Yiddish. Yiddish literature became a sphere of negotiating the tensions of being a Polish Jew outside of Poland and becoming a Jewish Argentine. The borderline between those two identifications was fluid and the same authors could glorify the beauty of Argentina while falling into nostalgia about the European landscapes that, as they believed, they would never see again. Only later did some authors (like José Rabinovich) switch to Spanish, though it was Yiddish that dominated the country's Jewish literary scene well into the 1940s. Despite the fact that Argentine Yiddish literature was assessed by many contemporaries as "low class" or as not achieving the greatness of other diaspora centers, it offers a unique mirror into early twentieth-century Argentina and the challenges faced by Jewish immigrants. Samuel Rollansky argued that Jewish literature in Argentina did not use all the potential and inspiration that was available in Argentina. Rollansky noted that the urban Yiddish literature of Buenos Aires "had limited themselves to barely commenting on what the eye sees"; whereas, Yosef Horn wrote "it seems that there is a hardened cover over the abundant Argentina that prevents its Jewish writers from reaching for greater heights." [87]

The problems of immigrant Jews in Argentina were largely also the problems of Argentina's Jewish literati. These two groups coincided. Most of the writers came from poor families and were employed in menial professions in Argentina. For many, literature was an "after-hours" activity. This was true both for the landsman writers, who wrote their poems or shorts stories for landsman publications, and for those who later became part of the Argentine Yiddish canon. In three key anthologies of Argentine Yiddish literature, the biographies of the authors always pointed out their underprivileged background and belonging to the folk. We read about those who originated from Polish shtetels or about those who came from working-class families in industrializing cities. The biographical notes reveal that on coming to Argentina, the future writers often faced financial misery and worked in blue-collar professions. Many were carpenters, typesetters, or tailors. An immediate success as a writer was hardly possible in Argentina. An Argentine landsman from the town of Ostróg recalled that "everyone needed to survive the period of *green years*, for it was not easy for anyone to make it in 'America.'"[88] The situation was no different from their condition in Poland, where authors could often barely make ends meet.

Within the Yiddish literature written in Argentina, we can differentiate a few generational-thematic groups. According to Pinie Katz (who was later followed by Yehiel Scheintuch), the first group of immigrant writers primarily focused on local life and described Argentine nature and life in the Jewish agricultural colonies.[89] Their writings expressed the experiences of the first group of eastern European immigrants who settled in agricultural colonies. These immigrants usually originated from areas located to the far east of the broadly understood Polish lands: from contemporary central Ukraine and south Russia, such as the first group of 1898 Jewish settlers, who came from Kamenets-Podolskiy. The experiences of Jewish colonization were portrayed by authors such as Borekh Benderski, Aharon Brodski, Marcos (Mordechai) Alpersohn, and Noah Vital, who lived or at least were brought up in the colonias. Like many others colonists' sons, they moved to Buenos Aires, where they defined life in the Jewish colonies as the main source of their creativity. Many of those authors criticized the colonization enterprise and described a sense of abandonment by the JCA.[90]

The second category of immigrant Jewish authors reflected the post-1918 immigration wave and included those who did not settle in the colonies. To this group of authors belonged numerous immigrant writers from Poland, like Moisés David Guiser, Moshe Goldstein, Nehemías Zucker, and Moshe Kaufman. Many of them grew up with the social-cultural revolution that hit eastern European Jews at the beginning of the twentieth century. As the Yiddishist journalist Lazaro Zhitnitsky put it, "they brought with them political, national and cultural unrest."[91] These immigrant authors were conditioned by the Yiddish press and literature bustling in eastern Europe after the 1905 revolution. Although in this case it was also primarily economic factors and anti-Semitism that pushed them out of Poland, their relationship to the alter heym was much more complex. Argentine literary critics commonly criticized the immigrants for what they regarded as an excessively intimate and deep attitude toward their eastern European homeland, describing it as problematic from the perspective of building Argentine Jewish identity. Pinie Katz and Yankev Botoshansky noted, "they often looked with nostalgia not only to the port, but also to the other side of the ocean."[92] Rollansky wrote that Polish Jewish authors who came to Argentina in the 1920s had difficulties with "liberating" themselves from the influence of the alter heym and nostalgia for it.[93] Similar views were held by Botoshansky, who wrote that the post-1918 immigrant "brought too much from the alter heym" and had a hard time finding a place in Argentina.[94]

Jewish immigrants from Poland reinvigorated the Buenos Aires Yiddish literary community.[95] For the writers who emerged from the post–World War I emigration wave, the strengthening of Yiddish culture was a central existential issue that was a part of a broader Yiddishist agenda that saw literature as a tool for raising Jewish Yiddish ethnonational questions. As Rollansky argued, the new migrants related to *veltlekhkayt* (secularism) and *groysshtotlekhkayt* (big city spirit) and challenged the provincialism and peripheral spatiality of Argentine Yiddish culture embedded in mythologizing Jewish agricultural colonization. Those immigrants who came to Argentina in the 1920s and 1930s were already very far away from the colonias and the atmosphere of Jewish land settlements.[96] Buenos Aires's urban life defined the dominant character of the postwar immigrant community and, consequently, also its literary manifestations. The 1920s were years of increasing proletarian struggle that found its expression in Yiddish literature. As Rollansky noted, the time between 1922 and 1930, the heyday of postwar Polish-Jewish immigration, was the golden age of Yiddish literature in Argentina.[97] The cultural trends arriving from the alter heym also influenced those who immigrated earlier. The newly arriving literati were transmitters of change not only concerning their own creativity but spreading it all over the Argentine literary scene.[98] This re-Yiddishization was observable throughout the entire Jewish cultural life in Argentina.

Yiddish immigrant literature in Argentina often focused on the challenges of life in the new country. The writers portrayed immigrants who felt they were refused basic rights and found it hard to properly function in the new society.[99] These included, for instance, problematic family relations, poverty, thoughts about returning to Poland, and a general disappointment with life in Argentina. Moisés David Guiser often portrayed the intersection of Argentine misery, urban life, and the first harbingers of Argentinization. He was born in Radom in central Poland in 1893. In 1919, Guiser moved to Warsaw and was a member of a prominent local avant-garde literary group Khalyastre for a few years. He immigrated to Argentina in 1924 and began publishing in *Oyfsnay* and *Nayvelt*. In 1933, Guiser moved to Chile where he edited a local periodical, *Zid-amerike* (together with another Argentine-Yiddish author Noah Vital), and independently the *Pacific* journal. Guiser's early works included poems that praised Argentina and described the wonders of life in the big city. Yet, many of his poems were expressions of painful immigrant experiences ("Geyst fun oremkeyt," "Conventillo," "Almacen"). The variety of subjects that Guiser chose demonstrates the complexity of Argentine experiences. It was both nostalgia for what was left in Europe and a desire to be successful and respected, all mixed with the challenges of poverty and exploitation.[100] His work mirrored both the dark and rosy facets of immigrant life in post-1918 Argentina, offering heterogeneous representations of Argentine experiences. Guiser's poems frequently appeared in *Dos Naye Vort*, edited by the Poylisher Farband. The poet was considered an important figure of the Polish-Jewish colonia in Argentina: he edited the 1928 almanac of the Poylisher Farband and its members co-organized Guiser's jubilee banquet in 1932.[101]

His poems "Conventillo" and "Geyst fun oremkayt" (A spirit of poverty) offer the reader a glimpse into the daily life of a typical immigrant Jewish working-class house (fig. 23). The conventillo is pictured as a place of horror: constant shouting, conflicts with Italian neighbors, lice covering the beds, and a courtyard covered in garbage. At the same time, Guiser showed the reader the social and cultural changes that the immigrants adopted. The Jewish men no longer put on *tephilin* or read holy books but instead drank mate. Their daughters twirled their curls preparing for an evening walk with their boyfriends. The whole house was covered with the aroma of the quintessential Argentine *asado*. Guiser's poem pointed to the hard conditions of life, yet at the same time pictured the willingness of immigrants to adapt certain aspects of the Argentine lifestyle. In a later (1931) poem "A briv" (A letter), Guiser described the hard economic reality of Buenos Aires.[102] In curt and sharp words, he referred to starving immigrants and the Buenos Aires reality, "where no one could be bothered if you died in the street." The author complained about the painful suggestions for their problems that immigrants often received from families back in Poland. For a jobless and hungering person receiving advice about "having two hands and being young and fit to work" was like salt on their wounds. The misery of immigrant life was also portrayed in "Vi orem ikh bin" (How poor I am) and "Foran aze ayner" (That one there). The first poem is narrated by a destitute immigrant, complaining about his fate in Buenos Aires, while the second one referred to the discrimination faced by the poor immigrant on behalf of the more successful ones.[103]

A fellow Polish-Jewish writer and Guiser's friend, Pinchas Bizberg noted in a posthumous anthology of Guiser's poems that "life did not smile upon him [Guiser] in Argentina . . . and his bitterness and disappointment were visible in his poems."[104] For Guiser, "the streets of Buenos Aires were a horrible labyrinth"; "he could not enjoy the blue skies of Argentina and the hopeful language did not speak to him at all." As Bizberg continued, Guiser experienced poverty and the indifference of the Jewish community that did not consider poetry a decent occupation. Guiser, who finally left Argentina for Chile in 1933, bade the country farewell in a poem entitled "Argentina." He accused Argentina of making his life bitter. Despite all the hopes he had for his life in the new country, "Argentina closed its ears" to his complaints. Guiser felt the heavy ballast of Argentina on his shoulders, perceiving it as a "tough country."[105]

Rollansky wrote that Guiser represented a whole generation of unemployed Jews, searching for consolation in the proletarian struggle.[106] Guiser saw himself

Figure 23. Conventillo in the first decade of the twentieth century, Archivo General de la Nacion, Argentina

as the voice of Argentine and Chilean Jewry and wanted Latin American Yiddish literature to be noticed in Europe and North America.[107] The general impression of Guiser's poems was also symptomatic of other immigrants from Poland. Many were disappointed with the situation in their new country. David Szyszacki of IWO Institute wrote that unlike Spaniards or Italians, "[Jews] didn't come here to make money and come back home. They arrived here to build a home.

Yet, many were not able to make a living in Argentina, or became sick, and were forced to go back. Many needed to ask the landslayt for money to buy a return ticket."[108] Jerzy Szeferblum recalled in an interview that his father Herman left for Buenos Aires in 1924 when Jerzy was only one year old. The suitcase factory that Herman Szeferblum opened in Buenos Aires burned down and the unfortunate immigrant had to return to Poland.[109] Likewise, León Menin recalled that his father was in Argentina from 1909 until 1914 but decided to come back to Poland.[110] Yet, taken as whole, the rates of return migration from Argentina to Poland were relatively low, oscillating between 10 and 15 percent.[111]

Emigration unsettled traditional gender roles and relations within the nuclear and extended family.[112] The emigration of single men challenged family life, and family reunification was often a painful disappointment. Landsman Borekh Ismach recalled that because of the lack of stable employment, the immigrants preferred not to risk bringing their families to Argentina. Yet, many men broke contact with their families on purpose and landsmanshaftn received letters from worried families that remained in Poland. Then landsmanshaftn often intervened, persuading the "confused" landsman to get back in touch with family and to bring them to Argentina.[113] Abraham Milberg, another Polish-Jewish landsman, remembered that at the beginning he felt estranged in Buenos Aires—he could not find any job, and he had "sinister feelings in his heart" and began to have doubts if emigrating was a good idea.[114] Samuel Blutrajt recalled that he worked twelve to fifteen hours a day in a textile factory.[115] Guitl Kanutsky, a tailor and Bundist activist, remembered that immigrant Jews were commonly exploited, including by the Jewish *talleristas* (workshop owners). She struggled for proper work conditions and a salary that would permit living with dignity.[116] Flora Abzac, another female immigrant, recalled that in the 1930s her economic situation was very bad, and even as an adolescent, she needed to work hard in exchange for poor pay.[117]

In the many stories and poems written by Polish-Jewish immigrants, emigration appeared as a factor that tore families apart. "Almacen" by Moisés David Guiser described a group of miserable immigrant men, who went out to Buenos Aires "watering holes." Guiser's poem revealed that the young men who lived alone in Buenos Aires spent long nights drinking because of despair and longing. Their wives were alone on the other side of the ocean, hardly aware of the psychological challenges that their husbands faced in remote Buenos Aires.[118] The challenges of single men in Argentina were also mentioned in testimonies. Samuel Blutrajt recalled that his brother, who immigrated to Argentina as an eighteen-year-old boy had suffered greatly because he missed his family. In his letters, he indirectly discouraged Samuel from joining him in Argentina.[119] The family left in Europe was also featured in Zalman (Salomón) Wassertzug's poem, "Hoben im geshoynt di merder."[120] The main character is an immigrant who resides in rich, plentiful Argentina, while his aging father lives alone in Poland. The immigrant is ashamed of leaving his parents in their old age, forcing them to face suffering and neglect alone.[121]

The tension between the Old World and Argentina was visible in "Opgebrokhene tsvayg" (A broken branch), a short story written by Moshe Goldstein.[122] In it, we deal with a classic example of emigration when a man sets out abroad alone to arrange a soft landing for his family that temporarily stayed in the Old Country. The main character, who already goes by the gentile name León rather than Leyzer, finally sends a *llamada* (an invitation) to his fiancée, who stayed behind in Poland. Yet, when she comes to Argentina, the situation is far from rosy. León is not as successful as he reported in his letters. What bothers his fiancée the most is his indifference to the European homeland. She is shocked that León does not want to listen to anything about his own parents. Despite his misfortunes, for better or for worse, León has already become Argentine. Old World problems do not mean anything to him. To the disbelief of his newly arrived fiancée, he prefers to focus on his new Argentine life.[123] The short story pictured the family tensions that were a result of separation and diverse experiences. Many years in Argentina changed the main character in a way that was unrecognizable to his fiancée.

A similar problem was featured in a short story "Shabes likhter" (Shabbat lights) by Kraków-born Nehemías Zucker. The male character, Volf, feels estranged in Argentina. He not only does not achieve spectacular success but is financially devastated. Volf feels sad and uprooted from eastern European Jewish life, yet with the passing of time, he "hardens" and finally decides to bring his wife, Rivka, to Argentina. For Volf, the arrival of the woman is a painful reminder of what he left behind. The golden candelabra Rivka brings with her is his only reminder of the Old World. Yet, it seems to Volf that the precious object does not find a proper place in his poor Argentine home, "where instead of prayers, the candelabra heard only the monotonous knockings of the neighbor." The candelabra seems to be miserable to Volf, even crying overs its misfortunes. It is unable to provide enough light in the dark room of the conventillo. The candelabra functions in Zucker's story as a personification of the very problems of Volf, a disillusioned, frustrated Jewish immigrant in Argentina. The candelabra brought from his hometown of Radomyśl, Poland, reminds him of where he grew up and where he actually belonged. This and other stories and poems touched on the problem of social and cultural adaptation in Argentina, with the hardships and disappointments of reuniting with family members, but finally promised coming to terms with Argentina.[124]

In Argentine Yiddish texts from the late 1930s, we notice a tendency to portray the social progress of Jewish immigrants, alongside doubts about their evolving Jewishness and weakening yidishkayt. The economic changes that immigrants experienced were often accompanied by social and cultural transformations. Berl Grinberg, born in 1906 in Warsaw, in a short story titled "Senyorita esters shabesdike likhtlekh" (The Shabbat lights of Miss Ester), depicted the family of Raquel Rozen, an old Jewish immigrant matron.[125] Four of her daughters marry Catholics and distance themselves from Jewishness. To Rozen's great satisfaction, their assimilation by marriage is a part of the process of becoming Argentine. They not only marry Christians but also the members of higher strata, elevating their own social status. Ester, the fifth daughter, is the family's black sheep. When she turns thirty, she is still unmarried, is active on the job market, and earns more than many men. To make things even worse, Ester returns to Judaism. On Friday evenings, she rushes to her religious aunt and is thrilled to participate in the *kabalat shabat* ceremony. To her mother, Ester's behavior is crazy. She describes the daughter as *a narishe moyd* (stupid girl) and a *puste kop* (empty head). Instead of following the example of her sisters, Ester seems willing to come back to the Jewish ghetto.[126] The figure of Ester was emblematic of many second-generation immigrant women. Although most of the immigrant Jewish women were confined to house chores, their daughters often entered the job market, with the most ambitious among them becoming teachers.[127]

A number of post-1918 immigrant Yiddish writings provide a significant source of eulogistic literature about Argentina. The texts analyzed below prove that attachment to the new country could be expressed also in the language of the Old World. A great example of the Argentine Jewish experience, combining both a desire to feel at home in Argentina and nostalgia after the lost alter heym, is visible in the poem "Boydem shtiber" by Grodno-born Moshe Kaufman. The author "singing a song of his *green brothers*," claimed to represent the voice of other immigrant Jews. On the one hand, he praises the sun of Argentina that "burned inside him as a big fire," is "deadly in love with Argentine skies," and states that the big city life had "swallowed" him. The immigrant-narrator is ready to hug the Argentine soil, a foreign soil that is slowly becoming his own. On the other hand, he does not avoid mentioning "stinky, dark conventillos." The main character already feels Argentinized, filled with Argentine air and the local lifestyle. He is aware that now he would not recognize his European homeland. He does not have a passport from his country anymore and is afraid of the "new flags blowing on the wind" of growing nationalism in Poland. Kaufman wrote about his feeling of being uprooted but simultaneously expressed the hope that one day he would feel at home in Argentina. His poem was a well-articulated description of Argentinization: a process that might be painful and arduous but in the end was very rewarding. The poet titled his 1944 poetry volume *Fun ale mayne heymer* (From all my homes), emphasizing a multiplicity of his homes-homelands.

Other Yiddish texts by Kaufman were a sign of an embracing of Argentina as a new homeland. In his 1935 "Taykh Parana" (Parana River), the poet represented the amazement that Argentine nature supposedly evoked in greenhorn immigrants.[128] Kaufman mentioned the essential symbols of Argentineness: mate, gauchos, or the indigenous population, marking them as a new cultural code that the immigrants needed to acquire. The newcomers experienced a "wild, hot sun" and were proud of the local earth "pregnant with coal and petrol." Kaufman was amazed by the immigrant diversity of Argentina, "where old criollos mix with Jews, Czechs and Italians." His poem was a description of a process of discovering Argentina, its nature, people, and customs. Kaufman was full of curiosity and willing to accept his new homeland as it was. The ethnic diversity of Buenos Aires and its big city flair also attracted Kohet Kliguer.[129] Kliguer's poetry is a firsthand testimony of everyday life in the city. Reading his texts, we pass by a bar "En Ancla," meet the patrons of the cafes or together with tango dancers immerse ourselves in the heat of a Buenos Aires summer. Further, the reader wanders through calle Lavalle and meets the poor folks at Plaza Once. In Kohet Kliguer's texts, Buenos Aires, but not the Argentine nature, become an object of immigrant fascination.[130]

The devotion and gratitude to Argentina is traceable in the Yiddish poetry of Aba Kliger. Born in Łuck in 1893, Kliger moved to Warsaw in 1906 and left for Argentina in 1912. In his poem, "Oyf di bregn fun plata" (On the shores of La Plata River), Argentina appears as a land of satisfaction and peace. La Plata river brings on its back "ships and nations filled with hope." Argentina represented for Kliger a new world, a new order that called all *farbenkte* (longing) from the Old World to its shores.[131] Argentina was for Kliger an embodiment of his dreams: already in Europe he was stretching his hands toward the Argentine "summerland."[132] In the poetry of Aba Kliger, we notice a neophyte fascination with Argentina. In "Tango," the poet describes the eroticism of this local dance. Tango was for him wild, seductive, and ecstatic. Similar scenes are visible in "Karnaval." Buenos Aires appears here as vicious and drunk but exciting and charming.[133] In "Mendoza," the Andean city is portrayed as Garden Eden, filled with flowers, palm trees, the air smelling like perfume. The Yiddishist Samuel Rollansky described Kliger's poetry as full of pathos and called him "the most Spanish" of the Argentine Yiddish poets.[134] Lazaro Shallman also pointed to the Argentinization visible in Kliger's poetry, especially in the high number of Latin-based words.[135]

Many Polish-Jewish immigrants from the 1920s turned to the so-called proletarian poetry, a *kampf-poezye* (poetry of struggle) and took sides in discussions on the rights of immigrant workers and the responsibility of poetry to be close to the folk. Among them were Hirsh Blostein and Yankev Plafon.[136] A strong example of these sentiments is Blostein's story "A lid fun a emigrant." The narrator of the poem depicts his immigration to Argentina as a painful experience. His dreams of success and wealth prove to be a lie. He can barely handle the separation from his child. Dreaming on the steamship to Argentina, the emigrant sees the outstretched arms of his son, who is calling him to return. Buenos Aires confuses him, he does not understand what people around him are saying, he suffers a lot while working as a cuentenik and feels humiliated knocking on the doors of the rich trying to sell his cheap merchandise. A cuentenik in Simkha Granievitch's short story is trapped in a similar situation. He is ashamed of being a peddler and feels like "a beaten-up dog." A picture of the hardships of immigrant life in Argentina was portrayed in "Lirisher peizazh" by Moshe Kaufman. The houses of the suburb (probably Villa Crespo in Buenos Aires) are gray, similar to the hearts of the hopeless immigrants. The streets, dotted with palm trees, are filled with the homeless at night. From this perspective, the rich center of Buenos Aires looks to Kaufman like a "made-up prostitute." In a working-class neighborhood, there are no fancy boulevards, but muddy, unpaved streets. Local children are hungry, their mothers pale white and fathers ashamed of unfulfilled dreams that they had back in Poland. Kaufman summarizes the situation in Buenos Aires as "little hills of gold, and mountains of poverty."[137]

Mendel Pschepiurka also brought to life the poverty of immigrant life within the bustling city. Pschepiurka was born in Węgrów, central Poland, and served as a year-long editor of *Dos Naye Vort*, a journal of the Poylisher Farband. Pschepiurka also expressed his opinions in *Di Presse*, where he published articles regularly.[139] Pschepiurka, an outspoken communist, complained that in Buenos Aires one only heard the "rhythm of money." He pointed to the enclaves of the rich, which were surrounded by hundreds of impoverished immigrants. According to Pschepiurka, city life had a terrible influence on the people. The poor men, instead of saving money, spent their last penny on the lottery.[138] The newspapers, instead of serving as a credible source of information, turned to yellow journalism. Hirsh Blostein deals with the problem of inequality in Buenos Aires in "Oyfn Avenida Alvear."[140] In the poem, a poor immigrant from Poland observes the wealth of neighborhoods such as Recoleta, with their magnificent palaces and spacious gardens. Understanding the contrast between Recoleta and poor immigrant districts, the immigrants learn about economic inequalities in Argentina and the meager chances for quick economic advancement. Blostein's depictions are similar to Schneur Wasserman's impressions of calle Florida in Buenos Aires.[141] The downtown street, a prestigious avenue of bohemians and "romantic women," is full of flowers. Yet, it is also calle Florida on which stones are thrown by hungry proletarian protesters. For the new immigrants, who usually lived in extremely poor households, the exaggerated wealth of central Buenos Aires districts was a reminder of their precarious conditions. They were living in the same city as the rich men, but their lives hardly ever coincided.

Another well-known writer to describe the Jewish poverty of Buenos Aires was José (Yosef) Rabinovich. Born in Białystok in 1903, he arrived in Argentina in 1924 and soon afterward began publishing his poems and short stories in the local Yiddish press. In 1937, he ceased to write in Yiddish and switched to Spanish. His short story "Unter rod" (1927) is a powerful description of the first days of the new immigrant in Buenos Aires. A character named Yelin is homeless and unemployed. He cannot express himself in Spanish, and the people he meets make jokes about his miserable situation. In a moment of despair, Yellin starts to have hallucinations/reminiscences of his family. In another text, "In der fremd" (In foreignness), originally published in 1934 in *Di Presse*, Rabinovich depicts the Argentine lives of two immigrant brothers.[142] Whereas the family reunification was often pictured as one of the first ambitions of the new immigrants, the relations between family members in Argentina were often conflicting. The younger brother, who arrived in Argentina a few years earlier, welcomes Leyzer in his home; yet, the new immigrant desperately wants to be independent. He is willing to take any job, just to become independent from his brother, who is the first to make a career in Argentina. Other texts by Rabinovich offer a glimpse into the interactions between Jewish and non-Jewish porteños. In the 1928 volume of poetry *Conventizhes* we look at relations between neighbors, landlords and tenants, between Jewish and Catholic children. The early texts of Rabinovich represented questions shared by many Polish-Jewish immigrants of his generation: cultural-linguistic dilemmas, poverty, and anti-Jewish prejudice.[143]

Whereas the New York peddler and the Buenos Aires cuentenik earned the respect of later generations, contemporaries hardly saw these professions as a "mythical threshold" to being American or Argentine.[144] Taking into account the personal and collective progress that became part of the second- and third-generation Argentine Jewish experience, it is tempting to imagine the cuentenik as a mythological figure, who through his suffering and hard work laid the foundations for the successes of his children and grandchildren. Yet, this angle ignores the experience of the immigrants themselves and attempts to reduce the importance of their experience, designating it as a necessary step for the success of the future generations. A sense of humiliation, estrangement, and despair shared by many immigrants was for many a part and parcel of Argentine reality in the 1920s and 1930s.

Conclusion

The relationship with the eastern European past was an omnipresent motive in Argentine Jewish cultural discussions and press debates throughout the 1920s and 1930s. The radicals demanded that Argentina would be either a Yiddish-speaking extension of eastern Europe or that Argentine Jews would be devoted exclusively to their new homeland. Most of the immigrants likely tried to balance voicing their belonging to the new homeland, while remembering the Old

Country to the extent that it served their needs in Argentina. The fierce cultural debates about the role of eastern Europe showed that memory of alter heym had important functions also in the New World.

The voices of ethnic leaders such as Katz, Granitstein, or Kibrick are reflected in Argentine Yiddish immigrant literature. The texts of Argentine Yiddish authors such as Blostein, Guiser, or Grinberg portray their own challenges as authors writing in a minority language. They are also a reflection of broader immigrant trends. They reflect disillusionment, nostalgia, or frustration with their situation as poor migrants or, more rarely, an expression of devotion to Argentina. In this context, as the travelogues of Hirschbein and Nomberg showed, many immigrants turned to eastern Europe and wanted to remember it as a simpler and better place, albeit from afar. Simultaneously, immigrant Jews were building a sense of *Argentiness*, also reflected in local Yiddish literature, for instance in pertaining to local motives, as demanded by Pinie Katz. From the 1920s through the 1930s, relations to the Old World were one of the key defining lines of Jewish life in Buenos Aires. The issue was a tense matter, poignantly showing internal conflicts within Argentine Jewish cultural leadership and the broader immigrant public.

Epilogue

Jewish migration from Poland to Argentina signifies processes of diasporism and competing nationalisms, while highlighting emergent hybrid transnational forms of ethnonational belonging and identity. The process of migration shaped individual and group incorporation into a nation, while simultaneously linking both individuals and groups to transnational social and cultural networks. Within the Argentine context, the identities of Polish-Jewish migrants were shaped by the Argentine powers of acculturation and nationalization but were also tied to the cultural and national dimensions of Yiddish. Jewish migrants negotiated their status between nation-states, while locating their linguistic, cultural, and ethnic ties to promote global interests and transnational narratives. Nostalgia for homeland and sustained dialogue with Poland proved to be a useful cultural resource in Argentina. A transatlantic *writing territory* emerged between Poland and Argentina, allowing Jewish migrants to remain in conversation with their land of origin, while engaging in new sociocultural exchanges.

The impact of pre-emigration imaginaries of Argentina in Poland played a role in the formulation of transnational Jewish identities. By looking at Polish Jewish discourse on Argentina, we can better understand future cultural and social developments among immigrants in Latin America. The ways in which Jews in Argentina defined their identities was, in part, conditioned and nurtured by Old World conceptualizations of Argentina. The importance of Poland in Jewish mythscape of that era gave opinions there formulated a special position and authority. There was constant dialogue between Polish and Argentine Jewish worlds, as evidence by Warsaw's *Literarishe Bleter*, Poland's Yiddish novels and dramas, along with periodicals, which made regular references to Argentina. In the Polish Jewish imaginary, Argentina was not a real country at first; rather, it was an imagined space, constructed through a mixture of gossip, newspapers news, and emigration guidebooks. In the early twentieth century, Polish Jews had little knowledge about Argentina and could hardly tell the difference between the United States of America and the rest of the Americas. Throughout the interwar period, however, this imagined territory became increasingly Jewish and familiar.

Polish Jewish discourse on Argentina was a polyphonic and complex amalgam of stories, opinions, gossip, and policies. Argentine narratives that developed in Poland traced the transformation that Polish and world Jewry were undergoing in interwar years. Migration and secularization changed the geographic scope of Jewish possibilities. This process was far from smooth but rather filled with tensions and fears and also hope for a better future. Unsurprisingly, Polish Jewish Argentina narratives reflected the conflicting interests of the young generation and of the religious or assimilationist establishment. For many Jews of Poland, Argentina was a promise for a better tomorrow. It was a chance to escape poverty and anti-Semitism and, often, an opportunity to leave behind a family that did not understand the worldview of the young. For some Yiddish activists in Poland, Argentina was a place where a modern secular Yidish culture could set roots.

This coincided with the narrative promoted by Argentine Yiddishists (like Pinie Wald, Yankev Botoshansky, Pinie Katz, Samuel Rollansky) and landsman leaders who saw Jews in Argentina as a part of a global Jewish nation.[1] Throughout the interwar years, particularly in the 1930s, Argentine Jews began to claim belonging to Yiddishland in general and to the Polish-Jewish world in particular. By confirming their loyalty to the Jewish madre patria in eastern Europe, the activists gave visibility to a web of intersecting interests among Polish Jews in diaspora. Polish Jews in Argentina developed a new form of diasporic belonging that was rooted in a shared memory of home and a sense of collective ethnic responsibility. The Argentine Jewish involvement was not based on Zionist nationalism but rather a transnational ethnic belonging that acknowledged and valorized Jewish diasporism (and Jewish embeddedness into Poland and Argentina). During the interwar years, the sustained dialogue between Polish-Jewish migrants in Argentina and their relatives in Poland helped create a diasporic ethnic network that spanned the Atlantic.

In 1920s and 1930s, the landsman movement was one of the main arenas to voice the transnational rootedness between Poland and Argentina. The Polish-Jewish landsmanshaftn, especially the Poylisher Farband, constructed and conveyed a specific narrative about Jewish immigration to Argentina throughout the interwar years. According to landsman discourse, immigrants were imagined as the "children" of Jewish Poland, implicitly responsible for improving the situation of Jews in their country of birth. These landsman actors called for a popular commitment to their native land and argued for a transnational and interconnected global diaspora of Yiddish-speaking Polish Jews; this diaspora would be made up of transnational networks of ethnic solidarity, a shared Jewish Polish identity and global Polish-Jewish interests. This approach found its expression in numerous aid campaigns for the Jews in Poland, chiefly concerning Yiddish secular school system. Even those who never officially registered as members often manifested their Polish-Jewish ethnicity in landsman parties or by supporting fund-raising campaigns for the benefit of Jews in Poland. The landsman welfare initiatives and their cultural discourse created an ethnic network that even attracted unaffiliated Jews.

Polish-Jewish immigrants in Argentina used the transnational engagement with Poland to argue in favor of their belonging to the new country. Polish Jews in Argentina saw transnational engagement as a source of pride, prestige, and social capital.[2] Ethnic engagement was used for building ethnic empowerment, which was supposed to stabilize the position of Jewish immigrants in Argentina. At the same time, the issue of an Argentine Jewish ethnic image and respectability entered a transnational dimension. Contributing to and taking financial responsibility for Jews in Poland was a way to prove one's prosperity and reflected positively on the broader Argentine Jewish community. Local Jewish leaders argued that Argentine Jewry was mature and sufficiently developed to become an active global actor, rather than a peripheral community. By organizing campaigns to help the Jews in Poland and protesting against Poland's anti-Semitism, the Polish-Jewish community in Argentina presented themselves as a significant, powerful branch of the Polish-Jewish diaspora. The claims of the landslayt were increasingly seen as legitimate, as Jewish institutions in Poland, such as TSYSHO schools, were in need of Argentine money and international support.

Finally, the development of Yiddishland networks, which paralleled the rise of Argentine nationalism, made space for the construction of a uniquely Jewish-Argentine identity. For immigrant Jews, Argentina offered the promise of secular citizenship and inclusive national ethos. In particular, the 1920s was a period of growing democratization and relative economic prosperity that helped many Jews to construct strong Argentine identities. The devotion of immigrants to the new homeland was visible in the Jewish communal narratives that emphasized Jewish belonging and gratitude to Argentina for the freedoms and chances it offered. It was also visible in the efforts and agendas of the first Argentinized Jewish generation centered around the Asociación Hebraica Argentina as they searched for cultural ways of combining Jewish and Argentine belonging. The 1930s signified a period of emergent Jewish rootedness to Argentina, as linguistic and cultural Argentinization became visible. Translations from Yiddish to Spanish began to appear, and landsmanshaftn engaged in typical Argentine activities, such as *bailes* and outings in quintas. The 1930s in Argentina were also a time of renewed and intensified suspicion toward immigrants, a time of growing anti-Semitism, and a time of a certain Jewish disillusionment toward the liberal-integrationist ethos.

In the 1920s and 1930s, waves of about sixty thousand Polish Jews arrived in Argentina, significantly reshaping the dominant identities in the community. In Argentina of the 1920s, the debates about Jewish belonging to Argentina coincided with the arrival of Yiddishist cultural nationalism from Europe. In the early 1920s, diverse secular Yiddishist schools were created, and in 1928, the Argentine branch of the Yiddishist authority—Yiddish Scientific Institute, the IWO (YIVO)—opened. Importantly, Argentinization and re-Yiddishization were mutually constitutive processes. The Argentine debates about the meaning of the Old Home, the responsibilities of Jewish Argentina toward the broader diaspora, the Argentine Jewish experience continued into the 1930s. These debates were documented in both Yiddish and Spanish, highlighting the community's simultaneous identification with the Argentine patria and the Jews in eastern Europe. Local and transnational belonging coincided and the fault lines between the two were rather blurred. Argentine Yiddishist figures like Pinie Katz voiced Jewish belonging and rootedness in Argentina, whereas many acculturated israelitas argentinos acknowledged the need for a broader, global approach toward the Jewish future. As such, the hybridity of the Argentine-Jewish experiences and identities in the 1920s and 1930s reached unprecedented levels of visibility. During the interwar period a hybrid Argentine Jewish culture, a synthesis of Argentine and Jewish Eastern European elements, first emerged.

Looking Back, Looking Ahead: Jewish Argentina after 1939

World War II (1939–45) completely reconfigured the Jewish world. Nazi Germany annihilated six million Jews, including three million Polish Jews. In Jewish Argentina, the Holocaust was described as a national catastrophe. In 1945, all major Jewish newspapers in Buenos Aires were busy publishing lists of survivors.[3] The testimonies of Argentine Jews who had relatives in Poland reveal that the Shoah dramatically influenced their daily lives and shifted individual and collective priorities. Around 350,000 Polish Jews survived the Holocaust (most of them in the Soviet Union), and around 280,000 temporarily returned to Poland after 1945. Most of them swiftly emigrated to Palestine-Israel, the United States, and Canada; by 1947, only 90,000 Jews remained in Poland. Around 30,000 Jewish Polish survivors left for Latin America. However, Argentina and Brazil continued their immigration restrictions, prompting many Polish Jews to seek refuge in smaller countries in the region. Many of those who managed to obtain Bolivian or Paraguayan visas ultimately crossed into Argentina without legal documentation. Jewish Polish–Argentine relations did not return to their prewar level, due to the new communist political order in Poland, Argentina's disinterest in accepting Holocaust survivors, and the emergence of Palestine as an alternative site of refuge. The Shoah was a transformative point in Jewish Argentine history, reshaping the social and cultural status of Yiddish and the ways in which Argentine Jews categorized themselves within Latin America and within a broader Jewish world.

Although the interwar immigration of Polish Jews reinvigorated Yiddish culture, journalism, and education, the simultaneous process of Argentinization was also at work. In the early 1930s, the strong efforts to modernize and financially secure the Jewish educational establishments appeared. A nonpartisan central Jewish educational institution Vaad Hakhinukh was founded in 1935. It united schools of diverse political profiles (including a part of secular Yiddishists) in a matter of a few years and secured financial subsidies for them. In the late 1930s, the economic recuperation of the Jewish community, mixed with fear of the growing sense of detachment from the Yiddish heritage, prompted many Argentine Jews to invest more money and time in Yiddishist schooling, especially its infrastructure. The secular-progressive Sholem Aleichem school opened in Villa Crespo in 1934, and a year later, two additional branches in Buenos Aires (Villa Crespo and Matadores) were added, and in 1936, three more schools followed.[4] The concerns about the future of Yiddish education came to fruition especially during and after World War II, and paradoxically, the Holocaust temporarily strengthened the importance of Yiddish in Argentina. Between 1940 and 1945, the number of those attending Jewish schools rose by 57 percent.[5]

Realizing that the eastern European center of Yiddish civilization was destroyed, some Argentine Yiddish culturists saw Argentina as an important new Yiddish center in the postwar order and perceived the development of Jewish schooling as compensation for the largely annihilated Eastern European Jewish heritage. For about two decades following the Holocaust, Argentina managed to re-create and safeguard the idea of a secular Yiddish culture to an extent. In 1941, a Yiddish teachers' seminary was opened in Buenos Aires. In 1942, more than 3,000 children attended Jewish schools in Buenos Aires, and by 1946, enrollment increased to 4,800 across 60 schools, staffed by 120 teachers.[6] The cornerstone for the new building of the Yiddishist TSVYSHO Sholem Aleichem school in Villa Crespo (on Serrano Street) in Buenos Aires was laid in 1940 and opened two years later. The impressive two-story building was imagined as an embodiment of the existential powers of Argentine Jewry and its willingness to continue the cultural tradition of European Jewry that the Nazis destroyed. The call to support the construction of the building read: "Our community . . . needs now, more than ever, to assume responsibility for the development of Jewish culture. When the Jewish cultural center in Europe is destroyed, when the heart of Jewish cultural life is torn out, when our existence as a nation is in danger, this is our obligation, the Jews of countries free from a devastating war, to receive from our brothers from the other side of the ocean the luminous cultural heritage. . . . We were called to preserve the holy fire of Jewish national culture. . . . In order to save this culture, to continue shaping it, we ought to do it from the foundations, that is, starting from the school."[7]

Calls to rebuild and invest in Jewish life in Argentina were strengthened during and after World War II when the erasure of Europe's Yiddish cultural center allowed the growth of new centers in Buenos Aires, Montreal, or Tel Aviv. Yiddishist propaganda suggested an increased responsibility on the part of Argentine Jews for Jewish continuity and the preservation of Yiddish. The Holocaust and the anti-Semitic tendencies in Argentina at the turn of the 1930s and 1940s gave an additional impulse to Jewish activism. In 1945, Yankev Vengrover, a leader of Poylisher Farband and AMIA's (Asociación Mutual Israelita Argentina) secretary general, argued that mourning the victims of the war in Europe was not enough and in fact paralyzed creativity. He argued for the existence of Jewish and Yiddish life in the diaspora, envisioning Argentine Jews as fighters for Jewish national and cultural continuity. Vengrover stressed the need for Argentina-produced and Argentina-inspired Jewish culture. The ethnic leader argued that since Jewish life in Poland lay in ruins, Jewish Argentina needed to stand on its own legs and meet its new role in a postwar order.[8]

The late 1940s and 1950s proved that Argentine Yiddish culture was in relatively good shape. Prior to 1939, Buenos Aires was largely a receiver of cultural content produced in Europe or the United States. However, by the 1940s and 1950s, Argentina emerged as a prolific cultural producer in its own right. This was seen as an expansion of Yiddish schooling but also in the development of Yiddish publishing. Several new Yiddish publishers appeared in the late 1940s and 1950s (Idisch, ICUF, Idbuj, Altveltlekher Yidisher Kultur-Kongres, IWO). Even though Polish Jews in Argentina increasingly preferred to speak Spanish in the daily public sphere, the community was strikingly secular and thus ideologically linked to prewar concepts of Yiddish-centered cultural and national belonging. These connections were made possible, in large part, by a generation of devoted ethnic leaders including Marek Turkow, Abraham Mitelberg, and Samuel Rollansky, as well as from the support of the landsmanshaftn.

The Poylisher Farband published 175 Yiddish books in their book series, *Dos poylishe yidntum* (The Polish Jewry, 1946–66). In sponsoring the book series, and drawing on its prewar activism, the Poylisher Farband saw its responsibility to assist survivors economically but also to maintain what they imagined as Polish Jewish culture. After 1945, Argentine Jewry felt an obligation to publish in Yiddish to preserve the memory of Polish Jewry. Wolf Bressler and Abraham Mitelberg, both members of Poylisher Farband and the founders of Idisch publishing house, wrote: "The world Jewish catastrophe elevated our yishev and appointed us with a tragic and great privilege. . . . Via the Idisch Publishers the Argentine yishev is starting to rebuild what the enemy had destroyed."[9] By publishing the collected works of Y. L. Peretz, the newly established publishing house drew on a tradition of cultural life in Poland and seemed to argue that the cultural treasures could be re-created and made useful in a postwar time. The case of *Dos poylishe yidntum* is especially informative for the study of transnational Polish-Jewish identities. By collectively mourning the Holocaust and the destruction of Jewish Poland, the Polish landslayt referred to the prewar transnational discourses that imagined Poland as the heartland of the Yiddish nation. The publishing endeavor was sponsored by community institutions (Poylisher Farband, Folks-bank of Buenos Aires) and featured content from contributors around the world (including Polish-Jewish landsman organizations in the United States).[10] For its part, *Dos poylishe yidntum* helped to establish Argentina as the central point on the Jewish world map.[11]

Buenos Aires–born scholar Abraham Nowersztern mentioned that in the 1950s "in hundreds of homes in Argentina one would recognize the black covers of *Dos poylishe yidntum* volumes."[12] Many books quickly sold out and were reprinted in new editions. After establishing the cooperation with survivors in Poland, hundreds of books were shipped to Europe and many were translated into Polish. Another Argentine, Poland-born Yiddishist Samuel Rollansky, published the book series *Musterverk fun der yidisher literatur* (Masterpieces of Yiddish literature) between 1957 and 1984. Rollansky relied on the heritage and Yiddishist legacy of Argentine IWO, of which he was the head. He was successful in recruiting philanthropists and individual subscribers, which allowed him to publish one hundred titles, including anthologies and works of fiction. The *Musterverk* was sponsored by South African philanthropist Yosef Lifshitz, which again underscored the pre- and postwar transnational networks among Yiddishists. Novels, memoirs of the prewar life in Poland, and Holocaust narratives were to bear witness to unspeakable crimes perpetrated against the Jews.[13] In 1955, when the one hundredth volume of *Dos poylishe yidntum* was published, its editors and Poylisher Farband began to consider their project as "erecting an eternal monument to Polish Jewry." The book series became a *lieux de memoire*, a portable site of remembrance that mourned the murder of Polish Jews but attempted to envision a bright future for Yiddish culture in a post-1945 world in general and in Argentina specifically. Both Argentine memorial series were secular endeavors and a testament to the enduring power of Yiddish peoplehood and their progressive national ideals.

If the Holocaust and the annihilation of eastern European Jewry redefined the dynamics within the Argentine Jewish community and its perception among world Jewry, this was further strengthened by the establishment of the State of Israel. Book publishing, schooling, and power relations in Jewish institutions witnessed a reorientation of culture and identity that mirrored the vision of ethnic leaders, publishers, and educators. This was also linked to the political transformation in Argentina with the rise of Juan Domingo Perón to power in 1943 and his pro-Israel attitude.[14] In the 1950s, Hebrew became more and more present in the school curricula, and some schools defined earlier as Yiddishist even supported Zionism. The Argentine Jewish school system at the turn of the 1940s and 1950s experienced a period of Hebraization. The director of Yiddishist TSVYSHO schools, Chaim Finkelstein, wrote in 1947: "Jewish education needs to develop in children an awareness that the idea of [national] redemption is concrete and near to them, and not something abstract. . . . In the diaspora, there is a need to enjoy the power of Israel, the spirit of the State and its national content, in order to fill them with Jewish life."[15] In 1950, the TSVYSHO opened a Hebrew course for adults; Sholem Aleichem schools reduced the number of Yiddish classes in order to make room for Hebrew. After the establishment of the state of Israel, Argentine Yiddishists seemed to increasingly acknowledge that both Yiddish and Hebrew needed to be taught in Argentina.

The reorientation toward Zionism was also visible within the publishing market. *Editorial Israel,* launched as early as 1938, advocated a pro-Zionist transition within Argentina's cultural realm. It published works in Spanish by the founding fathers of Zionism, including Herzl, Jabotinsky, Ahad Haam (and excluded socialist Zionists like Borokhov and Syrkin), as well as a number of fiction translations from Hebrew.[16] *Editorial Israel,* similar to the tendencies found in Argentine Jewish schooling, drew on historical and religious aspects of Jewishness, presenting them as an alternative to a narrative centered around Yiddish and secularism. Its editors, Maximo Yagupsky and José Mirelman, envisioned Israel as a sign of Jewish national revival and took a pride in the victories of the young state after 1948. This was also reflected in the books they published that praised militant Jewishness and Jewish heroism.[17] The Hebrew-Zionist tendencies in Jewish literary culture were strengthened after the establishment of Israel. In 1953, *Editorial Candelabro* was founded, publishing a so-called Zionist Library and cooperating with the Jewish Agency.[18] Most of the pro-Zionist books were published in Spanish rather than in Hebrew to make them more accessible to young Argentine Jewish readers. By the mid-1950s, the sale of the books "of Jewish interest" published in Spanish exceeded those in Yiddish.[19] The Hebrew and Zionist turn in Argentina reflected the developments in Israel, where a wedge between Yiddishness and Jewishness was being forged.[20]

The strongest opposition to the linguistic and ideological evolution was adopted by Yidisher Kultur Farband (ICUF or IKUF). In 1941, the ICUF, founded on the ideals of secular progressive Jewishness and social justice, was established in Argentina. The organization grouped together a number of local communist organizations and housed its own literary press between 1946 and 1967.[21] One of its leaders was the veteran ethnic activist and journalist Pinie Wald. The *progresistas,* the nickname of ICUF supporters, were an important political power at the turn of the century. They opposed what they saw as Zionist homogenization of Argentine Jewish schooling and defended the value of social and political diversity.[22] In the AMIA (the kehilla of Buenos Aires) elections of 1949, the procommunist progressives won an impressive share of 40 percent of the votes. Tensions between communist and Zionist Jews were extremely high and the Zionist supremacy was stabilized only around 1955, especially after the communists were boycotted in AMIA and DAIA (Delegación de Asociaciones Israelitas Argentinas).[23] In the 1950s, the ICUF school continued to teach according to the ideals of secularism and Yiddishism and placed a strong emphasis on the value of Jewish rootedness in the Argentine diaspora.[24]

The Holocaust and its aftermath closed an important era in Jewish Argentine history. The war signified a violent disruption of the debates surrounding Jewish peoplehood, ethnicity, and Yiddish culture across the Atlantic. The transnational, cultural, and ethnonational linkages that emerged following the immigration of Polish Jews to Argentina were largely dismantled. Similarly, the imagined polity of Yiddishland was shattered into pieces, as the commemorative projects that appeared in Argentina and other countries in the 1940s and 1950s were a distant memory of the formerly intensive cultural dialogue between Argentina and Jewish Poland. After 1945, the geographies of the Jewish world were redefined and the Jewish polacos of Argentina were compelled to search for new sites of individual and collective identity.

Glossary

alter heym: Literally old home, expression used by eastern European emigrants when referring to their home countries. Old Country bears a similar meaning; pl. alte heymen

Ashkenazi Jews: Jews historically originating from central and eastern Europe for whom Yiddish was a common vernacular language

Botoshansky, Yankev: Argentine Yiddish journalist and writer, who was born in Bessarabia in 1895 and died in Buenos Aires in 1964

criollo: Inhabitant of the Argentine interior, often of mixed indigenous and white ancestry

Der Moment: Warsaw Yiddish daily, published 1910–39

Di Presse: Buenos Aires Yiddish left-wing daily edited by Pinie Katz, published 1918–78

Di Yidische Zaitung: Buenos Aires Yiddish daily, published 1914–73

Dos Naye Vort: Poylisher Farband journal, published 1928 until late 1930s

gaucho: Argentine cowboy inhabiting the local lowlands (pampas), usually of mixed white and indigenous heritage

Haynt: Warsaw Zionist-Liberal Yiddish daily, published 1908–39

Hirschbein, Peretz: Yiddish writer and traveler, author of Argentine travelogue in Yiddish (*Fun vayte lender*, 1916)

Izraelita: Warsaw integrationist Jewish journal in Polish, published 1866–1912

Jewish Colonization Association (JCA): Philanthropic organization started in 1888 that coordinated Jewish agricultural settlements in Argentine, funded by Baron Maurice Hirsch

Katz, Pinie: 1881–1959, Argentine Yiddish activist, translator, and journalist and founder of *Di Presse* in Argentina

landsmanshaft: Organization uniting Jewish immigrants from the same town or region (who are called landslayt). Landsman is a member of a landsmanshaft.

Literarishe Bleter: Warsaw literary journal in Yiddish, published 1924–39

Mundo Israelita: Argentine-Jewish journal in Spanish, published 1923–2014

Nomberg, Hersh Dovid: Yiddish writer and traveler, author of Argentine travelogue in Yiddish (*Dos bukh felyetonen*, 1924)

Poylisher Farband: The biggest Polish-Jewish immigrant institution in interwar Argentina, established in 1916, in existence probably until 1980s

Resnick, Salomón: Jewish-Argentine writer and editor, founder of the Jewish journal in Spanish *Judaica*

Socieded Hebraica Argentina: Organization grouping Argentinized Jewish youth, established in 1928

TSYSHO: Tsentrale Yidishe Shul Organizatsye, Central Jewish School Organization, a Yiddishist educational institution

Wald, Pinie (Pedro): Argentine Jewish leader and left-wing activist, born in Tomaszów, Poland, in 1886, in Argentina from 1906, died in Buenos Aires in 1966

yishev: Settlement, Jewish community in a specific country; pl. yishevim

Notes

Introduction

1. Hersh Dovid Nomberg, introduction to Mordechai Alpersohn, *Kolonye Mauricio: Draysik yerike JCA kolonizatsye in argentine: A historishe shilderung* (Berlin: Jüdischer Verlag, 1923), 7.

2. In Polish, it is Centralny Związek Żydów Polskich w Argentynie, and in Spanish, Unión Central Israelita Polaca en la Argentina. I later abbreviate the name to Poylisher Farband.

3. Hasia Diner, *Roads Taken. The Great Jewish Migrations to the New World and the Peddlers who Forged the Way* (New Haven, CT: Yale University Press 2015), 20–23.

4. José Moya, *Cousins and Strangers: Spanish Immigrants in Buenos Aires* (Berkeley: University of California Press, 1998), 3–4.

5. As Daniel Soyer explained, the Yiddish word *landsman* denotes an immigrant from the same town, region, or country as the speaker. The plural form is *landslayt*. *Landsmanshaft* is an organization of landslayt, or an informal community of landslayt. The plural form of landsmanshaft is *landsmanshaftn*. I also use the word *landsman* as an adjective referring to the activity of the landslayt. See Daniel Soyer, *Jewish Immigrant Association and American Identity in New York, 1880–1939* (Cambridge, MA: Harvard University Press, 1997), 1.

6. Israel Bartal and Scott Ury, "Between Jews and Their Neighbours. Isolation, Confrontation, and Influence in Eastern Europe," in *Jews and Their Neighbours in Eastern Europe since 1750*, ed. Israel Bartal, Antony Polonsky, and Scott Ury, 5–8, vol. 24 of *Polin: Studies in Polish Jewry* (Oxford: Littman Library of Jewish Civilization, 2012).

7. Judith Laikin Elkin, *Jews of the Latin American Republics* (Chapel Hill: University of North Carolina Press, 1980); Robert Weisbrot, *The Jews of Argentina: From the Inquisition to Perón* (Philadelphia: Jewish Publishing Society of America, 1979); Haim Avni, *Argentina y la historia de la inmigración judía (1810–1950)* (Jerusalem: Magnes Press, Hebrew University of Jerusalem, 1983).

8. Judith Butler, *Parting Ways: Jewishness and the Critique of Zionism* (New York: Columbia University Press, 2012), 3–6.

9. Zulma Recchini de Lattes and Alfredo E. Lattes, eds., *La población de Argentina* (Buenos Aires: Ediciones C.I.C.R.E.D, 1974), 30–33.

10. Haim Avni and Sibila Seibert, "La agricultura judía en Argentina ¿éxito o fracaso?" *Desarollo Economico* 22, no. 88 (1983): 537. In 1935, it was 11 percent, compared to 22 percent in 1920. See Weisbrot, *Jews of Argentina*, 70.

11. José Moya, "Spanish Emigration to Cuba and Argentina," in *Mass Migration*

to Modern Latin America, ed. Samuel L. Baily and Eduardo José Míguez, 14 (Wilmington, DE: Jaguar Books, 2003).

12. Haim Avni, *Argentina y las migraciones judías. De la Inquisición al Holocausto y después* (Buenos Aires: Editorial Mila, 2005), 194.

13. Vicente Vázquez-Presedo, *Estadísticas históricas argentinas II (Comparadas). Segunda Parte 1914–1939* (Buenos Aires: Ediciones Macchi, 1976), 29.

14. In three five-year cycles, immigration contributed to around 50 percent of the population growth: 1895–1900, 1905–10, 1910–15. In the 1920s, it was respectively 34.6 percent in 1920–25 and 31.2 percent in 1925–30. Recchini de Lattes and Lattes, *La población de Argentina*, 33.

15. Vázquez-Presedo, *Estadísticas históricas argentinas II*, 31.

16. Ricardo Feierstein, *Historia de los judíos en la Argentina* (Buenos Aires: Ameghino, 1999), 141.

17. Jacob Shatzky, *Comunidades judías en Latinoamerica* (Buenos Aires: Ediciones del American Jewish Committee, 1952), 10. Another Jewish demographer, Jacob Lestschinsky, estimated that, between 1840 and 1947, 225,000 Jews immigrated to Argentina, Jacob Lestschinsky, *Di lage fun yidn in latayn-amerikaner lender* (New York: World Jewish Congress, 1948), 3–4.

18. Lestschinsky, *Di lage fun yidn*, 3.

19. N. Reif, "Rozwój emigracji żydowskiej z Polski." Referat na posiedzeniu Komitetu Emigracyjnego, May 20, 1936, quoted in Stanisław Pawłowski, *O emigracji żydów z Polski i ich kolonizacji* (Warsaw: Liga Morska i Kolonialna, 1937), 15.

20. Konrad Zieliński, "Emigracja żydowska z Rosji i Królestwa Polskiego (1881–1918)," *Kwartalnik Historii Żydów* no. 201 (2002): 32.

21. Arie Tartakower, *Emigracja żydowska z Polski* (Warsaw: Instytut Badań Narodowościowych, 1939), 11.

22. Jacob Lestschinsky, *National Groups in Polish Emigration* (New York: Conference on Jewish Relations, 1943), 109. Reprinted from *Jewish Social Studies* 5, no. 2.

23. Emigracja polska w Argentynie, sprawozdanie za rok 1931, AAN (Archiwum Akt Nowych) MSZ (Ministerstwo Spraw Zagranicznych) 9618-B26028, 2–27, following the data of Dirección General de Migraciones.

24. Katarzyna Porada, *Procesos de formación de la identidad étnica de un grupo de origen migratorio: Los desciendentes de polacos en Buenos Aires y Misiones* (Madrid: Ediciones Polifermo, 2016).

25. Arie Tartakower, *In Search of Home Freedom* (London: World Jewish Congress, 1958), 44.

26. Marta Kowalska, "La emigración judía de Polonia a la Argentina en los años 1918–1939," *Estudios Latinoamericanos* 12 (1989): 258–59.

27. Victor A. Mirleman, *En búsqueda de una identidad. Inmigrantes judíos en Buenos Aires, 1890–1930* (Buenos Aires: Editorial Mila, 1988), 14.

28. Rebecca Kobrin, "Conflicting Diasporas, Shifting Centers: Migration and Identity in Transnational Polish Jewish Community," (PhD diss., University of Pennsylvania, 2002), 5–6.

29. Gershon Bacon, "National Revival, Ongoing Acculturation: Jewish Education in Interwar Poland," *Simon Dubnow Institut Jahrbuch*, 1 (2002): 71–92.

30. Scott Ury, "Who, What, When, Where, and Why Is Polish Jewry? Envisioning, Constructing, and Possessing Polish Jewry," *Jewish Social Studies* 6, no. 3 (2000): 205–28.

31. Ezra Mendelsohn, *Żydzi Europy środkowo-wschodniej w okresie międzywojennym* (Warsaw: Wydawnictwo Naukowe PWN, 1992), 31–57.

32. Kenneth Moss, "Negotiating Jewish Nationalism in Interwar Warsaw," in *Warsaw. The Jewish Metropoli Essays in Honor of the 75th Birthday of Professor Antony Polonsky*, ed. Glenn Dynner and François Guesnet, 407 (Leiden, Netherlands: Brill 2015). See also Celia Stopnicka-Heller, "Poles of Jewish Background—The Case of Assimilation without Integration in Interwar Poland," in *Studies on Polish Jewry 1919–1939*, ed. Joshua A. Fishman, 266–70 (New York: YIVO Institute for Jewish Research, 1974).

33. See David Aliano, "Identity in Transatlantic Play: Il Duce's National Project in Argentina" (PhD diss., City University of New York, 2008), 249–55.

34. See Ronald C. Newton, *German Buenos Aires 1900–1933: Social Change and Cultural Crisis* (Austin: University of Texas Press, 1977).

35. Oscar A. Troncoso, *Buenos Aires se divierte* (Buenos Aires: Centro Editor de América Latina SA, 1971), 83–84.

36. Moss, "Negotiating Jewish Nationalism," 398–99. Moss explains that Jewish Diaspora Nationalism was eclectic and included a variety of practices that were often formed by engaging with Zionism.

37. Daniel Boyarin and Jonathan Boyarin, "Diaspora: Generation and Ground of Jewish Identity," *Critical Inquiry* 19, no. 4 (1993): 712–17.

38. Julie E. Cooper, "Diasporic Critic of Diasporism: The Question of Jewish Political Agency," *Political Theory* 43, no. 1 (2015): 95–97.

39. Roza Tsagarousianou, "Rethinking the Concept of Diaspora: Mobility, Connectivity and Communication in a Globalised World," *Westminster Papers in Communication and Culture* 1, no. 1 (2004): 52.

40. Yosef Yerushalmi, "Exile and Expulsion in Jewish History," in *Crisis and Creativity in the Sephardic World, 1391–1648*, ed. Benjamin R. Gampel (New York: Columbia University Press, 1997), 12, 14.

41. Robin Cohen, *Global Diasporas: An Introduction* (Seattle: University of Washington Press, 1997), 5–9.

42. Rebecca Kobrin, *Jewish Bialystok and Its Diaspora* (Bloomington: Indiana University Press, 2010).

43. Mays and Brodsky offer corrective moves in their works on Sephardi Diaspora. Devi Mays, "Transplanting Cosmopolitans: The Migrations of Sephardic Jews to Mexico, 1900–1934," PhD diss., Indiana University, 2013; Adriana M. Brodsky, *Sephardi, Jewish Argentine: Community and National Identity* (Bloomington: Indiana University Press, 2016).

44. Mays, "Transplanting Cosmopolitans"; Brodsky, *Sephardi, Jewish, Argentine.*

45. Joy Owen, "Transnationalism as a Process, Diaspora as Condition," *Journal of Social Development in Africa* 30, no. 1 (2014): 42.

46. Eliezer Ben-Rafael and Yitzhak Sternberg, "Introduction: Debating Transnationalism," in Ben-Rafael and Sternberrg, *Transnationalism*, 1.

47. Ava F. Kahn and Adam D. Mendelsohn provide a balance to this tendency in *Transnational Traditions: New Perspectives on American Jewish History* (Detroit, MI: Wayne State University Press, 2014).

48. Steven Vertovec, *Transnationalism* (New York: Routledge, 2009), 13–15.

49. Glick Shiller, Basch, and Blanc-Szanton, "Transnationalism: A New Analytic Framework for Understanding Migration," in Glick Shiller, Basch, and Blanc-Szanton, *Towards a Transnational Perspective*, 1–2.

50. Steven Vertovec, "Conceiving and Researching Transnationalism," *Ethnic and Racial Studies* 22, no. 2 (1999): 447–62.

51. Brodsky, *Sephardi, Jewish, Argentine*, 85.

52. Brodsky, *Sephardi, Jewish, Argentine*, 14–16.

53. Christian Joppke and Ewa Morawska, "Integrating Immigrants in Liberal Nation States: Policies and Practices," in *Toward Assimilation and Citizenship*, ed. Christian Joppke and Ewa Morawska (Basingstoke, UK: Palgrave, 2003), 3.

54. Sarah Albiez, and Nelly Castro, Lara Jüssen, Eva Youkhana, introduction to *Etnicidad, ciuadadanía y partenecía: Practicás, teoria y dimensiones espaciales*, ed. Sarah Albiez et al., 17 (Madrid: Iberoamericana/Vervuert, 2011).

55. Jeffrey Lesser, *A Discontented Diaspora: Japanese-Brazilians and the Meanings of Ethnic Militancy* (Durham, NC: Duke University Press, 2007); Ignacio Klich and Jeffrey Lesser, eds., *Arab and Jewish Immigrants in Latin America: Images and Realities* (London: Frank Cass, 1998); Edmundo Murray, *Becoming Gauchos Ingleses: Diasporic Model in Irish-Argentine Literature* (Bethesda, MD: Mausnel, 2009).

56. Jeffrey Lesser and Raanan Rein, eds., *Rethinking Jewish-Latin Americans* (Albuquerque: University of New Mexico Press, 2008).

57. Raanan Rein, "Historiografía judeo-latinoamericana: Desafios y propuestas," in Kahan et al., *Marginados y consagrados*, 27–46.

58. Roni Gechtman, "Creating a Historical Narrative for a Spiritual Nation: Simon Dubnow and the Politics of the Jewish Past," *Journal of the Canadian Historical Association* 22, no. 2 (2011): 98–124.

59. Dovid Katz, "Language: Yiddish," YIVO Encyclopedia of Jews in Eastern Europe, October 31, 2011, accessed January 24, 2019, http://www.yivoencyclopedia.org/article.aspx/Language/Yiddish.

60. Benedict Anderson, *Imagined Communities: Reflections on the Origin and Spread of Nationalism* (London: Verso, 2006).

61. Kalman (Keith) Weiser, "The Capital of the 'Yiddishland'?" in Dynner and Guesnet, *Warsaw*, 298–322.

62. Yehiel Scheintuch, "Veidat tshernovitz ve-tarbut yidish," *Huliot* 6 (2000): 260–261.

63. Tatjana Soldat-Jaffe, *Twenty-First Century Yiddishism* (Brighton, UK: Sussex Academic Press, 2012), 14.

64. Kenneth B. Moss, *Jewish Renaissance in the Russian Revolution* (Cambridge, MA: Harvard University Press, 2009), 10–16.

65. Jeffrey Shandler, *Adventures in Yiddishland: Postvernacular Language and Culture* (Berkeley: University of California Press, 2006), 36–37.

66. Dovid Katz, *Yiddish and Power* (London: Palgrave Macmillan, 2014), 272–73.

67. Soldat-Jaffe, *Twenty-first Century Yiddishism* 39.

68. Pinie Katz, "Di yidish-argentinishe yugent un ir kultur," in *Geklibene shriftn*, vol. 4 (Buenos Aires: Gezelshaftlekher komitet baym farlag "IKUF," 1946), 23, first presented at the Congress of Jewish Youth in Argentina in Rosario, February 24, 1940. Pinie Katz was born in southern Ukraine (Kherson region) in 1882 and arrived in Argentina in 1906. He was one of the most important figures of Argentine cultural Yiddishism, as well as editor of the *Di Presse* daily and a convinced communist.

69. Pinie Katz, "Argentiner yidn," in *Geklibene shriftn*, vol. 4, 11–13, first printed in a journal of the Jewish Youth Federation in Argentina.

Chapter 1

1. Peretz Hirschbein, *Fun vayte lender. Argentine, brazil, yuni, november 1914* (New York: Farlag Tog, 1916), 35.

2. Roberta Strauss Feuerlicht, *The Fate of the Jews: A People Torn Between Israeli Power and Jewish Ethics* (New York: Times Books, 1983), 61, quoted in Zieliński, "Emigracja żydowska," 18.

3. Maskilim were the followers of the Haskalah, the Jewish Enlightment, who from the late eighteenth century until the 1880s sought to adapt the Jews to European modernity. Haskalah explored the possibilities of social, economic, and cultural integration within the surrounding societies.

4. "Warszawskie Biuro informacyjne dla emigrantów żydów," *Izraelita*, no. 28, July 12, 1912, 6–7.

5. "Mikhtavey sofreynu," *Hazefirah*, no. 141, July 6, 1888, 2–3.

6. *Hazefirah*, no. 412, June 3, 1889, page unknown, quoted in Yaacov Rubel, "Di opklangen vegn der yidisher emigratsye fun rusland un yidisher kolonizatsye in argentine," *Argentiner IWO Shriftn* 15 (1989): 16.

7. *Hazefirah* in 1900 had a circulation of around five thousand copies. Since 1888, it appeared as a daily. See Marcin Wodziński and Agnieszka Jagodzińska, "*Izraelita" 1866–1915. Wybór źródeł* (Kraków: Austeria, 2015), 26–29.

8. The Hebrew phrase Erets Ha-kesef could be translated as "A Land of Silver," from the La Plata River, a "silver river" that passes through Argentina. It was often used in early Hebrew texts on emigration to Argentina.

9. Nahum Slouschz, "Tsiyon ve-argentina," *Hazefirah*, July 23, 1894, no. 155, 2 (666).

10. Yosef Halevy, "Be-argentina. Ha-limudim ha-ivri'im," *Hazefirah*, no. 276, December 20, 1912, 4.

11. Victor A. Mirelman, *En búsqueda de una identidad. Los inmigrantes judíos en Buenos Aires 1890–1930* (Buenos Aires: Editorial Milá, 1988), 27.

12. Pinie Katz, Yankev Botoshansky, Salomón Suscovich, Wolf Bressler, and Abraham Mitelberg, eds, *Antologye fun der yidisher literatur in argentine* (Buenos Aires: a gezelshaftlekher komitet le-koyved dem 25-yorikn yubiley fun der teglekher tsaytung Di Prese, 1944), 416. Liachovitzky also wrote for *Der Yud* from Kraków, *Hameltiz* from St. Petersburg, and the Viennese *Di Velt*. For instance, in 1901 he provided updates on Jewish education in Argentina. Yankev Shimon Liachovitzky, "Brif fun argentine. Unzere kinder-ertsiyung," *Der Yud*, no. 5, January 31, 1901, 7–9.

13. Quoted in Rubel, "Di opklangen vegn der yidisher emigratsye," 32.

14. *Izraelita* was founded in 1861 by Samuel Peltyn and reached the circles of Warsaw's progressive Jewish intelligentsia (lawyers, doctors, teachers, etc.). *Izraelita* held a Polonocentric integrationist position, rooted in the concept of a "Jewish-Polish brotherhood" that appeared in the 1860s. *Izraelita*'s circles saw themselves as "Polacy-Żydzi," or "Poles-Jews," rather than simply Jews or Polish Jews. Following Peltyn's death in 1896, the weekly was directed by his wife and son. Its editorship was later assumed by Nahum Sokolow, but other editors criticized his neophyte Zionism, and he was ultimately ousted. In the final period, its pro-Polish attitude was sharply criticized by the Yiddish dailies. The new social and political reality on the verge of the Great War led to the dissolution of the journal in 1912. See Zuzanna Kołodziejska, "*Izraelita" (1866–1915). Znaczenie kulturowe i literackie czasopisma* (Kraków: Wydawnictwo Uniwersytetu Jagiellońskiego, 2014).

15. "Kolonje I.C.A.," *Izraelita*, no. 33, August 16, 1912, 1.

16. "Walne Zebranie Żydowskiego Towarzystwa Emigracyjnego," *Izraelita*, no. 33, August 18, 1911, 7–8.

17. Samuel Peltyn, "Co z kolonizacji żydów sobie rokujemy?" *Izraelita*, no. 36, 1891, 241–42, quoted in Wodziński and Jagodzińska, "*Izraelita,*" 329.

18. Adolf Jakub Cohn, "Argentyna," *Izraelita*, no. 15, 1901, 173–174.

19. This was rooted in *Izraelita*'s approach towards the Jewish masses. The journal regarded them as "dark" and the circles of *Izraelita* as the illustrious leaders, who should "save the poor fanatics" and show them how to love Poland and live in unity with the Poles. See "Od Redakcji," *Izraelita*, no. 1, 1909, 1, quoted in Wodziński and Jagodzińska, "*Izraelita,*" 42.

20. Nahum [probably Sokolow], "Trudne początki," *Izraelita*, no. 17, April 29, 1892, 135–36.

21. "Ze świata. Z Argentyny," *Izraelita*, no. 10, March 4, 1892, 81.

22. Nahum [probably Sokolow], "Trudne początki," *Izraelita*, no. 17, April 29, 1892, 135–36.

23. Wodziński and Jagodzińska, "*Izraelita,*" 329.

24. "Co piszą z Argentyny," *Izraelita*, no. 14, April 1, 1892, 111–12.

25. Some rabbis even forbade emigration. Zieliński, "Emigracja żydowska," 21.

26. "Ba-israel," *Hazafirah*, no. 185, August 30, 1991, 2 (748).

27. Quoted in Rubel, "Di opklangen vegn der yidisher emigratsye," 33.

28. "Inyaney dyuma," *Hazefirah*, no. 135, July 2, 1889, 2 (552).

29. Leon Chasanovitch, *Die Krise der jüdischen Kolonisation in Argentinien und der moralische Bankerott der J.C.A.-Administration* (Stanislau: Verlag Bildung, 1910).

30. Alan Astro, *Yiddish South of the Border: An Anthology of Latin American Yiddish Writing* (Albuquerque: University of New Mexico Press, 2003), 46.

31. Nakhmen Mayzel, ed., *Y. L. Peretz. Briv un redes. Gezamelt un ibergezetst mit araynfir un bemerkungen fun nakhmen mayzel* (Vilna: Vilner Farlag B. Kletskin Farlag, 1929), 55, quoted in Rollansky, "Y. L. peretzes batsiyung tsu argentine," *Argentiner IWO Shriftn* 1, 1941, 120.

32. Baal Machshoves, "Ver iz JCA?" *Der Jud*, no. 8, February 21, 1901, quoted in Rollansky, "Y. L. Peretzes," 126.

33. *Shtet un shtetlekh* in *Ale verk fun Y.L. Peretz* (Vilna: Vilner Farlag fun Kletzkin, 1925), vol. 17, 243, quoted in Rollansky, "Y. L. Peretzes," 126.

34. Yitskhok Leybush Peretz, "Yudishe shtot un shtetlekh," *Der Yud*, November 20, 1902, 9–11, quoted in Rollansky, "Y. L. Peretzes," 128.

35. Rollansky, "Y. L. Peretzes," 121.

36. Jerzy Mazurek, *Kraj a emigracja: Ruch ludowy wobec wychodźstwa chłopskiego do krajów Ameryki Łacińskiej (do 1939 r.)* (Warsaw: Biblioteka Iberyjska, 2006), 9.

37. Mazurek, 29–30.

38. Krzysztof Groniowski, "Emigracja z ziem zaboru rosyjskiego (1864–1918)," in *Emigracja z ziem polskich w czasach nowożytnych i najnowszych (XVIII-XX w.)*, ed. Andrzej Pilch, 230–40 (Warsaw: Państwowe Wydawnictwo Naukowe, 1984).

39. One of the critics of peasant emigration was the nationalist politician Roman Dmowski. See Michał Starczewski, "Mrzonki racjonalnej kolonizacji w duchu narodowym: Roman Dmowski i polska emigracja do Brazylii," *Przegląd Historyczny* 52 no. 2 (2015): 63–74.

40. Maria Paradowska, *Podróżnicy i emigranci: Szkice z dziejów polskiego wychodźstwa w Ameryce Południowej* (Warsaw: Interpress, 1984), 159–62.

41. *Wiadomości o Argentynie do użytku wychodźców wraz z samouczkiem języka hiszpańskiego*, Biblioteczka Syndykatu Emigracyjnego, vol. 2 (Warsaw: Syndykat Emigracyjny, 1937).

42. Wacław Dostal, *Argentyna: Monografie Geograficzno-Handlowe Informatora Eksportowego*, vol. 4 (Warsaw, 1937).

43. *Pamiętniki Emigrantów z Ameryki Południowej* (Warsaw: Instytut Gospodarstwa Społecznego, 1937).

44. Gustaw Załęcki, *Kilka słów o nowoczesnym imperializmie narodowym* (Warsaw: Naukowy Instytut Emigracyjny, 1928).

45. Mieczysław Fularski, *Kryzys emigracyjny a polska polityka kolonialna* (Warsaw, Instytut Wydawniczy Ligi Morskiej i Kolonialnej, 1927).

46. Stanisław Pawłowski, *O emigracji żydów z Polski i ich kolonizacji* (Warsaw: Liga Morska i Kolonialna, 1937).

47. A. I. Piątkowski, "Jak pozbyć się Żydów," *Lud Polski*, no. 5, January 29, 1914, 1–2, quoted in Mazurek, *Kraj a emigracja*, 267.

48. "Monitor Polski," no. 43, February 21, 1925, pos. 168.

49. Leon Alter, "Wychodźstwo żydowskie," *Kwartalnik Instytutu Naukowego do Badań Emigracji i Kolonizacji* 1 (1926): 80–91; Mieczysław Goldsztejn, "Wychodźstwo żydowskie z ziem polskich," *Kwartalnik Naukowego Instytutu Emigracyjnego i Kolonialnego* 1 (1931): 388–425.

50. "A zitsung mitn delegat fun HIAS h. alter," *Dos Naye Vort*, no. 124, July 1931, 13.

51. Alter, "Wychodźstwo żydowskie," 81.

52. In the late 1930s, emigration from Poland was rather difficult. The United States and Argentina limited immigration possibilities, and Palestine, which received huge emigrant contingents in 1935 and 1936, was sealed by the British in the following years. Whereas 18,000 Polish Jews emigrated to Palestine in 1934 and 25,000–27,000 in 1935, the numbers dropped drastically to 3,636 in 1937. See Harry Schneiderman, ed., *American Jewish Yearbook 5699. September 26, 1938 to September 13, 1939, vol.* 40 (Philadelphia: Jewish Publication Society of America), 574.

53. Tara Zahra, *The Great Departure: Mass Migration from Eastern Europe and the Making of the Free World* (New York: W. W. Norton, 2016), 158.

54. Problem emigracji żydowskiej, 39–68, AAN MSZ 9914 B26324. The delegation included Henryk Rosmarin and Mojżesz Schorr, members of the Jewish Colonization Committee.

55. Ezra Mendelsohn, *The Jews of East Central Europe between the World Wars* (Bloomington: Indiana University Press, 1983), 36–37; Rogers Brubaker, *Nationalism Reframed: Nationhood and the National Question in the New Europe* (Cambridge: Cambridge University Press, 1996), 86–90.

56. Władysław Grabski, *Projekt programu polityki ekonomicznej i finansowej* (Warsaw: 1920), 13.

57. Quoted in Mazurek, *Kraj a emigracja*, 351.

58. Halina Janowska, "Emigracja z Polski w latach 1918–1939," in Pilch, *Emigracja z ziem polskich*, 409–11.

59. Józef Okołowicz, *Wychodźstwo i osadnictwo polskie przed wojną światową* (Warsaw: Urząd Emigracyjny, 1920), 402, quoted in Wojciech Wrzesiński, "Polacy zagranicą w polityce II Rzeczpospolitej (1918–1939)," in *Problemy dziejów Polonii*, ed. Marian M. Drozdowski (Warsaw: PWN, 1979), 22..

60. "Polska emigracja zarobkowa," *Wychodźca*, no. 6 (1925), 3–5.

61. See Emanuel Melzer, "Ha-diplomatiyah ha-polanit u-ve'ayat ha-hagirah ha-yehudit ba-shanim 1935–1939," *Gal-Ed* 1 (1973): 211–49.

62. Quoted in Mazurek, *Kraj a emigracja*, 145.

63. Yfaat Weiss, *Deutsche und polnische Juden vor dem Holocaust. Jüdische Identität*

zwischen Staatsbürgerschaft und Ethnizität 1933–1940 (Munich: Oldenbourg Verlag, 2000), 138.

64. J. Sawicki, director of MSW, letter to MSZ, October 29, 1937, Międzyministerialna Komisja Emigracyjna (Interministerial Emigration Commission, MKE), 120–21, AAN MSZ 9898, quoted in Mazurek, *Kraj a emigracja*, 157.

65. Protokół z posiedzenia MKE from February 24, 1938 (a report from the MKE meeting), AAN MSZ, 9898 B26308 Międzyministerialna Komisja Emigracyjna, quoted in Mazurek, *Kraj a emigracja*, 35.

66. Secret note to the Head of the Emigration Division of MSZ concerning tourist emigration, Problem emigracji żydowskiej, 44–48, AAN MSZ 9907 B26318.

67. A note from the Polish Embassy in Buenos Aires concerning Polish Jewish immigrants in Argentina, Emigracja polska do Argentyny, 96–102, AAN MSZ 9620 B2630.

68. *Wiadomości o Argentynie do użytk uwychodźców wraz z samouczkiem języka hiszpańskiego*, Biblioteczka Syndykatu Emigracyjnego, vol. 2 (Warsaw: Syndykat Emigracyjny, 1937), 39.

69. Eastern European Jews were popularly associated with communism and anarchism. See José Moya, "What's in a Stereotype? The Case of Jewish Anarchists in Argentina," in *The New Jewish Argentina: Facets of Jewish Experiences in the Southern Cone*, ed. Adriana M. Brodsky et al., 55–88 (Leiden: Brill, 2013).

70. Argentyna. Przyjęcie posła argentyńskiego przez prezydenta RP, sprawy emigracji polskiej, Freyre, AAN MSZ 3412 B19632, 5–7.

71. Rodolfo Freyere to Carlos Saavedra Lamas, AMREC (Archivo General del Ministerio de Relacions Exteriores y Culto), nota no. 28, Warsaw, 13.11.937.

72. Marcos Savon to Carlos Saavedra Lamas, Gdynia, 14.7.1937, AMREC, D.P. Polonia, 1937, Exp. 1, Nota no. 1.

73. On July 12, 1938, Argentine minister of Foreign Affairs José María Cantilo issued a secret circular which forbade Argentine from issuing visas to "undesirable immigrants," which was understood to be Jews. This limitation did not refer to Polish Jews specifically.

74. Utrudnienia wizowe dla emigrantów polskich do Argentyny 1938, 1–30, AAN MSZ, 9621 B26031. This was confirmed in the report by the US consulate in Buenos Aires: "The Jewish Refugee and the Argentine Immigration Problem," April 16, 1938, republished in John Mendelsohn, ed. *The Holocaust*, vol. 5 (New York: Garland Publishing, 1982), 201.

75. Rozporządzenie Prezydenta Rzeczypospolitej z dnia 11 października 1927 r. o emigracji., Dziennik Ustaw 127, nr 89, poz. 799.

76. Weiss, *Deutsche und polnische Juden*, 134–36.

77. Harry Schneiderman ed., *American Jewish Yearbook 5699. September 14, 1939 to October 2, 1940*, vol. 41 (Philadelphia: Jewish Publication Society of America), 597. Emigration to Palestine was limited by the quota system and the requirement to receive an immigrant permit.

78. Mark Tolts, "Population and Migration. Migration Since World War I," YIVO Encyclopedia of Jews in Eastern Europe.

79. Jacob Lestschinsky, *National Groups in Polish Emigration* (New York Conference on Jewish Relations, 1943), 110–11.

80. Tartakower, *Emigracja żydowska*, 48. Between 1929 and 1937, 43.7 percent of Polish Jews immigrated to Palestine and 18.8 percent to Argentina.

Chapter 2

1. Israel Makranski, "Poylishe yidn in der argentiner yidisher kolonizatsye," in *Poylishe yidn in doyrem amerike. 25 yor gezelshaftlekhe tetikayt. Zamlbukh tsum 25-yoriken yuvl fun organizirtn poylishn yidntum in argentine, 1916–1941* (Buenos Aires: Tsentral farband fun poylishe yidn in argentine, 1941), 129.

2. Former Russian Lipava is Liepāja in Latvia. See Irving Howe, *The World of Our Fathers* (New York: Galahad Books, 1994), 28–29, and Hans Rogger, *Jewish Policies and Right-Wing Politics in Imperial Russia* (Hampshire-London: Palgrave Macmillan, 1986), 183–84, quoted in Zieliński, "Emigracja żydowska," 20.

3. Michał Starczewski, "Z dziejów emigracji zarobkowej: Agenci emigracyjni na ziemiach polskich przed 1914 r." *Przegląd Historyczny* 103, no. 1 (2012): 48.

4. Starczewski, 48.

5. "Emigracja żydów z Rosji," *Izraelita*, no. 30, July 28, 1911, 8.

6. Warszawskie Biuro Emigrantów Żydów (Warsaw Information Bureau for Emigrant Jews) was directed by Leon Lichtenstein, a lawyer and coeditor of *Izraelita* in the late 1900s. See Wodziński and Jagodzińska, "*Izraelita" 1866–1915*, 40.

7. "Warszawskie Biuro informacyjne dla emigrantów żydów," *Izraelita*, no. 28, July 12, 1912, 6–7.

8. Starczewski, "Z dziejów emigracji zarobkowej," 47–80. See also Gur Alroey, "Bureaucracy, Agents, and Swindlers: The Hardships of Jewish Emigration from the Pale of Settlement in the Early 20th Century," in *Jews and the State: Dangerous Alliances and the Perils of Privilege. Studies in Contemporary Jewry*, vol. 19, ed. Ezra Mendelsohn, 214–31 (New York: Oxford University Press, 2003).

9. Bargash Shakhbar, *Argentina. Leyent un veyst vohin ir fort* (Berdichev, 1892), 4–5.

10. Shakhbar, 6–8.

11. Shakhbar, 12–13. Gauchos, in Argentine context, were inhabitants of the rural Argentine interior, a South American counterpart of other horse-based cultures, such as cowboys. Gauchos were often of mixed European and Amerindian heritage and were imagined as holders of Argentine national spirit.

12. Shakhbar, 14.

13. Shakhbar, 23.

14. Compare with Peretz Hirschbein's and Hersh Dovid Nomberg's accounts on the Jewish colonies in Argentina in chapter 3.

15. Yaakev Yedvabnik, *Di beshraybung fon argentina un ire kolonyen* (Warsaw, 1893).

16. Yedvabnik, 39–41.

17. Yedvabnik, 54.

18. Yedvabnik, 39.

19. Arie Tartakower, *Dos yidishe emigratsye-problem un der yidisher velt-kongres* (Paris: Ekzekutiv-komitet forn yidishn velt-kongres, 1935), 3.

20. Tartakower, 8, 18. Tartakower claimed that the professional structure of the Jewish population did not reflect the needs of Poland, nor did it allow Jews to earn a living. For every one hundred Jews, only 32.5 percent were professionally active.

21. Letter from the Polish Embassy in Buenos Aires to the Ministry of Foreign Affairs in Warsaw, January 28, 1935, MSZ AAN B24051, 3–4.

22. Letter from the Polish Embassy in Buenos Aires to the Ministry of Foreign Affairs, January 28, 1935.

23. Letter from the Polish Embassy in Buenos Aires to the Ministry of Foreign Affairs in Warsaw, April 19, 1934, AAN B24051, 19. *Di Presse* was a left-wing Yiddish daily in Buenos Aires published since 1918.

24. For more information on *Haynt* and *Der Moment*, see Joanna Nalewajko-Kulikov, ed., *Studia z dziejów trójjęzycznej prasy żydowskiej na ziemiach polskich* (Warsaw: Neriton, 2012); Joanna Nalewajko-Kulikov, *Mówić we własnym języku: Prasa jidyszowa a tworzenie żydowskiej tożsamości narodowej (do 1918 roku)* (Warsaw: Neriton 2016).

25. Marian Fuks, "Dwudziestolecie międzywojenne: Od '5 rano' do popołudnia," *Rzeczpospolita*, October 27, 2008, http://www.rp.pl/artykul/210885.html (accessed July 26, 2013).

26. Avni, *Argentina y las migraciones*, 236.

27. Centro Mark Turkow, Buenos Aires, Archivo de Palabra, no. 366, Ester Rollansky, daughter of Samuel Rollansky.

28. "Vosere dokumentn muzn hobn di emigrantn kdey tsu bakumen di amerikaner, argentiner oder brazilianer vize?" *Der Moment*, September 17, 1924, no. 219, 4.

29. "Ver ken forn keyn argentine?" *Hayntige Nayes*, May 16, 1930, no. 113, 3.

30. "HIAS komunikat tsu der lage in argentine," *Der Moment*, January 13, 1924, no. 11, 6. HIAS stands for Hebrew Immigrant Aid Society.

31. "Tsu der lage in argentine," *Haynt*, January 13, 1924, no. 11, 3.

32. "Argentine zukht bekers," *Der Moment*, September 17, 1924, no. 219, 6.

33. "Ver ken forn keyn argentine?" *Hayntige Nayes*, May 16, 1930, no. 113, 3.

34. For a study of Polish gentile re-emigration from Latin America, see Tadeusz Paleczny, *Idea powrotu wśród emigrantów polskich w Brazylii i Argentynie* (Warsaw: Polska Akademia Nauk, Komitet Badania Polonii, 1992).

35. "Fort nit dervayl keyn argentine," *Der Moment*, November 3, 1924, no. 252, 3.

36. Despite ongoing industrial development and growth of exports, the unemployment level in Argentina was always around a 10 percent margin between 1914 and 1939. In some years, it was close to 20 percent (1915–17.7 percent, 1916–19.4 percent). In the early 1920s, Patagonia witnessed a bloody labor unrest (Patagonia Trágica) that followed Semana Trágica in Buenos Aires in 1919. In 1924, seventy-seven strikes took place in Buenos Aires, which involved around 277,000 strikers (an increase from 19,000 in 1923). See Diego Rubinzal, *Historía económica argentina (1880–2009). Desde los tiempos de Julio Argentino Roca hasta Cristina Fernández de Kirchner* (Buenos Aires: Centro Cultural de la Cooperación Floreal Gorini, 2010), 114–22.

37. "Emigranten tsurikgekumen," *Der Moment*, October 16, 1924, no. 239, 5.

38. "Tsu der lage in argentine," *Haynt*, January 13, 1924, no. 11, 3.

39. Hersh Dovid Nomberg, "Vohin yo forn?" *Der Moment*, July 26, 1926, no. 172, 3.

40. *Haynt*, June 21, 1923, no. 142, 1.

41. *Haynt*, February 22, 1923, no. 46, 1.

42. "K.H.L. do Argentyny, Brazylji, Urugwaju," Królewski Holenderski Lloyd, Warsaw 1928, DŻS XIIA 5, National Library of Poland.

43. *Der Moment*, February 17, 1924, no. 41, 1.

44. *Haynt*, January 4, 1923, no. 4, 1.

45. Donna Guy, *Sex and Danger in Buenos Aires: Prostitution, Family, and Nation in Argentina* (Lincoln: University of Nebraska Press, 1991), 6.

46. Guy, 5.

47. Nicole F. Bromfield, "Sex Slavery and Sex Trafficking of Women in the United States: Historical and Contemporary Parallels, Policies, and Perspectives in Social Work," *Afflia: Journal of Women and Social Work* vol. 31, 1 (2016): 129–39.

48. "Walka z handlem żywym towarem," *Nasz Przegląd*, May 16, 1923, 4.

49. "A tragedye fun a yidishe tokhter fun poyln in argentina," *Der Moment*, December, 31, 1924, no. 302, 6.

50. "A yidishe meydl in gefangenshaft bay froyen-handler," *Hayntige Nayes*, March 23, 1931, no. 70, 1.

51. "Avekgeroybt durkh froyenhandler yidishe meydl vert geratevet durkh a biznesmen," *Hayntige Nayes*, April 27, 1931, no. 96, 1.

52. "Farnart tsvey lodzer yidishe froyen in a shand hoyz in argentine," *Hayntige Nayes*, January 5, 1931, no. 4, 1.

53. Guy, *Sex and Danger*; Sandra McGee Deutsch, *Crossing Borders, Claiming a Nation: A History of Argentine Jewish Women, 1880–1955* (Durham, NC: Duke University Press, 2010).

54. Abe Lang, Izaak Lesz, Izaak Nożyk, *Oyfn veg keyn Buenos Aires* (Warsaw, 1931).

55. Albert Londres, *The Road to Buenos Aires* (London: Constable, 1928). The Yiddish translation *Oyf veg keyn Buenos-Aires: di soydes fun froyenhandel* by Joel Szwajger was published by A. Szklar in Warsaw.

56. "Arestirt 24 yidishe imigrantn in argentine," *Der Moment*, September 24, 1924, no. 225, 4

57. "Falshe argentiner peser keyn tsfon amerike," *Der Moment*, April 24, 1924, no. 98, 2.

58. "A get fun buenos aires," *Hayntige Nayes*, January 15, 1930, no.13, 1.

Chapter 3

1. "Peretz hirschbein komitet: Konferents in avallaneda," *Di Yidische Zaitung*, October 20, 1925, no. 3289, 1.

2. Peretz Hirschbein, "Doyrem (briv fun veg)," 1926, YIVO Institute, Peretz Hirschbein Papers, folder 123, 2.

3. Berta Singerman was born in 1901 in Russia and immigrated to Argentina at the age of four. In the following decades, she made a career as one of the most popular Argentine actresses and singers. See her biography: Berta Singerman, *Mis dos vidas* (Buenos Aires: Ed. Tres Tiempos, 1981).

4. Invitation, *Di Yidische Zaitung*, April 6, 1922, 1

5. A. Reziner, "Aynike momentn mit nombergn in buenos aires," *Di Presse*, November 21, 1928, 7.

6. Biographic data from Samuel Rollansky, ed., *Peretz Hirschbein, drames, veltrayzen, zikhroynes* (Buenos Aires: Yosef Lifshitz-fond fun der literatur gezelshaft baym IWO, 1967).

7. Peretz Hirschbein, "Unzer tseshpoltene tsung," *Literarishe Bleter*, no. 51 (July 27, 1927): 1002–3.

8. Peretz Hirschbein, "In neblen fun der fargangenhayt," 1, unpublished memoirs, YIVO Institute, Peretz Hirschbein Papers, folder 123.

9. Peretz Hirschbein, "Argentine (bletl zikhroynes)," 1; "Ikh kum on keyn buenos aires (a bletl zikhroynes)," 3, unpublished memoirs, both YIVO Institute, Peretz Hirscbein Papers, folder 123.

10. Israel Osman, "Peretz Hirschbein (biografye)," in *Peretz Hirschbein. Tsu zayn zekhtsiksten geboyrntog* (New York: Hirschbein yovl komitet, 1941), 20.

11. For instance, Peretz Hirschbein, "Fun mayne rayzes keyn argentina. Tsum vayten goles-land," *Der Moment*, no. 248, October 27, 1922, 5.

12. "Peretz hirschbein dertselt in moment vos er hot gezen un ibergelebt in erets yisroel," *Der Moment*, August 9, 1927, 1.

13. Peretz Hirschbein, "Argentine (briv fun veg)," 2. 1926, YIVO Institute, Peretz Hirschbein Papers, folder 123.

14. Hirschbein, 6.

15. Hirschbein, "In neblen fun der fargangenhayt," 1.

16. Hirschbein, "Doyrem," 1–2.

17. Hirschbein, "Doyrem," 3.

18. *Literarishe Bleter*, no. 15, April 8, 1932.

19. "Kronik," *Literarishe Bleter*, no. 31 (274), August 2, 1929, 612.

20. "Peretz Hirschbein arestirt un befrayt in varshe," *Forverts*, November 6, 1922, 2. Hirschbein was arrested for a short time under suspicion of being a spy, due to more than two hundred visas in his passport.

21. "Der kabalas-ponim far peretz hirschbein un froy," *Haynt*, June 28, 1922, 3.

22. "Di forlezungn fun peretz hirschbein in poyln," *Der Moment*, December 15, 1927, 5.

23. "Peretz hirschbein un froy schumiatcher gekumen keyn varshe," *Der Moment*, December 18, 1927, 6.

24. See Eli Lederhendler, *Jewish Responses to Modernity: New Voices in Modernity and Eastern Europe* (New York: New York University Press, 1997), 23–103; Israel Bartal, *The Jews of Eastern Europe, 1772–1881* (Philadelphia: University of Pennsylvania Press, 2006), 90–101.

25. Avrom Reyzen, *Yidishe filologye*, vol. 1 (Warsaw: Kultur-Lige, 1924), 97.

26. Angelika Glau, *Jüdisches Selbstverständnis im Wandel: Jiddische Literatur zu Beginn des zwanzigsten Jahrhunderts* (Wiesbaden, Germany: Harrassowitz Verlag, 1999), 133.

27. Quoted in Glau, *Jüdisches Selbstverständnis im Wandel*, 131.

28. See Keith Weiser and Joshua A. Fogel, eds., *Czernowitz at 100: The First Yiddish Language Conference in Historical Perspective* (Lanham, MD: Lexington Books, 2010).

29. Yehiel Scheintuch, "Veidat tshernovitz ve-tarbut yidish," *Huliot* 6 (2000): 259–60.

30. Scheintuch, 261.

31. Scheintuch, 258.

32. Nomberg's article from September 1908, quoted in Itsche Goldberg, "Di tshernovitzer shprakh konferents 80 yor shpeter," *Yidishe kultur. Hodesh-zhurnal fun yidishn kultur farband*, 1988, 17.

33. Scheintuch, "Veidat tshernovitz," 277.

34. "Grindungs-farzamlung fun a yidisher folks-partay," *Der Moment*, March 17, 1917, 2. Its cofounders also included Hillel Zeitlin and Noyekh Prilutsky.

35. Hersh Dovid Nomberg, "Natsyonalism," in *Dos bukh felyetonen* (Warsaw: Sz. Jaczkowski, 1924), 310–14.

36. Hersh Dovid Nomberg, *Eretz yisroel* (Warsaw: Wydawnictwo Yacobson i Goldberg, 1925).

37. Hersh Dovid Nomberg, "Brif fun veg. A kleyn bisl vint," *Der Moment*, May 19,

1922, no. 115, 3, "Fun mayn rayze keyn argentine. Mayses fun patagonye," *Der Moment*, March 30, 1923, no. 77, 5.

38. "Nomberg fort keyn argentine," *Forverts*, March 12, 1922, 1.

39. Hersh Dovid Nomberg, "Yidn, eyrope," *Di Yidische Zaitung*, April 5, 1922, page unknown.

40. Samuel Rollansky, *Dos yidishe gedrukte vort un teater in argentine* (Buenos Aires, 1941), 53.

41. Nomberg, *Dos bukh felyetonen*.

42. M. N. Shpirnberg, "Unzer gast peretz hirschbein," *Penimer un penimlekh*, July 3, 1925, 1.

43. Shpirnberg.

44. Yid. "equal with the people."

45. "Unzer gast peretz hirschbein," *Di Presse*, July, 3, 1925, unknown page.

46. "Peretz Hirschbein," *Mundo Israelita*, June 27, 1925, 1.

47. "Fun rosarier yidisher gezelshaft," *Penimer un penimlekh*, undated newspaper clipping, Fundación IWO, Buenos Aires, Peretz Hirschbein clippings collection.

48. Mollie Lewis Nouwen, *Oy My Buenos Aires! Jewish Immigrants and the Creation of Argentine National Identity* (Albuquerque: University of New Mexico Press, 2013), 91.

49. "Fun rosarier yidisher gezelshaft."

50. "Peretz Hirschbein in Santa Fe," *Di Tribune*, 1925, undated clipping, Fundación IWO, Buenos Aires, Peretz Hirschbein clippings collection.

51. Poster, Shmuel Niger Papers, YIVO Institute for Jewish Research, New York, folder 2162.

52. "Groyse tsugreytungen tsu peretz hirschbein bezukh in rosario," *Di Yidische Zaitung*, undated clipping, Fundación IWO, Buenos Aires, Peretz Hirschbein clippings collection.

53. "Peretz Hirschbein," *Mundo Israelita*, July 11, 1925, page unknown.

54. Pinie Katz, "Der sotsyaler beshtand fun di poylishe yidn in Argentine," *Almanakh 1928. Aroysgegeben fun poylish yidishn farband in argentine*, ed. Moíses David Guiser (Buenos Aires: Poylish Yidisher Farband in Argentine, 1928), 57.

55. Children's drawing and compositions—from the Worker's School Ber Borokhov in Buenos Aires, 1925, YIVO Institute for Jewish Research, New York, Peretz Hirschbein Papers, folder 307.

56. "Di forlezungn fun peretz hirschbein in poyln," *Der Moment*, December 15, 1927, 5.

57. "Dray yor yidisher visenshaftlekher insititut," in *Yedies fun yidishn visenshaftlekhen institut*, no. 26, September 14, 1928. Published in *Literarishe Bleter*, no. 37, September 14, 1928, 728.

58. Aharon Zeitlin, "Peretz Hirschbein," in *Peretz Hirschbein. Tsu zayn zekhtsiksten geboyrntog*. (New York: Hirschbein yovl komitet, 1941), 28.

59. Moss, *Jewish Renaissance*, 105.

60. Peretz Hirschbein, "Doyrem," 3.

61. Hirschbein, "In neblen fun der fargangenhayt," 2–3.

62. Nomberg, Di argentinishe rayze, 70–71.

63. Hirschbein, "Doyrem," 4.

64. Rollansky, *Dos yidishe gedrukte*, 53–54.

65. Tamar Lewinsky, "Eastern Europe in Argentina: Yiddish Travelogues and Ex-

ploration of Jewish Diaspora," in *Writing Jewish Culture: Paradoxes in Ethnography*, ed. Andreas Kilcher and Gabriella Safran, 257 (Bloomington: Indiana University Press, 2016).

66. Hirschbein, *Fun vayte lender*, 13. Translation from Lewinsky, "Eastern Europe in Argentina," 252.

67. I refer here to Yiddishist ethnonational vision, a Jewish national concept that was not equivalent to but competed with Zionism.

68. Lazaro (also Pinkhas Elozer) Zhitnitsky was a left-wing Yiddishist activist and journalist. Zhitnitsky was born in 1894 in Ukraine, served in the tsarist army, studied law in Vienna, Berlin, and Königsberg and immigrated to Argentina in 1928. He worked for the daily *Di Presse*. In the 1930s, he headed the educational *Tsentrale veltlekhe yidish shul organizatsye in argentine* and chaired the Argentine branch of the IWO Institute.

69. Lazaro Zhitnitsky, "Funm zaydens kval," *Literarishe Bleter*, no. 25, June 22, 1928, 484, 489.

70. Zhitnitsky, "Funm zaydens kval."

71. Ana Weinstein and Eliahu Toker, *La letra ídish en tierra argentina: Bio-bibliografía de sus autores literarios* (Buenos Aires: Editorial Milá, 2004), xxx.

72. Yosef (José) Mendelson, *Oyf di bregen fun plata: Zamelbukh* (Buenos Aires: Farlag Ydische Zaitung, 1919), 23.

73. Hersh Dovid Nomberg, "Literarishe pruvn in argentine," *Der Moment*, November 7, 1924, no. 256, 4.

74. "Der funandervuks fun der yidisher literatur in argentine," *Haynt*, no. 38, February 13, 1931, 7.

75. Nathan Cohen, "Literarishe Bleter," YIVO Encyclopedia of Jews in Eastern Europe.

76. Yankev Botoshansky wrote a travel text from the Tierra del Fuego; Yankev Botoshansky, "Fayerland," *Literarishe Bleter*, no. 16, April 21, 1933, 262, 264.

77. Melech Ravitch, "Berl Grinberg—a nayer, ekhter prozaiker fun argentine," *Literarishe Bleter*, December 9, 1938, no. 44, 726–27.

78. Berl Grinberg, "30 zaydene tikhlekh," *Literarishe Bleter*, no. 25, July 22, 1934, 397–98, and no. 26, July 29, 1934, 415–16.

79. According to data of the AJC, 3,602,000 Jews lived in the United States and 2,845,000 in Poland in 1927, *American Jewish Committee Yearbook*, vol. 29, 1927–28, 231.

80. "Kronik," *Literarishe Bleter*, no. 26, June 29, 1929, 512.

81. TSYSHO was a network of Yiddishist schools in Poland, corun by the Bund and Poaley Tsiyon.

82. *Literarishe Bleter*, February 3, 1933, no. 6.

83. Y. B. (probably Yankev Botoshansky), "Yidishe bukh produktsye in argentine," *Literarishe Bleter*, April 1, 1933, no. 14, 221–23.

84. "Di yidishe literatur un prese in argentine (a shmues mit pinye katz)," *Literarishe Bleter*, no. 43, October 25, 1929, 286.

85. Yankev Botoshansky was born in 1895 in Bessarabia (now Moldova) and immigrated to Buenos Aires in 1926. He was a journalist of the local daily *Di Presse* and was engaged in progressive cultural Yiddishism throughout his life. In the 1930s, he was a secretary of the *Gezelshaft far yidishe veltlekhe shuln in argentine*.

86. Yankev Botoshansky, "A yubiley fun drey," *Literarishe Bleter*, March 23, 1928, 247–48.

87. "Buenos-aireser zhurnalist yaakov botoshansky in varshe," *Unzer Express*, no. 192, August 13, 1935, 10. Botoshansky's wife, Miriam Lerer, a star of the Argentine-Yiddish theater, traveled with him.

88. Aaron Mark, "Portretn fun yidishe shrayber," *Literarishe Bleter*, no. 34, August 25, 1933, 548–49.

89. The talk on May 13, 1931, titled "Di vershidene teritories fun yidisher literatur un kultur," was attended by the stars of the Warsaw Yiddish scene: Alter Kacyzne, Aharon Zeitlin, "Haynt gezegunsovent far yankev botoshansky," *Haynt*, no. 210, May 13, 1931, 5.

90. "A lebediger grus fun yudish lebn un yudisher kultur in argentina. Vos derzelt der bekanter yudisher shriftsteler fun argentina, yankev botoshansky," *Grodner Moment Express*, no. 62, May 13, 1931, 7.

91. "Zerubavel vegn dem yidishn kultur-lebn in argentine," *Literarishe Bleter*, September 30, 1927, 767.

92. Invitation for Zerubavel's lecture, Łuków, 1927, DŻS IK 2f, National Library of Poland.

93. Nakhman Mayzel, "Oyfs gots barot," *Literarishe Bleter*, no. 4, January 22, 1932, 55.

94. For more information on Zygmunt Turkow, see Mirosława M. Bułat, "Cosmopolitan or Purely Jewish? Zygmunt Turkow and the Warsaw Yiddish Art Theater," in *Inventing the Modern Yiddish Stage: Essays in Drama, Performance, and Show Business*, ed. Joel Berkowitz and Barbara Henry, 116–35 (Detroit, MI: Wayne University Press, 2012), and Turkow's autobiography, *Di ibergerisene tkufe: Fragmentn fun mayn lebn* (Buenos Aires: Tsentral farband fun poylishe yidn in argentine, 1961).

95. *Literarishe Bleter*, December 14, 1934, no. 50, 836.

96. Nakhmen Mayzel, "Fun vokh tsu vokh," *Literarishe Bleter*, October 11, 1929, no. 41, 812. Zasławski was born in Uman, Ukraine, and, before associating with Kamińska and moving to Poland, he played in numerous Russian and Yiddish theaters in Russia.

97. Zasławski lived in Argentina from 1916 until 1926, at which point he went to New York. In 1928, he returned to Poland but left it for another tour in Romania, France, and Brazil. Shortly before his death on February 19, 1937, he returned to Buenos Aires.

98. Nakhmen Mayzel, "Fun vokh tsu vokh," *Literarishe Bleter*, June 9, 1933, no. 23, 378; the same column on July 7, 1933, no. 27, 442, and July 14, 1933, no. 28, 458.

99. H. Gold, "In argentiner yidishn kultur-lebn," *Literarishe Bleter*, no. 8, February 19, 1932, 117–18.

100. Gold, "In argentiner yidishn kultur-lebn," 117–18.

101. Yosef Mendelson, "Dos yidishe dertsiyungs-vezn in argentine," *Literarishe Bleter*, no. 20, May 19, 1933, 320, 322.

102. The PEN Club is an international organization of writers. It was established in 1921 and regards literature as a tool of international cooperation. A broad discussion of the 1936 Buenos Aires debates can be found in Celina Manzoni, "Vacilaciones de un rol: los intelectuales en 1936," in *Rupturas,* vol. 7 of *Historia crítica de la literatura argentina*, ed. Celina Manzoni, 541–69 (Buenos Aires: Emecé, 2009).

103. Yankev Botoshansky, "H. leivik in argentine," *Literarishe Bleter*, no. 41, October 9, 1936, 645–47.

104. B. Walter, "Shaul tchernichovsky un h. leivick oyfn internatsyonaler PEN-kongres in buenos aires," *Haynt*, no. 218, September 21, 1936, 4.

105. Yosef Horn, *Arum yidisher literatur un yidishe shrayber: ophandlungen un fartsaykhenungen shrayber* (Buenos Aires: Altveltlekher yidisher kultur-kongres, argentiner aptayl, 1973), 78.

106. Yankev Botoshansky, "Der 14-ter pen-kongres in buenos aires," *Literarishe Bleter*, no. 42, October 16, 1936, 662–69.

107. Botoshansky, "Der 14-ter pen-kongres."

108. Edward Said, *Representations of the Intellectual: The 1993 Reith Lectures* (New York: Pantheon Books, 1994).

Chapter 4

1. Arjun Appadurai, *Nowoczesność bez granic. Kulturowe wymiary globalizacji* (Kraków: Universitas, 2005), 235–36.

2. Nomberg, "Di argentinishe rayze," in *Dos bukh felyetonen*; Hirschbein, *Fun vayte lender*. In 1922, Hirschbein's book was also serialized in *Der Moment* in Warsaw.

3. Yedvabnik, *Di beshraybung fon argentina*, 25–27. Yedvabnik referred here to the so-called Conquest of the Desert that until 1880 erased or subdued the indigenous population of Patagonia. See Andrés Bonatti, *Una guerra infame: La verdadera historia de la Conquista del Desierto* (Buenos Aires: Edhasa, 2015).

4. Nomberg, "Di argentinishe rayze," 45.

5. Nomberg, 89–95.

6. Nomberg, 90–91.

7. Nomberg, 78. Alberto Gerchunoff also referred to presumably violent and impulsive criollos. See Alberto Gerchunoff, *Los gauchos judíos* (Buenos Aires: Aguilar, 1975), 79–82. Porteños inhabit the capital city of Buenos Aires and often claim their belonging to a different (more cosmopolitan) cultural tradition than the rest of Argentina.

8. Oscar Chamosa, "People as a Landscape: The Representation of the *Criollo* Interior in Early Tourist Literature in Argentina," in *Rethinking Race in Modern Argentina*, ed. Paulina Alberto and Eduardo Elena, 53–72 (Cambridge: Cambridge University Press, 2016).

9. Rosana Gruber, "La construcción de la identidad étnica. Integración y diferenciación de los inmigrantes judíos ashkenazim en la Argentina," in *Ensayos de Antropologia Argentina* (Buenos Aires: Editorial Belgrano, 1984), 197–211.

10. May E. Bletz, *Immigration and Acculturation in Brazil and Argentina, 1890–1929* (New York: Palgrave Macmillan, 2010), 4.

11. Hirschbein, *Fun vayte lender*, 15.

12. Nomberg, "Di argentinishe rayze," 18–19.

13. Nomberg, 55–59.

14. Hirschbein, "Doyrem," 2.

15. Nomberg, "Di argentinishe rayze," 74.

16. Nomberg, 76

17. A. Reziner, "Aynike momentn mit nombergn in buenos aires," *Di Presse*, November 21, 1928, 7; "Tsu nombergs aktuatsye in argentine far der fertaydigung fun der yidishe kolonizatsye," *Di Presse*. November 21, 1928, 7.

18. Peretz Hirschbein, "Unzere kolonisten in argentine," unpublished text, 1925, Peretz Hirschbein Papers, folder 123, YIVO Archive in New York, 2–3.

19. Hirschbein, *Fun vayte lender*, 61–66.

20. Hirschbein, 71.

21. Hirschbein, 71–76.

22. For a study of the conflict between JCA and the colonists, see Iván Cherjovsky, "La faz ideológica del conflicto colonos/JCA: el discurso del ideal agrario en las memorias de Colonia Mauricio," in *Marginados y consagrados: nuevos estudios sobre la vida judía en la argentina*, ed. Emmanuel Kahan, Laura Schenquer, Damian Setton, and Alejandro Dujovne, 47–66 (Buenos Aires: Lumiere, 2011).

23. Nomberg, "Di argentinishe rayze," 81.

24. Hirschbein, *Fun vayte lender*, 70.

25. Nomberg, Di argentinishe rayze, 66–71.

26. Nomberg, 73.

27. Nomberg, 35.

28. See Simon G. Hanson, *Argentine Meat and the British Market: Chapters in the History of the Argentine Meat Industry* (Stanford, CA: Stanford University Press, 1983).

29. Hirschbein, *Fun vayte lender*, 62–71.

30. Peretz Hirschbein, "Ich kum on keyn buenos aires," unpublished memoirs, Peretz Hirschbein Papers, RG 833, YIVO Archive New York.

31. Nomberg, "Di argentinishe rayze," 42.

32. Hirschbein, *Fun vayte lender*, 132–34.

33. Centro Mark Turkow, Archivo de Palabra, no. 68, Maximo Yagupsky.

34. Lea Literat-Golombek, *Moíses Ville crónica de un shtetl argentino* (Jerusalem: La Semana Publicaciones, 1982), 89–91.

35. Nomberg, "Argentinishe rayze," 87.

36. Peretz Hirschbein, "Argentine (briv fun veg)," 1–2.

37. Nomberg, "Di argentinishe rayze," 23

38. For a study of the educational system in Jewish agricultural colonies, see Daniel Bargman, "Construcción de la Nación entre la asimilación de los inmigrantes y el particularismo. Las escuelas de las colonias agrícolas judías," in *Patrimonio Cultural y Diversidad Creativa en el Sistema Educativo*, ed. Leticia Maronese, 19–36 (Buenos Aires: Gobierno de la Ciudad Buenos Aires, 2006); Efraim Zadoff, "La educación general y judía en las colonias agrícolas judías en La Argentina y Eretz Israel a fines del siglo XIX," *Coloquio* 19 (1988): 95–108.

39. Hirschbein, *Fun vayte lender*, 96.

40. Moroccan Jews were often employed by the Argentine government as Jewish teachers. See Brodsky, *Sephardi, Jewish, Argentine*, 17.

41. Peretz Hirschbein, "Doyrem (briv fun veg)," 1.

42. For the sociocultural meaning of gaming, horse races, and lotteries in Buenos Aires, see Ana Cecchi, *La timba como rito de pasaje. La narrativa del juego en la construción de la modernidad porteña (Buenos Aires 1900–1935)* (Buenos Aires: Ediciones Biblioteca Nacional Teseo, 2012).

43. Hirschbein, *Fun vayte lender*, 43–45.

44. Centro Mark Turkow, Archivo de Palabra, no. 55, Lazaro Pinchuk.

45. Nomberg, "Di argentinishe rayze," 64–65.

46. Hirschbein, *Fun vayte lender*, 51; Hirschbein, "Argentine (briv fun veg)," 3–4.

47. Hirschbein, *Fun vayte lender*, 50.

48. Hirschbein, 54–56.

49. Sandra McGee Deutsch noted that women often took various paid domestic jobs, including as seamstresses or cooks. Some women joined their husbands in family-

run businesses. Technology was assigned to men, whereas women focused on painstaking and onerous manual labor. In the 1930s, the situation began to change and female employment outside the home became much more common. See Deutsch, *Crossing Borders, Claiming a Nation*, 49–52.

50. Martin Grinstein, *Recuerdos de Entre Rios. Colonia San Antonio y Pueblo Cazés* (Buenos Aires: Acervo Culural Editores, 1998), 60.

51. See Scott Ury, *Barricades and Banners: The Revolution of 1905 and the Transformation of Warsaw Jewry* (Redwood City, CA: Stanford University Press, 2012), 141–72.

52. Nomberg, "Di argentinishe rayze," 64–65.

53. Peretz Hirschbein, "Argentine (briv fun veg)," unpublished, 1926, YIVO Archive, Peretz Hirschbein Papers, Folder 126, 4–5.

54. Centro Mark Turkow, Archivo de Palabra, no. 207, Raquel Minces.

55. Centro Mark Turkow, Archivo de Palabra, no. 207, Raquel Minces.

56. Peretz Hirschbein, "Argentine (briv fun veg)," 1.

57. Nomberg, "Di argentinishe rayze," 7–67.

58. Anne Godlewska and Neil Smith, eds., *Geography and Empire* (Oxford: Blackwell, 1994); Walter Mignolo, "Putting the Americas on the Map (Geography and Colonization of Space)," *Colonial Latin American Review* 1 (1992): 25–63.

59. Mary Louise Pratt, *Imperial Eyes: Travel Writing and Transculturation* (Abingdon, UK: Routledge, 1992), 5.

60. Isabella Bird (1831–1904) was a British explorer and travel writer. She traveled widely, including tours of China, Central Asia, and Australia; Jelena Dimitrijević (1862–1945) was a Serbian feminist and traveler. Her writings include travel books from North America, Egypt, and India.

61. Consider, for example, the Vladimir Rusanov expedition of 1912 to Svalbard, Siberia.

62. See Stephen Clark, *Travel Writing and Empire: Postcolonial Theory in Transit* (London: Zed Press, 1999).

63. Kristine L. Jones argued that Argentina became a popular destination for travel writers only in the 1820s, a decade after the country's declaration of independence in 1810. During the period of mass emigration in the second half of the nineteenth and early twentieth centuries, Argentina became "too popular" and stopped being considered an important place for travel writers. Kristine L. Jones, "Nineteenth Century British Travel Accounts on Argentina," *Ethnohistory* 33, no. 2 (Spring 1986): 95–211.

64. Zahra, *The Great Departure*, 73.

65. Bernard Mark, "A bukh vegn yidishe kolonizatsye problemen. Mark Turkow, *Oyf yidishe felder (a nesiye iber di yidishe kolonies in argentine)*," *Literarishe Bleter* 43, no. 754, November 11, 1938, 716–17.

66. Melech Ravitch, "Fun di masoes binyomin hashlishi biz di masoes peretz hirschbein," in *Peretz Hirschbein. Tsu zayn zekhtsiksten geboyrntog*, 106.

67. Sara Mills, *Discourses on Difference: An Analysis of Women's Travel Writing and Colonialism* (London: Routledge, 2003), 61–62.

68. Yet, in relation to the indigenous population, they were considered white.

69. Karen Brodkin, *How Jews Became White Folks and What That Says about Race in America* (New Brunswick, NJ: Rutgers University Press, 1998); Melanie Kaye/Kantorowitz, *The Colors of Jews: Racial Politics and Radical Diasporism* (Bloomington: Indiana University Press, 2007).

70. Hirschbein, *Fun vayte lender*, 13–14, 38.

71. Ella Shohat and Robert Stam, *Unthinking Eurocentrism: Multiculturalism and the Media* (London: Routledge, 1994), 1–7.

72. Mónica Szurmuk, *Women in Argentina: Early travel narratives* (Gainesville: University Press of Florida, 2000), 8.

73. Lewinsky, "Eastern Europe in Argentina," 253.

74. Carolyn Ellis, Tony Adams, and Arthur Bochner, "Autoethnography: An Overview," *Forum Qualitative Sozialforschung/Forum: Qualitative Social Research* 12 (November 24, 2010), http://www.qualitative-research.net/index.php/fqs/article/view/1589/3095.

75. Tartakower, *Emigracja żydowska z Polski*, 45.

76. Zieliński, "Emigracja żydowska," 19.

77. John Klier, "Pale of Settlement," YIVO Encyclopedia of Jews in Eastern Europe. See Benjamin Nathans, *Beyond the Pale: The Jewish Encounter with Late Imperial Russia* (Berkeley: University of California Press, 2002).

78. Using James Clifford's typology, Garrett examined Jewish travels by applying a set of criteria of "good travel." Good travel had to be "heroic, educational, scientific, adventurous and ennobling." Leah V. Garrett, *Journeys Beyond the Pale: Yiddish Travel Writing in the Modern World* (Madison: Wisconsin University Press, 2003), 16–18.

79. Samuel Kassow, "Travel and Local History as a National Mission: Polish Jews and the *Landkentenish* Movement in the 1920s and 1930s," in *Jewish Topographies: Visions of Space, Traditions of Place*, ed. Alexandra Nocke, Julia Brauch, and Anna Lipphardt, 241–65 (Aldershot: Ashgate, 2008).

80. Hersh Dovid Nomberg, *Erets-yisroel: Ayndrikn un bilder* (Warsaw: T. Yacobson-M. Goldberg, 1925); *Mayne rayze iber rusland* (Warsaw: Kultur-Lige, 1928).

81. Elimelech Neufeld, *A rayze keyn erets-yisroel* (Warsaw: Grafia, 1935); Boruch Glazman, *Step un yishev: Bilder fun a rayze iber di yidishe kolonyes fun soviet-rusland un ukraine* (Warsaw: Kultur-Lige, 1928); Shemarya Gorelik, *In vander-lebn: Rayzebilder un felyetonen* (Warsaw: Gitlin, 1918); Schulim Gottlieb, *Tsvishn sinay un zanzibar: Togbukh fun a rayze iber mizreh-afrike (mit ilustratsyes un mapes)* (Warsaw: Grafia, 1937); Bentsiyon Hoffman, *Mayne rayze in erets-yisroel* (Warsaw: Di Velt, 1923).

82. Poster, DŻS XVIIC 1c, Polona Library, National Library of Poland.

83. Poster, DŻS IK 2f, Polona Library, National Library of Poland.

84. Poster, DŻS IK 2f, Library, National Library of Poland.

85. For instance *Di Velt: Ilustrirt wokhnblat far unterhaltung, rayze un turistik* (Warsaw,1939).

86. Nakhmen Mayzel, "Peretz hirschbein erets yisroel," *Literarishe Bleter*, no. 34, August 25, 1929, 658–59.

87. "Peretz hirschbein kumt keyn varshe," *Haynt*, December 8, 1927, 6.

88. "Kronik," *Literarishe Bleter*, no. 4, January 27, 1928, 83.

89. "Di forlezungn fun peretz hirschbein in poyln," *Moment*, December 15, 1927, 5.

90. Peretz Hirschbein, "Fir hundert milion (briv fun khina)," *Literarishe Bleter*, November 12, 1926, 752; "A yapanisher revolutsyoner," June 11, 1926, 379–81; "Di geysha," October 8, 1926, 667–68.

91. "Peretz Hirschbein dertselt in moment vos er hot gezen un ibergelebt in erets yisroel," *Moment*, 9.8.1927, 1; Peretz Hirschbein "Bet lekhem," *Moment*, January 20, 1928, 6.

92. Peretz Hirschbein, "Di yidishe ibervanderung tsu erd-arbeyt in soviet rusland," *Haynt*, July 30, 1929, 6.

93. Jacob Lestchinsky estimated that between 1920 and 1937 around 1.4 million

non-gentiles and 395,000 Jews emigrated from Poland. Jacob Lestchinsky, *National Groups in Polish Emigration* (New York: Conference on Jewish Relations, 1943), 109.

94. See Fularski, *Argentyna, Paragwaj, Boliwja: Wrażenia z podróży* (Warsaw: Wydawnictwo M. Arcta, 1929). Two years earlier, Fularski published a book entirely devoted to Polish agricultural colonies in Argentina: *Polskie kolonje rolnicze w Argentynie* (Warszawa: Wydawnictwo Polskiego Towarzystwo Emigracyjnego, 1927).

95. See, for example, Tadeusz Chrostowski, *Parana. Wspomnienia z podróży w roku 1914* (Poznań: Księgarnia św. Wojciecha, 1922); Mieczysław Lepecki, *Argentyna* (Warsaw: Międzynarodowe Towarzystwo Osadnicze, 1936); or a much earlier account by Józef Siemiradzki, *Szlakiem wychodźców* (Warsaw: A. T. Jezierski, 1900).

Chapter 5

1. Rollansky, *Dos yidishe gedrukte*, 136.

2. Alejandro Dujovne, *Una historía del libro judío. La cultura judía argentina a través de sus editores, libreros, traductores, imprentas y bibliotecas* (Buenos Aires: Siglo Veintiuno Editores, 2014), 80–81.

3. "Somos distinos," *Mundo Israelita*, June 22, 1923, 3.

4. Eduardo D. Faingold, "Educational Attitudes and Language Choice at the Birth of a Progressive Yiddish-Language Folks Shule in Argentina," *International Journal of Jewish Education Research* 7 (2014): 55–76.

5. "Żydzi w Ameryce," *Izraelita*, no. 12, March 22, 1912, 5.

6. As a private communal endeavor, Jewish education in the colonies, and later in Buenos Aires, was a subject of a heated debate between the JCA, colonists, intellectuals, and Jewish institutions such as Hevra Kadisha. Similar to the situation in Poland, until the 1930s, parents were required to pay tuition, while the schools received very little support. Since the passage of Ley de Educacción Común in 1884, Argentina offered free access to state schools. See Celia Gladys Lopez, *El sistema de educación no formal implantado por las cooperativas agrarias en las colonias judías entrerrianas* (Concepción del Uruguay: Instituto de Investigación Ibarra Grasso, 1993),

7. Yankev Shimon Liachovitzky, "Brif fun argentine. Unzere kinder-ertsiyung," *Der Yud*, no. 5, January 31, 1901, 7–9.

8. Frank Wolff, "The Home That Never Was: Rethinking Space and Memory in Late Nineteenth and Early Twentieth Century," *Historical Social Research* 38, no. 3 (2013): 198.

9. Efraim Zadoff, *Historia de la educacción judía en Buenos Aires 1935–1957* (Buenos Aires: Editorial Milá, 1994), 34–37.

10. Rollansky, *Dos yidishe gedrukte*, 214.

11. Rollansky, 216–17.

12. "Z. Turkow un der yid. teater in buenos aires," *Literarishe Bleter*, no. 50, December 14, 1935, 836. For a short overview text on Argentine Yiddish theater, see Susanna Skura, Leonor Slavsky, "El treatro ídish como patrimonio cultural judío argentino," in *Encuentro: Recreando la cultura judeoargentina 2*, ed. Ricardo Feierstein and Stephen A. Sadow, 41–50 (Buenos Aires: Editorial Mila, 2004). For a longer study see: Nora Glickman and Glora F. Waldman, *Argentine Jewish Theater: A Critical Anthology* (Lewisbug, PA: Bucknell University Press, 1996).

13. Raanan Rein, *Argentine Jews or Jewish Argentines? Essays on Ethnicity, Identity and Diaspora* (Leiden, Netherlands: Brill, 2010).

14. Pinie Katz defined the *yidishkayt* of Argentine Jews as the feeling that they were part of the Jewish nation and their *argentinishkayt* was love for their Argentine home. See Pinie Katz, "Argentiner yidn (esey)," in Katz et al., *Antologye fun der yidisher literatur in argentine*, 395–99.

15. Alan Astro, "Persistencía del ídish en Argentina: Reflexiones comparativas con Estados Unidos y Canadá," unpublished work in progress, available at the website of IDES, http://ides.org.ar/archivos/7675 (accessed March 10, 2016).

16. Katz, "Der sotsyaler bashtand," 55.

17. Mark, "A bukh vegn yidishe kolonizatsye problemen," 716–17.

18. Lewinsky, "Eastern Europe in Argentina," 262.

19. "A lebediger grus fun yudish lebn un yudisher kultur in argentina. Vos dertselt der bekanter yudisher shriftshteler fun argentina, yankev botoshansky," *Grodner Moment Express*, no. 62, March 13, 1931, 7.

20. David Ajzensztat, "Ver vet farzetsen unzer arbet?," in *Poylishe yidn in doyrem amerike*, 155.

21. "Di yidishe yugent un di yidishe kultur," *Dos Naye Vort*, no. 140, October 1932, 17.

22. Shatzky, *Comunidades judías*, 51.

23. For a study of the emergence of the Argentine middle class, see Ezequiel Adamovsky, *Historia de la clase media argentina: Apogeo y decadencía de una ilusión, 1919–2003* (Buenos Aires: Planete, 2009).

24. Leonardo Senkman, "Ser judío en Argentina: Las transofrmaciones de la identidad nacional," in *Identidades judías, modernidad y globalización*, ed. Paul Mendes-Flohr, Yom Tov Assis, and Leonardo Senkman (Jerusalem: Hebrew University of Jerusalem and Ediciones Lilmod, 2007), 403–54.

25. Isaias Lerner, "A Half Century Ago: The Jewish Experience in Argentina," in *Identity in Dispersion: Selected Memoirs from Latin American Jews*, ed. Leon Klenicki, 60–61 (Cincinnati: Jacob Rader Marcus Center of American Jewish Archives, 2000).

26. Lerner, 60–65.

27. See Juan Carlos Tedesco, *Educación y sociedad en la Argentina (1880–1945)* (Buenos Aires: Solar 1993); Lilia Ana Bertoni, "Nacionalidad o cosmopolitismo. La cuestión de las escuelas de las colectividades extranjeras a fines del siglo XIX," *Anuario del IEHS* 11 (1996): 179–99.

28. Luis E. García Fanlo, *Genealogía de la argentinidad* (Buenos Aires: Gran Aldea Editores, 2010), 113–40.

29. García Fanlo.

30. For details of Alberdi's views, see Juan Bautista Alberdi, *Bases y puntos de partida para la organización política de la República de Argentina* (Buenos Aires, 1853).

31. Domingo Faustino Sarmiento, *Civilización i barbarie. Vida de Juan Facundo Quiroga*. First published in 1845. This reference is taken from an edition by Editorial Huemul: *Facundo*, Introducción, 57–64 (Buenos Aires, 1978). For a broader discussion on Sermiento's vision of Argentina and immigration, see Joséph T. Criscenti, ed., *Sarmiento and His Argentina* (Boulder: Lynne Rienner Publishers, 1993).

32. Jean H. Delaney, "Imagining 'El Ser Argentino': Cultural Nationalism and Romantic Concepts of Nationhood in Early Twentieth-Century Argentina," *Journal of Latin American Studies*, 34, no. 3 (2002): 626–28; Earl T. Glauert, "Ricardo Rojas and the Emergence of Argentine Cultural Nationalism," *Hispanic American Historical Review* 43, no. 1 (1963): 1–13.

33. María Fernanda Astiz, "Jewish Acculturation: Identity, Society and Schooling Buenos Aires, Argentina (1890–1930), *Journal of Jewish Identities* 3, no. 1 (2010): 45.

34. García Fanlo, *Genealogía de la argentiniadad*, 91–112.

35. See Adolfo Prieto, *El discurso criollista en la formación de la Argentina moderna* (Buenos Aires: Siglo Veintinuno, 2006).

36. *Medio siglo en el surco argentino. Cincuentenario de la Jewish Colonization Association (J.C.A). Homenaje de la Delegación de Asociaciones Israelitas Argentinas (D.A.I.A) a la Jewish Colonization Association (J.C.A.) con motivo de su cincuentenario. 1891 agosto 1941* (Buenos Aires: D.A.I.A, 1942), 22–23.

37. José C. Moya, "The Jewish Experience in Argentina in a Diasporic Comparative Perspective," in *The New Jewish Argentina: Facets of Jewish Experiences in the Southern Cone*, ed. Adriana M. Brodsky and Raanan Rein (Leiden, Netherlands: Brill, 2013), 109.

38. Paulina L. Alberto and Eduardo Elena, "Introduction: The Shades of the Nation," in *Rethinking Race in Modern Argentina*, ed. Paulina L. Alberto and Eduardo Elena (New York: Cambridge University Press, 2016).

39. Józef Włodek, *Argentyna i emigracja. Ze szczególnym uwzględnieniem emigracji polskiej* (Warsaw: Wydawnictwo M. Arcta, 1923), 275–76.

40. Julio Mafud, "El desarraigo del inmigrante. La influencía migratoria en el carácter nacional," in *Inmigración y nacionalidad*, ed. Dardo Cúneo, Julio Mafud, Amalia Sánchez Sivori, and Lazaro Schallman, 74 (Buenos Aires: Editorial Paidós, 1967).

41. Fanlo, *Genealogía de la argentiniadad*, 17–22.

42. Carlos Ibarguren, "La suerte del pueblo hebreo," *Vida Nuestra*, no. 1, July 1917, 1. Later in life, Ibarguren became a fierce critic of the radical government of Hipólito Yrigoyen and turned to nationalism and fascism.

43. Carlos Ibarguren, "A los judíos en la Argentina," *Vida Nuestra*, no. 3, September 1918, Buenos Aires, 34.

44. May E. Bletz, *Immigration and Acculturation in Brazil and Argentina: 1890–1929* (New York: Palgrave Macmillan, 2010), 101.

45. Bletz, 101–14.

46. Ezequiel Gomez Caride, "'Catholic Secularism' and the Jewish Gaucho School: Salvation Themes of the 19th Century Argentinean Citizen," in *The "Reason" of Schooling: Historicizing Curriculum Studies, Pedagogy and Teacher Education*, ed. Thomas S. Popkiewitz (New York: Routledge, 2015), 130.

47. Astiz, "Jewish Acculturation," 52.

48. Shatzky, *Comunidades judías*, 43–46.

49. Monitor de la Educación Común 1908 (Buenos Aires: Consejo Nacional de la Educación, 1908), 602.

50. Włodek, *Argentyna i emigracja*, 312.

51. Włodek.

52. García Fanlo, *Genealogía de la argentiniadad*, 24–25.

53. Astiz, "Jewish Acculturation," 53–54.

54. Desmond King, *Making Americans: Immigration, Race, and the Origins of the Diverse Democracy*, (Cambridge, MA: Harvard University Press, 2000), quoted in Anat Helman, "Hues of Adjustment: Landsmanshaftn in Interwar New York and Tel Aviv," *Jewish History* 20, no. 1 (2006): 55.

55. Juan A. Alsina, *La inmigración en el primer siglo de la indepdendencía* (Buenos Aires: Felipé S. Alsina, 1910), 8, quoted in Włodek, *Argentyna i emigracja*, 308

56. Julián Martel (1867–96) was a conservative writer and editor of *La Nación*.

57. Nora Glickman, *The Jewish White Slave Trade and The Untold Story of Raquel Liberman* (New York: Routledge, 2000), 29–30.

58. David Rock, *Authoritarian Argentina: The Nationalist Movement, Its History and Impact* (Berkeley: University of California Press, 1993), 104–10.

59. Lerner, "A Half Century Ago," 61.

60. Oscar Kornblit estimated that in 1914 only around 1.4 percent (33,203 persons) of immigrants in Argentina were naturalized citizens, whereas in the United States it was 24.1 percent in the case of Jewish and 21.6 percent in the case of Polish immigrants (in 1914). See Oscar Kornblit, "Inmigrantes y empresarios en la politica argentina," in *Los fragmentos del poder: de la oligarquía a poliarquía argentina*, ed. Torcuato S. Di Tella and Tulio Haperin Donghi (Buenos Aires: Alvarez, 1969), 416–18. The Argentine naturalization law enabled applications for Argentine citizenship after two years of living in the country. Yet, as *Di Presse* commented, the naturalization process was hard, lengthy, expensive, and often humiliating. Consequently, only a small fraction of immigrants applied for citizenship. See: "Natualizatsye," *Di Presse*, November 29, 1929, page unknown. The Polish Ministry of Foreign Affairs estimated that in 1933 a mere 1,069 Polish citizens were naturalized in Argentina, out of them three-quarters were Jews. In the same year, the number of Polish citizens in Argentina was estimated at fifty thousand, including twenty-five thousand Jews. AAN, MSZ, 9618, 147, quoted in Izabela Klarner-Kosiński, "Polonia w Buenos Aires," in *Dzieje Polonii w Ameryce Łacińskiej*, ed. Marcin Kula, 236 (Wrocław, Poland: Polska Akademia Nauk, Komitet Badań Polonii, Zakład Narodowy im. Ossolińskich, 1983).

61. Frank Wolff, "Als Wilna neben Buenos Aires lag: Die Transnationalität jüdischen Lebens am Rio de La Plata, 1904–1939," in *Migration—Religion—Identität. Aspekte transkultureller Prozesse*, ed. Kerstin Kazzazi, Angela Treiber, and Tim Wätzold, 60–62 (Wiesbaden, Germany: Springer Fachmedien, 2016).

62. Bletz, *Immigration and Acculturation*, 89–91.

63. Edgardo Bilsky, *La Semana Trágica* (Buenos Aires: Ediciones Ryr, 2011), 35.

64. Mollie Lewis Nouwen, *Oy, my Buenos Aires: Jewish Immigrants and the Creation of Argentine National Identity* (University of New Mexico Press: Albuquerque, 2013), 17–18.

65. Leandro H. Gutiérrez and Luis Alberto Romero, "La conctrucción de la ciudadanía 1912–1955," in *Sectores populares, cultura y política. Buenos Aires en la entreguerra*, ed. Luis H. Gutiérrez and Luis Alberto Romero, 155–74 (Buenos Aires: Siglo Veintinuno Editores, 2007).

66. Michael Humphrey, "Ethnic History, Nationalism and Transnationalism in Argentine Arab and Jewish Cultures," in Klich and Lesser, *Arab and Jewish Immigrants*, 167–88.

67. Lazaro Zhitnitsky, "Transformatsyes inem yishev fun argentine," in *Zamlbukh fun h.d. nomberg shrayber farayn in argentine* (Buenos Aires, 1962), 77.

68. Manuel Bronstein, "Origenes de la Sociedad Hebraica Argentina," *Davar* 119 (October–December1968): 71, quoted Mirelman, *En búsqueda de una identidad*, 295.

69. *Juventud*, no. 49 (1916): 1, quoted in Astiz, "Jewish Acculturation," 58.

70. "25 de Mayo," *Semanario Hebreo*, no. 68, May 24, 1924, 1, quoted in Astiz, "Jewish Acculturation," 58.

71. *Medio siglo en el surco argentino, Cincuentenario de la Jewish Colonization Association*, 42.

72. Sociedad Hebraica Argentina, *Memoria y Balance 1928* (Buenos Aires, 1928), 14, quoted in Mirelman, *En búsqueda de una identidad*, 298.

73. Liliana Ruth Feierstein, "The New Midrash. The Jewish Press in Argentina," in *The PRESSA: International Press Exhibition Cologne 1928 and the Jewish Contribution to Modern Journalism*, ed. Susanne Marten-Finnis and Michael Nagel, 570–74 (Bremen, Germany: Edition Lumiere, 2012).

74. Humphrey, "Ethnic History, Nationalism and Transnationalism," 181. For a broader study of the rise of the right in the 1930s in Argentina, see Sandra McGee Deutsch, *Las Derechas. The Extreme Right in Argentina, Brazil, and Chile, 1890–1939* (Stanford, CA: Stanford University Press, 1999).

75. Dujovne, *Una historía del libro judío*, 147–57.

76. Dujovne, 125–29.

77. Yosef (José) Mendelson, "Discurso de José Mendelson," *Judaica*, no. 62, August 1938, 45–47.

78. Sh. Feinberg, "Cuentos judíos," *Di Presse*, November 21, 1920, 4.

79. Pinie Katz, "Salomón Resnick el enamorado del ídish," 1947, republished in *Noaj: Revista Literaria*, no. 12–13 (1997), Homenaje a Salomón Resnick y la revista *Judaica*, 138–40.

80. "Alejamiento, no asimilación," *Mundo Israelita*, August 16, 1924, 1.

81. Yosef (José) Mendelson "Unzer svive, unzer geshtalt," in *Oyf di bregn fun plata. A zamelbukh* (Buenos Aires: Farlag Yidische Zaitung, 1919), 3–15.

82. Rollansky, *Dos yidishe gedrukte*, 193.

83. "A lebediger grus fun yudish lebn un yudisher kultur in argentina. Vos dertselt der bekanter yudisher shriftshteler fun argentina, yankev botoshansky," *Grodner Moment Express*, no. 62, March 13, 1931, 7.

84. "Dos yidishe kultur-lebn in argentine. A shmues mit yankev botoshansky," *Literarishe Bleter*, no. 12, March 20, 1931, 229, 230.

85. Wolff, "Als Wilna neben Buenos Aires lag," 59, 68.

86. Cecile Esther Kuznitz, *YIVO and the Making of Modern Jewish Culture: Scholarship for Yiddish Nation* (New York: Cambridge University Press, 2014), 17–18.

87. "La colectividad israelita en la Argentina," *Mundo Israelita*, January 5, 1924, 1

88. See Yardena Fain, *Dos yingl fun karaskal* (Buenos Aires, 1941).

89. "Ha regresado el director del Diario Israelita," *Mundo Israelita*, August 31, 1935, 1.

90. "Partirá para Europa el señor M. Regalsky," *Mundo Israelita*, July 20, 1935, no. 632, 1.

91. "La conferencia de la IWO," *Mundo Israelita*, August 25, 1935, 1.

92. "El escritor judío S. Niger, nuestro ilustre huésped, emite interesantes juicios sobre la actualidad cultural y la política judía," *Mundo Israelita*, May 4, 1935, 2.

93. Yaakov Zerubavel was a Labor Zionist leader, yet a strong supporter of Yiddish as a Jewish national language. Born in 1886, Zerubavel immigrated to Palestine in 1910 but was forced to leave in 1915. Between 1918 and 1935, he lived in Poland, working as an editor and leader of Poaley Tsiyon Left. He immigrated to Palestine again in 1935.

94. "Por las escuelas judías de Polonia," *Mundo Israelita*, April 30, 1928, 1. For a broader study of Jewish schooling in Argentina, see Zadoff, *Historia de la educacción.*

95. "Por las escuelas de Polonia," *Mundo Israelita*, May 21, 1928, 4.

96. Zachary M. Baker, "Gvald, Yidn, Buena Gente. Jevel Katz, Yiddish Bard of the Rio de la Plata," in *Inventing the Modern Yiddish Stage: Essays in Drama, Performance, and Show Business*, ed. Joel Berkowitz and Barbara Henry, 202–24 (Detroit, MI: Wayne State University Press, 2012).

97. Yosef Horn, "Poylishe yidn: Di shefer fun unzer kultur-svive un boyer fun a aygn yidish lebn in argentine," in *Poylishe yidn in doyrem amerike*, 151.

98. The 1920s saw to the establishment of supplementary Borokhov schools related to Labor Zionism, communist Arbetershulorg schools, Folks-schul-rat schools that combined Yiddish and Argentine elements, and a free Bundist school established in 1925. In 1930, authorities closed the schools and reopened them with changed structures around 1931 (with a Gezelshaft far yidishe veltlekhe shuln in argentine and Tsentrale fun di yidishe veltlekhe shuln in argentine). See Frank Wolff, *Neue Welten in der neuen Welt. Die Transnationale Geschichte des Allgemeinen Jüdischen Arbeiterbundes 1897–1947* (Köln, Germany: Böhlau Verlag, 2014), 380.

99. Centro Mark Turkow, Archivo de la palabra, no. 11 José Chiaskelevitz, no. 32 Guitl Kanutsky.

100. In the early 1930s, two competing Yiddishist educational networks were in existence in Argentina: Gezelshaft and Tsentrale.

101. Centro Mark Turkow, Archivo de la palabra, no. 54, Zalman Orensztein.

102. Wolff, *Neue Welten in der neuen Welt*, 387.

103. Wolff, 289.

104. "Por la enseñanza judía," *Mundo Israelita*, no. 213, July 2, 1927, 1.

105. "Alejamiento, no asimilación," *Mundo Israelita*, August 16, 1924, 1.

106. Salomón Resnick, *Esquema de la literatura judía* (Buenos Aires: M. Gleizer Editor, 1933; repr., Buenos Aires: Mario Saban, 2006), 165–66. During the 1936 PEN Club congress, Resnick served as a Spanish translator of H. Leivick representing Yiddish literature.

107. Leonardo Senkman, "La construcción de un espacio de transculturción judeo-iberoamericano," Homenaje a Salomón Resnick y la revista Judaica, *Noaj. Revista Literaria*, no. 12–13 (1997): 1–3.

108. "El Instituto Científico Judío ampliara su labor en la America," *Judaica*, no. 37, July 1936, 44–45.

109. Rosa Perla Resnick, "Salomón Resnick, pionero de la cultura judía en lengua castellana en Latinoamérica," Homenaje a Salomón Resnick y la revista Judaica, *Noaj. Revista Literaria* no. 12–13 (1997): 10.

110. Teofilo Wechsler, "El castellano idioma nacional para los judíos," *Vida Nuestra*, no. 3, September 1918, Buenos Aires, 58–61.

111. Salomón Resnick, "El idioma nacional de los judíos," *Vida Nuestra*, no. 4, October 1919, 82–85.

112. See Iaacov Rubel, "Salomón Resnick y su revista JUDAICA como factores de mediación e intercambio entre la cultura judía, la literatura ídish y la sociedad argentina," in *Buenos Aires ídish*, ed. Perla Sneh, 161–66 (Buenos Aires: Comisión para la Preservación del Patrimonio Histórico Cultural de la Ciudad de Buenos Aires, 2006).

113. F. Fridman, "El historiador Meier Balaban, Sexuagenario," *Judaica*, no. 45, March 1937, 93–95.

114. Moses Merkin, "El problema judeo-polaco. A proposito de la campania en favor de los judíos de Polonia," *Judaica*, no. 45, March 1937, 96–98.

115. Jacob Lestschinsky, "Situacíon catastrófica de los judíos en Europa Oriental y Central," *Judaica*, no. 48, June 1937, 209–17.

116. Israel Friedlender, "Breve historia de los judíos de Polonia," *Judaica*, no. 55, January 1938, 29–36, no. 56, 73–83, 135–140.

117. Resnick, "Salomón Resnick," 8.

118. In 1938, Ravitch was in Argentina as an envoy of the YIVO Institute in Vilna.

119. Melech Ravitch, "Bigamia cultural," *Judaica*, no. 59–61, May–July 1938, 196–201.

120. Pinie Katz, "Ídish e Judaica," *Judaica*, no. 59–61, May–July1938, 251–52.

121. Katz, "Der sotsyaler bashtand," 55–59.

122. Beatriz Sarlo, "Oralidad y lenguas extranjeras: El conflicto en la literatura argentina durante el primer tercio del siglo XX," in *Oralidad y argentinidad, estudios sobre la fúncion del lenguaje hablado en la literatura argentina*, ed. Walter Brune Berg and Markus Klaus Schäffauer, 28–32 (Tübbingen, Germany: Gunter Narr Verlag, 1997).

123. Raanan Rein and Jeffrey Lesser claim that the fact that the sources for the study of Latin American history are often in Yiddish makes a false impression that Jews lived in closed communities. I do not entirely agree with this statement. Of course, the general Argentine social and political problems influenced the lives of Argentina's Jews. Yet the discussions taking place in the Yiddish press did indeed to a certain degree leave the gentiles aside. Whereas the daily lives of Jews in Buenos Aires were influenced by interactions with the gentile word, a part of intellectual discussion and media discourse happened and was located within the transnational Yiddishland, rather than in Buenos Aires. See Jeffrey Lesser and Raanan Rein, "Challenging Particularity: Jews as a Lens on Latin American Ethnicity," *Latin American and Caribbean Ethnic Studies* 1, no. 2 (2006): 254.

124. Astro, *Yiddish South of the Border*, 7.

125. Alejandro Dujovne, "The Books That Should Not Be Missing in Any Jewish Home: Translation as a Cultural Policy in Argentina, 1919–1938," in Amalia Ran and Jean Axelrad Cahan, eds., *Returning to Babel. Jewish Latin American Experiences, Representations and Identity* (Leiden, Netherlands: Brill, 2013), 164.

126. Humphrey, "Ethnic History, Nationalism and Transnationalism," 168. Turco (a Turk) is an Argentine nickname for non-Ashkenazi Jews.

127. Samuel Glusberg, "Mate Amagro," in *La levita gris. Cuentos judíos de ambiente porteño* (Buenos Aires: Editorial Babel, 1924). The positive picture of immigration offered in "Mate Amagro" was challenged in the story's ending: Potacovsky's wife dies following the escape of their daughter Eliza with a *goy*, while Potacovsky himslef is murdered in the Semana Trágica. Other stories in the volume present figures of successful Jews: those becoming doctors or publishing articles in the national Spanish press.

128. As Ariana Huberman noted, *Los gauchos judíos* does not avoid portraying the hardships of immigration. The book also encapsulates fragments that reflect the fear of assimilation, violent interactions with the *gauchos*, or memories of a better life in eastern Europe. See Ariana Huberman, *Gauchos and Foreigners: Glossing Culture and Identity in the Argentine Countryside* (Plymouth, UK: Lexington Books, 2011), 102.

129. Dardo Cúneo, Julio Mafud, Amalia Sánchez Sivori, and Lazaro Schallman, eds. *Inmigración y nacionalidad* (Buenos Aires: Instituto Judío Argentino de Cultura e Información, Editorial Paidós, 1967), 13.

130. Edna Aizenberg, *Parricide on the Pampa: A New Study and Translation of Alberto Gerchunoff's Los Gauchos judíos* (Madrid: Vorvuert, Iberoamericana, 2000), 12.

131. Humphrey, "Ethnic History, Nationalism and Transnationalism," 187.

132. Lesser and Rein, "Challenging Particularity," 257.

133. Class differences often coincided with generational ones. Those who arrived in Argentina earlier often had access to middle-class professions, especially in the private sector. For an in-depth study of the 1919 Semana Trágica, see John Dizgun, "Immigrants of Different Religion: Jewish Argentines and the Boundaries of Argentini-

dad, 1919–2009" (PhD diss., Rutgers University, 2010), chapter "Semana Tragica," 14–67 and the references.

134. Poster, "150.000 Israelitas al pueblo de la Republica," quoted in Pinie Wald, *Los judíos en la Semana Trágica*, reprint (Buenos Aires: Instituto Hebreo de Ciencias 1985), 27. For a study of Semana Trágica see Bilsky, *La Semana Trágica*; Marcelo Dimenstein, "En busca de un pogrom perdido," in *Marginados y consagrados: Nuevos estudios sobre la vida judía en la Argentina*, ed. Emmanuel Nicolás Kahan, Laura Schenquer, Damián Setton, and Alejandro Dujovne, 121–41 (Tel Aviv: Tel Aviv University, Lumiére, 2011).

135. "Encuesta de *Vida Nuestra* sobre la situación de los judíos en la Argentina," *Vida Nuestra* 8 (February 1919), page unknown, quoted in Wald, *Los judíos*, 31. Wald's text was originally published in *Argentiner IWO Shriftn*, "Yidn in der tragisher wokh," no. 4 (1947): 5–55.

136. Huberman, *Gauchos and Foreigners*, 100.

137. Wald, *Los judíos*, 55.

138. Pinie Wald, *Koshmar* (Buenos Aires: n.p., 1929), 42.

139. María Silva Ospital, *Inmigración y nacionalismo: Liga Patriótica y la Asociación del Trabajo (1910–1930)* (Buenos Aires: Centro Editor de America Latina, 1994), 44–72.

140. Samuel Rollansky, even in 1989, wrote about the Jewish colonization enterprise with great passion, even though it was not part of his personal experience. Rollansky ascribed the guilt for the failures of colonization to the frauds of JCA that "did not share the folk spirit of Baron Hirsch." He continued by stating that the colonists "washed away" the bad name of the Jews as female traffickers and that colonization was a "mikveh for Jewish Argentina." See Samuel Rollansky, "100 yor yidishe kolonizatsye un der yishev in argentine," *Argentiner IWO Shriftn* 15 (1989): 11–14.

141. "Unzer (. . .) raykhtum: Der nayer beis yetoymim," *Penimer un penimlekh*, October 22, 1926, 17.

142. Marcos (Mordecai) Regalsky, "IWO," in *Tsvishn tsvey velt mikhomes. Di goyrl yorn 1918–1945* (Buenos Aires, 1946), 412.

143. Marcelo Dimenstein, "The Building of the Once Neighborhood in Buenos Aires: Immigrant Bourgeoisie, Ethnic Architects and Jewish Elites (1900–1930)," *Perush: An Online Journal of Jewish Scholarship and Interpretation* 2 (2010): unpaginated.

144. For an analysis of German migrants, see Benjamin Bryce, "Paternal Communities: Social Welfare and Immigration in Argentina, 1880–1930," *Journal of Social History* 49, no. 1 (2015): 213–36.

145. It took more than twenty years to construct the first building of the Jewish hospital. The organization that raised money for it was already founded in 1900. See Shatzky, *Comunidades judías*, 20.

146. See Donna Guy, "Women's Organizations and Jewish Orphanages in Buenos Aires, 1918–1955," in *Rethinking Jewish-Latin Americans*, ed. Jeffrey Lesser and Raanan Rein, 187–206 (Albuquerque: University of New Mexico Press, 2008).

147. "Sociedad de Protección de Inmigrantes Israelitas. Su actividad desde 20.5.1922 al 30.6.1926," *Mundo Israelita*, July 10, 1926, no. 162, page unkown.

148. Aharon Leyb Schussheim, *Tsu der geshikhte fun yidishn yishev in argentine* (Buenos Aires, 1954), 64.

149. "Ken es den azoy vayter geyen?" *Dos Naye Vort*, no. 140, October 1931, 3.

150. Leizer Kochan, "Tsu der geshikhte vengrover yidn in argentine," *Yuvl oysgabe*

tsu der 15 yoriker gezelshaftlekher tetigkayt fun vengrover landslayt farayn in argentine (Buenos Aires, 1940), 8.

151. *50 Años de colonización judía en la Argentina* (Buenos Aires: DAIA, 1939), 5.

152. *Medio siglo en el surco argentine. Cincuentenario de la Jewish Colonization Association.*

153. *Poylishe yidn in doyrem amerike*, 8, 9 in the Yiddish section and pages 6–8 in the Spanish section.

Chapter 6

1. Katz, "Der sotsyaler bashtand," 57.

2. Hannah Kliger estimated that in the case of New York every fourth Jewish immigrant belonged to a landsmanshaft. Hannah Kliger, ed., *Jewish Hometown Associations and Family Circles in New York*, WPA Yiddish Writers' Group Study (Bloomington: Indiana University Press, 1992), I.

3. Lazaro Zhitnitsky, "Di landsmanshaftn in argentine," *Argentiner IWO Shriftn* 3 (1945): 155–61.

4. "Oyftuen, dergraykhungen un begangene feler fun der landsmanshaftn bevegung in argentine," *Argentiner IWO Shriftn* 15 (1989): 65–66.

5. Poselstwo RP w Buenos Aires do MSZ, 13.11.1937, AAN MSZ 11497, 8.

6. "Poylish yidisher farband in argentine. Zayn entshteyung un entviklung," *Dos Naye Vort*, September 1932, 19; "Oyfruf fun der komision direktiva tsu di mitglider fun farband," *Dos Naye Vort*, July 1933, 1.

7. Michael Weisser, *A Brotherhood of Memory: Jewish Landsmanshaftn in the New World* (New York: Basic Books, 1985), 5.

8. "Poylish yidisher farband," *Dos Naye Vort*, September 1933, 4.

9. Nouwen, *Oy, My Buenos Aires*, 90–106.

10. "Espiritu localista," *Mundo Israelita*, no. 218, August 6, 1928, 1.

11. Tobias Brinkmann, "We Are Brothers! Let Us Separate! Jews and Community Building in American Cities during the 19th Century," *History Compass* 11/10 (2013): 869–79.

12. Ronaldo Munck, "Mutual Benefit Societies in Argentina: Workers, Nationality, Social Security and Trade Unionism," *Journal of Latin American Studies* 30, no. 3 (1998): 580.

13. In Argentina, social welfare was a patchwork system made up of the state, the Catholic church, private philanthropies, and immigrant associations. Bryce, "Paternal Communities," 216.

14. Ben Gidley, "Diasporic Memory and the Call to Identity: Yiddish Migrants in Early Twentieth Century East London," *Journal of Intercultural Studies* 34, no. 6 (2013): 650–664.

15. Leonardo Senkman, "Klal Yisrael at the Frontiers: The Transnational Jewish Experience in Argentina," in *Jewish Identities in an Era of Globalization and Multiculturalism: Latin America in the Jewish World*, ed. Judit Bokser de Liwerant, Eliezer Ben-Rafael, Yosef Gorny, and Raanan Rein, 129–33 (Leiden, Netherlands: Brill, 2008).

16. Rebecca Kobrin, "The Other Polonia: The Responses of Yiddish Immigrant Writers in New York and Buenos Aires to the New Polish State, 1920–1925," in *Choosing Yiddish: New Frontiers of Language and Culture*, eds. Lara Rabinovitch, Shiri Goren, and Hannah S. Pressman, 103–5 (Detroit: Wayne State University Press, 2013).

17. Daniel Soyer, "Transnationalism and Americanization in East European Jew-

ish Immigrant Public Life," in *Imagining the American Jewish Community*, ed. Jack Wertheimer, 47 (Waltham, MA: Brandeis University Press, 2007).

18. Kobrin, *Jewish Bialystok*.

19. Prior to 1939, eastern Europe and the new Jewish diasporas boasted many non-Zionist forms of national expression, including territorialism, autonomism, Diaspora Nationalism, folkism and to some extent also Yiddishism. Joshua Shanes argued that the failure of Diaspora Nationalism to achieve a lasting cultural or political autonomy, combined with the subsequent success of Zionism, led historians to discount nationalist alternatives to Zionism. See Joshua Shanes, "Yiddish and Jewish Diaspora Nationalism," *Monatshefte* 90, no. 2 (1998): 178–88.

20. See Jan Schwarz, "A Library of Hope and Destruction: The Yiddish Book Series Dos poylishe yidntum, 1946–1966," in *Making Holocaust Memory*, vol. 20 of *Polin: Studies in Polish Jewry* (Oxford: Littman Library of Jewish Civilization, 2008), 173–96.

21. Soyer, *Jewish Immigrant Association*.

22. The precise date of the establishment of Agudas Ahim is uncertain. Its establishment is confused (in landsman publications) with the establishment of their subcommittee of help for war victims in Europe (in 1916). Some sources mention August 1, 1916, as the day of the establishment, others list October 1, 1916.

23. Kobrin, "The Other Polonia," 111.

24. Opinions regarding the problematic reputation of Polish Jews in Argentina also reached the Polish diplomatic mission in Argentina. In a 1938 note to the Ministry of Foreign Affairs (MSZ) in Warsaw, the embassy stressed that negative opinions about Polish Jews led to a limitation of Poland's immigration quotas to Argentina. *Notatka w sprawie wartości imigracji żydowskiej z Polski*, AAN, MSZ, 9915, 56–62. An earlier report, from 1931, stated that the bad reputation of Jewish immigrants from Poland also had an influence on the situation of gentile Polish workers, who were sometimes refused employment. The problem of prostitution and accusations of anarchism and communism allegedly discouraged employers. Emigracja polska w Argentynie. Sprawozdanie za 1931, 123, AAN, MSZ 9618.

25. Anat Helman, "Hues of Adjustment: Landsmanshaftn in Interwar New York and Tel Aviv," *Jewish History* 20, no. 1 (2006): 55.

26. Helman, 54.

27. Abraham N. Polak, "Yehudei polin be-eretz yisrael," in *Kiyum ve-shever. Yehudey polin le-doroteyhem*, ed. Israel Bartal and Israel Gutman, 218–21 (Jerusalem: Zalman Shazar Center, 1997–2001).

28. This was true for 1924 when the name Poylish yidisher farayn "Agudas Ahim" appeared in the organization's almanac. The words "Poylish yidisher" were added at the very beginning, probably in 1916.

29. *Poylishe yidn in doyrem amerike*, 83; according to *Dos Naye Vort*, the name "Agudas Ahim" was considered "provincial" in 1925. See "Der ershter president fun poylish-yidishn farband," *Dos Naye Vort*, September 1935, 25.

30. "Der nomen," *Almanakh 1925. Tsvayter almankh aroysgegeben fun poylish yidishen farband in argentine*, ed. Leib Malach (Buenos Aires: Poylish yidisher farband in argentine, 1925), 10.

31. David Aizenberg, "A virdike matone tsum 20 yubileum fun poylish yidishn farband—di faraynikung fun poylishn yidntum in argentine," *Dos Naye Vort*, September 1935, 10.

32. See *Belchatow. Memorias de residentes judíos en Argentina* (Buenos Aires: Asociación Judeo Argentina de Estudios Históricos, 1986); Fiszel Trybiarz, *Villa Lynch en silencio: Inmigrantes judíos de Bialystok, Belchatow y Lodz y la industria textil* (Buenos Aires: Editorial Milá, 2006); Frank Wolff, "Eastern Europe Abroad: Exploring Actor-Networks in Transnational Movements and Migration History, the Case of the Bund," *International Review of Social History* 57, no. 2 (2012): 229–55.

33. "Aynike biografishe shtikhn fun abraham fridman z"l," *Dos Naye Vort*, March 1937, 1.

34. In the case of New York, early anarchist and socialist societies opposed subethnic immigrant associations, as both types of institutions struggled for limited financial resources, political power, and space. See Helman, "Hues of Adjustment," 50–51, and Daniel Soyer, "Landsmanshaftn and the Jewish Labor Movement: Cooperation, Conflict, and the Building of Community." *Journal of American Ethnic History* 7, no. 2 (1988), 22–45.

35. Nouwen, *Oy, My Buenos Aires*, 118–20; Pinie Wald, "Der poylish-yidisher arbeter in argentine. Fun 1901 bis 1941," in *Poylishe yidn in doyrem amerike*, 157.

36. Kochan, "Tsu der geshikhte vengrover yidn," 8.

37. Meir Lerner, "Di oyfagaben fun poylish-yidishn farband in itstikn moment," *Dos Naye Vort*, October 1933, 3.

38. As Mir Yarfitz showed, in 1924 Jewish prostitutes constituted 33.3 percent of all Buenos Aires registered prostitutes. The remaining 30.5 percent of them were French and 6.4 percent Italian, see Mir Yarfitz, "Polacos, White Slaves, and Stille Chuppahs: Organized Jewish Prostitution and the Jews of Buenos Aires, 1890–1939," PhD. diss., University of California Los Angeles, 2012, 92.

39. Lerner, "A Half Century Ago," 60.

40. Abraham Fridman, "Di grindung fun agudas ahim un vaytere perspektiv," in *Almanakh 1924. Ershter zamlbukh aroysgegeben fun poylish yidisher farayn "agudas ahim,"* ed. Leyb Malach, 14–16 (Buenos Aires, 1924). Fridman was then the president of the Farband. See also David Szyszacki, "Agudas ahim un dos poylishe agudas ahim," *Argentiner IWO Shriftn* 14 (1988): 123–129.

41. Jacobo Pukach, "Oyfbli un yeride fun landsmanshaftn," *Argentiner IWO Shriftn* 15 (1989): 69.

42. "Hoypt punktn fun di statutn," par. 6, *Almanakh 1924*, 23.

43. Pedro Chapov, "40 yor gezelshaftlekhe tetigkayt fun di vengrover," in *Yuvl oysgabe tsu der 15 yoriker gezelshaftlekher tetigkayt fun vengrover*, 11.

44. Felix Hershkovich, "Vos der poylish yidisher farband hot durkhtsufirn un der hov fun poylishe yidn legabey dem zelbn," in Guiser, *Almanakh 1928*, 14.

45. "Yo defiendo a sus polacas," *Dos Naye Vort*, September 1933, 3.

46. Bryce, "Paternal Communities," 214.

47. Next to some of the most successful immigrants, the majority of left-wing proletarian immigrants also did not join the landsmanshaftn because of their political convictions. Consequently, landsmanshaftn mirrored the Argentine experiences of only a fraction of Polish Jews. Despite their relative under-representativeness, landsmanshaft involvement is a great lens for exploring the process of becoming Jewish Argentine, while also negotiating the place of Argentina within the Yiddishland.

48. Natan Fruchter, "Di galitsianer yidn in buenos aires," in *Tsvayter almanakh fun farband fun galitsianer yidn in buenos aires* (Buenos Aires: Farband fun galitsianer yidn in Buenos Aires, 1929), 11.

49. Katz, "Der sotsyaler bashtand," 55–56.

50. Eduardo José Míguez, "Introduction: Foreign Mass Migration to Latin America in the Nineteenth and Twentieth Century—An Overview," in *Mass Migration to Modern Latin America*, ed. Samuel Baily, Eduardo José Míguez, xx (Wilmington, DE: Jaguar Books, 2003).

51. "Der ershter president fun poylish-yidishn farband," *Dos Naye Vort*, September 1925, 25. Abraham Fridman was born in 1877 in Lublin, Poland. For a few years, he worked in the textile industry in Łódź, before arriving in Buenos Aires in 1907. In 1915, he cofounded the Poylisher Farband Agudas Ahim and later worked in SOPROTIMIS (Society for the Protection of Jewish Immigrants). For a detailed biography, see "Aynike biografishe shtikhn fun abraham fridman, z"l," *Dos Naye Vort*, March 1937, 1.

52. Wolf Bressler, ed., *Lexicón de los hombres de bien de la colectividad israelita en la Argentina* (Buenos Aires, 1941), 167.

53. Guiser, *Almanakh 1928*, 78.

54. Bressler, *Lexicón de los hombres*, 198.

55. Advertisement, *Almanakh 1924*, 30.

56. Advertisement, *Dos Naye Vort*, July 1933, 8.

57. The Vengrover Farayn was established in 1906/1907. Later, it went defunct and was re-established in 1925. Chapov, "40 yor gezelshaftlekhe tetigkayt," 11. Another vengrover, Leizer Kochan argued that the first association of Węgrów Jews was formed in 1900 and in fact was the basis for Poylisher Farband Agudas Ahim. Kochan, "Tsu der geshikhte vengrover yidn."

58. David Szyszacki, "Tsu der geshikhte fun di yidishe landsmanshaftn in argentine," *Argentiner IWO Shriftn* 13 (1981): 132–33.

59. Meier Iagodinsky, "Di poylish-yidishe landslayt-faraynen un di gezelshaftlekhkayt," in *Poylishe yidn in doyrem amerike*, 223.

60. Marek Turkow, "Tsi iz noytik a farband fun poylishe yidn?" *Dos Naye Vort*, August–September 1937, 5.

61. Kobrin, "When a Jew Was a Landsman," 358.

62. Weisser, *Brotherhood of Memory*, 13.

63. The same was true for mutualist societies in other parts of the world. See Marcel van der Linden, "Introduction," in *Social Security Mutualism: The Comparative History of Mutual Benefit Societies*, ed. Marcel van der Linden, 9–38 (Bern, Switzerland: Peter Lang, 2006).

64. Borekh Ismach, "Vos hobn landsmanshaftn oyfgeton far di imigrant in zayere naye heymer," *Argentiner IWO Shriftn* 15 (1989): 68.

65. Michl Grines, "In loyf fun zvantsik yor," in *Almanakh fun ostrog-voliner landslayt farayn un umgegent in argentine 1924–1944* (Buenos Aires: Ostrog-voliner landslayt farayn un umgegent in argentine, 1944), 10.

66. Szyszacki, "Tsu der geshikhte fun yidishe landslayt-faraynen in argentine," 133.

67. Abraham Milberg, "A por verter tsu unzer hayntigker yuvl," *Yuvl oysgabe tsu der 15 yoriker gezelshaftlekher tetigkayt fun vengrover*, 12.

68. Milberg, 6.

69. Malach, *Almanakh 1925*, 152.

70. Grines, "In loyf fun zvantsik yor," in *Almanakh fun ostrog-voliner landslayt farayn*, 11.

71. "Unzer kultur-arbet," in *Poylishe yidn in doyrem amerike*, 58–59.

72. "Der Varshever Yidisher Klub," in *Landsmanshaftn. Spetsyele oysgabe fun di tsen-*

trale fun di faraynikte poylish-yidishe landsmanshaftn in argentine tsum dritn zid amerikaner tsuzamenfor (Buenos Aires: Di tsentrale fun di faraynikte poylish-yidishe landsmanshaftn in argentine, 1939), 42.

73. Malach, *Almanakh 1924*, 152–59.

74. Flyer, Galitsianer Farband collection, documents no. 1053/82 and 1053/96, Fundación IWO, Buenos Aires.

75. Malach, *Almanakh 1924*, 110.

76. Guiser, *Almanakh 1928*, 9.

77. "Poylish yidisher farband in argentine," in *Landsmanshaftn. Spetsyele oysgabe*, 37–38; "Shpanishe ovnt kursn," *Dos Naye Vort*, August 1933, 6.

78. Flyer, Galitsianer Farband collection, document no. 43, Fundación IWO, Buenos Aires.

79. Y. Horn, "In a mazaldiker sho. Tsu der aktsye far tsentrale yidishe biblyotek in buenos aires," in *Landsmanshaftn. Spetsyele oysgabe*, 27.

80. Leandro H. Gutiérrez and Luis Alberto Romero, "Sociedades barriales, bibliotecas populeres y cultura de los sectores populares: Buenos Aires 1920–1945," *Desarollo Economico* 29, no. 113 (1989): 33–62.

81. Two private Jewish libraries examined by Dujovne, Biblioteca Vainstoc and Biblioteca Kamenszain, held 50.4 percent and 37.4 percent of books published in Poland (between 1910 and 1938), respectively. Books published in Buenos Aires became dominant only after 1939; Alejandro Dujovne, "Buenos Aires en geografía de diaspora judía. Una aproximación desde la producción y circulación transnacional de libros entre 1900 y 1980," unpublished, available at the website of Nucleo de Estudios Judios (IDES), http://estudiosjudios.ides.org.ar/files/2012/02/bibliotecas_Buenos_Aires_en_la_geografia_de_la_diaspora_judia.pdf (accessed on February 3, 2017).

82. Malach, *Almanakh 1924*, 124; "Vegn der oysshtelung funem yidish bukh," *Dos Naye Vort*, October 1932, 15.

83. Alejandro Dujovne, "'The Books That Should Not Be Missing in Any Jewish Home': Translation as a Cultural Policy in Argentina, 1919–1938," in Kahan et al., *Marginados y consagrados*, 159–77.

84. Centro Minkovsky opened on May 16, 1931. "In farband," *Dos Naye Vort*, June 1931, 19.

85. "Poylish-yidisher farband in argentine," *Di Yidische Zaitung*, October 5, 1925, page unknown.

86. "Kultur-tsenter M. Minkovsky," *Dos Naye Vort*, September 1933, 5.

87. "Centro Cultural y Deportivo M. Minkovsky," *Dos Naye Vort*, May 1938, 12.

88. Centro Mark Turkow, Archivo de Palabra no. 6, Samuel Blutrajt.

89. "Landsmanshaftn un zayere oyfagaben," *Ershter almanakh fun hilfs farayn fun lemberger un umgegent* (Buenos Aires: Hilfs farayn fun lemberger un umgegent, 1934), 7.

90. "Unzer kultur-arbet," in *Landsmanshaftn. Spetsyele oysgabe*, 24–25.

91. Nouwen, *Oy, My Buenos Aires*, 90–98.

92. Leandro H. Gutiérrez and Luis Alberto Romero, "La construcción de la ciudadanía," 82–89.

93. Ofelia Targovnik, "S'iz noytik a damen-komisye baym farband," *Dos Naye Vort*, September 1933, 3.

94. Felix Hershkovich, "A vort vegen a damen-komisye baym farband," *Dos Naye Vort*, October 1933, 4.

95. Bryce, "Paternal Communities," 220–23.

96. Flyer, Galitsianer Farband collection, document no. 56, Fundación IWO, Buenos Aires.

97. See Adrian Gorelik, *La grilla y el parque: Espació publico y cultura urbana en Buenos Aires, 1887–1936* (Buenos Aires: Universidad Nacional de Quilmes, 2010); Ana Cecchi, *La timba como rito de pasaje. La narrativa del juego en la construción de la modernidad porteña (Buenos Aires 1900–1935)* (Buenos Aires: Ediciones Biblioteca Nacional Teseo, 2012).

98. Flyer, TSYSHO campaign materials, document no. 1036/64, Fundación IWO, Buenos Aires.

99. Flyer, TSYSHO campaign materials, document no. 1036/6, Fundación IWO, Buenos Aires.

100. Invitation, *Dos Naye Vort*, August–September 1937, 16.

101. Invitation, *Dos Naye Vort*.

102. Flyer, Galitsianer Farband collection, document no. 1053/83, Fundación IWO, Buenos Aires.

103. I. Singer, "Di yugnt in galitisianer farband," in *Driter almanakh fun farband fun galitsianer yidn in buenos aires* (Buenos Aires: Farband fun galitsianer yidn in Buenos Aires, 1933), June 1933, 32.

104. Marcos Gottdenker, "Sport als optsvayg fun galitsianer farband," in *Driter almanakh, 32.*

105. "Di yidishe yugent un yidishe kultur," *Dos Naye Vort*, October 1932, 17.

106. S. R. "Vos hoben di landsmanshaftn oyfgeton far sharias haplitim," *Argentiner IWO Shriftn* 15 (1989): 76. S. R. argued that the eastern European Jewish landsmanshaftn did not do enough to attract the youth (in comparison with other ethnic groups).

107. Centro Mark Turkow, Archivo de Palabra, no. 47 León Menin

108. "Naye mitglider farn farband," *Dos Naye Vort*, September 1932, 6.

109. Kobrin, "The Other Polonia," 110.

110. Wolff, "Home That Never Was," 197–215.

111. Dujovne, *Una historia del libro judío. La cultura judía argentina a través de sus editores, libreros, traductores, imprentas y bibliotecas* (Buenos Aires: Siglo Veintiuno Editores, 2014), 91.

112. Katz, "Der sotsyaler bashtand," 57.

113. Efraim Kleiman, "Poyln," in *Almanakh 1926. Driter zamlbukh aroysgegeben fun poylish yidishn farband in argentine* (Buenos Aires, 1926), 54–59.

114. Letter from the Polish Embassy in Buenos Aires to the Ministry of Foreign Affairs in Warsaw, November 13, 1931, AAN MSZ 11497, 9.

115. Volf Orzech, "Dos Naye Vort," *Dos Naye Vort*, January 1937, 4.

116. Rollansky, *Dos yidishe gedrukte*, 119–21.

117. Apart from the Poylisher Farband, which started to publish regular yearbooks in 1924, the Galitsianer Farband (established in 1925) was one of the first landsmanshaftn to print regular publications.

118. Pinchas Bizberg, "Poylishe yidn in der heym, poylishe yidn in der fremd," in *Poylishe yidn in doyrem amerike*, 195–202.

119. Rein, *Argentine Jews or Jewish Argentines*, 3–4.

120. Pinie Wald, "Argentinish-yidishe interesn un problemen," in *Yor-bukh fun yidishn yishev in argentine 1945–1946*, ed. Nehemías Zucker and Volf Bressler (Buenos Aires, 1946), 29.

121. Gidley, "Diasporic Memory," 654–655.

Chapter 7

1. "Yankel piotrovski dertseylt a por verter," *Dos Naye Vort*, September 1935, 17.

2. *Poylishe yidn in doyrem amerike*, 50–52.

3. A similar discourse was visible among other ethnic communities. Benjamin Bryce argued that German immigrants, in their fund-raising efforts, likewise often referred to a sense of honor and solidarity with less fortunate fellow Germans. See Bryce, "Paternal Communities," 224.

4. "Tsuzamenfor un kongres fun poylishe yidn," in *Poylishe yidn in doyrem amerike*, 75–79.

5. According to the 1921 census, 2,855,318 Jews lived in Poland (10.5 percent of the general population), whereas in 1931, the Jewish population grew to 3,113,933 (9.8 percent of the general population). Data from Ezra Mendelsohn, *The Jews of East Central Europe between the World Wars* (Bloomington: Indiana University Press, 1983), 23.

6. Tartakower, *Emigracja żydowska z Polski*, 44.

7. *1791–3 Maj-1916, uroczysty pochód w Warszawie: Rabinat warszawski ze 105-letnim rabinem Perlmutterem na czele*; photography by Marjan Fuks, Pocz. 20343, National Library of Poland.

8. In 1916, Jews fighting in the Polish Legions called on Jewish youth to join the struggle of the Polish nation. Flyer *Do młodzieży żydowskiej! [Inc.:] Gdy wybiła godzina dziejowa dla Narodu Polskiego, gdy zaświtała jutrzenka swobody dla wszystkich mieszkańców ziem polskich bez różnicy stanu i wyznania [. . .]: Królestwo Polskie. W marcu 1915 r. / Żydzi-Legioniści*; DŻS IA 5 Cim., National Library of Poland.

9. "Mizrah-galitsishe yidn far di feraynikung mit poyln?" *Di Presse*, October 22, 1920, page unknown.

10. Tartakower, *Emigracja żydowska*, 17–19. See also Tomasz Schramm, "Żydzi wobec odradzania się państwowości polskiej," in *Przełomy Historii, XVI Powszechny Zjazd Historyków Polskich, Wrocław, 15–19 września 1999*, vol. 2, part 2 (Toruń, Poland: Adam Marszałek, 2000), 223–43.

11. A flyer of Żagiew, 1918, DU IV P.8[425], Warsaw University Library.

12. Leopold Halpern, *Polityka żydowska w Sejmie i Senacie Rzeczpospolitej Polskiej, 1919–1933* (Warsaw: Instytut Badań Spraw Narodowościowych, 1933), 9.

13. Halpern, 9–10.

14. "Di farkonfernts tsum yidishn kongres in poyln," *Di Yidische Zaitung*, undated newspaper clipping, late 1918.

15. "Di rekht fun di minoriteten. Unzer dopelte befrayung," *Di Yidische Zaitung*, undated clipping (around May–July 1919).

16. "Di rekht fun di minoriteten."

17. "Di befrayung fun poyln," *Dos Naye Vort*, September 1935, 20.

18. "Der protest shtrom gegen di pogromen oyf yidn in poyln, *Di Yidische Zaitung*, July 2, 1919, page unknown.

19. "Hungerlaydn fun di yidn in poyln," *Di Yidische Zaitung*, May 9, 1919, page unknown.

20. "Protesten un yidishe prese unterdrikt," *Di Yidische Zaitung*, May 28, 1919, page unknown.

21. "In der yidisher velt," *Di Yidische Zaitung*, July 6, 1919, 5.

22. *Balance General del Comité Central Pro-Victimas Israelitas de la Guerra, desde 1.12.1917 hasta 30.11.1918* (Buenos Aires, 1918), 5.

23. Szyszacki, "Tsu der geshikhte fun yidishe landslayt-faraynen," 134.

24. "A brif fun poyln," *Di Yidische Zaitung*, undated clipping, July 1919.

25. "Der goyrl fun di yidn in mizhrekh-eyrope," *Di Yidische Zaitung*, undated clipping, June 1919.

26. "Di yidishe imigratsye fun mizhrekh-eyrope," *Di Yidische Zaitung*, undated clipping, July 1919.

27. Guiser, *Almanakh 1928*, 11.

28. See, for example, a reprint from the book by Poland's national hero, Marshal Józef Piłsudski, who praised Jewish participation in the January uprising of 1863 against tsarist Russia: Józef Piłsudski, "Der ontayl fun yidn in poylishn opshtand fun 1863," *Dos Naye Vort*, September 1935, 12.

29. Reprinted in *Poylishe yidn in doyrem amerike*, 60, from the first (October 5, 1928) issue of *Dos Naye Vort*.

30. "Delegaten farzamlung hayst gut di handlung fun poylishn farband vegen intsident mitn dom polski," *Dos Naye Vort*, August–September 1937, 15.

31. "Di oyfname funem marshalek in poylish-yidishn farband," *Dos Naye Vort*, August 1933, 4.

32. "Dos gezets vegn farlirn di poylishe birgershaft," *Dos Naye Vort*, May 1938, 6.

33. *Dos Naye Vort*, May 1931, 22.

34. The Polish patriotism expressed by Poylisher Farband was not a new Jewish Argentine invention. Similar attitudes were a strategy characteristic of many Jews living in Poland. A loyalist stand was typical of the leaders of Poland's orthodox Jewry, represented politically by Agudas Isroel.

35. In 1938, *Dos Naye Vort* published a letter congratulating Poland on the twentieth anniversary of its independence, *Dos Naye Vort*, November 1938, 9.

36. Sh. Freilech, "Di tragedye fun 3 milion yidn," in *Almanakh 1926*, 15–16; in the same volume, Y. Okon, "Di ekonomishe lage fun yidn in poyln," 9–14; *Dos Naye Vort* published a regular column entitled "*Briv fun poyln*" (Letters from Poland) or "*Vos hert zikh in poyln?"* (What's going on in Poland?), which featured descriptions of the Jewish situation in Poland. David Aizenberg, "Hilf un solidaritet," *Dos Naye Vort*, August–September 1937,13.

37. Kochan, "Tsu der geshikhte vengrover yidn in argentine," 8.

38. Humphrey, "Ethnic History, Nationalism and Transnationalism," 167.

39. Katz, "Der sotsyaler bashtand," 55.

40. "Hilfs-farayn fu varshe un umgegent," *Zaitschrift*, April 1938, 10.

41. Natan Fruchter, "Ver iz shuldik? A nokhvort tsum durkhgefirten peretz hirschbein yovl-akt," *Di Presse*, October 18, 1941, unknown page; collection of Hersh Dovid Nomberg Association of Jewish Writers and Journalists in Argentina, Fundación IWO, Buenos Aires.

42. "15 yor tetigkeyt fun vengrover landslayt farayn," in *Yuvl oysgabe tsu der 15 yoriker gezelshaftlekher tetigkayt fun vengrover*, 9.

43. *Poylishe yidn in doyrem amerike*, 69. Yankev Vengrover, Boris Knobel, and Gregorio Pachter later served as representatives of the World Union of Polish Jews for South America.

44. In the campaign call, published in Yiddish and Spanish, we read about *judaísmo argentino*—Argentine Jewry. "A los judios de Argentina," help campaign materials 1035/2, Fundación IWO, Buenos Aires.

45. In Spanish, Comité de las Sociedades Israelitas Argentinas Pro-Ayuda a los Israelitas en Polonia.

46. *Memoria de gran campaña del million en Republica Argentina*, 1939, help-campaigns collection, Fundación IWO Buenos Aires.

47. Marcos Regalsky, "Tsum ershtn hilfs-tsuzamenfor in argentine," in *Tsvishn tsvey velt milkhomes. Di goyrl yorn 1918–1945* (Buenos Aires, 1946), 402–3. First published on May 1, 1920.

48. Letter from July 5, 1927, no. 1036/14, help-campaigns collection, Fundación IWO, Buenos Aires.

49. *Di Presse*, 5.3.1922, 7.3.1922.

50. It is unclear if Poylisher Farband sent an envoy to Poland. *Di Presse* from ("In poylish yidishen agudas ahim," *Di Presse*, 24.10.1920, 5) wrote about a meeting of the Farayn, in which delegate who would travel to Poland was supposed to be chosen. Some ethnic activists, like Marcos Regalsky, believed that Argentine Jews themselves were unable to coordinate the help action. See Marcos Regalsky, "Tsum ershtn hilfs-tsuzamenfor in argentine," *Tsvishn zvey velt milkhomes. Di goyrl yorn 1918–1945* (Buenos Aires, 1946), 402–403. First published on May 1, 1920.

51. "Vegn di delegatsyes keyn mizrah eyrope," *Di Presse*, November 18, 1920, 4.

52. Guiser, *Almanakh 1928*, 11.

53. Emanuel Melzer, "Antisemitism in the Last Years of the Second Polish Republic," in *The Jews of Poland Between Two World Wars*, ed. Yisrael Gutman, 126–40 (Hannover, NH: Brandeis University Press, 1989).

54. Y. M. Puchacz, "Oyfbli und yeride fun di landsmanshaftn," 70.

55. The report from this campaign was published in Vilnius in 1934: *Argentine un uruguay far dem YIVO. Barikht fun der aktsye far dem yidishn visenshaftlekhn institut* (Vilna, Poland: YIVO 1934). During this campaign, money was raised both for the YIVO in Vilna and for the building of its Argentine branch (transliterated as IWO), opened in 1928 in Buenos Aires. In 1934, a second YIVO campaign was organized in Argentina, with Herts Gilishanski as a delegate.

56. "Spetsyeler numer gevidmet dem argentiner yidishn kampeyn-komitet letoyves di yidn in poyln," *Dos Naye Vort*, April 1937.

57. "Ratevet dos poylish-yidishe kind!," *Zaitschrift*, April 1938, 2.

58. Gidley, "Diasporic Memory," 658.

59. *Dos Naye Vort*, April 1937, 5, 13, 14.

60. Pachter was then president of Poylish Yidishen Farband. Wolf Bressler, born in Łódź in 1892, was a Yiddishist cultural activist and journalist. Bressler immigrated to Argentina in 1933 and since the mid-1930s was an editor of a popular weekly, *Penimer un penimlekh*. In 1944, together with Abraham Mitelberg, Bressler established the publishing house Idisch.

61. A. Schleien, "Unzere pflikhten in dozikn moment," in *Landsmanshaftn. Spetsyele oysgabe*, 23.

62. "A los Judíos de la Argentina," flyer, help-campaigns collection, document no. 1035/2, Fundación IWO, Buenos Aires.

63. See Jack Jacobs, *Bundist Counterculture in Interwar Poland* (Syracuse, NY: Syracuse University Press, 2009); Daniel Blatman, "National-Minority Policy, Bundist Social Organizations, and Jewish Women in Interwar Poland," in *The Emergence of Modern Jewish Politics: Bundism and Zionism in Eastern Europe*, ed. Zvi Gitelman, (Pittsburgh: University of Pittsburgh Press, 2003), 54–70.

64. The supporters of TSYSHO schools came from various groups within progressive Jewry: some were Bundist, others socialist, communist, or Labor Zionist.

65. Samuel Rollansky, "100 yor yidishe kolonizatsye un der yishev in argentine," *Argentiner IWO Shriftn* 15 (1989): 5.

66. Wolff, "Eastern Europe Abroad,"236.

67. See Nerina Visacovsky, *Argentinos, judíos y camaradas. Tras la utopía socialista* (Buenos Aires: Ed. Biblos, 2015).

68. "Hilfs-kampeyn far di yidishe shuln in poyln," *Penimer un penimlekh*, no. 145, 1927, 17.

69. In the 1920s, progressive Jewish schools in Argentina were affiliated with various political movements: Bundism, communism, anarchism, and Labor Zionism, combined with differing attitudes on linguistic and social problems. The 1930s brought a structural change and stabilization inspired by the TSYSHO schools in Poland. In 1931, the Gezelshaft far yidish-veltlekhe shuln in argentine school was founded, and in 1934, the TSVYSHO (Tsentrale veltlekhe yidishe shul organizatsye), which together educated around one thousand students. See Wolff, "Als Wilna neben Buenos Aires lag," 53–74.

70. Wolff, *Neue Welten in der neuen*, 442–43.

71. Schussheim, *Tsu der geshikhte*, 60.

72. "Dos poylish-argentiner yidntum hot dos vort," *Dos Naye Vort*, June 1934, 1.

73. Zalmen Reyzen, "Briv fun vilne," *Di Presse*, November 11, 1929, 7.

74. In the same issue of *Di Presse*, the 1929 affair was followed by B. Abramson, who reported on the issue directly from Warsaw. Abramson called the anti-TSYSHO efforts of the Zionists "a pogrom." See B. Abramson, "A haylike milkhome kegn 20 toysend yidisher kinder," *Di Presse*, November 3, 1929, 8.

75. "Der proklamirungs-akt funem hilfs-komitet far yidishe shuln in poyln," *Di Presse*, November 7, 1929, 6.

76. "Morgn der proklamirungs akt (. . .)," *Di Presse*, November 4, 1929, 4.

77. "Shtitst di yidishe veltlekhe shuln in poyln," *Di Presse*, November 5, 1929, 6.

78. Volf Orzech, "Mir, un der yidisher shul-vezn in poyln," *Dos Naye Vort*, September 1931, 22.

79. Education in Polish state schools was free. Bundist and other private Jewish schools had to arrange for their own funding, as states and municipalities rarely offered any financial support.

80. A letter from Poylisher Farband, signed by president Abraham Fridman, August 15, 1931, unnumbered, help-campaigns collection, Fundación IWO, Buenos Aires.

81. Letter from the Peretz Hirschbein Biblyotek, November 19, 1929, unnumbered, help-campaigns collection, Fundación IWO, Buenos Aires.

82. Letter from Poylisher Farband, signed by president Abraham Fridman, August 19, 1931, unnumbered, help-campaigns collection, Fundación IWO, Buenos Aires.

83. Letter from Poylisher Farband, signed by president Abraham Fridman, August 18, 1931, unnumbered, help-campaigns collection, Fundación IWO, Buenos Aires.

84. Letter from Galitisianer Farband, November 29, 1929, unnumbered, help-campaigns collection, Fundación IWO, Buenos Aires.

85. Letter from Unión Israelita de Residentes de Polonia en Tucumán, October 20, 1931, unnumbered, help-campaigns collection, Fundación IWO, Buenos Aires.

86. Letter from Unión Israelita de Residentes de Polonia en Tucumán, October 23, 1931, unnumbered, help-campaigns collection, Fundación IWO, Buenos Aires.

87. Flyer, 1931, "A las mases populares y a la mujer israelita," help campaigns-collection, document no. 62, Fundación IWO, Buenos Aires.

88. Pinie Wald, "Di aktsye vos mir hoben durkhgefirt," in *Barikht fun der aktsye durkhgefirt in argentine fun sof may biz november* (Buenos Aires: Hilfs komitet far di yidish veltlekhe shuln in poyln, 1931), 1–7.

89. Wald.

90. Leyb (Aaron Leyb) Schussheim, "A vort tsu di raykhe yidn," *Dos Naye Vort*, April 1937, 5.

91. Wolff, *Neue Welten in der neuen*, 441.

92. Wolff, 385–89.

93. Wolff, 445–51.

94. A letter of Jacobo Setton, Poylisher Farband's secretary to the committee president, protest materials, document no. 1036/75, Fundación IWO, Buenos Aires.

95. Letter from July 19, 1919, from Poylish Yidisher Agudas Ahim, no. 1036/14, unit 19, Help campaigns collection, Fundación IWO, Buenos Aires.

96. Poster, protest campaigns collection, document no. 236/42, Fundación IWO, Bueno Aires.

97. A letter from the Committee against the Pogroms in Romania to the president of Liga de Maestros Israelitas, February 3, 1928, protest.

98. Zvi Cohen, "Di poylishe regirung un di yidn baym itstigen moment," Malach, *Almanakh 1925*, 16.

99. "Rede fun dep. noah prilutsky," *Di Yidische Zaitung*, November 22, 1925, page unknown.

100. The status of Jews in interwar Poland was in constant negotiation between inclusion and exclusion in the nation. Jews were recognized as citizens and entitled to participate in the political struggle yet excluded from the ethnonational community. See Marcos Silber, "Ambivalent Citizenship—The Construction of Jewish Belonging in Emergent Poland, 1915–1918," *Simon Dubnow Institute Yearbook* 10 (2011): 161–83.

101. "Otra vez Polonia," *Mundo Israelita*, Februay 7, 1925, page unknown.

102. Przemysław Różański, "The Attitude of American Jews and American Diplomacy towards the Bill Banning *Shehitah* in Poland in the Second Half of the 1930s," in *Jews and Their Neighbours in Eastern Europe since 1750*, ed. Israel Bartal, Antony Polonsky and Scott Ury, 342–62, vol. 24 of Polin*: Studies in Polish Jewry* (Oxford: Littman Library of Jewish Civilization, 2012).

103. Z. Weinfer, "Vi azoy matern zikh itst di yidn in poyln. A lebendiker grus fun bezukh in poyln," *Zaitschrift. In di interesn fun di karbones fun eyrope*, April 1938, 6–7.

104. "Di faralgemaynerung fun hilfs arbet," *Zaitschrift*, 3

105. "Di faralgemaynerung fun hilfs arbet," *Zaitschrift*, 3.

106. "Zakhn vos kumen for in poyln," *Zaitschrift*, 8.

107. Although the protest propaganda materials presented the situation in Poland as horrible (phrases like "Jews are expelled," "Jews are hunted"), the Jews of Poland were not presented as passive victims. See "Barikht fun solidaritets manifestatsye in teater excelsior," *Dos Naye Vort* August–September 1937, 20.

108. Mordechai Vengrover, "Di geshenishn in poyln un di yidishe protest in argentine," *Dos Naye Vort*, January 1931, 13.

109. Leyzer Stokhammer, "Vi azoy reagirn mir oyf di antiyudishe oystretungen in poyln," in Malach, *Almanakh 1924*, 129.

110. "Protest note fun poylish yidishn farband kegen di onfalen oyf yidn in poyln," *Dos Naye Vort*, December 1932, 14.

111. "Protest note."

112. *Barikht un balans fun protest-akt kegn pogromen oyfn yidn in poyln durkhgefirt 15.12.1932 in salon prince george hall* (Buenos Aires, 1933), 17.

113. *Barikht un balans.*

114. Polish-Jewish organizations in Argentina established a committee that coordinated the protests (in Spanish, Comité de las Sociedades Israelitas Argentinas Pro Ayuda a los Israelitas en Polonia, in Yiddish, Gezelshaftkekher hilfs-komitet letoyves di yidn in poyln).

115. "The New York Protest Meeting Called by Federation of Polish Jews in America (. . .)," December 2, 1931, Jewish Telegraphic Agency. A similar protest was also held in New York on January 8, 1933; "To Protest Pogroms in Poland on January 8th," JTA, January 3, 1933. For a panoramic study of Jewish American involvement in the situation of Jews in post-1918 Poland, see Przemysław Różański, *Stany Zjednoczone wobec kwestii żydowskiej w Polsce 1918–1921* (Gdańsk, Poland: Wydawnictwo Uniwersytetu Gdańskiego, 2007).

116. "Der impozanter protest miting kegn di ekstsesn oyf yidn in poyln," *Dos Naye Vort*, December 1932, 14–15.

117. Gidley, "Diasporic Memory," 654.

118. "Protestn un politishe aktsyes," *Poylishe yidn in doyrem amerike*, 72–75.

119. "Protestn un politishe aktsyes," 15.

120. *Barikht un balans*, 10–12.

121. "For vos un kegn vos protestirn mir?" *Dos Naye Vort*, December 1932, 3.

122. Document no. 236/42, protest campaigns collection, Fundación IWO, Buenos Aires.

123. Tobias Brinkman, "From Immigrants to Supranational Transmigrants and Refugees: Jewish Migrants in New York and Berlin before and after the Great War," *Comparative Studies of South Asia, Africa and the Middle East* 30, no. 1 (2010): 51.

CHAPTER 8

1. Mendelson "Unzer svive, unzer geshtalt," 4.

2. In Katz et al., *Antologye fun der yidisher literatur in argentine*, we find a whole section of "Shrayber-gast" (Visiting writers) that featured Peretz Hirschbein, Hersh Dovid Nomberg, Melech Ravitch, and Borekh Schefner.

3. "Como nos conocen," *Mundo Israelita*, December 13, 1924, no. 80, 1.

4. "Como nos conocen."

5. Katz was invited to visit Soviet Russia as a delegate of *Procor* to promote Jewish colonization there. After visiting Russia, he traveled for a week to Vilna. Afterward, Katz continued to Warsaw, where he also gave a lecture to the Association of Jewish Writers and Journalists.

6. Sh. Erzet, "Pinie katz in vilne," *Di Presse*, November 1, 1929, 6. The article was written in Vilna on October 17, 1929.

7. Erzet.

8. Vilna was often imagined as the capital of the Yiddishland. See Gennady Estraikh, "Yiddish Vilna: A Virtual Capital of a Virtual Land," *Zutot* 3, no. 1 (2003): 135–141.

9. "A lebediger grus fun yudish lebn un yudisher kultur in argentina. Vos dertselt der bekanter yudisher shriftshteler fun argentina, yankev botoshansky," *Grodner Moment Express*, no. 62, March 13, 1931, 7.

10. "A lebediger grus."

11. Yarfitz, "Polacos, White Slaves, and Stille Chuppahs," 77–81.

12. "Gálvez y el anti-Semitismo," *Mundo Israelita*, October 22, 1932, 1–2, quoted in Leonardo Senkman, *La identidad judía en la literatura argentina* (Buenos Aires: Pardes, 1983), 426–27.

13. León Kibrick, "Un falso problema," *Mundo Israelita*, August 18, 1926, no. 172, 1.

14. Kibrick.

15. "Hilfs kampeyn," in Guiser, *Almanakh 1928*, 11.

16. Hershkovich, "Vos der poylish yidisher farband," in Guiser, *Almanakh 1928*, 14–15.

17. Katz, "Der sotsyaler bashtand," 58–59.

18. Eliahu Toker and Ana E. Weinstein, *Trayectoria de una idea: Nueva Sión, 50 años de periodismo judeo-argentino con compromiso: 1948–1998* (Buenos Aires: Ediciones Fundación Mordejai Anilevich, 1999), 7.

19. Feierstein, "New Midrash," 568.

20. Samuel Rollansky, "Y. L. peretzes batsiyung tsu argentine," *Argentiner IWO Shriftn*, no. 1, 1941, 121.

21. *Portretn* did not include any writer working in Argentina. The book received a positive review by Vilna educator and translator Aharon Mark; Aharon Mark, "Portretn fun yidishe shrayber," *Literarishe Bleter*, no. 34, August 25, 1933, 548–49.

22. Nakhmen Mayzel, "Fun vokh tsu vokh," *Literarishe Bleter*, September 1, 1933, 570.

23. Yosef Horn, "La nueva literatura judía en Polonia," *Judaica*, no. 49, July 1937, 7–12.

24. Melech Ravitch, "Di ydishe shilern fun shiler," *Di Presse*, September 8, 1929, no. 4494, 11. The article featured Else Lasker-Schüller, "In der poylisher literatur," *Di Presse*, December 20, 1928, 7.

25. I. Shames, "Danzig un Gdynia," *Di Presse*, September 8, 1929, no. 4494, 13. "Konflikt in farayn fun yidishe literatn un zhurnalistn in varshe iber palestiner geshenishn," *Di Presse*, October 30, 1929, 7; "Shtimen fun yidishe dikhter un literatn vegn di haynt anfaln oyfn literatn farayn," *Di Presse*, January 6, 1929, 8. "Far di yidishe veltlekhe shuln in poyln," *Di Presse*, October 31, 1929, 6. When the Warsaw *Haynt* called for stopping municipal and kehilla support for the TSYSHO schools, TSYSHO accused *Haynt* of "being a tool in the hands of Polish reactionaries."

26. B. Abramson, "'Di sheyne helene' hot ongehoybn den politishn sezon in poyln," *Di Presse*, November 1, 1929, 8. The problem was followed in subsequent issues.

27. Borekh Schefner, "A yidisher kontsert in a poylish shtetl," *Di Presse*, April 8, 1933, 6.

28. Yaakov Zerubavel, "Alveltlekhe konferents fun yidishn visenshaftlekhn institute," *Di Presse*, December 1, 1929, 7; "Likvidirt di milkhome tsvishn yidish aktyorn org. in nord amerike un in poyln," *Di Presse*, December 18, 1929, 8.

29. "A par sho bay der arbet fun opatoshu 'poylishe velder,'" *Di Presse*, clipping in Fundación IWO, Buenos Aires, unknown page and issue, 1928.

30. Abraham Goldberg, "Ydishe karbones fun revolutsye," *Yidische Zaitung*, June 24, 1926, 4(?).

31. Abraham Goldberg, "Tragishe forfalen un shlagerayen in yamim noraim in poyln," *Yidishe Zaitung*, October 24, 1926, page unknown; "Men zukht in poyln a yidishn minister," *Yidische Zaitung*, June 10, 1926, 3(?).

32. Abraham Goldberg, "Kalman un zelde forn keyn argentine," in *10 yor Yidishe Zaitung* (Buenos Aires, 1924), 74–75.

33. Commissioning foreign versus Argentine authors was a result of the growing financial prosperity of the Yiddish journals. See Rollansky, *Dos yidishe gedrukte*, 131.

34. "Haynt vern benayt di sitzungen fun poylishn sejm," *Di Presse*, September 5, 1929, no. 4549, 1.

35. S. Lvovski, "Oys klezmer in galitsie," *Di Presse*, November 5, 1929, 8.

36. "A 'bakhurte' vos iz gor geven a manparshoyn," "Bilder un pasirungen fun alter heym," *Di Presse*, November 9, 1929, unknown page. "Shoyderlekhe selbst-mordn in varshe," *Di Presse*, October 3, 1928, 4.

37. K. Israel (probably Israel Kahan) "Yidishe nekome," *Di Yidische Zaitung*, October 7, 1925, 7.

38. Hirschbein, *Fun vayte lender*, 41–44.

39. Hirschbein, 45.

40. Hirschbein, 44.

41. Hirschbein, 48–49.

42. Hirschbein, "Argentine (briv fun veg)," 2.

43. Rebecca Kobrin, "The Shtetl by the Highway: The East European City in New York's Landsmanshaft Press, 1921–39," *Prooftexts* 26 (1 and 2) 2006: 107–37.

44. Hirschbein, *Fun vayte lender*, 58.

45. Hirschbein, "Argentine (briv fun veg)," 2.

46. Some Jewish immigrants did travel back to eastern Europe, a practice that was probably more frequent in the United States than in the Argentine context. See, for instance, Daniel Soyer, "Revisiting the Old World: American Jewish Tourists in Interwar Eastern Europe," in *Forging Modern Jewish Identities*, ed. Susan Tananbaum, Sam Bloom, and Michael Berkowitz (London: Valentine-Mitchell, 2003).

47. Nomberg, "Di argentinishe rayze," 63.

48. Nomberg, 82–83.

49. Nomberg, 59–66.

50. Hirschbein, *Fun vayte lender*, 59.

51. Hirschbein.

52. Hirschbein.

53. Dan G. Hertz, "Psychological and Psychosocial Adjustments of Migrants: Families in a Changing Environment," in *Psychological Aspects of Geographical Moves: Homesickness and Acculturation Stress*, ed. Miranda van Tilburg and Ad Vingerhoets, 77–79 (Amsterdam: Amsterdam University Press, 2005).

54. Eugene Tartakovsky, "Cultural Identities of Adolescent Immigrants: A Three-Year Longitudinal Study Including the Pre-Migration Period," *Journal of Youth and Adolescence* 5 (2009): 654–71.

55. Nomberg, "Di argentinishe rayze," 62.

56. Hirschbein, *Fun vayte lender*, 60–61.

57. Hirschbein, 56–60.

58. Nomberg, "Di argentinishe rayze," 62.

59. Schussheim, *Tsu der geshikhte*, 11–12.

60. Hirschbein, *Fun vayte lender*, 58.

61. Hirschbein, 60.

62. Nomberg, "Di argentinishe rayze," 61.

63. Nomberg, 60. Aaron Leib Schussheim of the Poylisher Farband also recalled

that many Jewish immigrants chose Argentina only because it was not possible to go to the United States, Schussheim, *Tsu der geshikhte*, 11–12.

64. Centro Mark Turkow, Archivo de Palabra, no. 6, Samuel Blutrajt. In 1925, at the age of seventeen, Blutrajt immigrated to Argentina from Polish Volhynia.

65. Hirschbein, *Fun vayte lender*, 60.

66. Hirschbein, 14.

67. Pinie Katz, "Der argentiner tsvayg fun der yidisher literatur. Forvort," in Katz et al., *Antologye fun der yidisher literatur*, 12.

68. Eliahu Toker, *El ídish es también Latinoamérica* (Buenos Aires: Ediciones Desde la Gente, Instituto Movilizador de Fondos Cooperativos, 2003), 17. These neologisms are a mix of the words *castellano* and *español* for Spanish and the Spanish transliteration of the word Yiddish—*ídish*.

69. Gershon Henekh Zakhak, "Ayngevanderte un argentiner yidn," *Di Yidische Zaitung*, September 8, 1926, 3–5.

70. Zakhak.

71. Wolff, "Home That Never Was," 197–215.

72. Katz, "Argentiner yidn (esey),"395.

73. Katz.

74. *Di Presse yubiley numer 1918–1928* (Buenos Aires, 1928).

75. Katz touched on the subject of Yiddish localism in numerous articles in *Di Presse* in 1925. Rollansky, *Dos yidishe gedrukte*, 137.

76. Pinie Katz, "Der argentiner tsvayg," 12.

77. Quoted in "Bibliografia," *Judaica*, no. 62, 36. Underlining Jewish immersion and interest in the Argentine public sphere, Katz also included in the volume a number of Spanish works translated into Yiddish.

78. Pinie Katz, *Geklibene shriftn*, vol. 7 (Buenos Aires: Gezelshaftlekher komitet baym farlag "IKUF," 1947), 122–23, quoted in Scheintuch, "Safrut yidish be-argentina ksafrut me'agrim," 200–201, in *Proceedings of the World Congress of Jewish Studies*, vol 4 of Division D (Hebrew Language, Yidish Literature, Jewish Languages) (Jerusalem: World Union of Jewish Studies, 1973),

79. Rollansky, *Dos yidishe gedrukte*, 137.

80. Moyshe Granitstein was born in Kovel (Kowel), Poland in 1897. After World War I, he published for *Di Yidishe Tribune* (Warsaw), *Voliner Gedank* (Lutsk), and *Di Yidishe Vokh* (Rivne). After immigrating to Argentina in 1927, he worked as a teacher in Jewish schools and published in *Di Presse*. He published numerous books, yet usually in very small editions. Granitstein died in Buenos Aires in 1956.

81. Moyshe Granitstein, "Tsi ken argentiner yidishe literatur zikh farneymen durkhoys mit lokaln shtayger? (a politishn artikl)," in *Fun tkhum tsu tkhum. Zikhroynes un betrakhtungen iber shtetl* (Buenos Aires, 1933), 36–37.

82. Granitstein, 31–38.

83. H. Gold, "Fun dem argentiner yidishn kultur-front," *Literarishe Bleter*, no. 6 (561), February 8, 1935, 89.

84. Katz et al., *Antologye fun der yidisher literatur*, 12.

85. Claudia Ferman, "Nuevas localidades para la producción cultural: diáspora, identidad y escritura," paper presented at the conference of Latin American Studies Association in Gaudalajara, Mexico, April 17–19, 1997, printed proceedings, 9.

86. Liliana Ruth Feierstein, "*Oyf di bregn fun Plata*—Am Ufer des Silberflusses.Versuch einer Topographie jüdischer Erfahrungen in Argentinien," in *Der Ort des Juden-*

tums in der Gegenwart, Michael Kümper, Johannes Schwarz, Jens Neumann, Anna Lipphardt, Maria Vassilikou, and Hiltrud Wallenborn eds., 93–118 (Berlin: Bebra Verlag, 2006).

87. Samuel. Rollansky, ed., *Tsvishn shtotishe vent*, vol. 2 of *Argentinish* (Buenos Aires: Literatur gezelshaft baym iwo in argentine, 1976), 9–16; Horn, *Arum yidisher literatur*, 60–62.

88. Grines, "In loyf fun zvantsik yor," in *Almanakh fun ostrog-voliner landslayt farayn*, 10.

89. Scheintuch, "Safrut yidish be-argentina," 197–98.

90. Samuel Rollansky described Alpersohn as the strongest critic of the JCA. His criticism was voiced as early as 1911 in his text "Halutsim ha-rishonim," Rollansky, *Dos yidishe gedrukte*, 142.

91. Zhitnitsky, "Transformatsyes," 77.

92. Katz, "Der argentiner tsvayg," in Katz et al., *Antologye fun der yidisher literatur*, 14.

93. Rollansky, *Dos yidishe gedrukte*, 137.

94. "Dos yidishe kultur-lebn in argentine. A shmues mit yankev botoshansky," *Literarishe Bleter*, no. 12, March 20, 1931, 229, 230.

95. Rollansky, *Dos yidishe gedrukte*, 135–38.

96. Samuel Rollansky, *Argentine. Fun land un yishev. Poezye, proze, publitsistik un bilder* (Buenos Aires: Alter-Rozental-Fond, 1960), 15–19.

97. Rollansky, *Dos yidishe gedrukte*, 136.

98. Rollansky, 149–50. Rollansky gave the example of Russian-born Yankev Eisenstein and Yankev Streicher, who adopted a new modernist style in the 1920s and expressed the pain and misery of proletarian immigrants.

99. Amalia Sánchez Sivori, "La inmigración y la literatura argentina," in Cúneo et al., *Inmigración y nacionalidad*, 114.

100. Samuel Rollansky noted that nostalgia (*benkshaft* in Yiddish) and dreaming (*farkholemkay*t) were two of the main themes of Argentine Yiddish writing. Rollansky, *Dos yidishe gedrukte*, 147.

101. "15 yoriker yubileum fun m.d. guiser shafn," *Dos Naye Vort*, October 1932, no. 140, 12.

102. Moisés David Guiser, "A briv," *Argentinish*, vol. 2, 93.

103. Moisés David Guiser, "Vi orem ikh bin," "Foran aze ayner," *Argentinish*, vol. 2, 155–56.

104. Pinchas Bizberg, "Moisés David Guiser," in *Dos gezang fun a lebn* by Moisés David Guiser (Buenos Aires: Tsentral farband fun poylishe yidn in argentine, 1953), 10–16.

105. Moisés David Guiser, "Argentina," from the poem "Der blonder gaucho," originally 1933, in *Argentinish*, vol. 2, 200.

106. Rollansky, *Dos yidishe gedrukte*, 155.

107. Bizberg, "Moisés David Guiser," in Guiser, *Dos gezang fun a lebn*, 15; Rollansky, *Dos yidishe gedrukte*, 155.

108. David Szyszacki, "Tsu der geshikhte fun di yidishe," 137.

109. Interview with Jerzy Szeferblum, Cyfrowe Archiwum Historii Lokalnej w Buenos Aires in cooperation with Biblioteka Domeyki w Buenos Aires: recorded by Fundacja Ośrodka Karta, sig. CATL 63 L / 8.2.3.

110. Centro Mark Turkow, Archivo de la Palabra, no. 47, León Menin.

111. The 1931 report of the Polish Embassy specified that re-emigration from Argentina to Poland in the 1921 to 1937 period was at a 14.5 percent level. That figure included both Jewish and gentile immigrants.

112. Zahra, *Great Departure*, 69.

113. Ismach, "Vos hobn landsmanshaftn oyfgeton," 67.

114. Milberg, "A por verter tsu unzer hayntiker yuvl," 12.

115. Centro Mark Turkow, Archivo de la Palabra, no. 6, Samuel Blutrajt.

116. Centro Mark Turkow, Archivo de la Palabra, no. 32, Guitl Kanutsky.

117. Centro Mark Turkow, Archivo de la Palabra, no. 1, Flora Abzac. Mrs. Abzac was born near Łódź in 1917 and immigrated to Argentina in 1930.

118. Moisés David Guiser, "Almacen," in Katz et al., *Antologye fun der yidisher literatur*, 160.

119. Centro Mark Turkow, Archivo de la Palabra, no. 6, Samuel Blutrajt.

120. Zalman Wassertzug was born in 1904 in Lubin, Włocławek county, Poland. Between 1923 and 1925, he studied in a state and Jewish religious teacher seminary in Warsaw. Between 1925 and 1927, Wassertzug worked as a teacher in Janusz Korczak's orphanage. In 1927 he immigrated to Argentina. There, Wassertzug initially taught in a Jewish school in a JCA colony and later moved to Buenos Aires, where he wrote articles and children's stories for *Di Yidische Zaitung*.

121. Zalman Wassertzug, "Hoben im geshoynt di merder," in Katz et al., *Antologye fun der yidisher literatur*, 331

122. Goldstein was born in 1900 in Łosice, which is one hundred kilometers east of Warsaw, immigrated to Argentina in 1923, and was forced to go to the Soviet Union in 1932.

123. Moshe Z. Goldstein, "Opgebrokhene tsvayg," originally 1935, in Katz et al., *Antologye fun der yidisher literatur*, 137–42.

124. Nehemías Zucker, "Shabes likhter," in Katz et al., *Antologye fun der yidisher literatur*, 663.

125. Berl Grinberg was born in Warsaw in 1906, where he studied both in a religious and an assimilationist school. From a young age, he worked as a shoemaker and hatter. He became involved early in the proletarian movement. In 1923, Grinberg immigrated to Argentina, lived for two years with his uncle in Cordoba and from 1925 in Buenos Aires. Grinberg worked as a linotypist in *Di Presse*, where he published most of his short stories. He was also an editor of almanacs of the Poylisher Farband and a regular contributor to Warsaw's *Literarishe Bleter*.

126. Berl Grinberg, "Senyorita esters shabesdike likhtlekh," *Argentinish*, vol. 2, 1939, 392–403.

127. Deutsch, *Crossing Borders*, 48.

128. Moshe Kaufman, "Der taykh parana (poeme)," in Katz et al., *Antologye fun der yidisher literatur*, 698–701.

129. Kohet Kliguer, born in Volodimir Volinsk in 1904, later lived in Warsaw, where he began to publish in *Wokhenshrift for literatur un kunst* and *Literarishe Bleter*, as well as a number of regional periodicals. He immigrated to Argentina in 1936.

130. Horn, "Poylishe yidn: di shefer," in *Poylishe yidn in doyrem amerike*, 72.

131. Aba Kliger, "Oyfn di bregn fun plata," in Katz et al., *Antologye fun der yidisher literatur*, 708–9.

132. Aba Kliger, "Zumerland," in Katz et al., *Antologye fun der yidisher literatur*, 720.

133. Aba Kliger, "Tango," 707; "Karnaval," 709 in Katz et al., *Antologye fun der yidisher literatur*.

134. Rollansky, *Dos yidishe gedrukte*, 147.

135. Lazaro Shallman, untitled, in *Comunidad judia de Buenos Aires 1894–1994: AMIA 100 años* (Buenos Aires: AMIA, Editorial Milá, 1995), 74.

136. Hirsh Blostein was born in Kiejdany, Lithuania, in 1895. He worked as a Hebrew teacher in the Caucasus and later moved to Minsk. He immigrated to Argentina in 1925. In Buenos Aires, he worked for the journals *Di Presse* and *Nayvelt*. In 1931, following accusations of endorsing communism, Blostein was forced to leave for the Soviet Union. He was a major figure in the so-called *komlit* (communist literature) and attracted many other writers to working-class themes. His poems also featured the Jewish proletarian schools, their students, and the parents of the immigrant generation.

Yankev Plafon was born in Grodzisk Mazowiecki near Warsaw in 1897. He spent his youth in Kovna (Kaunas), Lithuania, and studied literature in Berlin for a year before immigrating to Argentina in 1924. In Argentina, he was close to the proleterian publishing house Nayvelt. He died in 1936.

137. Moshe Kaufman, "Lirisher peizazh," *Argentinish*, 87–89.

138. Mendel Pschepiurka, "Miniaturn,"in Katz et al., *Antologye fun der yidisher literatur*, 573–80.

139. Mendel Pschepiurka, "Epes vegn der geystikn geshtaltung fun di yidishe masn," *Di Presse*, October 22, 1928, page unknown.

140. Hirsh Blostein, "Oyfn Avenida Alvear," in Katz et al., *Antologye fun der yidisher literatur*, 88.

141. Schneur Wassernam, "Florida," *Argentinish*, vol. 2, 77–78.

142. Yosef Rabinovich, "In der fremd," in Katz et al., *Antologye fun der yidisher literatur*, 753–56.

143. Leonardo Senkman, *La identidad judía en la literatura argentina* (Buenos Aires: Pardes, 1983), 106–22.

144. See Diner, *Roads Taken*.

EPILOGUE

1. Marcos Regalsky, "Konstituirung fun der yidisher natsye," in Regalsky, *Tsvishn tsvey velt milkhomes*, 403–8.

2. Luis Roniger, "Latin American Jews and Processes of Legitimization and De-Legitimization," *Journal of Modern Jewish Studies* 9, no. 2 (2010): 185.

3. Malena Chinski, "Incertidubre, búsqueda y duelo: la Shoá desda la perspectiva de los familiares de las víctimas en Argentina," *Temas de Nuestra América* 32, no. 60 (2016): 187–202.

4. Mendel Meiern-Laser, *Dos yidishe shulvezn in argentine* (Buenos Aires, 1948), 129.

5. Zadoff, *Historia de la educacción judía*, 331.

6. Meiern-Laser, *Dos yidishe shulvezn in argentine*, 178.

7. Flyer, "Boy komitet farn aygenem binyen fun der sholem aleichem shul," Laser collection, folder TSVYSHO, Central Archive for the History of Jewish People, quoted in Zadoff, *Historia de la educacción judía*, 329–30.

8. Nehemías Zucker, ed., *Yor-bukh fun yidishn yishev in argentine 5706* (Yearbook of the Argentine Jewry 1945–1946), vol. 1 (Buenos Aires, 1946), quoted in Le-

ondardo Senkman, "Los sobrevivientes de la Shoa en Argentina: su imagen y memoria en la sociedad general y judía: 1945–1950," *Arquivo Maaravi: Revista Digital de Estudos Judaicos da UFMG* 1, 1(2007): 68–70.

9. Dujovne, *Una historia del libro judío*, 96–100.

10. Alejandro Dujovne, "The Book as a Combat Weapon: Intellectuals, Patronage and Institutions in the Establishment of the Argentine Jewish Publishing Field, 1920–1980," *Perush: Online Journal of Jewish Scholarship and Interpretation*, vol. 2 (2010), unnumbered.

11. Jan Schwarz, *Survivors and Exiles: Yiddish Culture after the Holocaust* (Detroit, MI: Wayne State University Press, 2015), 93.

12. Abraham Nowersztern, "Dos poylishe yidntum," *Book Peddler: Newsletter of the National Yiddish Book Exchange* 15 (1993): 18.

13. Schwarz, *Survivors and Exiles*, 116.

14. See Raanan Rein, *Los muchachos peronistas judíos: Los argentinos judíos y el apoyo a justicialismo* (Buenos Aires: Sudamericana, 2015); Lawrence D. Bell, "The Jews and Perón. Communal Politics and National Identity in Peronist Argentina, 1946–1955" (PhD diss., Ohio State University, 2002).

15. Zadoff, *Historia de la educación judía*, 391–92.

16. Dujovne, *Una historia del libro judío*, 172–77.

17. Dujovne, 229–32.

18. Dujovne, 177–82.

19. Dujovne, 271.

20. Shandler, *Adventures in Yiddishland*, 48.

21. See Visacovsky's works, *Argentinos, judíos*; "Una historia antifascista: Argentina, Brasil y la identidad icufista," *Travesía. Revista de Historia Económica y Social* 17, no. 1 (2015): 79–103.

22. Zadoff, *Historia de la educacción*, 446.

23. Lawrence D. Bell, "Bitter Conquest: Zionists against Progressive Jews and the Making of the Post-War Jewish Politics in Argentina," *Jewish History* 17 (2003): 285–308.

24. In 1955, the ICUF school had around twenty thousand students. See Visacovsky, *Argentinos, judíos*, 23.

Selected Bibliography

Primary Sources

Archives and Libraries

Archivo General del Ministerio de Relacions Exteriores y Culto (AMREC)
Archiwum Akt Nowych, Warsaw
Biblioteca Nacional, Buenos Aires
Central Archive for the History of Jewish People, Jerusalem
Centro Marc Turkow, Buenos Aires
Cyfrowe Archiwum Historii Lokalnej, Ośrodek Karta, Warsaw
Fundación IWO, Buenos Aires
Jewish Historical Institut (ŻIH), Warsaw
National Library of Israel, Jerusalem
National Library of Poland, Warsaw
National Yiddish Book Center, Amherst, Massachusetts
Tel-Aviv University Library
Warsaw University Library
YIVO Institute for Jewish Research, New York

Newspapers and Periodicals

In Argentina

Di Presse
Di Yidische Zaitung
Dos Naye Vort
Far grois un klein
Judaica
Juventud
Mundo Israelita
Penimer un penimlekh
Semanario Hebreo
Vida Nuestra

In Poland

Chwila
Der Moment
Der Yud

Emigrant w Argentynie
Grodner Moment Express
Haynt
Hayntige Nayes
Hazefirah
Izraelita
Literarishe Bleter
Monitor Polski
Nasz Przegląd
Pinsker Lebn
Tygodnik Żydowski
Unzer Expres
Wiadomości ŻTK
Yidishe Emigratsye Tsaytung

Books, Memoirs, and Brochures

Almanakh 1926. Driter zamlbukh aroysgegeben fun poylish yidishen farband in argentine. Buenos Aires: Poylish yidisher farband in argentine, 1926.

Almanakh fun ostrog-voliner landslayt farayn un umgegent in argentine 1924–1944. Buenos Aires: Ostrog-voliner landslayt farayn un umgegent in argentine, 1944.

Alsina, Juan A. *La inmigración en el primer siglo de la indepdendencía.* Buenos Aires: Felipé S. Alsina, 1910.

Alter, Leon. "Wychodźstwo żydowskie." *Kwartalnik Instytutu Naukowego do Badań Emigracji i Kolonizacji* 1 (1926): 80–91.

Alter, Victor. *Tsu den yidn frage in poyln.* Warsaw, 1937.

Argentine un uruguay far dem YIVO. Barikht fun der aktsye far dem yidishn visenshaftlekhn institut. Vilna, Poland: YIVO Yidisher visenshaftlekher institut, 1934.

Balance General del Comité Central Pro-Victimas Israelitas de la Guerra, desde 1.12.1917 hasta 30.11.1918. Buenos Aires, 1918.

Barikht fun der aktsye durkhgefirt in argentine fun sof may biz november. Buenos Aires: Hilfs komitet far di yidish veltlekhe shuln in poyln, 1931.

Barikht un balans fun protest-akt kegn pogromen oyfn yidn in poyln durkhgefirt 15.12.1932 in salon prince george hall. Buenos Aires, 1933.

Bizberg, Pinchas. "Konflikt tsvishn di yidishe kolonistn in argentine un der lokaler JCA-administratsye." *Argentiner IWO Shriftn* 4 (1947): 85–107.

Botoshansky, Yankev. *Portretn fun yidishe shrayber.* Warsaw: Literarishe Bleter, 1933.

Bressler, Wolf, and Samuel Glazerman eds. *Lexicón de los hombres de bien de la colectividad israelita en la Argentina.* Buenos Aires: Drukeray Kultur, 1941.

Chasanovitch, Leon. *Die Krise der jüdischen Kolonisation in Argentinien und der moralische Bankerott der J.C.A.-Administration.* Stanislau, Austrian Galicia: Verlag Bildung, 1910.

Comunidad judía de Buenos Aires 1894–1994: AMIA 100 años. Buenos Aires: AMIA, Editorial Milá, 1995.

Di Presse yubiley numer 1918–1928. Buenos Aires, 1928.

Dostal, Wacław. *Argentyna: Monografie Geograficzno-Handlowe Informatora Eksportowego*, vol. 4. Warsaw, 1937.

Driter almanakh fun farband fun galitsianer yidn in buenos aires. Buenos Aires: Farband fun galitsianer yidn in buenos aires, 1933.

Ershter almanakh fun hilfs farayn fun lemberger un umgegent. Buenos Aires: Hilfs farayn fun lemberger un umgegent, 1934.

50 Años de colonización judía en la Argentina. Buenos Aires: DAIA, 1939.

Finkelstein, Chaim. *Egalitishe lern-program far zeks-klasiker tsugab-shul.* Buenos Aires: Tsentrale veltlekhe yidishe shul-organizatsye in argentine, 1943. Reprint, edited by Bernardo Danker. Buenos Aires: Asociación Judeo-Argentina de Estudios Históricos, 1985.

Fuftsik yor yidisher yishev, tsvantsig yor "Di Presse." Buenos Aires: Di Presse, 1938.

Fularski, Mieczysław. *Kryzys emigracyjny a polska polityka kolonialna.* Warsaw, Instytut Wydawniczy Ligi Morskiej i Kolonialnej, 1927.

Gerchunoff, Alberto. *Los gauchos judíos.* La Plata, Argentina, 1910. Reprint, Buenos Aires: Aguilar, 1975.

Granitstein, Moshe. *Avantures fun haver hamerl.* Buenos Aires, 1934

———. *Fun tkhum tsu tkhum. Zikhroynes un betrakhtungen iber shtetl.* Buenos Aires, 1933.

Grinstein, Martin. *Recuerdos de Entre Rios. Colonia San Antonio y Pueblo Cazés.* Buenos Aires: Acervo Culural Editores, 1998.

Guiser, Moisés David, ed. *Almanakh 1928. Ferter zamlbukh aroysgegeben fun poylish yidishn farband in argentine.* Buenos Aires: Poylish Yidisher Farband in Argentine, 1928.

———. *Dos gezang fun a lebn.* Buenos Aires: Tsentral farband fun poylishe yidn in argentine, 1953.

Halpern, Leopold. *Polityka żydowska w Sejmie i Senacie Rzeczpospolitej Polskiej, 1919–1933.* Warsaw: Instytut Badań Spraw Narodowościowych, 1933.

Hirschbein, Peretz. *Fun vayte lender. Argentine, Brazil, yuni, November 1914.* New York: Farlag Tog, 1916.

Horn, Yosef. *Arum yidisher literatur un yidishe shrayber: Ophandlungen un fartsaykhenungen.* Buenos Aires: Altveltlekher yidisher kultur-kongres, argentiner aptayl, 1973.

Ismach, Borekh "Vos hobn landsmanshaftn oyfgeton far di imigrantn in zayere naye heymer." *Argentiner IWO Shriftn* no. 15 (1989): 67–68.

Katz, Pinie. *Geklibene shriftn,* vol. 4. Buenos Aires: Gezelshaftlekher komitet baym farlag "IKUF," 1946.

———. *Geklibene shriftn,* vol. 7. Buenos Aires: Gezelshaftlekher komitet baym farlag "IKUF," 1947.

———.*Tsu der geshikhte fun yidisher zhurnalistik in argentine.* Buenos Aires: Yidishn literaten un zhurnalistn farayn, 1929.

Katz, Pinie, Yankev Botoshansky, Salomón Suscovich, Wolf Bressler, and Abraham Mitelberg, eds. *Antologye fun der yidisher literatur in Argentine.* Buenos Aires: A gezelshaftlekher komitet 1ekoyved dem 25-yorikn yubiley fun der teglekher tsaytung Di Prese, 1944.

Landsmanshaftn. Spetsyele oysgabe fun di tsentrale fun di faraynikte poylish-yidishe landsmanshaftn in argentine tsum dritn zid amerikaner tsuzamenfor. Buenos Aires: Di tsentrale fun di faraynikte poylish-yidishe landsmanshaftn in argentine, 1939.

Lang, Abe, Izaak Lesz, and Izaak Nożyk. *Oyfn veg keyn Buenos Aires.* Warsaw: Folks-Teater, 1931.

Lestschinsky, Jacob. *Di lage fun yidn in latayn-amerikaner lender.* New York: World Jewish Congress, 1948.

———. *Di onhoybn fun der emigratsye un kolonizatsye bay yidn: in 19-tn yorhundert.* Berlin: Emigdirect, 1929.

———. *National Groups in Polish Emigration.* New York: Conference on Jewish Relations, 1943.

Literat-Golombek, Lea. *Moisés Ville crónica de un shtetl argentino.* Jerusalem: La Semana Publicaciones, 1982.

Londres, Albert. *The Road to Buenos Aires.* London: Constable, 1928.

Malach, Leyb, ed. *Almanakh 1924. Ershter zamlbukh aroysgegeben fun poylish yidishen farayn "agudas ahim."* Buenos Aires: Poylish yidisher farayn "agudas ahim," 1924.

———, ed. *Almanakh 1925. Tvayter almankh aroysgegeben fun poylish yidishn farband in argentine.* Buenos Aires: Poylish yidisher farband in argentine, 1925.

———. *Ibergus.* Buenos Aires, 1926).

Medio siglo en el surco argentino. Cincuentenario de la Jewish Colonization Association (J.C.A). Homenaje de la Delegación de Asociaciones Israelitas Argentinas (D.A.I.A) a la Jewish Colonization Organization (J.C.A.) con motivo de su cincuentenario 1891 agosto 1941. Buenos Aires: D.A.I.A, 1942.

Meiern-Laser, Mendel. *Dos yidishe shulvezn in argentine.* Buenos Aires, 1948.

Memoria de gran campaña del million en Republica Argentina. Buenos Aires, 1939.

Mendelson, Yosef (José), ed. *Oyf di bregn fun plata. Zamelbukh.* Buenos Aires: Farlag Yidische Zaitung, 1919.

Niger, Samuel, and Jacob Shatzky, eds. *Leksikon der nayer yidisher literatur.* New York: Altveltlekher yidisher kultur-kongres, 1956.

Nomberg, Hersh Dovid. "Di argentinishe rayze." In *Dos bukh felyetonen.* Warsaw: Sz. Jaczkowski, 1924.

———. *Mayne rayze iber rusland.* Warsaw: Kultur-Lige, 1928.

Pamiętniki Emigrantów z Ameryki Południowej. Warsaw: Instytut Gospodarstwa Społecznego, 1937.

Pawłowski, Stanisław. *O emigracji żydów z Polski i ich kolonizacji.* Warsaw: Liga Morska i Kolonialna, 1937.

Peretz Hirschbein. Tsu zayn zekhtsiksten geboyrntog. New York: Hirschbein yovl komitet, 1941.

Poylishe yidn in doyrem amerike. Zamlbukh tsum 25-yoriken yuvl fun organizirtn poylishn yidntum in argentine, 1916–1941. Buenos Aires: Tsentral farband fun poylishe yidn in argentine, 1941.

Regalsky, Marcos. *Tsvishn tsvey velt milkhomes. Di goyrl yorn 1918–1945.* Buenos Aires: Yovl komitet tsum 60-tn geboyrn tog funem mahber, 1946.

Reysen, Zalmen. *Leksikon fun der yidisher literatur, prese un filologye.* Vilna: Vilner Ferlag fun B. Kletskin, 1926–29.

Rollansky, Samuel. *Argentine. Fun land un yishev. Poezye, proze, publitsistik un bilder.* Buenos Aires: Alter-Rozental-Fond 1960.

———. *Dos yidishe gedrukte vort un teater in argentine.* Buenos Aires, 1941.

———"Y.L. peretzes batsiyung tsu argentine," *Argentiner IWO Shriftn* 1, 1941.

———, ed. *Peretz Hirschbein, drames, veltrayzen, zikhroynes.* Buenos Aires: Yosef Lifshitz-fond fun der literatur gezelshaft baym IWO, 1968.

———, ed. *Tsvishn shtotishe vent.* Vol. 2 of *Argentinish.* Buenos Aires: Literatur gezelshaft baym iwo in argentine, 1976.

Schussheim, Aharon Leyb. *Tsu der geshikhte fun yidisher yishev in argentine.* Buenos Aires, 1954.

Shakhbar, Bargash. *Argentina. Leyent un veyst vohin ir fort.* Berdichev, 1892.
Shatzky, Jacob. *Comunidades judías en Latinoamerica.* Buenos Aires: Ediciones del American Jewish Committee, 1952.
Sociedad Hebraica Argentina. *Memoria y Balance (1927–1928).* Buenos Aires: Sociedad Hebraica Argentina, 1928.
Szyszacki, David. "Tsu der geshikhte fun di yidishe landsmanshaftn in argentine." *Argentiner IWO Shriftn* 13 (1981): 132–34.
Tartakower, Arie. *Dos yidishe emigratsye-problem un der yidisher velt-kongres.* Paris: Ekzekutiv-komitet forn yidishn velt-kongres, 1935.
———. *In Search of Home Freedom.* London: World Jewish Congress, 1958.
———. *Emigracja żydowska z Polski.* Warsaw: Instytut Badań Narodowościowych, 1939.
Triwaks, Hirsch, ed. *Yovl bukh: A sakhakl fun 50 yor yidishen lebn in argentine, lekoved "Di Ydische Zaitung" tsu iren 25-yorigen yubileum.* Buenos Aires: Yidische Zaitung, 1940.
Tsvayter almanakh fun farband fun galitsianer yidn in buenos aires. Buenos Aires: Farband fun galitsianer yidn in Buenos Aires, 1929.
Wald, Pinie. *Koshmar.* Buenos Aires, 1929.
Wiadomości o Argentynie do użytków użytku wychodźców wraz z samouczkiem języka hiszpańskiego. Biblioteczka Syndykatu Emigracyjnego, vol. 2. Warsaw: Syndykat Emigracyjny, 1937.
Włodek, Józef. *Argentyna i emigracja ze szczególnym uwzględnieniem emigracji polskiej.* Warsaw: Wydawnictwo M. Arct, 1923.
Yedvabnik, Yankev. *Di beshraybung fon argentina un ire kolonyen.* Warsaw, 1893.
Yuvl oysgabe tsu der 15 yoriker gezelshaftlekher tetigkayt fun vengrover landslayt farayn in argentine. Buenos Aires, Vengrover landslayt farayn,1940.
Załęcki, Gustaw. *Kilka słów o nowoczesnym imperializmie narodowym.* Warsaw: Naukowy Instytut Emigracyjny, 1928.
Zamlbukh fun h.d. nomberg shrayber farayn in argentine. Buenos Aires, 1962.
Zhitnitsky, Lazaro. "Di landsmanschaftn in argentine." *Argentiner IWO Shriftn* 3 (1945): 155–61.
———. "Yidn in Buenos Aires loyt der munitsipaler tseylung fun 1936." *Argentiner IWO Shriftn* 3 (1945): 5–22.
Zucker, Nehemías. *Fun alts tsu bislekh.* Buenos Aires: Farlag "Kundas," 1935.
Zucker, Nehemías, and Wolf Bressler, eds. *Yor-bukh fun yidishn yishev in argentine 1945–1946.* Buenos Aires: Farlag Idish 1946.

Secondary Sources

Adamovsky, Ezequiel. *Historia de la clase media argentina: Apogeo y decadencía de una ilusión, 1919–2003.* Buenos Aires: Planete, 2009.
Aizenberg, Edna. *Parricide on the Pampa? A New Study and Translation of Alberto Gerchunoff's Los gauchos judíos.* Madrid: Iberoamericana, 2000.
Alberto, Paulina, and Eduardo Elena. *Rethinking Race in Modern Argentina.* Cambridge: Cambridge University Press, 2016.
Albiez, Sarah, Nelly Castro, Lara Jüssen, and Eva Youkhana. Introduction to *Etnicidad, ciudadanía y partenecía: Practicás, teoria y dimensiones espaciales,* edited by Sarah Albiez, 11–34. Madrid: Iberoamericana, 2011.

Aliano, David. "Identity in Transatlantic Play: Il Duce's National Project in Argentina." PhD diss., City University of New York, 2008.

Anderson, Benedict. *Imagined Communities: Reflections on the Origin and Spread of Nationalism*. London: Verso, 2006.

Appadurai, Arjun. *Nowoczesność bez granic. Kulturowe wymiary globalizacji*. Kraków: Universitas, 2005.

Astiz, María Fernanda. "Jewish Acculturation: Identity, Society and Schooling Buenos Aires, Argentina (1890–1930)." *Journal of Jewish Identities* 3, no. 1 (2010): 41–66.

Astro, Alan. "Persistencía del ídish en Argentina: Reflexiones comparativas con Estados Unidos y Canadá." Unpublished work in progress, July 8, 2014, http://ides.org.ar/archivos/7675.

Avni, Haim. *Argentina y las migraciones judías. De la Inquisición al Holocausto y después*. Buenos Aires: Editorial Milá, AMIA, Hebrew University of Jerusalem, 2005.

Avni, Haim, and Sibila Seibert. "La agricultura judía en Argentina ¿éxito o fracaso?" *Desarollo Economico* 22, no. 88 (1983): 535–48.

Bacon, Gershon. "National Revival, Ongoing Acculturation: Jewish Education in Interwar Poland." *Simon Dubnow Institut Jahrbuch* 1 (2002): 71–92.

Baily, Samuel L. *Immigrants in the Lands of Promise: Italians in Buenos Aires and New York City, 1870–1914*. Ithaca, NY: Cornell University Press, 2004.

Bargman, Daniel. "Construcción de la Nación entre la asimilación de los inmigrantes y el particularismo. Las escuelas de las colonias agrícolas judías." In *Patrimonio Cultural y Diversidad Creativa en el Sistema Educativo*, edited by Leticia Maronese, 19–36. Buenos Aires: Gobierno de la Ciudad Buenos Aires, 2006.

Bartal, Israel. *The Jews of Eastern Europe, 1772–1881*. Philadelphia: University of Pennsylvania Press, 2006.

Bartal, Israel, Antony Polonsky, and Scott Ury, eds. *Jews and Their Neighbours in Eastern Europe since 1750*. Vol. 24 of *Polin: Studies in Polish Jewry*. Oxford: Littman Library of Jewish Civilization, 2012.

Bartal, Israel, and Israel Gutman, eds. *Kiyum ve-shever. Yehudey polin le-doroteyhem*. Jerusalem: Zalman Shazar Center, 1997–2001.

Bell, Lawrence D. "Bitter Conquest: Zionists against Progressive Jews and the Making of the Post-War Jewish Politics in Argentina." *Jewish History* 17 (2003): 285–308.

———. "The Jews and Perón. Communal Politics and National Identity in Peronist Argentina, 1946–1955." PhD diss., Ohio State University, 2002.

Bletz, May E. *Immigration and Acculturation in Brazil and Argentina, 1890–1929*. New York: Palgrave Macmillan, 2010.

Ben-Rafael, Eliezer, and Yitzhak Sternberg. "Introduction: Debating Transnationalism." In Ben-Rafael and Sternberg, *Transnationalism*, 1–25.

Ben-Rafael, Eliezer, and Yitzhak Sternberg, eds. With Judit Bokser and Liwerant Yosef Gorny. *Transnationalism: Diaspora and the Advent of a New (Dis)order*. Leiden, Netherlands: Brill, 2009.

Berkowitz, Joel, and Barbara Henry, eds. *Inventing the Modern Yiddish Stage: Essays in Drama, Performance, and Show Business*. Detroit: Wayne University Press, 2012.

Bertoni, Lilia Ana. *Patriotas, cosmopolitas y nacionalistas. La construcción de la nacionalidad argentina a fines del siglo XIX*. Buenos Aires: Fondo de Cultura Económica, 2001.

Bilsky, Edgardo. *La Semana Trágica*. Buenos Aires: Ediciones Ryr, 2011.

Bonatti, Andrés. *Una guerra infame: La verdadera historia de la Conquista del Desierto*. Buenos Aires: Edhasa, 2015.

Boyarin, Daniel, and Boyarin, Jonathan. "Diaspora: Generation and Ground of Jewish Identity." *Critical Inquiry* 19, no. 4 (1993): 693–725.

Brinkmann, Tobias. "We Are Brothers! Let Us Separate! Jews and Community Building in American Cities during the 19th Century." *History Compass*, 11/10 (2013): 869–79.

Brodkin, Karen. *How Jews Became White Folks and What That Says about Race in America*. New Brunswick, NJ: Rutgers University Press, 1998.

Brodsky, Adriana M. *Sephardi, Jewish, Argentine: Community and National Identity*. Bloomington: Indiana University Press, 2016.

Brodsky, Adriana M., and Raanan Rein, eds. *The New Jewish Argentina: Facets of Jewish Experiences in the Southern Cone*. Leiden, Netherlands: Brill, 2013.

Bromfield, Nicole F. "Sex Slavery and Sex Trafficking of Women in the United States: Historical and Contemporary Parallels, Policies, and Perspectives in Social Work." *Afflia: Journal of Women and Social Work* vol. 31, 1 (2016): 129–39.

Brubaker, Rogers. *Nationalism Reframed: Nationhood and the National Question in the New Europe*. Cambridge: Cambridge University Press, 1996.

Bryce, Benjamin. "Paternal Communities: Social Welfare and Immigration in Argentina, 1880–1930." *Journal of Social History* 49, no. 1 (2015): 213–36.

Butler, Judith. *Parting Ways: Jewishness and the Critique of Zionism*. New York: Columbia University Press, 2012.

Cecchi, Ana. *La timba como rito de pasaje. La narrativa del juego en la construción de la modernidad porteña (Buenos Aires 1900–1935)*. Buenos Aires: Ediciones Biblioteca Nacional Teseo, 2012.

Cherjovsky, Iván. "La faz ideológica del conflicto colonos/JCA: el discurso del ideal agrario en las memorias de Colonia Mauricio." In *Marginados y consagrados: nuevos estudios sobre la vida judía en la argentina*, edited by Emmanuel Kahan, Laura Schenquer, Damian Setton, and Alejandro Dujovne, 47–66. Buenos Aires: Lumiere, 2011.

Chinski, Malena. "Incertidubre, búsqueda y duelo: La Shoá desda la perspectiva de los familiares de las víctimas en Argentina." *Temas de Nuestra América* 32, no. 60 (2016): 187–202.

Clark, Stephen. *Travel Writing and Empire: Postcolonial Theory in Transit*. London: Zed Press, 1999.

Comunidad judia de Buenos Aires 1894–1994: AMIA 100 años. Buenos Aires: AMIA, Editorial Milá, 1995.

Cohen, Robin. *Global Diasporas: An Introduction*. Seattle: University of Washington Press, 1997.

Cooper, Julie E. "Diasporic Critic of Diasporism: The Question of Jewish Political Agency." *Political Theory* 43, no. 1 (2015): 80–110.

Criscenti, Joseph T. ed. *Sarmiento and His Argentina*. Boulder: Lynne Rienner Publishers, 1993.

Cúneo, Dardo, Julio Mafud, Amalia Sánchez Sivori, and Lazaro Schallman, eds. *Inmigración y nacionalidad*. Buenos Aires: Instituto Judío Argentino de Cultura e Información, Editorial Paidós, 1967.

Delaney Jean H. "Imagining 'El Ser Argentino': Cultural Nationalism and Romantic Concepts of Nationhood in Early Twentieth-Century Argentina." *Journal of Latin American Studies* 34, no. 3 (2002): 626–58.

Deutsch, Sandra McGee. *Crossing Borders, Claiming a Nation: A History of Argentine Jewish Women, 1880–1955*. Durham, NC: Duke University Press, 2010.

———. *Las Derechas. The Extreme Right in Argentina, Brazil, and Chile, 1890–1939*. Stanford, CA: Stanford University Press, 1999.

Devoto, Fernando J., and Eduardo José Míguez. *Asociacionismo, trabajo e identidad etnica: Los italianos en América Latina en una perspectiva comparada*. Buenos Aires: CEMLA Centro de Estudios Migratorios Latinoamericanos, 1992.

Dimenstein, Marcelo. "The Building of the Once Neighborhood in Buenos Aires: Immigrant Bourgeoisie, Ethnic Architects and Jewish Elites (1900–1930)." *Perush: An Online Journal of Jewish Scholarship and Interpretation* 2 (2010): unpaginated.

Diner, Hasia. *Roads Taken. The Great Jewish Migration to the New World and the Peddlers Who Forged the Way*. New Haven, CT: Yale University Press, 2015.

Dizgun, John. "Immigrants of Different Religion: Jewish Argentines and the Boundaries of Argentinidad, 1919–2009." PhD. diss., Rutgers University, 2010.

Dujovne, Alejandro. "The Book as a Combat Weapon: Intellectuals, Patronage and Institutions in the Establishment of the Argentine Jewish Publishing Field, 1920–1980." *Perush: Online Journal of Jewish Scholarship and Interpretation* vol. 2 (2010): unnumbered.

———. "Buenos Aires en geografía de diaspora judía. Una aproximación desde la producción y circulación transnacional de libros entre 1900 y 1980." Accessed February 3, 2017. http://estudiosjudios.ides.org.ar/files/2012/02/bibliotecas_Buenos_Aires_en_la_geografia_de_la_diaspora_judia.pdf.

———. *Una historia del libro judío. La cultura judía argentina a través de sus editores, libreros, traductores, imprentas y bibliotecas*. Buenos Aires: Siglo Veintiuno Editores, 2014.

Dynner, Glenn, and François Guesnet, eds. *Warsaw. The Jewish Metropolis Essays in Honor of the 75th Birthday of Professor Antony Polonsky*. Leiden, Netherlands: Brill 2015.

Elkin, Judith Laikin. *Jews of the Latin American Republics*. Chapel Hill: University of North Carolina Press, 1980.

Ellis, Carolyn, Tony Adams, and Arthur Bochner. "Autoethnography: An Overview." *Forum Qualitative Sozialforschung/Forum: Qualitative Social Research* 12 (November 24, 2010). http://www.qualitative-research.net/index.php/fqs/article/view/1589/3095.

Estraikh, Gennady. "Yiddish Vilna: A Virtual Capital of a Virtual Land." *Zutot* 3, no. 1 (2003): 135–41.

Faingold, Eduardo D. "Educational Attitudes and Language Choice at the Birth of a Progressive Yiddish-Language Folks Shule in Argentina." *International Journal of Jewish Education Research* 7 (2014): 55–76.

Feierstein, Ricardo. *Historia de los judíos en la Argentina*. Buenos Aires: Ameghino, 1999.

Feierstein, Ricardo, and Stephen A. Sadow, eds *Encuentro: Recreando la cultura judeo-argentina 2*. Buenos Aires: Editorial Mila, 2004.

Feuerlicht, Roberta Strauss. *The Fate of the Jews: A People Torn between Israeli Power and Jewish Ethics*. New York: Times Books, 1983.

Fishman, Joshua A. *Ideology, Society, Language: The Odyssey of Nathan Birnbaum*. Ann Arbor, MI: Karoma, 1989.

———, ed. *Studies on Polish Jewry 1919–1939*. New York: YIVO Institute for Jewish Research, 1974.

Gampel, Benjamin R. ed. *Crisis and Creativity in the Sephardic World, 1391–1648.* New York: Columbia University Press, 1997.

García Fanlo, Luis E. *Genealogía de la argentiniadad.* Buenos Aires: Gran Aldea Editores, 2010.

Garrett, Leah V. *Journeys beyond the Pale: Yiddish Travel Writing in the Modern World.* Madison: Wisconsin University Press, 2003.

Gechtman, Roni. "Creating a Historical Narrative for a Spiritual Nation: Simon Dubnow and the Politics of the Jewish Past." *Journal of the Canadian Historical Association* 22, no. 2 (2011): 98–124.

Gidley, Ben. "Diasporic Memory and the Call to Identity: Yiddish Migrants in Early Twentieth Century East London." *Journal of Intercultural Studies* 34, no. 6 (2013): 650–64.

Gitelman, Zvi, ed. *The Emergence of Modern Jewish Politics: Bundism and Zionism in Eastern Europe.* Pittsburgh: University of Pittsburgh Press, 2003.

Glau, Angelika. *Jüdisches Selbstverständnis im Wandel: Jiddische Literatur zu Beginn des zwanzigsten Jahrhunderts.* Wiesbaden, Germany: Harrassowitz Verlag, 1999.

Glauert, Earl T. "Ricardo Rojas and the Emergence of Argentine Cultural Nationalism." *Hispanic American Historical Review* 43, no. 1 (1963): 1–13.

Glickman, Nora, and Gloria F. Waldman. *Argentine Jewish Theater: A Critical Anthology.* Lewisbug, PA: Bucknell University Press, 1996.

Gruber, Rosana. "La construcción de la identidad étnica. Integración y diferenciación de los inmigrantes judíos ashkenazim en la Argentina." In *Ensayos de Antropologia Argentina*, 197–211. Buenos Aires: Editorial Belgrano, 1984.

Gutiérrez, Leandro H., and Luis Alberto Romero. "La conctrucción de la ciudadanía 1912–1955." In *Sectores populares, cultura y política. Buenos Aires en la entreguerra*, edited by Luis H. Gutiérrez and Luis Alberto Romero, 155–74. Buenos Aires: Siglo Veintinuno Editores, 2007.

———. "Sociedades barriales, bibliotecas populeres y cultura de los sectores populares: Buenos Aires 1920–1945." *Desarollo Economico* 29, no. 113 (1989): 33–62.

Gutman, Israel. *The Jews of Poland between Two World Wars.* Hannover, NH: Brandeis University Press, 1989.

Guy, Donna J. *Sex and Danger in Buenos Aires: Prostitution, Family, and Nation in Argentina.* Lincoln: University of Nebraska Press, 1991.

Helman, Anat. "Hues of Adjustment: Landsmanshaftn in Interwar New York and Tel Aviv." *Jewish History* 20, no. 1 (2006): 41–67.

Howe, Irving. *The World of Our Fathers.* New York: Galahad Book, 1994.

Huberman, Ariana. *Gauchos and Foreigners: Glossing Culture and Identity in the Argentine Countryside.* Plymouth, UK: Lexington Books, 2011.

Humphrey, Michael. "Ethnic History, Nationalism and Transnationalism in Argentine Arab and Jewish Cultures." In *Arab and Jewish Immigrants in Latin America. Images and Realities*, edited by Ignacio Klich and Jeffrey Lesser, 167–88. London: Frank Cass, 1998.

Jacobs, Jack. *Bundist Counterculture in Interwar Poland.* Syracuse, NY: Syracuse University Press, 2009.

Jones, Kristine L. "Nineteenth Century British Travel Accounts on Argentina." *Ethnohistory* 33, no. 2 (Spring 1986): 95–211.

Joppke, Christian, and Ewa Morawska. "Integrating Immigrants in Liberal Nation

States: Policies and Practices." In *Toward Assimilation and Citizenship*, edited by Joppke and Morawska, 1–36. Basingstoke, UK: Palgrave, 2003.

Kahan, Emmanuel, Laura Schenquer, Damián Setton, and Alejandro Dujovne, eds. *Marginados y consagrados. Nuevos estudios sobre la vida judía en Argentina*. Buenos Aires: Lumiére, 2011.

Kahn, Ava F., and Adam D. Mendelsohn. *Transnational Traditions: New Perspectives on American Jewish History*. Detroit: Wayne State University Press, 2014.

Katz, Dovid. *Yiddish and Power*. London: Palgrave Macmillan, 2014.

Kaye/Kantorowitz, Melanie. *The Colors of Jews: Racial Politics and Radical Diasporism*. Bloomington: Indiana University Press, 2007.

Kazzazi, Kerstin, Angela Treiber, Tim Wätzold, eds. *Migration—Religion—Identität. Aspekte transkultureller Prozesse*. Wiesbaden, Germany: Springer Fachmedien, 2016.

King, Desmond. *Making Americans: Immigration, Race, and the Origins of the Diverse Democracy*. Cambridge, MA: Harvard University Press, 2000.

Klenicki, Leon, ed. *Identity in Dispersion: Selected Memoirs from Latin American Jews*. Cincinnati: Jacob Rader Marcus Center of American Jewish Archives, 2000.

Klich, Ignacio, and Jeffrey Lesser, eds. *Arab and Jewish Immigrants in Latin America: Images and Realities*. London: Frank Cass, 1998.

Kliger, Hannah, ed. *Jewish Hometown Associations and Family Circles in New York*. The WPA Yiddish Writers' Group Study. Bloomington: Indiana University Press, 1992.

Kobrin, Rebecca. "Conflicting Diasporas, Shifting Centers: Migration and Identity in Transnational Polish Jewish Community." PhD diss., University of Pennsylvania, 2002.

———. *Jewish Bialystok and Its Diaspora*. Bloomington: Indiana University Press, 2010.

———. "The Other Polonia: The Responses of Yiddish Immigrant Writers in New York and Buenos Aires to the New Polish State, 1920–1925." In *Choosing Yiddish: New Frontiers of Language and Culture*, edited by Lara Rabinovich, Hannah Pressman, and Shiri Goren, 99–119. Detroit: Wayne State University Press, 2012.

———. "The Shtetl by the Highway: The East European City in New York's Landsmanshaft Press, 1921–39." *Prooftexts* 26, nos. 1 and 2 (2006): 107–37.

———. "When a Jew Was a Landsman." *Journal of Modern Jewish Studies* 7, no. 3 (2008): 357–76.

Kołodziejska, Zuzanna. *"Izraelita" (1866–1915). Znaczenie kulturowe i literackie czasopisma*. Kraków: Wydawnictwo Uniwersytetu Jagiellońskiego, 2014.

Kornblit, Oscar. "Inmigrantes y empresarios en la politica argentina." In *Los fragmentos del poder: De la oligarquía a poliarquía argentina*, edited by Torcuato S. Di Tella and Tulio Halperin Donghi, 389–437. Buenos Aires: Alvarez, 1969.

Kowalska, Marta. "La emigración judía de Polonia a la Argentina en los años 1918–1939." *Estudios Latinoamericanos* 12 (1989): 249–72.

Kula, Marcin, ed. *Dzieje Polonii w Ameryce Łacińskiej*. Wrocław, Poland: Polska Akademia Nauk, Komitet Badań Polonii, Zakład Narodowy im. Ossolińskich, 1983.

Kümper, Michael, Johannes Schwarz, Jens Neumann, Anna Lipphardt, Maria Vassilikou, and Hiltrud Wallenborn, eds. *Der Ort des Judentums in der Gegenwart*. Berlin: Bebra Verlag, 2006.

Kuznitz, Cecile Esther. *YIVO and the Making of Modern Jewish Culture: Scholarship for the Yiddish Nation*. New York: Cambridge University Press, 2014.

Lederhendler, Eli. *Jewish Responses to Modernity: New Voices in Modernity and Eastern Europe*. New York: New York University Press, 1997.

Lesser, Jeffrey. *A Discontented Diaspora: Japanese-Brazilians and the Meanings of Ethnic Militancy*. Durham, NC: Duke University Press, 2007.

Lesser, Jeffrey, and Raanan Rein. "Challenging Particularity. Jews as a Lens on Latin American Ethnicity." *Latin American and Caribbean Ethnic Studies* 1, no. 2 (2006): 249–63.

———, eds. *Rethinking Jewish-Latin Americans*. Albuquerque: University of New Mexico Press, 2008.

Lewinsky, Tamar. "Eastern Europe in Argentina: Yiddish Travelogues and Exploration of Jewish Diaspora." In *Writing Jewish Culture: Paradoxes in Ethnography*, edited by Andreas Kilcher and Gabriella Safran, 251–71. Bloomington: Indiana University Press, 2016.

Lopez, Celia Gladys. *El sistema de educación no formal implantado por las cooperativas agrarias en las colonias judías entrerrianas*. Concepción del Uruguay: Instituto de Investigación Ibarra Grasso, 1993.

Mafud, Julio "El desarraigo del inmigrante. La influencía migratoria en el caracter nacional." In *Inmigración y nacionalidad*, edited by Dardo Cúneo, Julio Mafud, Amalia Sánchez Sivori, and Lazaro Schallman, 63–91. Buenos Aires: Editorial Paidós, 1967.

Manzoni, Celina, ed. *Rupturas*. Vol. 7 of *Historia crítica de la literatura argentina*.. Buenos Aires: Emecé, 2009.

Maronese, Leticia, ed. *Patrimonio Cultural y Diversidad Creativa en el Sistema Educativo*. Buenos Aires: Gobierno de la Ciudad Buenos Aires, 2006.

Marten-Finnis, Susanne, and Michael Nagel. *The PRESSA: International Press Exhibition Cologne 1928 and the Jewish Contribution to Modern Journalism*. Bremen, Germany: Edition Lumiere, 2012.

Mays, Devi. "Transplanting Cosmopolitans: The Migrations of Sephardic Jews to Mexico, 1900–1934." PhD diss., Indiana University, 2013.

Mazurek, Jerzy. *Kraj a emigracja: Ruch ludowy wobec wychodźstwa polskiego do krajów Ameryki Łacińskiej (do 1939r.)*. Warsaw: Biblioteka Iberyjska, 2006.

Melzer, Emanuel. "Ha-diplomatiyah ha-polanit u-ve'ayat ha-hagirah ha-yehudit bashanim 1935–1939." *Gal-Ed* 1 (1973): 211–49.

Mendelsohn, Ezra, ed. *Jews and the State: Dangerous Alliances and the Perils of Privilege*. Vol. 19 of *Studies in Contemporary Jewry*. New York: Oxford University Press, 2003.

———. *The Jews of East Central Europe between the World Wars*. Bloomington: Indiana University Press, 1983.

———. *Żydzi Europy środkowo-wschodniej w okresie międzywojennym*. Warsaw: Wydawnictwo Naukowe PWN, 1992.

Mendes-Flohr, Paul, Yom Tov Assis, and Leonardo Senkman, eds. *Identidades judías, modernidad y globalización*. Jerusalem: Hebrew University of Jerusalem and Ediciones Lilmod, 2007.

Mills, Sara. *Discourses on Difference: An Analysis of Women's Travel Writing and Colonialism*. London: Routledge, 2003.

Mirelman, Víctor A. *En búsqueda de una identidad. Los inmigrantes judíos en Buenos Aires 1890–1930*. Buenos Aires: Editorial Milá, 1988.

Moss, Kenneth B. *Jewish Renaissance in the Russian Revolution*. Cambridge, MA: Harvard University Press, 2009.

Moss, Kenneth. "Negotiating Jewish Nationalism in Interwar Warsaw." In Dynner and Guesnet, *Warsaw*, 390–436.

Moya, José C. *Cousins and Strangers: Spanish Immigrants in Buenos Aires*. Berkeley: University of California Press, 1998.

———. "Spanish Emigration to Cuba and Argentina." In *Mass Migration to Modern Latin America*, edited by Samuel L. Baily and Eduardo José Míguez, 9–29. Wilmington, DE: Jaguar Books, 2003.

———. "What's in a Stereotype? The Case of Jewish Anarchists in Argentina." In *The New Jewish Argentina: Facets of Jewish Experiences in the Southern Cone*, edited by Adriana M. Brodsky et al., 55–88. Leiden, Netherlands: Brill, 2013.

Munck, Ronaldo. "Mutual Benefit Societies in Argentina: Workers, Nationality, Social Security and Trade Unionism." *Journal of Latin American Studies* 30, no. 3 (1998): 573–90.

Murray, Edmundo. *Becoming Gauchos Ingleses: Diasporic Model in Irish-Argentine Literature*. Bethseda, MD: Mausnel, 2009.

Nalewajko-Kulikov, Joanna. *Mówić we własnym języku: Prasa jidyszowa a tworzenie żydowskiej tożsamości narodowej (do 1918 roku)*. Warsaw: Neriton, 2016.

———, ed. *Studia z dziejów trójjęzycznej prasy żydowskiej na ziemiach polskich*. Warsaw: Neriton, 2012.

Nathans, Benjamin. *Beyond the Pale: The Jewish Encounter with Late Imperial Russia*. Berkeley: University of California Press, 2002.

Newton, Ronald C. *German Buenos Aires 1900–1933: Social Change and Cultural Crisis*. Austin: University of Texas Press, 1977.

Nocke, Alexandra, Julia Brauch, and Anna Lipphardt. *Jewish Topographies: Visions of Space, Traditions of Place*. Aldershot, UK: Ashgate, 2008.

Nouwen, Mollie Lewis. *Oy, My Buenos Aires: Jewish Immigrants and the Creation of Argentine National Identity*. Albuquerque: University of New Mexico Press, 2013.

Nowersztern, Abraham. "Dos poylishe yidntum." *Book Peddler: Newsletter of the National Yiddish Book Exchange* 15 (1993): 16–19.

Owen, Joy. "Transnationalism as a Process, Diaspora as Condition." *Journal of Social Development in Africa* 30, no. 1 (2014): 31–46.

Paleczny, Tadeusz. *Idea powrotu wśród emigrantów polskich w Brazylii i Argentynie*. Warsaw: Polska Akademia Nauk, Komitet Badania Polonii, 1992.

Paradowska, Maria. *Podróżnicy i emigranci. Szkice z dziejów polskiego wychodźstwa w Ameryce Południowej*. Warsaw: Interpress, 1984.

Pilch, Andrzej, ed. *Emigracja z ziem polskich w czasach nowożytnych i najnowszych (XVIII-XX w.)*. Warsaw: Państwowe Wydawnictwo Naukowe, 1984.

Popkiewitz, Thomas S., ed. *The "Reason" of Schooling: Historicizing Curriculum Studies, Pedagogy and Teacher Education*. New York: Routledge, 2015.

Porada, Katarzyna. *Procesos de formación de la identidad étnica de un grupo de origen migratorio: Los desciendentes de polacos en Buenos Aires y Misiones*. Madrid: Ediciones Polifermo, 2016.

Pratt, Mary Louise. *Imperial Eyes: Travel Writing and Transculturation*. Abingdon, UK: Routledge, 1992.

Rabinovitch, Lara, Shiri Goren, Hannah S. Pressman, eds. *Choosing Yiddish: New Frontiers of Language and Culture*. Detroit: Wayne State University Press, 2013.

Ran, Amalia, and Jean Axelrad Cahan, eds. *Returning to Babel: Jewish Latin American Experiences, Representations and Identity*. Leiden, Netherlands: Brill, 2012.

Recchini de Lattes, Zulma, and Alfredo E. Lattes, eds. *La población de Argentina*. Buenos Aires: Ediciones C.I.C.R.E.D, 1974.

Rein, Raanan. *Argentine Jews or Jewish Argentines: Essays on Ethnicity, Identity and Diaspora*. Leiden, Netherlands: Brill, 2010.

———. *Los muchachos peronistas judíos: Los argentinos judíos y el apoyo a jusicialismo*. Buenos Aires: Sudamericana, 2015.

Resnick, Rosa Perla. "Salomón Resnick, pionero de la cultura judía en lengua castellana en Latinoamérica." Homenaje a Salomón Resnick y la revista Judaica, *Noaj.Revista Literaria* no. 12–13 (1997): 4–12.

Rock, David. *Authoritarian Argentina: The Nationalist Movement, Its History and Impact*. Berkeley: University of California Press, 1993.

Rogger, Hans. *Jewish Policies and Right-Wing Politics in Imperial Russia*. Hampshire-London: Palgrave Macmillan, 1986.

Roniger, Luis. "Latin American Jews and Processes of Legitimization and De-Legitimization." *Journal of Modern Jewish Studies* 9, no. 2 (2010): 185–207.

Różański, Przemysław. "The Attitude of American Jews and American Diplomacy towards the Bill Banning Shehitah in Poland in the Second Half of the 1930s." In *Jews and Their Neighbours in Eastern Europe since 1750*, edited by Israel Bartal, Antony Polonsky, and Scott Ury, 342–62. Vol. 24 of *Polin: Studies in Polish Jewry*. Oxford: Littman Library of Jewish Civilization, 2012.

———. *Stany Zjednoczone wobec kwestii żydowskiej w Polsce 1918–1921*. Gdańsk, Poland: Wydawnictwo Uniwersytetu Gdańskiego, 2007.

Rubel, Yaacov. "Di opklangen vegn der yidisher emigratsye fun rusland un yidisher kolonizatsye in argentine." *Argentiner IWO Shriftn* 15 (1989): 15–42.

Rubinzal, Diego. *Historia económica argentina (1880–2009). Desde los tiempos de Julio Argentino Roca hasta Cristina Fernández de Kirchner*. Buenos Aires: Centro Cultural de la Cooperación Floreal Gorini, 2010.

Said, Edward. *Representations of the Intellectual: The 1993 Reith Lectures*. New York: Pantheon Books, 1994.

Sánchez Sivori, Amalia. "La inmigración y la literatura argentina." In *Inmigración y nacionalidad*, edited by Dardo Cúneo, Julio Mafud, Amalia Sanchez Sivori, Lazaro Schallman, 93–143. Buenos Aires: Editorial Paidós, 1967.

Scheintuch, Yehiel. "Safrut yidish be-argentina ksafrut me'agrim." In *Proceedings of the World Congress of Jewish Studies*, 197–205. Vol 4 of Division D (Hebrew Language, Yidish Literature, Jewish Languages). Jerusalem, 1973.

———. "Veidat tshernovitz ve-tarbut yidish." *Huliot* 6 (2000): 255–85.

Schramm, Tomasz. "Żydzi wobec odradzania się państwowości polskiej." In *Przełomy Historii, XVI Powszechny Zjazd Historyków Polskich, Wrocław, 15–19 września 1999*, vol. 2, 223–43. part 2. Toruń, Poland: Adam Marszałek, 2000.

Schwarz, Jan. "A Library of Hope and Destruction: The Yiddish Book Series Dos poylishe yidntum, 1946–1966." In *Making Holocaust Memory*, 173–96. Vol. 20 of *Polin: Studies in Polish Jewry*. Oxford: Littman Library of Jewish Civilization, 2008.

———. *Survivors and Exiles: Yiddish Culture after the Holocaust*. Detroit, MI: Wayne State University Press, 2015.

Senkman, Leonardo. "La construcción de un espacio de transculturción judeo-iberoamericano." Homenaje a Salomón Resnick y la revista Judaica, *Noaj.Revista Literaria*, nos. 12–13 (1997): 1–3.

———. *La identidad judía en la literatura argentina.* Buenos Aires: Pardes, 1983.

———. "Los sobrevivientes de la Shoa en Argentina: Su imagen y memoria en la sociedad general y judía: 1945–1950." *Arquivo Maaravi: Revista Digital de Estudos Judaicos da UFMG,* vol. 1, 1 (2007): 67–97.

Shandler. Jeffrey. *Adventures in Yiddishland: Postvernacular Language and Culture.* Berkeley: University of California Press, 2006.

Shanes, Joshua. "Yiddish and Jewish Diaspora Nationalism." *Monatshefte* 90, no. 2 (1998): 178–88.

Shiller, Nina Glick, Linda Basch, and Cristina Blanc-Szanton, eds. *Towards a Transnational Perspective on Migration: Race, Class, Ethnicity, and Nationalism Reconsidered.* New York: New York Academy of Sciences, 1992.

Shohat, Ella, and Robert Stam. *Unthinking Eurocentrism: Multiculturalism and the Media.* London: Routledge, 1994.

Silber, Marcos. "Ambivalent Citizenship—The Construction of Jewish Belonging in Emergent Poland, 1915–1918." *Simon Dubnow Institute Yearbook* 10 (2011): 161–83.

Silva Ospital, María. *Inmigración y nacionalismo: Liga Patriótica y la Asociación del Trabajo (1910–1930).* Buenos Aires: Centro Editor de América Latina, 1994.

Sneh, Perla, ed. *Buenos Aires ídish.* Buenos Aires: Comisión para la Preservación del Patrimonio Histórico Cultural de la Ciudad de Buenos Aires, 2006.

Soldat-Jaffe, Tatjana. *Twenty-First Century Yiddishism.* Brighton, UK: Sussex Academic Press, 2012.

Soyer, Daniel. *Jewish Immigrant Associations and American Identity in New York, 1880–1939.* Cambridge, MA: Harvard University Press, 1997.

———. "Landsmanshaftn and the Jewish Labor Movement: Cooperation, Conflict, and the Building of Community." *Journal of American Ethnic History* 7, no. 2 (1988): 22–45.

Starczewski, Michał. "Mrzonki racjonalnej kolonizacji w duchu narodowym: Roman Dmowski i polska emigracja do Brazylii." *Przegląd Historyczny* 52, no. 2 (2015): 63–74.

———. "Z dziejów emigracji zarobkowej: Agenci emigracyjni na ziemiach polskich przed 1914 r." *Przegląd Historyczny* 103, no. 1 (2012): 47–80.

Tananbaum, Susan, Sam Bloom, and Michael Berkowitz, eds. *Forging Modern Jewish Identities.* London: Valentine-Mitchell, 2003.

Tartakovsky, Eugene. "Cultural Identities of Adolescent Immigrants: A Three-Year Longitudinal Study Including the Pre-Migration Period." *Journal of Youth and Adolescence* 5 (2009): 654–71.

Tedesco, Juan Carlos. *Educación y sociedad en la Argentina (1880–1945).* Buenos Aires: Solar, 1993.

Toker, Eliahu. *El ídish es también Latinoamérica.* Buenos Aires: Ediciones Desde la Gente, Instituto Movilizador de Fondos Cooperativos, 2003.

Toker, Eliahu, and Ana E. Weinstein. *Trayectoria de una idea: Nueva Sión, 50 años de periodismo judeo-argentino con compromiso: 1948–1998.* Buenos Aires: Ediciones Fundación Mordejai Anilevich, 1999.

Troncoso, Oscar A. *Buenos Aires se divierte.* Buenos Aires: Centro Editor de América Latina, 1971.

Tsagarousianou, Roza. "Rethinking the Concept of Diaspora: Mobility, Connectivity and Communication in a Globalised World." *Westminster Papers in Communication and Culture* 1, no. 1 (2004): 52–65.

Ury, Scott. *Barricades and Banners: The Revolution of 1905 and the Transformation of Warsaw Jewry*. Stanford, CA: Stanford University Press, 2012.

———. "Who, What, When, Where, and Why Is Polish Jewry? Envisioning, Constructing, and Possessing Polish Jewry." *Jewish Social Studies* 6, no. 3 (2000): 205–28.

van Tilburg, Miranda, and Ad Vingerhoets, eds. *Psychological Aspects of Geographical Moves: Homesickness and Acculturation Stress*. Amsterdam: Amsterdam University Press, 2005.

Vázquez-Presedo, Vicente. *Estadísticas históricas argentinas II (Comparadas). Segunda Parte 1914–1939*. Buenos Aires: Ediciones Macchi, 1976.

Vertovec, Steven. "Conceiving and Researching Transnationalism." *Ethnic and Racial Studies* 22, no. 2 (1999): 447–62.

———. *Transnationalism*. New York: Routledge, 2009.

Visacovsky, Nerina. *Argentinos, judíos y camaradas. Tras la utopía socialista*. Buenos Aires: Ed. Biblos, 2015.

Weinstein, Ana E., and Eliahu Toker. *La letra ídish en tierra argentina: Bio-bibliografía de sus autores literarios*. Buenos Aires: Editorial Milá, AMIA, Comunidad Judía, 2004.

Weisbrot, Robert. *The Jews of Argentina: From the Inquisition to Perón*. Philadelphia: Jewish Publishing Society of America, 1979.

Weiser, Kalman, and Joshua A. Fogel, eds. *Czernowitz at 100: The First Yiddish Language Conference in Historical Perspective*. Lanham, MD: Lexington Books, 2010.

Weiss, Yfaat. *Deutsche und polnische Juden vor dem Holocaust. Jüdische Identität zwischen Staatsbürgerschaft und Ethnizität 1933–1940*. Munich: Oldenbourg Verlag, 2000.

Weiser, Kalman (Keith). "The Capital of the 'Yiddishland'?" In Dynner and Guesnet, *Warsaw*, 298–322.

Weisser, Michael. *A Brotherhood of Memory: Jewish Landsmanshaftn in the New World*. New York: Basic Books, 1985.

Wertheimer, Jack, ed. *Imagining the American Jewish Community*. Waltham, MA: Brandeis University Press, 2007.

Wodziński, Marcin, and Agnieszka Jagodzińska. *"Izraelita" 1866–1915. Wybór źródeł*. Kraków: Austeria, 2015.

Wolff, Frank. "Als Wilna neben Buenos Aires lag: Die Transnationalität jüdischen Lebens am Rio de La Plata, 1904–1939." In *Migration—Religion—Identität. Aspekte transkultureller Prozesse*, edited by Kerstin Kazzazi, Angela Treiber, and Tim Wätzold, 53–74. Wiesbaden, Germany: Springer Fachmedien, 2016.

———. "Eastern Europe Abroad: Exploring Actor-Networks in Transnational Movements and Migration History, the Case of the Bund." *International Review of Social History* 57, no. 2 (2012): 229–55.

———. "The Home That Never Was: Rethinking Space and Memory in Late Nineteenth and Early Twentieth Century." *Historical Social Research* 38, no. 3 (2013): 197–215.

———. *Neue Welten in der neuen Welt. Die Transnationale Geschichte des Allgemeinen Jüdischen Arbeiterbundes 1897–1947*. Köln, Germany: Böhlau Verlag, 2014.

Yarfitz, Mir. "Polacos, White Slaves, and Stille Chuppahs: Organized Prostitution and the Jews of Buenos Aires, 1890–1939." PhD diss., University of California, Los Angeles, 2012.

Yerushalmi, Yosef. "Exile and Expulsion in Jewish History." In *Crisis and Creativity in the Sephardic World*, 1391–1648, edited by Benjamin R. Gampel, 3–22. New York: Columbia University Press, 1997.

Zadoff, Efraim. *Historia de la educacción judía en Buenos Aires (1935–1957)*. Buenos Aires: Editorial Milá, 1994.

———. “La educación general y judía en las colonias agrícolas judías en la Argentina y Eretz Israel a fines del siglo XIX.” *Coloquio* 19 (1988): 95–108.

Zahra, Tara. *The Great Departure: Mass Migration from Eastern Europe and the Making of the Free World*. New York: W. W. Norton, 2016.

Zieliński, Konrad. “Emigracja żydowska z Rosji i Królestwa Polskiego (1881–1918).” *Kwartalnik Historii Żydów* no. 201 (2002): 16–36.

Index